Franciscan Institute Publications

THEOLOGY SERIES No. 8
Edited by George Marcil, O.F.M.

JUAN DE CARTAGENA, O.F.M.
(1563-1618)
The Mariology of his HOMILIAE CATHOLICAE
and its Baroque Scripturism

by

Sabino A. Vengco

THE FRANCISCAN INSTITUTE
ST. BONAVENTURE UNIVERSITY
ST. BONAVENTURE, NEW YORK 14778

This work was presented first as a doctoral dissertation and accepted by the Theological Faculty of Trier, West Germany, in 1974.

Printed in Italy
Tipografia Porziuncola Assisi
Assisi

Dedicated
to
my mother

My sincere gratitude is especially due to Prof. Klaus Reinhardt, who mentored me with competence and patience; to Dr. Anton Arens whose kind hospitality as Regens of the Trierer Priester-seminar made it possible for me to study in Trier; and to The Franciscan Institute of St. Bonaventure University, New York, for graciously including this book in its Theology Series. I am particularly grateful too to Fr. George Marcil, O.F.M., for all his assistance in preparing the manuscript for publication.

Fr. Sabino Vengco,
San Carlos Seminary,
Makati, Rizal, Philippines.

CONTENTS

phors: temple, tabernacle, ark of the covenant, garden
of paradise, six days, lily, cinnamon, neck, Esther, Eve.

ABBREVIATIONS

In addition to the common abbreviations of biblical books, the following are oft used in this study:

ARSJ   *Archivum Romanum Societatis Jesu.*

CCL   *Corpus Christianorum seu Nova Patrum Collectio* (Turnhout–Paris, 1953 ff.).

CSCO   *Corpus Scriptorum Christianorum Orientalium* (Paris, 1903 ff.).

CSEL   *Corpus Scriptorum Ecclesiasticorum Latinorum* (Wien, 1866 ff.).

ES   *Enchiridion Symbolorum, Definitionum et Declarationum de Rebus Fidei et Morum*, ed. H. Denzinger & A. Schönmetzer (Barcelona–Freiburg, edn 34, 1967).

DThC   *Dictionnaire de Théologie Catholique*, ed. A. Vacant, E. Mangenot, E. Amann (Paris, 1903–1950).

GCS   *Die griechischen christlichen Schriftsteller der ersten drei Jahrhunderte* (Leipzig, 1897 ff.).

HCUCRA   Juan de Cartagena, *Homiliae Catholicae in Universa Christianae Religionis Arcana* (Romae, 1609).

HCSADM   Juan de Cartagena, *Homiliae Catholicae de Arcanis Deiparae Mariae et Joseph* (Coloniae, 1613–1616).

LThK   *Lexikon für Theologie und Kirche*, ed. J. Höfer & K. Rahner (Freiburg, 2nd. edn, 1957–1967).

PG   *Patrologia Graeca*, ed. J.–P. Migne (Paris, 1857 ff.).

PL   *Patrologia Latina*, ed. J.–P. Migne (Paris, 1844 ff.).

PO   *Patrologia Orientalis* (Paris, 1903 ff.).

INTRODUCTION

Until a few years ago, it could be said with full justification that
Juan de Cartagena was a 17th century theologian, appending the
description with a question mark. Biographers, annalists and commentators of the past have unanimously sung his praise as a theology
lector of public renown.[1] His books were highly esteemed and saw
many reprintings. Only a short time after his death, a Dominican
could challenge a Franciscan adversary: *"Acrior tibi acies, quam Ioanni
de Carthagena?"* [2] Recently he has been referred to as a *"theologus
eximius"*.[3] His homiletical writings, which according to M. Grabmann
are deeply dogmatical,[4] have exerted in the opinion of F. Stegmüller
a great influence in the field of Mariology.[5] How deserved are these
words of recognition and these high compliments?

On the other hand, a theologian of his own generation branded
him a theological *"nugivendulus"* (a twaddle–retailer),[6] and further
characterized him as a *"laevus interpres"* as far as his use of Sacred
Scripture went.[7] Frenchmen were said to have found *"plaintes ma-*

---

[1] Lucas Wadding, *Scriptores Ordinis Minorum* (Romae, 1650 – Unveränderter Nachdruk: Frankfurt/Main, 1967), p. 198.

[2] Nicolaus Ianssenius, O.P., *Animadversiones et Scholia in Apologiam nuper
Editam de Vita et Morte Ioannis Duns Scoti, adversus R.P. F. Abraham Bzovium
eiusdem Ordinis SS. Th. Magistrum, et Historiae Ecclesiasticae Scriptorem* (Coloniae Agrippinae, 1622), pp. 89–90.

[3] T. Gallus, S.J., *Interpretatio Mariologica Protoevangelii Posttridentina
usque ad Definitionem Dogmaticam Immaculatae Conceptionis*. Pars prior. (Roma,
1953), p. 111.

The permission for publication of Juan de Cartagena's book *Praxis Orationis
Mentalis* (1618) referred to him also as "theologus eximius."

[4] M. Grabmann, *Die Geschichte der katholischen Theologie seit dem Ausgang
der Väterzeit* (Freiburg i. Br., 1933), p. 176.

[5] F. Stegmüller, "Carthagena, Johannes de," in *Lexikon der Marienkunde*,
hrsg. Konrad Algermissen et al., I (Regensburg, 1960), col. 1067.

[6] Claudius Dausquius, *Aplysiarum F. Minorum Audomarensium Spongia*
(Lugduni, 1631), p. 48.

[7] Idem, *Sancti Josephi Sanctificatio extra Uterum, seu Binoctium adversus
F. Marchanti Inanias* (Lugduni, 1631), p. 82.

lignes" against them in his books.[8] What was this Juan de Cartagena really as a theologian? What did he write and teach? This ex–Jesuit turned Franciscan was known to be a trusted friend of Pope Paul V. Was he just another partisan *"eifriger Verfechter des römischen Hofes,"* [9] as another writer described him?

Even the biographical data on the man are so inadequately established, that a great many of the primary details about him seem irrevocably lost in the clouds of the forgotten or of the simply unknown. This situation has been considerably improved, however, by the spade–work of one historian, Isaac Vazquez, O.F.M. His research has been so far the only comprehensive and critical effort to scale down the big question mark casting its shadow on Juan de Cartagena's life and works.[10] This first try has shown the way, and we propose to take the task up from there.

It is the intention of this study to tackle the uncertainties surrounding Juan de Cartagena, his works and teachings. We want at least to subtract from the unknown–quotient about the man and thus contribute to the knowledge about him, his theology and his time. We might not be able to erase the above–mentioned question mark completely, but surely it can be reduced.

In the present day discussion about the crisis in doctrinal and kerygmatic language of the Church, it has been more than once underlined, and appropriately so, that the Christian message is necessarily conveyed in, and by means of, a particular culture.[11] Set against the backdrop of a culture upon which it is dependent and which it transforms at the same time, the kerygma, as verbally communicated, can seem "strange" or at odds, say, with modern culture. The modern man's preoccupation with rationality and scientific objectivity easily finds incongruous the language of a bygone culture with its peculiar mythology and imagery. Hence it comes about that for many the means of communication replaces the very message of Christianity.

---

[8] Pierre Bayle, *Dictionaire Historique et Critique*, II, 5th ed. (Amsterdam, 1740), p. 66.

[9] Christian Gottlieb Jöcher, *Allgemeines Gelehrten Lexicon*, I (Leipzig, 1750), col. 1707.

[10] I. Vazquez, "Fr. Juan de Cartagena (1563–1618). Vida y Obras," *Antonianum*, 39 (1964) 243–301.

[11] Cf. Danièle Hervieu–Léger, "The Crisis in Doctrinal and Kerygmatic Language," *Concilium*, 9 (May 1973) 19–30.

The preaching of the Gospel has always been "situationally determined." It has been the clear duty of the Christian preacher from the very beginning to present the faith in terms that make sense to the intellectual and social climate of his time. An encounter therefore with the proclamation of the Word of God in the past demands a study of its distinct cultural basis. This is true too of Juan de Cartagena's principal work, his homiletical writings, the *Homiliae Catholicae de Sacris Arcanis Deiparae Mariae et Ioseph*. Its theological content, and its kerygmatic and doctrinal language should be understood as the product of a particular society. We intend to evaluate especially his use of Sacred Scripture in the mystical sense within the context of the social environment for which it was planned. Not just his language but even his hermeneutics was historically conditioned.

This study is divided into three main parts. Part One is concerned with Juan de Cartagena's *vida y obras*, presenting in three chapters as rounded a view as possible of his life and accomplishments. The third chapter is particularly occupied with the structure, mechanics and orientation of the *Homiliae Catholicae*. Part Two samples Cartagena's Mariology as contained in the aforementioned work. In a chapter each, we consider his teaching on Mary's Immaculate Conception, her perpetual virginity and her assumption into heaven. Special attention is given here to his use of Sacred Scripture in support of the above doctrines. Finally, Part Three attempts to round off our understanding of Juan de Cartagena and his thoughts within the context of the Baroque period during which he lived. An in–depth grasp of his methodology, kerygmatic language and hermeneutics is gained by gauging him in the perspective of his theological milieu, culture and time.

In this inquiry into the works of a past theologian, we want to examine to what extent he was a witness of the Christian faith, if clearly or obscurely, intelligibly or less intelligibly, powerfully or weakly — the extent to which he had been fertilized but also limited by the tradition before him, his milieu, his experience, thought–structure and *Weltanschauung*. It is only in thus taking into serious consideration the positive and negative experiences and conclusions of the theologians of former times that one in his own time can be spared from beginning at zero and being sidetracked into already well trodden areas. Karl Barth stressed this natural and indispensable connection between theology's past and present, when he wrote:

In order to serve the community of today, theology itself must be rooted in the community of yesterday. Its testimony to the Word and the profession of its faith must originate, like the community itself, from the community of past times, from which that of today arose. Theology must originate also from the older and the more recent tradition which determines the present form of its witness. The foundation of its inquiry and instruction is given to theology beforehand, along with the task which it has to fulfill. Theology does not labor somewhere high above the foundation of tradition, as though Church history began today. Nevertheless, the special task of theology is a critical one, in spite of its relative character. The fire of the quest for truth has to ignite the proclamation of the community and the tradition determining this proclamation. Theology has to reconsider the confession of the community, testing and rethinking it in the light of its enduring foundation, object, and content.[12]

---

[12] Karl Barth, *Einführung in die evangelische Theologie* (Zurich, 1962), p. 50.

PART ONE

JUAN DE CARTAGENA: HIS LIFE AND HIS WORKS

This first part of our investigation tries to give an exhaustive round–up of what we know about Juan de Cartagena. Our point of departure is the results of the research of I. Vazquez, which has rightly become the more reliable basis for any further inquiry into Cartagena's *vida y obras*. We shall double–check on Vazquez and, where necessary, correct him. The opening chapter deals with the life of the man Cartagena. The following one lines up as completely as possible all the writings penned by Cartagena. The libraries where his works are to be found are also listed. And the last chapter of this part is devoted to a detailed scrutiny of his principal work, the *Homiliae Catholicae*.

CHAPTER ONE

HIS LIFE

This chapter is a reconstruction of pieces of information about Juan de Cartagena. As in a jigsaw puzzle, piecing the parts together is the game. Much like a puzzle, however, some pieces are still missing, which, if found, would have given us a more complete picture of the man. Nonetheless, the biographical data available provide us with enough details to be able to form some definite ideas about him. And where there are unfilled slots, probable hypotheses are not lacking.

I. BIRTH AND ORIGIN

A. HISPANUS

Luke Wadding, the great historian of the Friars Minor, identified Juan de Cartagena some 30 years after his death with the one word *"Hispanus."* [1] Regarding his birth date and place, not another word. Nicolas Antonio,[2] Juan de San Antonio,[3] Pierre Bayle,[4] Christian Gottlieb Jöcher,[5] the unsigned writer in the *Biografia Eclesiastica Completa*,[6] Stanislaus Melchiorri de Cerreto,[7] the *Diccionario*

---

[1] Wadding, op. cit., p. 198. Wadding (1588–1657), a member of the Irish Observant Province, was called to Rome in 1618 shortly after Cartagena's death to act as an advocate for the definition of the Immaculate Conception. He resided where Cartagena had lived, and later set out to systematize the vast stores of information from all Franciscan provinces throughout the world in St. Isidore's College. He digested the material into the stupendous *Annales Ordinis Minorum*, eight of whose 25 volumes he himself published during the years 1625–1654. Cf. Manuel de Castro, O.F.M., "El Analista P. Lucas Wadding, O.F.M. (1588–1657), y sus Relaciones con la Peninsula Iberica," *Salmanticensis*, 5 (1958) 107–162.

[2] Nicolás Antonio, *Bibliotheca Hispana Nova sive Hispanorum Scriptorum qui Anno MD. ad MDCLXXXIV. Floruere Notitia.* Recognita emendata aucta ab ipso auctore. I (Madrid, 1788), p. 672. This work first came out in 1672 in Rome.

[3] Juan de San Antonio, O.F.M., *Bibliotheca Universa Franciscana* II (Madrid, 1732), p. 143.

[4] Bayle, loc. cit.

[5] Jöcher, loc. cit.

[6] *Biografía Eclesiastica Completa*, s.v. Cartagena, III (Madrid–Barcelona, 1850), p. 464,

[7] Stanislaus Melchiorri de Cerreto, *Annales Minorum*, XXV (Quaracchi, 1934²), p. 260. This volume was first published in 1860.

Enciclopedico Hispano–Americano,[8] Hugo Hurter,[9] Anscar Zawart,[10] E. Amann,[11] F. Stegmüller,[12] and Johann Baptist Schneyer [13] continued one way or another the tradition set forth by the Irish Franciscan and passed over in silence what were perhaps the formerly unimportant facts of the man's origin and birth. In comparison with a personage's more "historical" accomplishments, the little details about his birth and place of origin could have been earlier regarded as belonging to the insignificant area of a biography. Paradoxically enough, we are now occupied with these important omissions. To be fair, however, Wadding's one–word description of the bio–datum of Juan de Cartagena was not of his own invention. Cartagena's books themselves more often than not have in their title–pages this *"Hispanus"* appellation for their author.[14]

José Pío Tejera seems the first biographer to have tried to determine more precisely the particulars of the generic description, Spaniard. His posthumous work affirms of Juan de Cartagena: *"natural de la ciudad de su nombre."* [15] That would make Cartagena a native of the Mediterranean coastal town of Cartagena, thus entitling Tejera to include him in his list of distinguished sons and daughters of the southeastern province of Murcia. But this obvious possibility regarding Juan de Cartagena's place of origin did not seem to have impressed the Augustinian bio–bibliographer Agustin Renedo, who in turn claimed Cartagena for his own province. Five years before Tejera's book was published, Renedo came out with his own thesis that Cartagena was *"natural de Ampudia,"* in the northern province

---

[8] *Diccionario Enciclopedico Hispano–Americano*, s.v. Cartagena, Juan de, IV (Barcelona, 1888), p. 322.

[9] Hugo Hurter, S.J., *Nomenclator Literarius Recentioris Theologiae Catholicae*, I (Oenipote, 1892), p. 149.

[10] Anscar Zawart, O.F.M., *The History of Franciscan Preaching and of Franciscan Preachers* (New York, 1925), p. 490.

[11] E. Amann, "Jean de Carthagène," in *Dictionnaire de Théologie Catholique*, VIII (Paris, 1925), p. 754.

[12] F. Stegmüller, art. cit.

[13] Johann Baptist Schneyer, *Geschichte der katholischen Predigt* (Freiburg, 1969), p. 297.

[14] See the next chapter, p. 65 ff.

[15] José Pio Tejera y R. de Moncada, *Biblioteca del Murciano y Ensayo de un Diccionario biográfico y bibliográfico de la Literatura en Murcia*, I (Madrid, 1924), p. 120. Tejera died in 1902. It was Moncada who edited this book.

of Palencia.[16] The basis for this assertion, even if Renedo himself offered no reason for it, could be the fact that Cartagena later stayed in a Franciscan convent of that province. Another historian, anyway, seconded Renedo and criticized Tejera for numbering a *palentino* among the *murcianos*.[17] Toda y Güell for his part adopted a year later Tejera's position in an explicit rejection of Renedo's.[18]

B. DE MADRID

The above differences of opinions over the question of Juan de Cartagena's place of origin received yet a third side to it, when Manuel de Castro affirmed that in fact the man was born in Madrid.[19] This newest development is the fruit of Vazquez' research in the Archive of the Jesuit Curia in Rome. Formerly every Jesuit province used to send to the procurators in Rome a triennial catalogue. These records, compiled every three years in the months of March and April, contain all pertinent data on every Jesuit of a given province as they were grouped in various communities. Given are the religious' complete name, place of origin, age, health, length of time in the Society, studies completed, former and actual functions, academic grade, and status in the Society.

The triennial catalogues of the Jesuit province of Castilla for the years 1590, 1593 and 1597 have for Juan de Cartagena under the heading *Patria: "de Madrid."* [20] And as if to remove any possible doubt that the man might have come from the town of Madrid de las Caderechas in the province of Burgos, the last entry on Cartagena in the 1600 triennal catalogue specifies it as *"Madrid, del arzobispado de Toledo."*[21]

So, it was from the city of Madrid, which King Philip II selected

[16] Agustin Renedo, O.S.A., *Escritores Palentinos* (*Datos Bio–Bibliograficos*), I (Madrid, 1919), p. 124.

[17] Atanasio López in his review of Tejera's book in *Archivo Ibero–Americano*, 27 (1927) 141.

[18] Eduart Toda y Güell, *Bibliografia Espanyola d'Italia*, II (Escornalbou, 1928), p. 335: "Nasqué a Cartagena, com son nom de religio indica, per més que també se l'ha suposat fill d'Ampudia, Palencia."

[19] Manuel de Castro, O.F.M., "Juan de Cartagène," in *Catholicisme*, VI (Paris, 1967), p. 595.

[20] Roman Archive of the Society of Jesus (hereafter ARSJ), *Cat. Trien. Castell.* 14, I, f. 165v; II, f. 248v; f. 324v.

[21] Ibid., II, f. 380r.

to be the capital of the Spanish Monarchy only in 1561, that Juan de Cartagena originated. As a true *madrileño*, he could write to Philip III in dedicating to him his *Homiliae Catholicae de Sacris Arcanis Deiparae Mariae et Ioseph* in 1611: *"sum et ego tua in ditione natus."* [22] Juan de Cartagena was born therefore in the heart of the Castilian tableland, in the very center of Spain, in Madrid, the Monarch's own permanent capital.

C. DATE OF BIRTH

As we have mentioned above, Wadding and all the other commentators who imitated him simply passed in silence the question of Cartagena's date of birth. The first to offer a guess appears to be Renedo, who gave the rounded figure of 1550 as the year of Cartagena's birth in Ampudia.[23] And Toda y Güell, while contesting Renedo's claim that the man was from Ampudia, followed him nonetheless on this matter and set 1550 too as the year of birth of Cartagena.[24] Again, Vazquez [25] and Castro [26] presented the definitive date: 1563. The 1584 triennial catalogue of the Castilian province gives the age of Cartagena as *"21. años."* [27] And the records for 1600 list him to be 37 years of age.[28] Cartagena was born in 1563, the year of the end of the Council of Trent which laid the foundation for a Catholic Reformation.

D. FAMILY ORIGIN

The foregoing shows that the surname "de Cartagena" does not indicate Juan de Cartagena's place of immediate origin. How he or his family got the name is intriguing, if only because we have no information whatsoever about his family. "de Cartagenas" are not lacking among the prominent personages of Spain's "Who's Who"

---

[22] Juan de Cartagena, *Homiliae Catholicae de Sacris Arcanis Deiparae Mariae et Iosephi* I (Coloniae Agrippinae, 1613). We shall be using this Cologne edition in our study, and it shall hereafter be referred to as *HCSADM*.

[23] Renedo, loc. cit.

[24] Toda y Güell, loc. cit.

[25] Vazquez, art. cit.

[26] Castro, art. cit.

[27] ARSJ, *Cat. Trien. Castell.* 14, I, f. 23r.

[28] Ibid., II, f. 380r.

of the 16th and 17th centuries. To mention a couple, there was Pablo
de Santa Maria's family from Burgos taking the surname "de Cartagena" after the father became bishop of Cartagena.[29] Converted from
Judaism, this family produced high dignitaries in the Church and
in the State. There was also Antonio de Cartagena, the renowned
professor of medicine in the University of Alcalá (1518), commissioned by Cisneros himself to start there the faculty of medicine. Since
the surname was not common in that district of Alcalá, Juan Catalina
Garcia wondered if the parents of this Antonio were not perhaps
Juan de Cartagena and Maria de Uceda of Guadalajara (1520), whose
names came up in the proceedings of the Inquisition of Toledo.[30]

For us, a nagging question crops up in this connection: Could
this Juan de Cartagena be the grandfather or great-grandfather of
our Juan de Cartagena? In an apparently autobiographical allusion,
Cartagena once wrote, "It is clear from experience, that proper names
are very often given for some peculiar circumstance. Hence it happens,
that one born on St. Peter's day is called Peter, and one who has
a grandfather with the name Juan is assigned the same name." [31]
Antonio de Cartagena had a son in 1530. And the change of residence
of each new generation from Guadalajara to Alcalá, then to Madrid
would not be altogether unlikely. Unfortunately, we have nothing
more solid to hold on to than this wisp of speculation.

A hypothesis has been advanced by Vazquez, that the name
"de Cartagena" tells us the racial origin of the man. His foreparents
could have come from the Jewish ghetto in Cartagena.[32] Juan de
Cartagena then would be a descendant of *conversos* or *marranos*,
who where originally from the Murcian town of Cartagena. Unlike
other west European states during the Middle Ages, both Castile and
the Crown of Aragon tolerated their Jewish community which played

---

[29] Manuel Martinez Añibarro, *Intento de un Diccionario Biográfico y Bibliográfico de Autores de la Provincia de Burgos* (Madrid, 1890), pp. 88–116, 469–489.

[30] Juan Catalina Garcia, *Biblioteca de Escritores de la Provincia de Guadalajara y Bibliografia de la misma hasta el siglo XIX* (Madrid, 1899), pp. 50–51.
At about the same time, there was also another Jesuit in the Province of
Castilla by the name of Juan de Cartagena, a native of Medina del Campo and
older than our Cartagena. Cf. ARSJ, *Cat. Trien. Castell.* 14, I, f. 29r.

[31] Juan de Cartagena, *Homiliae Catholicae in Universa Christianae Religionis Arcana* (Romae, 1609), lib. V, hom. IV, col. 24. This volume will hereafter
be known as *HCUCRA*.

[32] Vazquez, art. cit., p. 248.

an outstanding part in the cultural and economic life of Spain. Following the wave of anti–Semitism towards the end of the 14th century, however, many of the Spanish Jews submitted to baptism, in order to save their lives. The wealth of these so–called *cristianos nuevos* gave them entry into the circle of the Court and aristocracy, and acquired for them power and influence as financiers, administrators, or members of the ecclesiastical hierarchy.[33] While speaking on how to select officials, Cartagena dropped a line which throws some tantalizing lead on his family background. In choosing officials, he said, one must use the care and diligence of a minter, whom he had observed *"non semel"* weighing first the quantity of gold and then according to its weight minting it.[34] A minting house is obviously

---

[33] A good example of this social mobility for the moneyed *conversos* is the grandfather of St. Theresa of Avila. A merchant of Toledo, Juan Sanchez married into the aristocratic family of Cepeda. In 1485 the Toledo Inquisition penanced him for Judaizing practices. He moved his family to Avila, got all his children to be married into families of the local nobility, and continued his very successful career as a cloth and silk merchant. The family later switched from trade to the administration of rents and the farming of taxes. Cf. *Obras Completas de Santa Teresa de Jesus*, I, Introduction (Madrid, Biblioteca de Autores Cristianos, 1951).

[34] "...id eis servandum est, quod in officina monetam cudentium non semel ego observavi, qui prius ponderabant auri quantitatem, et secundum pondus, signum, et figuram ei imprimebant..." *HCUCRA*, lib. VIII, hom. III, col. 23.

In view of the possibility that Juan de Cartagena might have come from a *converso* family, the question of his attitude towards the Jews assumes interest. In his writings, Cartagena never directly concerned himself with the matter. He had however in passing repeatedly referred to the Jews with the asperity common during his time. For instance, he entitled a homily: "Verba illa: Dispersit superbos mente cordis sui: explicantur de Iudaeis; ubi haec praecipue ostenditur, beneficium copia, quibus Deus eos cumulavit; ingratitudo illorum, filium eius occidentium varia supplicia quae ob id perpessi sunt." *HCSADM*, lib. VI, hom. XXI (I, 671b). – The Roman numeral within the parentheses stands for the volume of the *HCSADM*, while Arabic numbers indicate the page and the letter specifies the column. – In hom. XXVI of the same book (I, 698b), he writes: "Coelum Christum agnovit... soli tamen Iudaei non tantum dicam brutis animantibus, sed ipso inferno obstinatiores, semper illum spreverunt..." Cartagena also often uses the expression "perfidi Hebraei". Cf. *HCUCRA*, lib. V, hom. V, col. 26, and lib. VI, hom. II, col. 14. In one of the eight new homilies Cartagena later added in the 1612 Facciotti edition of the *HCUCRA*, he notes that: "rex Sissebutus... ardenter cupiens a iudaicae perfidiae labe totam Hispaniam emundari, omnes iudaeos ab ea longe primus relegare coepit; cuius pietatis aemulator extitit successor eius rex Scintillae; posteaquam ultimam ei manum apposuerunt reges catholici Ferdinandus et Isabella, nihil pendentes magni momenti tributa et vectigalia, quae a iudaeis sibi pendebantur, ne eos abire compellerent... ac tandem Philippus tertius

a pretty restricted place. To have been in one repeatedly, watching the operations, perhaps as a child wandering in with wide–eyed curiosity, connotes a ready access to the mint. Was Juan de Cartagena related to a financier or an administrator? If he were likewise related to the Juan de Cartagena of Guadalajara whom we have referred to above, the hypothesis of Vazquez could be really strengthened. This Juan de Cartagena's name came up in the proceedings of the Inquisition of Toledo, which was set up to handle the cases of the *conversos* who were regressing back to Jewish practices, or who were suspected of doing so. But this whole matter of Cartagena's possible Jewish origin is again nothing but guesswork.

Still another "hypothesis" about Cartagena's family origin surfaced some 14 years after his death. In the hefty controversy during the second quarter of the 17th century concerning St. Joseph's *sanctificatio in utero*, Cartagena received a major billing as a main protagonist of the teaching. We shall treat this event more fully in an excursus in Chapter Three below, so it suffices here to note that the controversy was carried on by the principal participants on a

---

Hispaniarum rex omnes agaraenos tanquam catholicae fidei hostes ab omnibus suis regnis tam prudenter quam religiose hac nostra tempestate exturbavit." *HCUCRA*, lib. VI, hom. VI. The 1614 Cologne edition does not have this passage, which refers to the 1492 expulsion of the Jews from Spain and to the 1610 expulsion of the Moriscos.

On the other hand, Cartagena did not subscribe to the then fashionable theory of the irremisibility of the Jews' guilt. Christ's reason for willing the circumcision is a universal invitation to his friendship also for the Jews: "Estne aliquis capitalis hostis meus, qui mihi reconciliari cupiat? Accedat securus, et sanguinem meum amicitiae pignus accipere non dubitet..." *HCUCRA*, lib. IV, hom. II, col. 14. Again, in connection with Christ's words of forgiveness on the cross, the author says: "...quam absurda loquendi ratio sit ea, quae multis fidelibus familiaris esse solet, contra proprium videlicet honorem esse, illatam iniuriam non vindicare. Id enim existimaverim implicite, et involute errorem contra fidem catholicam continere..." Ibid., lib. XI, hom. I, col. 16. He is directly talking about the forgiveness of personal offense, but in the context of what preceded in this homily, esp. cols. 5 & 9, included in the criticism is the racial discrimination against the Jews on the ground of their blood contaminated with the sin of deicide. And it used to be a matter of honor not to mix with the Jews. The 16th century development in Spain of the doctrine of *limpieza de sangre* — purity of blood — was actually a culmination of anti–Semitism, excluding all persons of Jewish ancestry from high office in Church and State. Cf. Peter Browe, S.J., "Die religiöse Duldung der Juden im Mittelalter," *Archiv für katholisches Kirchenrecht*, 118 (1938) 3–76.

very personal level with aspersions on personalities flying thick. Claudius Dausquius or Claude d'Ausque, the articulate crusader against the thesis that St. Joseph was sanctified in the womb, had strongly hinted that the dead Cartagena was Moorish. Pierre Marchant, the Franciscan Recollect who championed Cartagena's position, challenged the assertion as a calumny.[35] But as Dausquius retorted, to prove him false, Marchant had simply to name the Spanish city of Cartagena's origin, but Marchant did not or could not.[36] Juan de Cartagena's family background was that unknown! To be objective, Dausquius' reasons for his suspicion relayed in the form of a gossip that Cartagena was a Morisco are at best facetious, supercilious and

---

[35] Pierre Marchant, O.F.M., *Sanctificatio S. Josephi Sponsi Virginis Nutritii Iesus in Utero, Asserta pro R.P.F. Joanne Carthagena Ordinis S. Francisci olim in Academia Salmanticensis Professore, et in Urbe de Mandato Sanctissimi Generali Lectore contra R.D. Claudii Dausquii Tornacensis Canonici Calumnias* (Brugge, 1630), p. 41.

[36] Dausquius, *Sancti Joseph Sanctificatio extra Uterum...*, op. cit., p. 224. On p. 221 Dausquius entitles his chapter: "Cartagenam non esse Maurum non probat Marchantius. De natione cur dubitarit Dausquius."

With the completion of the *Reconquista* in 1492, the Moors' eight century long hold over Granada had been broken. At first the Christian administrators of the conquered kingdom were rather tolerant, guaranteeing the Moors among others the free exercise of their faith. Hernando de Talavera, the first Archbishop of Granada, especially had no sympathy for a policy of forcible conversion. Archbishop Cisneros of Toledo, however, coming to Granada with Ferdinand and Isabella in 1499, believed in a more forceful approach. The mild Talavera was eventually pushed aside and a campaign for mass baptism was launched. Predictably, Moors became nominal Christians by the thousands. But almost at the same time an uprising broke out in the Alpujarras of the Sierra Nevada. Ferdinand crushed the revolt in 1500, and the Moors now had to choose between emigration and conversion. A 1502 pragmatic ordered the expulsion of all unconverted adult Moors, thus assuring the automatic "Christianization" of the Moorish population in the south. The Moriscos of Granada, resenting the ever worsening treatment they were receiving, burst out once more in 1568–1570 in a savage racial and religious revolt. This Second Rebellion of the Alpujarras, as it is called, ended like the first in defeat and in more repressive measures from the hands of the Old Christians. Philip II ordered the dispersion of the Moriscos throughout Castile. This order only extended the problem of this unassimilated racial minority to other areas. In Valencia in 1609, for example, its 135,000 Moriscos, the largest concentration anywhere in the country, made up perhaps a third of the entire population, a closely-knit community of outsiders significantly known as *la nación de los cristianos nuevos de moros del reino de Valencia*. The popular feeling against them eventually led to the assumption that expulsion was the only remaining solution. And between 1608 and 1614, the expulsion of the Moriscos from Spain

self–contradictory.[37] He had never anywhere read Cartagena's birthplace. That was why he doubted. And why not a Moor? A Moor and a Spaniard are of the same color, as he had seen some of them in Paris, and they come just from neighbouring countries. In fact, a great part of Spain was formerly Moorish. He, Dausquius, considers the name *"Maurus"* no less honorable than the name *"Hispanus"* (which Cartagena banners in the title–pages of his books). As a friend of Dausquius said, writers from the villages want to be known to come from the cities. Yes, why not a Moor? Cartagena writes like one–without wit and without the Spanish acumen.[38]

The idea, though, that Juan de Cartagena might have come from a Morisco family is not altogether improbable. All things being equal, it has only the same probability as the other opinion that Cartagena perhaps had Jewish ancestry. The family designation "de Cartagena" could mean origin from the community of Moriscos in the city of that name as well as from its Jewish ghetto.[39] The province of Murcia by the time of the expulsion of the Moriscos had a population of 14,000 of them, while the neighboring Valencia harbored the largest concentration of these peoples.[40] We have noted before that Cartagena himself volunteered only one definite piece of information about his origin: he was a *Hispanus*. Was there something about his family background which he judged better to keep silent about in the light of the developments during his time? He was not so reticent as not to say anything at all about his person. But he was careful enough to say only what little personal tid–bits he wanted others to

---

was carefully executed. According to estimates, only 1 out of every 12 Moriscos in a probable total of 300, 000 managed to remain. Cf. J. H. Elliott, *Imperial Spain 1469–1716* (Middlesex, Pelican, 1970), pp. 43–53, 235–241, 305–308.

[37] Dausquius, op. cit., pp. 222–224.

[38] Ibid., p. 126.

[39] Again, Cartagena never considered the question of the Moriscos in itself, just as he did not concern himself directly with the matter of the Jews. But he definitely sees in their inclusion into the Church a divine ordination. Speaking in the context of the Epiphany, he writes with distinct universalism: "Video tandem nunc, quod in mysterio Salomonis templo praefiguratum fuerat (I Kg 5, 15–32), impletum: nam sicut illud ex lapidibus Iudaeae, ac lignis Gentium aedificatum erat; sic magnum hoc Ecclesiae templum a sapientissimo Salomone Christo, ex Iudaeis et Gentibus constructum est, in cuius rei testimonium pastores a Iudaea, et Reges a gentium regionibus illum adorare convenerunt." *HCUCRA*, lib. VI, hom. IV, col. 48.

[40] Cf. Elliott, op cit., p. 307.

know about him. Was he protesting too much in always affixing "Spaniard" to his name? But, again, such self–identification was not really that unusual, considering that Cartagena published all his books abroad, where he could simply be proudly proclaiming his nationality to his non–Spanish readers.

E. EARLY EDUCATION

One of the few morsels of biographical importance we can gather from the writings of Juan de Cartagena touches on his early education. In that dedication to Philip III we have referred to above, Cartagena spoke of himself: "I was educated in your kingdom and in your academies I grew up in the letters." [41] The allusion is probably to his studies of grammar and rhetoric, of the humanities in other words, prior to his *curso de artes*. These four years of *gramatica* were required for the higher university courses. For a command of Latin was necessary to follow the courses and speak the language of the universities. The academies mentioned could be the university colleges at Salamanca or Alcalá, Spain's two leading institutions of higher learning at that time. The latter would have been nearer to Madrid, his birth place, but Cartagena's subsequent entrance into the Society of Jesus in the Jesuit province of Castilla whose provincial house was in Salamanca suggests that he had contact with the Jesuits there. Was he a student in one of the more than 40 colleges clustered around the Salamancan center of learning, the *Athenas española*, which as early as the 14th century had already gained the same footing as Paris, Bologna and Oxford? These colleges, Cartagena would later muse, provide the State with officials outstanding in the letters and in virtue. And these alumni honor the founders of their colleges so much, that just the mention of their names was enough to move the former students to bare and bow their heads.[42] During the last quarter of the 16th century, Salamanca boasted of more than 6,700 students.[43]

---

[41] "...in tuo regno educatus, in tuis academiis in litteris adolevi." *HCSADM* (I, Dedication).

[42] "...in Hispaniae academiis varia sunt... Collegia, ex quibus, tanquam ex equo troiano, multi viri litteris et virtute praestantes ad reipublicae christianae diversos gravesque regendos magistratus prodeunt, qui tanta reverentia prosequuntur sui collegii conditores, ut, me teste, audito illorum nomine, statim capita detegant et demittant." *HCUCRA*, lib. V, hom. VII, col. 41.

[43] Cf. Raoul de Scorraille, S.J., *François Suarez*, I (Paris, 1912), pp. 26–27.

In this teeming student population, just what *beca* or colored sash worn over the soutane to represent a college did Cartagena have, we do not know. Was he a *camarista* renting an apartment like other students from well–to–do families, or an intern in one of the colleges?

II. A JESUIT

A. FORMATION AND STUDIES

The triennial catalogue for the year 1584 of the Jesuit province of Castilla lists Juan de Cartagena as 21 years of age with four years in the Society.[44] The catalogues for 1590, 1593, 1597 and 1600 establish the same conclusion that he must have joined the Society of Jesus in 1581 at the age of 17 years. Since the triennial catalogue for 1581 is missing from the Jesuit Archive in Rome, we do not know where Cartagena made his novitiate. Most probably it was at Medina del Campo, northeast of Salamanca and south of Tordesillas, established in 1562. It was there that the novitiate house for Castilla la Vieja was then located.

The 1584 catalogue also specifies that Juan de Cartagena "de Madrid," an "*escholar aprobado*" in his present occupation, has already "*3. años de artes.*" [45] If in his fourth year in the Society he had already behind him his three years of philosophy, it means that what should normally be his second year as a novice served actually as the first year of his philosophy course (1581–1582). Ordinarily the study of philosophy or *artes* in the training of the Jesuits begins only after the two years of the novitiate. Apparently Cartagena was dispensed from the second year of being a novice, or at least it was so adjusted, that he could start at once with his *curso de artes*.[46] Where did he study philosophy? In the spring of 1584, or at the time the triennial catalogue was edited, Cartagena was included among the Jesuits in the college of the Society in León. Whether he studied there the complete three–year course in philosophy or only the latter part of it, we do not know. The college's faculty record of that year lists neither professors of philosophy nor other students of the *artes*.

---

[44] ARSJ, *Cat. Trien. Castell.* 14, I, f. 23r.

[45] Ibid.

[46] Such exceptions are known to have been made. Suárez, for instance, had an even shorter novitiate of only three months. Cf. Scorraille, op. cit., pp. 52–53.

Castilla's catalogue for 1587, during which time Cartagena should be studying theology, inexplicably does not include his name. He could naturally have gone to another Jesuit province for his theological training. The 1587 catalogues for Toledo, Bética, Aragón, Luisitania and the Roman College in Rome contain however no entry whatsoever about him. In 1590 the catalogue of Castilla picks him up once more with the notation under *Studia: "Artes y theologia."* [47] So, he had completed by then his course in theology, most probably finishing it in 1588. Where? Most likely he spent those four years of theological studies in the province's faculty of theology in Salamanca. Reckoning all the years since he took up theology as one long preparation for the pastoral ministry of proclaiming the Word of God, Cartagena began his letter dedicating the first volume of the *Homiliae catholicae* to Pope Paul V towards the end of 1608 thus:

> What I have laboured at, Most Blessed Father, for almost twenty five years through continuous studies for the nourishment of the faithful... I begin now under your apostolic guidance to deposit gladly in the Lord's granary of the Catholic Church. [48]

From the summer of 1584 when he started his theological studies to the winter of 1608 would be almost 25 years.

Since we do not know for sure in which colleges Juan de Cartagena actually studied philosophy and theology, the names of his teachers remain unknown. One thing is certain, however, that he could not have been a student of Suárez, as has been claimed. [49] During the years of Cartagena's theological studies, the *Doctor Eximius* was teaching in Alcalá, whose 1587 catalogue list does not carry any Juan de Cartagena.

As a student of philosophy and later of theology, Cartagena must have resided in a Jesuit college nearby a university, where he went for the principal lectures and academic exercise. In the Jesuit college itself he would have classes to attend together with his fellow Jesuit students. Some of these classes were exclusively for the community

---

[47] ARSJ, *Cat. Trien. Castell.* 14, I, f. 165v.

[48] "Quae per annos ferme vigintiquinque (Beatissime Pater) continuis lucubrationibus elaboravi pro cibandis fidelibus... incipio nunc sub apostolicis suis auspiciis in Dominicum horreum Ecclesiae catholicae... feliciter inferre." *HCUCRA*, Dedication.

[49] F. Stegmüller, loc. cit., describes Cartagena as "Schüler u. Anhänger v. Suarez."

members, especially on matters of spiritual formation. But in the larger Jesuit colleges with their own professors, certain lectures were also held *a puerta abierta*, open to the public and at the hour corresponding to the university's titular *cátedras*. This was the case, for instance, in Salamanca, until the Jesuits were given a university hall for their lectures but with the proviso that these lectures be not given in conflict with the time of the main *catedráticos*, so as not to divide the students.

The Constitution of the Society specifies what the Jesuit students should study : the humanities and languages, logic, natural and moral philosophy, metaphysics, theology both scholastic and positive, and Sacred Scripture.[50] The classroom method would have been the so-called Parisian method, canonized by the Society whose founding fathers were formed in Paris. The main thing was the progress of the students under the immediate supervision of the teacher. The tools for that were, in addition to the lessons, written assignments, public discussions and repetitions. The learner's active participation in the classroom was taken for granted. Disputations were especially stressed.[51]

---

[50] *Constitutiones Societatis Jesu*, P. IV, c. V, 1. Cf. P. Leturia, "De 'Constitutionibus collegiorum' P. Joannis A. de Polanco ac de eorum influxu in Constitutiones Societatis Jesu," *Archivum Historicum Societatis Jesu*, 7 (1938) 1–30.

[51] *Constitutiones*, P. IV, c. VI, 10. Cf. P. Leturia, "La pedagogía humanista de San Ignacio," *Razon y Fe*, 121 (1940) 329–340, and Bernhard Duhr, S.J., *Die Studienordnung der Gesellschaft Jesu*, Bibliothek der katholischen Pädagogik IX (Freiburg im Breisgau, 1896), pp. 159–166.

Cartagena's comment about these disputations, apparently based on his experience both as a student and as a teacher, is very revealing of his own temperament: "Adfui ego non semel permultis publicis Academiarum disputationibus, quibus tanta erat vociferantium confusio, ut dicere compellerer: ecce imaginem inferni, 'ubi nullus ordo sed sempiternus horror inhabitabat.' Ferrarios malleatores, sapientiores his iudico; illi enim sic se gerunt, ut dum unus malleo super incudem ferri massam percutit, alius malleum suum elevat, nec pariter percutiunt, nec pariter elevant, sed alternantes; isti vero importunae suae vociferationis malleo semper nostras aures percutiunt, interrogationem et responsionem minime alternare volentes, sed omnia confundentes..." Moralizing, Cartagena says: "Sane, qui in disputatione ita inordinate se gerunt, stultitiae suae non obscurum praebent inditium (Prov. 18, 13)... Etenim, qui doctrinam auscultat, colligit et haurit, et cor implet; qui vero loquitur, erogat et exinanitur... Disputantes ergo moneo, cantores peritos imitentur, qui cantantes silentii pausam interponunt, alioquin molestum, et ingratum cantum ederent." *HCSADM*, lib. X, hom. X (II, 280a–b).

B. PADRE

In 1593 Juan de Cartagena's name was added by another hand and apparently at the last minute as the 87th and last entry in that year's triennial catalogue list of community members in the tertian house in Villagarcia de Campos.[52] The tertianship of the Jesuits is a "third" year of novitiate devoted to the deepening of one's spirituality following the completion of the normal studies and prior to a full-scale engagement in the ministry. This time Cartagena is referred to as *Padre*. But the assertion by Vazquez that Cartagena, 30 years of age, was probably ordained to the priesthood shortly before the catalogue of Castilla was completed in April, 1593, is contradicted by a careful reading of the records.[53] It was not first in 1593 that a triennial catalogue prefixes his name with a *"P"* signifying *"Padre."* Both in 1590 and 1600, the records have before Juan de Cartagena's name a *"Pe,"* an abbreviation for *Padre*.[54] That means that in 1590, at the age of 27 years, Cartagena had already been ordained a priest.

C. MINISTERIA

But even after Cartagena had received ordination, he still had another stage of his Jesuit formation to undergo, the stint at teaching normally lasting three years. These years of practise are gone through by the young Jesuits ordinarily after finishing philosophy and before starting theology. However, there have been and there are variations to this sequence. Cartagena himself had his practise-teaching after completing both his philosophical and his theological studies. This requirement in his formation would be capped, as already noted, with the "finishing touches" during the tertianship. Meanwhile, we are told by the 1593 catalogue that Cartagena had made the *"votos de dos años."* [55]

Having completed then his formal studies at the age of 27, Juan

---

[52] ARSJ, *Cat. Trien. Castell.* 14, II, f. 248v.

[53] Vazquez, art. cit., p. 253.

[54] ARSJ, *Cat. Trien. Castell.* 14, I, f. 165v; and II, f. 380r.

[55] Ibid., f. 165v. It is first here that we have any reference to Cartagena's religious vows. Vazquez, art. cit., p. 252, claims that the 1584 catalogue records that Cartagena has already made the vows "de los dos años." Perhaps Cartagena made the vows then, inasmuch as the Jesuits take the vows temporarily during the years of formation. But certainly the 1584 triennial catalogue does not say so.

de Cartagena commenced his teaching careeer. According to the 1590 catalogue of Castilla, he was once more in the Jesuit college in León, but this time as a teacher. "*Lee a(h)ora artes,*" observes the triennial catalogue.[56] He has been in the Society of Jesus for ten years now, and officially his status was still that of an "*Escholar aprobado,*" since these years as a teacher before the tertianship are considered part and parcel of the basic Jesuit training. In today's parlance among the Jesuits, Cartagena was still at this point a "scholastic." He taught philosophy in León for two years only. For the 1593 catalogue specifies that "he read the arts for two years." [57] Incidentally, one of his students there was Fernando de la Bastida, who years later would be defending in Rome the Molinism attacked among others by his former teacher in León.[58]

Following his "scholastic" years and the tertianship at Villagarcia de Campos, we find Cartagena once more listed in 1597 among the community members of the college in León.[59] (Somebody bungled with the catalogue and wrote his age as 25. That and his 17 years in the Society would have meant that he joined the Jesuits at the age of 8! Another hand therefore added "*34. ò 35.*") Under his *ministeria* are enumerated: "*Lector de artes, casos y theologia, y predicador.*" As a teacher of philosophy, Cartagena was just pursuing the work he had earlier performed in León as a "scholastic." New were his functions as preacher, about which we shall comment more later, and as lecturer of theology and in *casus conscientiae* or moral theology which was then not yet separated from dogma.

Cartagena's new assignment as lecturer in theology, after having taught philosophy for at least a couple of years in León, brings to mind Juan de Maldonado's, S.J. († 1583), prescription for an ideal professor of theology. Such a professor should preferably have already taught philosophy. He must likewise be well grounded in languages, Sacred Scripture, conciliar documents, patrology, and scholastic authors, especially St. Thomas.[60] St. Thomas, however, should not be slavishly followed in everything. We shall presently see what such

---

[56] ARSJ, ibid., I, f. 165v.

[57] Ibid., II, f. 248v: "Leyó dos años artes."

[58] Cf. Carlos Sommervogel, S.J., *Bibliothèque de la Compagnie de Jésus,* I (Brussels–Paris, 1890), p. 1006.

[59] ARSJ, *Cat. Trien. Castell.* 14, II, f. 324v.

[60] *Monumenta Paedagogica, Monumenta Historica Societatis Jesu* I, ed. Caecilius Gomez Rodeles et al. (Matriti, 1901), pp. 864–865.

an advice as this worked out in Cartagena's career as a theologian. But briefly now concerning the mechanics of Cartagena's work as a theology professor, the Constitution of the Society points out first of all regarding textbooks that only those teachings are to be advocated which are solid and certain. "And in theology are to be read the Old and New Testaments, and the scholastic teaching of St. Thomas, and for the so–called positive teaching, those authors are to be selected who are more compatible to our goal." [61] To this rule has been added a declaration by St. Ignatius that "The Master of the Sentences is also to be read. But should it appear in the course of time that another author shall be more useful for the students, such as, if some *summa* or book of scholastic theology should be composed, which seems more suited to our times, with serious deliberation... and with the approval of the General, it may be read." [62]

The basic matter to be covered in theology is supposed to be cycled in four years, so that anyone can join the course in any year and still complete it at the end of the fourth year. Two dogma professors, for instance, handling St. Thomas' *Summa* would have the following division of labor according to the 1599 *Ratio Studiorum:* The first professor takes up for the first year the first part of the *Summa* up to *Quaestio* 43 inclusive. The following year he has angelogy and the first 21 questions of the second part, from question 55 or 71 up to the end of the *Prima Secundae* for the third year, and *de fide, spe et caritate* for the fourth year. The second professor is responsible for *de iustitia, de iure* and *de religione* in the first year out of the *Secunda Secundae*, then *de incarnatione* and *de sacramentis in genere* for the second year. The third year has *de baptismo* and *de Eucharistia*, and if the time allows it, *de ordine, de confirmatione* and the anointing of the sick. *De poenitentia* and *de matrimonio* are had in the fourth year.[63] Cartagena himself must have started up with the subject matter of the first year for the second professor, when he was called upon to teach theology at Salamanca where we know he lectured at least on *de Voto*.[64]

The theology professors are told to leave exegetical questions to the Scripture professor and philosophical matters to philosophy, not

[61] *Constitutiones*, P. IV, c. XIV, 1.

[62] Ibid., 1B.

[63] Duhr, op. cit., pp. 206–207.

[64] See the following chapter, p. 97.

to devote too much time to apologetics against heretics, and to pass on to *casus conscientiae* what pertains more to it.[65] The procedure in handling the above–enumerated subject matters would be along the line the *cátedra de Prima* used to be conducted at Salamanca. In the order that St. Thomas gives them, the articles are to be treated, beginning with the title, then going to the body. Doubts and questions are then answered. The opinions of other authors and their reasonings should be brought in too. But anything brought in should be treated only in connection with the article in question.[66]

The *Ratio Studiorum* in 1599 set the distinction between moral theology or casuistry and dogmatic theology. The professor of the former is supposed to cover all the sacraments, the decalogue, *de statibus, censuris, et obligationibus* from the pastoral point of view in a cycle of two years. And every Saturday, in place of the lecture, there should be *casus conscientiae*.[67] At first it was probably only of such cases that Cartagena was in charge in León. And for that he could have used for example Bartolomé de Fumo's *Aurea Armilla*, a *summa casuum conscientiae* (1550).[68]

During Cartagena's assignment to the college in León, the Jesuit province of Castilla had more than 500 members, half of them priests. Distributed among the province's colleges were four professors of philosophy, nine for theology, one for Sacred Scripture (in Salamanca), and eight for *Casus conscientiae*.[69]

Cartagena's first assignment following his tertianship was therefore a teaching post at the college in León. It must have been shortly after taking his post there that he was named professor of theology in Salamanca. But his sojourn in Salamanca was of such a short duration, that Cartagena was back again in León just before the 1957 triennial catalogue was compiled.

---

[65] Duhr, op. cit., p. 207.

[66] *Monumenta Paedagogica*, op. cit., pp. 518–519. Fernando Pérez more fully described this method commonly employed by the Jesuits towards the end of the 16th century not just in their lectures but also in their writings. Cf. ibid., pp. 572–573.

[67] Duhr, op. cit., pp. 210–212.

[68] Jeronimo Nadal, S.J. († 1580), for one recommended this book for the Society. Cf. Melquiades Andres Martin, *Historia de la Teologia en España (1470–1570)*, I: Instituciones Teologicas (Roma, 1962), p. 209.

[69] Cf. Scorraille, op. cit., p. 316.

D. SALAMANCA

The Jesuit college of San Marcos in Salamanca had at this time some 50 community members. Less than half of these were theology students. The early inadequacies of the house — the college was begun in 1548 — were such that the death there of some Jesuit students lent it the reputation of being a *"studiosorum sepultura."* The building though had just been renovated. And the theology lecture *de prima*, open to the public, was attracting a sizable crowd.

It was evidently a big boost to the young Juan de Cartagena and a recognition of his abilities, when he was given the chance to read theology at Salamanca. This rightly renowned center of higher learning, where the Golden Age of Spanish theology fully blossomed, would have been the secret goal in the heart of any aspiring theologian. Unfortunately, it was here that Cartagena would have his first hard experience of uncharitable rivalry and intramural fighting. To comprehend the incident fully, we shall have to go into a detailed investigation of the circumstances.

In 1593 Francisco Suárez returned to Salamanca, where he had studied, to rest and to concentrate on his writings for which he needed the libraries of the university town. Behind him were 22 years in high repute as teacher in Rome and in Alcalá. His early published works had already spread his name far and wide. His homecoming to the *"cuidad del Tormes"* soon resulted, however, in a confrontation between two opposing camps extending outside the confines of that place. A long–simmering tension had been building up in the field of theology over the binding force of the teachings of St. Thomas Aquinas. The Jesuits were especially involved in the matter, because in addition to the fact that their schools had mushroomed all over Europe, an ever–growing number of Jesuit professors refused to accept that they had an obligation — notwithstanding the position of St. Thomas as the official doctor of the Society — to teach simply *"in verbo magistri,"* much less to agree with the interpretations of the Thomists.[70] That Suárez should be in Salamanca during the last decade of the 16th century, when his "non–Thomistic" and "unorthodox" ideas and methods were already well known, naturally

---

[70] Ibid., p. 215 ff. Cf. A. Inauen, S.J., "Stellung der Gesellschaft Jesu zur Lehre des Aristoteles und des hl. Thomas vor 1583," *Zeitschrift für katholische Theologie*, 40 (1916) 201-237; and *Monumenta Paedagogica*, op. cit., pp. 572-573.

promised an explosion of some proportion. Occupying theology's *cá-tedra de Prima* in Salamanca at that time was none other than the Dominican Domingo Bañez, who had been compaigning for years for a strict, pure Thomism. The inevitable show–down came, but not so much with the Dominicans as with Suárez' own fellow Jesuits. For, within the Society itself a polarization had been building up between the traditional Thomists and the more progressive theologians. Suárez' main opponent was Miguel Marcos, who had the first professorship in theology for the Jesuit college, where he had been assigned since 1573.

Although the Constitution of the Society of Jesus opts for St. Thomas as the text to be read in scholastic theology, the intention was always to leave an opening for some future developments. St. Ignatius himself was "waiting" for a *summa* which would be more suited to the times.[71] Jeronimo Nadal, S.J. († 1580), superintendent of the *Collegium Romanum*, spoke in his second outline for the *Ratio Studiorum* about putting together a *summa theologiae* with which to replace St. Thomas and which would take into consideration both Thomists, Scotists and Nominalists[72]. Diego de Ledesma, S.J. († 1575), another first generation Jesuit, in his rules for the teachers of theology, took it for granted that one could depart from the teaching of St. Thomas when the view of most other teachers contradicts him, but that care must be had that the authority of the Angelic Doctor does not unduly suffer.[73] This attitude of generally following Thomas Aquinas but also of disagreeing with him when necessary reflects the stance itself of Francisco de Vitoria, O.P. († 1546), who was the first one in 1526 to replace the Master of the Sentences with the *Summa* of St. Thomas for his lectures *de Prima* at Salamanca. Melchior Cano, O.P. († 1560), wrote how Vitoria had said that one must not follow Thomas Aquinas blindly and that one should especially examine his words when they seem improbable.[74] Cano himself followed the advice of his teacher scrupulously.

But by 1582 the intolerance among the various schools of thought and religious orders, which would prove to be the tragic undoing of the 16th century renaissance in theology, was already rearing its

---

[71] *Constitutiones*, P. IV, c. XIV, B.
[72] *Monumenta Paedagogica*, op. cit., p. 99.
[73] Ibid., pp. 570–571; cf. p. 146.
[74] Melchior Cano, *Loci Theologici* (Venetiis, 1567), XII, proemium, p. 671.

head. A theological arteriosclerosis was setting in. Ominously, for example, the Inquisition was brought into play in a controversy that broke out in Salamanca in 1582 involving Miguel Marcos himself. In January of that year, a disciple of Marcos, Prudencio de Montemayor, publicly defended some theses on the Incarnation.[75] Answering the interpellations from Bañez, Montemayor affirmed that an antecedent predetermination of Christ to die on the cross would be contrary to the will's freedom. Bañez retorted with the qualification of that statement as erroneous, even heretical. The Augustinian Luis de León sided with the Jesuit. Marcos stepped in to clear up the point at issue, but to no avail. Bañez was not satisfied. This event, which could be considered the first shot in what developed into the controversy *de auxiliis*, led to denunciations before the Inquisition. Luis de León was warned not to teach the proposition anymore. Montemayor was penanced by his Provincial and banned from teaching theology.

As the Inquisition proceedings on this matter were going on, Alonzo Deza, professor of theology in the Jesuit college in Alcalá, under whom Miguel Marcos studied and who was known for his fervid loyalty to St. Thomas, took the occasion to write the General of the Society, Aquaviva, making recommendations partly in the light of the recent developments and partly out of his own personal convinction that the Society of Jesus should follow Thomas Aquinas.[76] These two, Deza and Marcos, respected theologians in Spain's two leading universities, were the principal advocates within the Society for a strict Thomism. Significantly, Marcos had as early as 1579 taken a stand against Suárez, then teaching in Valladolid, in a letter to the Visitator of Castilla urging that measures be taken to put a stop to strange doctrinal innovations being introduced especially by the Granadian.[77]

---

[75] Cf. A. Astrain, S.J., *Historia de la Compañia de Jesus en la Asistencia de España*, IV (Madrid, 1913), pp. 129–146.

[76] Scorraille, op. cit., II, p. 212. The orthodoxy of Deza's Thomism as far as the Dominicans were concerned is mirrored by the story that Bañez in a public lecture in Salamanca was reported to have said that he could use for his commentaries on the *Summa* only the writings of Deza, which are faithful and without evasions. Cf. Valentin Serna, S.J., "Un comentario inedito de Miguel Marcos a a la cuestion 23 de la Suma de Santo Tomas de Praedestinatione," *Archivo Teologico Granadino*, 19 (1956) 239.

[77] Serna, ibid., p. 240; Scorraille, op. cit., I, pp. 320-324. Miguel Marcos was born in Villacastin in Segovia in 1542. Cf. Sommervogel, op. cit., V, p. 534.

Voices had not been wanting, however, which opposed from the very beginning an exaggerated commitment to St. Thomas, who admittedly had espoused doctrines now proven to be obsolete like his stand against the Immaculate Conception.[78] Pointing out the danger of putting a person ahead of the truth, Alfonso Salmeron quoted the Philosopher: "*Amicus Plato, amicus Socrates, sed magis amica veritas.*" [79] Suárez himself in 1579 in answering the accusation levelled against him that he was departing from St. Thomas, maintained that the *Constitutiones* of the Society has not prescribed the Angelic Doctor for everything, but only that he be adhered to as a general rule.[80] Thomas Aquinas' theology is a uniquely masterful accomplishment, but it is not perfect and should not be used to stifle intellectual freedom.

Meanwhile Miguel Marcos carried on his running battle against Bañez over theological matters, causing the disquietude of superiors who wanted a truce with the Dominicans. He also went once to Valladolid to help in the defense of four Jesuits accused of heresy by the Inquisition. His fearless defense of the Society against all outside threats was matched only by his zeal in combating all doctrinal novelties inside the Order. Anything not found in St. Thomas or in his classic commentators were for him proscribed. Anything new in matters of doctrine were for him dangerous or false. The inevitable collision of this man with Suárez was immediately preceded by his participation in the 5th General Congregation of the Society of Jesus which opened in Rome on November 3, 1593. Marcos was one of Castilla's representatives. This General Congregation, taking cognizance of the ever increasing attacks against the Society regarding doctrine, decreed among other things that St. Thomas must be followed by Jesuit theologians.[81] Incidentally, Marcos himself made a successful intervention during the General Congregation taking to task the *cristianos nuevos.* He asserted that those who make trouble within the Society were for the most part of Jewish ancestry.[82] On

---

[78] Cf. Inauen, art. cit., pp. 217-221.

[79] Quoted by Inauen, ibid., p. 219.

[80] Scorraille, op. cit., p. 221; Inauen, art. cit., p. 220.

[81] *Decreta Congregationum Generalium Societatis Iesu* (Antwerpiae, 1635), Decreta Quintae Congregationis generalis, XLI, in Ms. d. 55, pp. 299–300.

[82] Astrain, op. cit., III, pp. 565 & 593. The 5th General Congregation decreed: "Quoniam Societatis ministeria eo maiori cum fructu, in communi animarum salute procuranda exercentur, quo Nostri longius absunt ab iis hominum

this subject, the General Congregation yielded to outside pressures and decreed the debarment from the Society of postulants with Jewish or Moorish ancestry.

Suárez arrived in Salamanca in October of 1593. He was just on time for the opening of classes, and was pressed to substitute for Marcos who had already left for Rome. When the General Congregation ended on January 18, 1594, Marcos would not return to take over his teaching position again. In a sulk that Suárez of all persons was the one who was given his *c tedra*, he proceeded to the popular missions in Galicia instead of returning to Salamanca. It was just a ruse, however, for he believed himself to be indispensable and really wanted to return to his old post. Also he saw a chance to have Suárez removed from there. In a very revealing letter to Claudius Aquaviva on July 8, 1594, Marcos claimed that his efforts to repress the introduction of new opinions in the Society are no less than his continuous battles against the enemies of the Society. How could he return to teach in Salamanca and defend against the attacks of the *"frailes"*? Surely, there would be unavoidable conflicts between him and Suárez, *"uno de los principales inventores y defensores de nuevas opiniones en esta provincia."* [83] The Provincial and the Rector at Salamanca were of the view that Marcos should be returned there. And he did return to resume his lecturing in the summer of 1594, but without the satisfaction of being rid of Suárez, who stayed on to continue working on his books. Marcos, as the Prefect of Studies spurred on by the new decree about

---

conditionibus, quae aliis offendiculo esse possunt; ii autem, qui a progenitoribus modernis Christianis descendunt, plurimum et offendiculi et detrimenti (quemadmodum diuturna experientia compertum est) ordinarie in Societatem invehere consueverunt; ob eam causam multi efflagitarunt, ut praesentis congregationis auctoritate statueretur, ne ullus post hac in Societatem admittatur, qui ex Hebraeorum aut Saracenorum genere descendat: et si quispiam eorum per errorem admissus fuerit, cum primum de hoc impedimento constiterit, a Societate dimittatur. Placuit autem congregationi universae, statuere, quemadmodum praesenti suo Decreto statuit, ut nullus omnino ex huiusmodi hominibus, qui ex Hebraeorum aut Saracenorum genere descendunt, deinceps in Societatem recipiatur. ...Congregatio declaravit et statuit, hoc Decretum non essentialis, sed indispensabilis impedimenti vim obtinere." *Decreta Congregationum Generalium Societatis Iesu*, op. cit., LII, in Ms. d. 68, pp. 313–315. Cf. Albert A. Sicroff, *Les Controverses des Statuts de 'Pureté de Sang' en Espagne du XVe au XVIIe siècle* (Paris, 1960), pp. 381–285. See below footnote 159.

[83] Miguel Marcos' letter to Claudius Aquaviva, dated July 8, 1594; quoted by Serna, art. cit., pp. 244–245.

adhering to St. Thomas, expectedly could not find peace in such a close proximity to the Granadian. He wrote to the General that Suárez' example and protection of new opinions reduced to uselessness his own exertions among the Jesuit students to implement the new decree.[84] To his mind, Suárez must go, if orthodox doctrine and the peace of the Jesuit community were to be safeguarded. Moreover, the *"encuentros"* between the two of them had in the meantime leaked out to the public.

When no action on his recommendation was forthcoming, Marcos himself tried to force the issue and left Salamanca in May of 1595. He retired to Burgos, then to Villagarcia, but not without again writing the General a letter full of resentments against Suárez, who, he charged, was being patronized by the Rector and the Provincial. The departure of Marcos necessitated a readjustment in the line–up of Jesuit professors in Salamanca. Juan de Salas at first took over the vacated principal chair in theology.[85] Then Cristóbal de los Cobos, who was probably occupying the *catedra de Vísperas*, replaced Salas in 1596.[86] It was then, it seems, that Juan de Cartagena was summoned to take over the vespertine lectureship in theology. That would be the 1596–1597 winter semester. By this time, since the 1590 incorporation of the Jesuit college into the university, the Jesuits in Salamanca had already been given a *general*, i.e. a hall or aula in the university, where they could conduct public lectures at definite hours.

The seeming normalcy that followed the reshuffling of theology

---

[84] "Con el ejemplo y amparo del P. Francisco Suárez está tan valida la libertad de ¡opinión entre estos carisimos estudiantes de casa, que tengo por imposible irles a la mano ni reducirles al nuevo decreto de seguir la doctrina de Santo Tomás. ...Siempre turve por muy dificultoso que este decreto viniese a ejecución vièndo las dificultades que hubo en la congregación acerca del, y las opiniones comúnmente recibidas entre los nuestros que han escrito, que en muchas y muy graves materias van por caminos muy diferentes y aun contrarios al de Santo Tomás... y como veo que al Papa y al Rey y al Consejo de Inquisición tan recelosos de la doctrina de la Compañía y tan a la mira de cómo procedemos en esta parte, no sé cómo hacer oficio de lector con satisfacción de los nuestros y de los dichos príncipes." Miguel Marcos to Aquaviva. Salamana, July 17, 1594; quoted by Serna, ibid., p. 246.

[85] Salas was born in 1553. Cf. Sommervogel, op. cit., VII, pp. 448–449.

[86] Cobos himself from Avila had been teaching in Salamanca since 1586. Cf. Sommervogel, ibid., II, p. 1255.

professors did not last long. Aquaviva was displeased with Marcos' departure from Salamanca. Soon after, the province of Castilla received its Visitator in the person of García de Alarcón, who was especially instructed to reestablish peace in the community in Salamanca. Alarcón was a man of the mental cast of Miguel Marcos, who had in fact recommended him for that job. Meanwhile, through the Dominican Provincial and the Jesuit Visitator, King Philip II had personally stepped in to put a stop to the growing animosity between the two Orders. He banished from their *cátedras* the main *dramatis personae* in Salamanca and Valladolid. Marcos was included in the list, even if he had been absent from Salamanca for already a year. Alarcón however saw no reason why Marcos after his absence could not return to Salamanca. To give the Society's first chair of theology there to someone of proven orthodoxy and thereby to appease the campaign against the Jesuits and their ideas, the Visitator ordered that post to be handed back to Miguel Marcos. So, in January of 1597 Marcos triumphantly returned to Salamanca from his self–imposed exile, to assume once more the *cátedra de Prima* until his death in 1600. And three months after Marcos' return Suárez left Salamanca to teach in Coimbra. But even before Suárez reached his new assignment, two *"suaristas"* in the midst of their courses were summarily removed from their teaching positions in Salamanca: Cristóbal de los Cobos and Juan de Cartagena.[87] It would later be alleged that these two were not following St. Thomas Aquinas. Cartagena, as we have seen, is listed by the 1597 triennial catalogue to be once more in the college in León. Thus ended Juan de Cartagena's brief professorship in theology at Salamanca.

E. Defended by Suárez

Suárez's "banishment" was somewhat alleviated by Philip II's royal decree summoning him as a professor to Coimbra, the leading university of Portugal, which had been annexed by Spain in 1580. There was no such consolation, however, for the other two victims of the Salamancan intramural. The affair was particularly painful for Juan de Cartagena. A young professor just beginning a promising

---

[87] Scorraille, op. cit., pp. 325–326. As Scorraille puts it: "Les Pères Cristobal de los Cobos et Juan de Cartagena, partisans des doctrines de Suarez, en furent brusquement retirés en pleine année scolaire."

careeer as a theologian, he must have suffered from the high–handed
action, as he was ordered back to the college in León. The story
that shadowed him there was to the effect that his teaching was questionable in its fidelity to St. Thomas Aquinas. Incidentally, Dausquius
seemed to be alluding to this unhappy story, when in the heat of
the controversy over St. Joseph's sanctification in the womb he sar-
castically turned around Marchant's claim that Cartagena was
esteemed by his order. He interpreted Order here as the "Order of
the Ignatians" and recalled in turn that "he was so esteemed by his
'Order,' that in virtue of the profession he made in it the Ignatians
bridled Cartagena with gratings of restricting strings, etc." [88]

To clear up the dark clouds hanging over him, Juan de Cartagena thought it best to have Suárez' testimony in his favor. On
November 16, 1597, the new professor in Coimbra sent to Aquaviva
in Rome a long letter accompanying a shorter one by Cartagena. As
the leader — if unintentionally — of the persecuted *suaristas*, the
Granadian gladly assented to the latter's request for a letter of testimony, taking up the defense of his younger fellow Jesuit. The
letter by Suárez gives a rare personal glimpse into both men.[89] He
had not written a word of defense for himself, Suarez wrote the General, over the happenings at Salamanca, because his published works
testify to the truth. However, Cartagena had been dragged into the
affair and had suffered from it, and had consequently asked for help
to clear his name. "Although he is still very young and was just
starting to lecture there, he was afraid his reputation would suffer
much," spoke Suarez of Cartagena. The Visitator, Garcia de Alarcón, had told Suarez at that time, that Cartagena would be transferred
from Salamanca, in order to pacify some people. He even added that
Cartagena was still young and they would later call him back. The
Provincial, Cristóbal de Rivera, also said that the removal was
"*propter bonum pacis*," after questioning Suarez over the orthodoxy
of Cartagena's lectures and receiving a favorable answer. And now
they were justifying their action by placing a question mark on Cartagena's teaching. "In this," Suarez wrote taking an unequivocal
stand, "I really feel, that they do him wrong, because from what he

---

[88] Dausquius, op. cit., p. 294.

[89] ARSJ, *Epist. Virorum Illustrium S.J.*, V, 96, f. 215rv: Letter of Suárez
to Aquaviva, Coimbra, November 16, 1597. Scorraille has part of this letter in the
French translation, op. cit., p. 327.

had said there in some disputations and from the things he had talked over with me, and from some of his papers (although few) which I have seen, I have found nothing except correct doctrine and affection for St. Thomas." Suárez admitted that the young man was very fond of St. Thomas' works and method. Some would discredit him for that. Was Cartagena then not fit to teach? "There is no doubt that he is a good instrument for teaching and a man of great promise. And if they in Castilla do not want or cannot properly employ him, Your Paternity," he wrote to Aquaviva, "can send him to some other post in Italy, with much satisfaction and edification, since he is by nature gentle, obedient and not haughty, but moderate and is very outstanding in the letters."

Even before Cartagena and Suárez wrote to him, however, Aquaviva had already shown disapproval over the things that had transpired in Salamanca. He descried the conduct of Marcos, the Visitator and the Provincial. He commanded the return to his former assignment of Gonzalo de Hormaza, Rector of the college in Santiago. The latter had been called to take over Juan de Cartagena's position as *de Vísperas* professor in theology, after Pedro de Guzman, who first took it over, died. Replying to Cartagena in León on June 30, 1598, the Jesuit General expressed gratification at the man's humility and obedience in the whole affair and reassured him of the acceptability of his teaching. Aquaviva told Cartagena:

> It matters little what others said, if Your Reverence show that they are mistaken who feel or talk otherwise. I know well what occurred in Salamanca and the account of that transfer and the meekness with which Your Reverence took it. And I am far from thinking that your teaching is contrary to St. Thomas. On account of the information I have to the contrary, I have written Father Provincial, that it would be good to send you to teach in Valencia, where they lack a good lecturer.[90]

Suárez received an even earlier reassurance on June 2 from Aquaviva, that Juan de Cartagena, or anybody else who follows Suárez's doctrine, would never be molested, mentioning further that the young professor would probably be going to Valencia.[91] But a couple of months later,

---

[90] ARSJ, *Castell. Epist. Gener. 1588–1603*, Cast. 5, f. 291rv: Letter of Aquaviva to Cartagena in León, June 30, 1598.

[91] Ibid., f. 288r: Letter of Aquaviva to Suárez, June 2, 1598. Cf. Scorraille, op. cit., pp. 327–328.

the General somehow changed his mind as to the new assignment for Cartagena. To José de Acosta, the Rector at Salamanca, who was advocating Cartagena's return there, Aquaviva wrote in August, that the Provincial "does not see it proper to excite ill–feeling by putting Father Cartagena in that college, and so I believe that he will place there somebody else who may help establish unity and peace." [92] Then on October 7, 1598, Aquaviva closed the "Case Cartagena" in his letter to the Rector of the college in Valladolid with the words: "Regarding Father Juan de Cartagena, I am of the same opinion as those who would send him to read either in Valladolid or somewhere else more suitable." [93]

F. A Case of Conscience?

And so after an apparently prolonged discussion regarding the next place of assignment for Juan de Cartagena, it was in Valladolid's Jesuit college of St. Ambrose, the second most important in the province of Castilla, that he actually ended with a vote of confidence to resume his teaching career. In fact, he had already travelled from León to Valladolid. On May 17, 1598, Cartagena made there his final vows as a Jesuit before the Provincial Cristóbal de Rivera. [94] Indeed

---

[92] ARSJ, *Castell. Epist. Gener.*, op. cit., ff. 295v–296r: Letter of Aquaviva to Jose de Acosta, August 24, 1598.

But even before, towards the end of July of 1598, Aquaviva already wrote both to the Provincial Cristóbal de Rivera and to José de Acosta, that it might be better if Cartagena would teach in Valladolid. ARSJ, ibid., ff. 293v–294r: Letter of Aquaviva to José de Acosta, July 27, 1598; and f. 292rv: Letter of Aquaviva to Cristóbal de Rivera, July 27, 1598. In this latter letter the General said: "Supuesto lo que passo en Salamanca quando la buena memoria del Padre Garcia saco de la lectura los Padres Cobos y Cartagena tengo por conveniente, que V.P. provea aquel colegio le un lector que siendo suficiente, sea también a gusto del Padre Miguel Marcos, para que aya allí la paz que conviene, pues esta se deva estimar mas que las letras, esto digo porque el Padre Cartagena podia leer en Valladolid..."

On the Rector of Salamanca, José de Acosta, who seemed to have sided with Cartagena, see Sommervogel, op. cit., I, pp. 31–38.

[93] ARSJ, *Castell. Epist. Gener.*, op. cit., f. 300r: Letter of Aquaviva to Antonio de Padilla, October 7, 1598.

[94] Ego Joannes de Cartagena professionem facio et promitto omnipotenti Deo, coram eius Virgine matre, et universa coelesti curia, ac omnibus circumstantibus et tibi Rdo. Patri Christophoro de Ribera Provinciali Castellae vicepraepositi Generalis Societatis Jesu et successorum eius locum Dei tenenti perpetuam paupertatem, castitatem et obedientiam, et secundum eam peculiare curam

it could be that the Provincial had already temporarily assigned Cartagena to Valladolid, and Aquaviva's note was but his own official concurrence with the decision. Between giving up the young promising professor to Valencia as earlier suggested and returning him to Salamanca as some would want it, there was not much choice. To keep him for Castilla, Valladolid was the compromise assignment. It was there, consequently, that the triennial catalogue of 1600 locates Cartagena in all good health — the catalogues always describe his health as *"buenas"* — as a teacher of philosophy and theology, confessor and preacher.[95] The catalogue of 1600 remarks too that he had for two years professed the four vows. And that was the last time the Jesuit triennial records ever speak of him.

Hardly two years later on March 18, 1602, a letter came from Aquaviva, granting Juan de Cartagena the faculty *"ad maiorem Dei gloriam... to enter another Mendicant Order approved by the Holy See and where the regular observance is followed, and, taking profession, to remain there..."* [96] Why did Cartagena request such a transfer? What motivated this move? We do not have Cartagena's letter of petition stating his reasons. And Aquaviva's decree granting him the desired faculty offers no light, but simply makes the allusion that the petition was formulated in such a manner that the permission to join another religious Order was being asked for only if the General considers it for the greater glory of God. Definitely, there was no fluctuation in Cartagena's religious vocation. He had been a Jesuit for 23 years already and with final vows. Moreover, he did not want to leave the religious life altogether; he wished only to join

---

circa puerorum eruditionem juxta formam vivendi in Litteris Apostolicis Societatis Jesu et in eius constitutionibus contentam. Insuper promitto specialem obedientiam summo Pontifici circa missiones prout in eiusdem Litteris Apostolicis et constitutionibus continetur. Vallisoleti in ecclesia eiusdem Societatis die decima septima Mense Maii An. Milles. quingentes. nonagessimo octavo." ARSJ, *Hisp. 2,* f. 686: Cartagena's handwritten profession of his final vows.

[95] ARSJ, *Cat. Trien. Castell.* 14, II, f. 380r.

[96] "Quamvis Jo'es de Cartagena SJ aliquot annos in nostra Societate reponit, et in ea professionem emiserit: mittas tum ob eas nobis visum fuit ad maiorem Dei gloriam fore, si ipsi petenti facultatem concederemus... amitam nobis a Sancta Sede Apostolica indulam concedimus, ut intra tres menses a data patiam conputandos, quemvis aliam ordinem Mendicantium a S. Sede Apostolica approbatum, et in quo regularis vigeat observantia, ingredi et in eo, professione edita, remanere possit, praesentibus post dictos tres menses nullum robur habituris." ARSJ, *Hist. Soc.* 54, f. 17v: Aquaviva's decree, March 18, 1602.

another Mendicant Order. The guiding principle of the action was
not a do–or–die attitude but the Jesuits' motto for God's greater
glory, *AMDG*. Neither does it appear to be a delayed reaction to
the recriminations he suffered from his confreres at Salamanca.[97]

Was Juan de Cartagena in search of another type of spirituality
different from that of St. Ignatius? Did de feel himself called to another
form of religious self–dedication? Vazquez advances a hypothesis
that Cartagena left the Society of Jesus in connection with the controversy *"de auxiliis divinae gratiae."* [98] By 1602 the fight had reached
a high point. The Society had officially espoused the defense of Luis
de Molina's *Concordia* (1588), which the Dominicans had been trying
hard to have condemned by the Inquisition. After various investigations and commissions, 20 Molinist propositions have been submitted
to Pope Clement VIII for final judgment. Not all Jesuits, however,
were of the conviction that it was right for the Society to be officially
committed to the theology of one of its men.[99] For one thing not all
Jesuits accepted Molina's theology on grace and free will. Juan de
Cartagena was one of these dissenters. This will be evident in the next
chapter, where his writings portray him as a fervent opponent of
Molinism. Was he perhaps asked to assist in the peroration of the
Jesuit defense in Rome, being one of the Society's gifted younger
dialecticians? His fellow professor of theology at Salamanca, Cristóbal
de los Cobos, and his former student, Fernando de la Bastida, would
be summoned up by Aquaviva to Rome to help in the defense. Was
it at this juncture that Juan de Cartagena decided it would be better
for him to get out of the Society of Jesus whose official position on
a doctrinal question contradicted his own conviction? His theological
independence had already been recognized in Salamanca. This time
did he determine to make a stand and draw the consequences? It is
not hard to imagine that his experience in Salamanca influenced in
some way his decision to change religious Orders. Anyway, it is also

---

[97] Stegmüller, loc. cit., thought so.

[98] Vazquez, art. cit., pp. 263–264. On the historical background of this
theological drama, see Scorraille, op. cit., p. 352 ff. See also, E. Vansteenberghe,
"Molinisme," in *DThC*, X, 2142 ff.

[99] Cf. Jacobus Hyacinthus Serry, O.P., *Historia Congregationum de Auxiliis
Divinae Gratiae sub Summus Pontificibus Clemente VIII et Paulo V in quatuor
libros distributa*, V (Antwerpiae, 1709), col. 11–117. Henricus Henríquez, S.J.
(† 1608) in Salamanca & Juan de Mariana, S.J. († 1624) in Toledo, e.g., were
against Molina.

clear that as a "conscientious objector," if that was the case, Cartagena separated himself from the Society of Jesus in good terms and not as an embittered enemy. He would remain a great admirer of many of his former religious colleagues — of the *"religiosissimus pariterque doctissimus Alphonsus Salmeron,"* [100] of the *"sapientissimus Suarez,"* [101] and of the *"eruditissimus Maldonatus,"* [102] among others; Martinus del Rio even later was his *"charissimus amicus."* [103] Juan de Cartagena closed this formative chapter of his life as a Jesuit with no apparent rancour against the Society that nurtured him.

III. A FRANCISCAN

A. Starting Again

The release Cartagena received from the Jesuit Curia in Rome allowed him three months during which to join another Mendicant Order.[104] He did not need that much time really, and he did not have to wander far. It appears that his three years or so of stay in Valladolid brought Cartagena into close contact with the Friars Minor of the Observance, whose former Province of the Immaculate Conception, erected in 1518, had its main theological faculty in Valladolid. And with all due respect to Vazquez's theory regarding the reason for Cartagena's switch of religious Orders, it could very well be that the Observants' policy of closer adherence to the Rules of St. Francis had already attracted Cartagena even earlier and was in fact a big factor, if not the principal cause, in his decision to seek a transfer.[105]

---

[100] *HCUCRA*, lib. X, hom. X, col. 198. Cf. also lib. III, hom. VI, col. 43; lib. X, hom. XXV, col. 235; lib. XI, hom. XI, col. 94.

[101] *Propugnaculum Catholicum* (Romae, 1609), p. 141. Cf. *HCSADM*, lib. V, hom. VII, (I, 423b).

[102] *HCSADM*, lib. VII, hom. IX (I, 773b).

[103] *HCSADM*, lib. I, hom. I (I, 5b). Cf. Sommervogel, op. cit., II, pp. 1894–1905.

[104] ARSJ, *Hist. Soc.* 54, f. 17v.

[105] For a brief rundown on the Observance movement, see Ignacio Iparraguirre, S.J., "Nuevas Formas de Vivir el Ideal Religioso" in *Historia de la Espiritualidad*, II (Barcelona, 1969), pp. 144–153. For an exhaustive treatment of the origins of the Franciscan Observance in Spain, see F. Lejarza and A. Uribe, O.F.M., *Introducción a los origenes de la observancia en España. Las reformas en*

Anyway, it must have been shortly after the March 18, 1602 decree from Aquaviva reached him, that Juan de Cartagena joined the Friars Minor of the Observance. He received the Franciscan habit in the convent of El Abrojo on the banks of the river Duero, only a few kilometers outside the city of Valladolid. El Abrojo was one of the original convents of the reform group of Pedro de Villacreces († 1422) and was later incorporated into the Observance Province of the Immaculate Conception.

There is some confusion in the Franciscan records over the date of Cartagena's entrance into the Order. Francisco Calderon in his chronicle of the Province of the Immaculate Conception vaguely mentioned that Cartagena donned the habit of the Franciscans at El Abrojo around the time ("*por este tiempo*") that the Provincial Martin de Cepeda was elected in 1601.[106] And in the *Relación histórica* written by the same Calderon in 1678 and sent to Rome, reference is made to Cartagena's profession in 1600, consequently implying that the habit–taking was sometime in 1599.[107] In turn, the convent's own *Memoria y relación* claims the profession to have taken place in 1602, thus pushing the habit–taking back to 1601.[108] Well, we know for sure that Cartagena got the faculty to leave the Society and join another Mendicant Order only in March of 1603. He could not have become a Franciscan before that date. Also, his profession in the Franciscan Order came a year later when he was 40 years old, taking place in the convent in Palencia, where he completed his "second" novitiate, as the chroniclers unanimously note. Incidentally, this short sojourn in Palencia must be the explanation why Cartagena was included by Renedo among his "*Escritores palentinos.*" [109]

---

los siglos XIV y XV (Madrid, 1958). This work is a special number of the *Archivo Ibero–Americano* of the same year.

[106] *Primera Parte de la Chronica de la Santa Provincia de la Purissima concepción de Nuestra Señora de la Regular Observancia de N.S.P.S. Francisco*, a manuscript in the archive of the Franciscan Convent in Valladolid, p. 134; quoted by Vazquez, art. cit., p. 265.

[107] *Relación historica de la Provincia de la Concepción*, Archivum gen. O.F.M., Rome v. T/8, f. 270; Vazquez, ibid.

[108] *Memoria y relación... de algunos religiosos célebres en virtud y dignidades que moraron en el convento del Abrojo*, a manuscript in the convent archive of La Aguilera, f. 10; Vazquez, ibid.

[109] Cf. above, pp. 8–9.

B. ROME

At the time that Juan de Cartagena made his profession as a Franciscan, the top–ranking men of the Order were no strangers to him. The General, Francisco de Sosa, was a professor of theology in the college of San Francisco in Salamanca at the time that the young Jesuit was starting to lecture there.[110] The Procurator General in Rome, Juan de Rada, was also at that time a professor in Salamanca and at the moment a consultor to the Congregation *de auxiliis* and a major adversary of Molinism.[111] And it was an ex–Provincial of the Province of the Immaculate Conception, Juan de Cepeda, who was then the Vicar–General resident in Madrid for the Ultramontane Family of the Franciscans. A unique conjunction of happy circumstances, if we may say so, promised Cartagena a good start.

And the break that Suárez once suggested to Aquaviva, i.e. a teaching post for Cartagena in Italy, now came to pass for the newly professed Franciscan. The reason for Cartagena's assignment abroad does not seem to be primarily out of personal consideration.[112] It is true that it must have cost him some pain to move about and to function as a Friar Minor in Castilla, where for so long he had been known and active as a Jesuit. But he did so for two years before he actually left the country. So, it appears that it was not just to save him from embarassment and disconcerting "reacclimatization," that Cartagena was given work elsewhere. The real reason seems to be indicated by the circumstances of his new assignment, which we shall discuss below. Meanwhile, it was early in 1606 that we hear of Juan de Cartagena being already in Rome in the convent of San Pietro in Montorio across the Tiber. He evidently lost no time in getting himself actively involved in the principal issues of the day. By January and February of 1606, if not earlier, Cartagena was already writing papers on the various points at issue in the discussions of the Congregation *de auxiliis*.[113]

---

[110] Cf. J. de San Antonio, op. cit., p. 439.

[111] See I. Vazquez, "El arzobispo Juan de Rada y el molinismo. Sus votos en las controversias 'de auxiliis'," *Verdad y Vida*, 20 (1962) 351–396.

[112] Vazquez, "Fr. Juan de Cartagena...," art. cit., p. 266, suggests that Cartagena was sent abroad "para superar el impacto sicológico que no pudo menos de producir en su espiritu el hecho de haber tenido que abandonar... su primer instituto... Para evitar el escándalo que pudiera sobrevenir en el pueblo."

[113] See the next chapter, pp. 94–96.

To get to Rome, Cartagena must have made the long and arduous trip in the late months of 1605. At Milan he made a stop–over for rest. And there he came into contact with Spanish officials and diplomats managing the Lombardian State. For Milan became an imperial fief in 1535, was conferred by Charles V on his son, Prince Philip, in 1540, and thereafter remained attached to the Spanish Crown. Upon the request of Lorenzo Polo, President of the Extraordinary Magistrate for Milan and counsellor to Philip III, the travelling theologian wrote and published in Milan a short treatise on simony, which was then rampant.[114]

C. PRAELECTOR

Cartagena's Roman assignment to the convent of San Pietro in Montorio was not so uncomplicated as it might appear at first. In the General Chapter of the Order on May 13, 1606, held in Toledo, Cartagena was named to the chair of first lecturer in scholastic theol-

---

[114] *Disputatio Insignis... ad Extirpandum quoddam Latentis Simoniae Vitium* (Romae, 1607²). The circumstances surrounding his writing this short treatise are given in the dedicatory letter by the author: "Nimia longissimi itineris defatigatione decus et ornamentum, coactus sum per nonnullos dies apud Mediolanenses commorari; inimici tamen otii vitandi gratia, et ut publicae utilitati non nihil inservirem, propositam difficultatem, te iubente, enucleandam suscepi." Quoted by Vazquez, art. cit., p. 285.

Cartagena's encounter with simony and the practise of aspiring for an ecclesiastical office not out of a religious vocation but due to some personal profits makes him eloquent as he later denounces it. Speaking of the Magi, he observes that "...hos sanctos Reges intrasse in Ecclesiam, bona sua ei offerentes, quos minime imitantur, immo contra faciunt multi, qui ad illam veniunt, et ecclesiasticam vitam profitentur, ut bona Ecclesiae, et eius annuos redditus adipiscantur... Id genus ecclesiasticorum non ingreditur in Ecclesiam per ostium, sed per caminum, et ita videbitis in hoc fumare ignem concupiscentiae, in altero ambitionis; in illo avaritiae, in alio iracundiae: unde graviter dolendum est, sacratos Deo, quos vitam agere sanctam oportebat, nonnullos quandoque eorum supra ceteros saeculi homines moribus esse magis profanis et licentiosis. Ego existimo peculiari daemonis astutia fieri, ad suum regnum augendum, ut Ecclesiastici quidam male vivant: quoniam quemadmodum olim multorum animas ad inferorum barathrum detrusit, ...ita nostris temporibus simili utitur dolo ad multorum conscientias depravandas, efficiens, ut non pauci sacerdotum... libere ac licentiose vivant. Sic enim sperat saeculares vitia in Ecclesiasticis quasi honestata et commendata, cernentes illa, facilius et libentius imitaturos. Quod si volumus huius damne causam investigare, inveniemus inde esse, quod non sicut hi Reges ingrediuntur ecclesiam religiose, et lucri non appetentes, sed potius propter ecclesiasticos reditus, et honores obtinendos." *HCUCRA*, lib. VI, hom. VI, col. 50.

ogy for this house of studies.[115] The convent of San Pietro had been a general house of studies in the hands of the Italian Observants even before the turn of the century. By a decision of the General Chapter of the Congregation of the Cismontane Family in 1603, it was supposed to serve the Roman Province and the whole of Germany and of Poland.[116] And the Cismontane Constitution of that time stipulates that should a province not have enough professors, individuals outstanding in virtue and learning could be selected by the General from elsewhere, i.e. from other Cismontane provinces.[117] The first remarkable thing about Cartagena's appointment to San Pietro in Montorio was therefore the fact that he was an Ultramontane. The Toletan General Chapter named together with him three other professors for San Pietro, who were all *cismantanos*.[118] His nomination as the first lecturer, the *praelector*, could be in simple recognition of his talents and a further justification for this unusual assignment. But his being there at all must have been the result of some well–placed interventions. His nomination was in fact subsequent to his coming to San Pietro. Was it a "legalization" step of a previously conceived plan to get an *ultramontano* into this Cismontane house? Did Philip III intervene as a way of reasserting the somewhat forgotten royal *patronato* over some Franciscan churches and houses in Italy, one of which was San Pietro in Montorio? The issue had thus come to the fore and the Spaniard–heavy Ultramontane leadership of the Order was favorable to the *patronato*.[119] The ex–Jesuit, a former professor in Salamanca, was in possession of the right credentials to make such a move reasonable and acceptable. Besides serving him well, the assignment served the purposes of the su-

---

[115] Dominicus de Gubernatis, O.F.M., *Orbis Seraphicus, Historia de Tribus Ordinibus a Seraphico Patriarcha S. Francisco Institutis*, III (Romae, 1684), p. 596. Two of Cartagena's books mention in their title–pages that he is a theology *praelector: Disputatio... ad extirpandum quoddam latentis simoniae vitium* (Romae, 1607) and *Pro Ecclesiastica Libertate* (Romae, 1607).

[116] Gubernatis, ibid., p. 594.

[117] Ibid., p. 452.

[118] Ibid., p. 596. With Cartagena, as second lecturer in theology was Petrus de Rygio, while Salvator de Roma handled moral theology and Bonaventura de Monterolo took care of Hebrew.

[119] Cf. J. Pou y Marti, O.F.M., "Felipe III y los santuarios franciscanos de Italia," *Archivo Ibero–Americano*, 3 (1915) 212–233; 4 (1916) 74–79, 214–241. See esp. pp. 229–230 which give a report by Rada in favor of the *patronato*.

periors. In later dedicating the second volume of his *Homiliae Catholicae* to King Philip III, Cartagena would say:

> I shall put together in short the reason for sending to you
> the first volume of this Marian work, which was produced in your
> royal convent, to which I have been elected as general Lector of
> Sacred Theology by the Supreme Pontiff. Plainly, it is a fruit of
> your garden, and therefore is rightly presented to you.[120]

Significantly, Catagena referred to himself as "a general Lector
of Sacred Theology appointed by the Supreme Pontiff." He was
appointed *praelector* for San Pietro in Montorio by the General Chapter in 1605. But it was only in 1609 that the titlepages of Cartagena's
books began to mention the distinction that he was "a *Lector generalis*
in the royal convent of Saint Peter of the Golden Mountain by the
order of the Most Holy Father." [121] Was this special appointment by
the Pope a reward for Cartagena's services and dedication to the Papacy, and/or an intervention to consolidate Cartagena's position in
San Pietro? It is easy to think that some hardliners among the *cis-
montanos* found the Spaniard's extraordinary assignment to San Pietro ground for some protest. Cartagena, only three years in the Eternal City, felt particularly endebted to the Holy Father's goodwill
towards him. The first volume of the *Homiliae Catholicae* was dedicated to Pope Paul V, as Cartagena put it, "...because of the goodwill
too, which you have shown me not just in one but in many favors
on account of your extraordinary noble–mindedness." [122] Juan de
Cartagena had certainly gone a long way from being an innocent
victim in an intramural bickering at Salamanca.

---

[120] *HCSADM*, (I, Dedication).

[121] "...de mandato Sanctissimi Lectore generali in Regali conventu Sancti
Petri montis aurei," in the title–pages of *HCUCRA* (1609), *HCSADM* (1611),
and *Propugnaculum Catholicum* (1609).

[122] "...propter benevolentiam etiam, quam ob eximiam tui animi ingenui-
tatem, erga me non uno sed pluribus beneficiis ostendisti." *HCUCRA*, Dedication.

D. Emeritus

As the first lecturer in theology, Cartagena according to the statutes of 1603 handled the first book of the *Sententiae*.[123] And for a while in 1607 he even lectured on the sacred canons.[124] From 1608 or perhaps from the end of 1607 on, San Pietro in Montorio apparently ceased to be a general house of studies. The 1612 General Chapter in Rome, for instance, no longer listed it as one.[125] But the convent seemed to have continued to function as a provincial house of theology until 1628, when it passed over to the hands of the Reformed, who later turned it into a college for oriental languages.[126] The discontinuance of its status as a *Studium Generale* explains why Cartagena from 1608 on ceased too to be a *praelector*. Being no longer a full faculty, San Pietro could no longer retain the right of having a *praelector*. Cartagena, however, remained a professor of theology, a *lector generalis* by order of the Holy Father.[127]

Juan de Cartagena pursued his career as a theology professor with a fair measure of success. Luke Wadding characterized his public lectures as being attended by a large entourage of students.[128] N. Antonio, writing in Rome in 1672, mentioned that those who had heard Cartagena's lectures still accorded him unwonted praise up to that time.[129] It was then with such a reputation as a *"buen teólogo y excelente catedrático,"* [130] that Cartagena completed his ten years of uninterrupted professorship of theology in San Pietro in

---

[123] Gubernatis, op. cit., p. 594.

[124] The *Pro Ecclesiastica Libertate* (1607) names him also "sacrorumque canonum professore."

[125] Gubernatis, op. cit., pp. 603–604.

[126] Ibid., p. 389.

[127] Cartagena is termed "lector generalis" in the title–pages of his *Selectarum Disputationum in quartum Sententiarum*, which although dated 1607 was actually approved for publication only in 1608, of the *HCUCRA*, the *HCSADM*, and of the *Propugnaculum Catholicum*.

[128] Wadding, op. cit., p. 198: "...publice Theologiam, magno discipulorum profectu, praelegit." San Antonio, op. cit., p. 143, simply repeats these words of Wadding. Cerreto, op. cit., p. 260, has something similar: "...publice sacra dogmata miro auditorum lucro explanavit."

[129] N. Antonio, op. cit., p. 672: "...auditoribus solito frequentius usque ad hunc diem gloriatur."

[130] *Biografia Eclesiastica Completa*, op. cit., p. 464; and Renedo, op. cit., p. 124.

Montorio. In 1616, therefore, he became *lector emeritus*.[131] The jubilee
was celebrated early that year.[132]

At the same time that Cartagena retired from active teaching
in 1616, he seemed to have been granted the title of *Magister* in theology. Nicolaus Rodulphus, Lector of Sacred Theology in the Roman
college of St. Thomas Aquinas and one of the censors of the last
volume of the *Homiliae Catholicae*, referred to Cartagena as "*Sacrae
Theologiae Magister.*" [133] A year later in 1617, another Lector of
theology, who censored Cartagena's book *Praxis orationis mentalis*,
called him simply "*Magister.*" [134] A master of theology had come to
mean a doctor of theology. It is the top grade that one can attain,
after putting in at least two years more than the basic four years
of the theology course which ends with a *bacalaureus formatus* degree and the other two years for a *licentia ubique docendi*.[135] There
is no mention at all in the triennial catalogues of the Jesuits that
Cartagena ever obtained the grade of a master in theology. Most probably he later was given the title *honoris causa* upon being an *emeritus*
professor of theology.

E. CONCIONATOR

It was not only as a teacher that Juan de Cartagena distinguished
himself. As the *Memoria y relación* of the convent at El Abrojo says,
he left behind him in San Pietro in Montorio "*fama de docto y vir-*

---

[131] A statute of 1603 says: "Item Lectores illi, qui Sacram Theologiam per
annos duodecim legerint, privilegiis omnibus gaudeant iuxta statutum Capituli
Generalis Vallisoleti, quod specialiter confirmatur, et servetur prout in familia
Ultramontans ervatur. Quod si continuate, et sine interpollatione, sufficiat legisse
per decennium." Gubernatis, op. cit., p. 594.

Cartagena already termed himself an "emeritus" in the dedication of the
HCSADM, III (1616), and the same in the dedication of the *Praxis Orationis
Mentalis* (1618).

[132] Pedro Jover, Procurator General of the Friars Minor, in giving Cartagena on February 10, 1616, the permission to publish the last volume of the
HCSADM, referred to him as "Lectori Generali Iubilato." This faculty was not
given on January 22, 1616, as Vazquez claims, art. cit., p. 270, note 3, in his
effort to specify January as the month of the Jubilee. It was the letter of one of
the censors, Nicolaus Rodulphus, that was dated January 22, 1616.

[133] HCSADM, (III, censor's letter)

[134] *Praxis Orationis Mentalis*, letter by the censor Emanuel da Vila.

[135] Cf. M. Andres Martin, op. cit., pp. 78–84.

tuoso." [136] The *Memorie istoriche del convento di S. Pietro in Montorio* itself describes Cartagena's religious life as *"divotissimo."* [137] "A man with a golden heart" is a contemporary's picture of him.[138]

The same contemporary of Cartagena calls to our attention another occupation Cartagena had besides teaching theology. The writer points out that while living in San Pietro in Montorio, Cartagena was active as a Christian orator both with his voice and with his pen.[139] The products of his pen we shall go into later. That Cartagena was also actively involved in preaching is clearly to be gathered from the title–pages of some of his books which present him as a *concionator.*[140]

As a Franciscan preacher, Cartagena would be simply exercising a form of ministry he had practised as a Jesuit in León and Valladolid. The function or office of preacher, according to the Rules of St. Francis, is to be given by the Minister General only to one who has been examined, approved and commissioned as one.[141] In this connection, Cartagena most probably did not have to go through an examination in view of his obvious adequacy for the job and of his previous preaching apostolate.[142] Was Cartagena the official house preacher in San Pietro in Montorio? It is to be noticed that he was presented as a *concionator* on the title–pages of his books only as long as he was the *praelector.* He ceased using the title of preacher at the same time that he stopped being the latter, when San Pietro was no longer a general house of studies. We know that, in order that the Word of God may be properly honored and recognized in

---

[136] Cf. above, footnote 108. Incidentally, this manuscript mistakenly assigned Cartagena to have been a lecturer in Aracaeli in Rome instead of San Pietro in Montorio.

[137] This manuscript, found in the convent of San Pietro itself, is quoted by Vazquez, art. cit., p. 262, note 3.

[138] Ioannes Baptista Laurus, *Orchestra Theatri Romani. Dialogus de Viris Sui Aevi Doctrina Illustribus Romae 1618* (Romae, 1625), pp. 46–47.

[139] "...quondam in D. Petri ad Montem aureum voce et calamo christianae rhetoricantis." Ibid., p. 47.

[140] *Disputatio... ad Extirpandum quoddam Latentis Simoniae Vitium* (1607) and *Pro Ecclesiastica Libertate* (1607).

[141] Cf. Bartholomaeus Belluco, O.F.M., *De Sacra Praedicatione in Ordine Fratrum Minorum* (Roma, 1956), p. 9; cf. pp. 29 & 34.

[142] "Etenim cum ratio examinis in eo sit ut sufficientia candidati cognoscatur, si ea aliunde nota sit, deest ratio sufficiens examinis imponendi, cum effectus intentus iam habeatur." Ibid., p. 67.

the larger convents and general houses of studies, the General Chapter in Toledo in 1606 for the first time appointed two house preachers for S. Maria Aracaeli in Rome.[143] The same General Chapter which elected Cartagena *praelector* did not assign any *praedicator* for San Pietro. He could have been entrusted afterwards with the office of preaching the year round in the church of the convent. In later ceasing to be the house-preacher, if such was the case, Cartagena, however, did not give up the office of preaching altogether. For in 1609 when Luis de San Juan Evangelista, the Order's Commissary General in the Roman Curia, gave the permission for the publication of Cartagena's book *Propugnaculum catholicum*, he referred to him still as *praedicator*.[144] Three years later, the Minister General of the Franciscans, Arcángel de Mesina, in personally writing to Cartagena termed him as *"concionator praestantissimus."* [145] In the *imprimatur* of the *Praxis orationis mentalis* in 1617, Pedro Jover called Cartagena *"Concionator celeberrimus."* [146] And we know that the Friars Minor even then had a rule regarding the title of preacher which says: *"Nullus titulus absque exercitio."* [147]

Without going into the details of how Cartagena's understanding of the dynamics of preaching influenced his theologizing, which we shall discuss in the latter part of this study, we would like to note here what he said about preaching as a ministry. First of all, teaching and proclaiming the mysteries of the faith are so essential, that should men be lacking for the office, even women according to Cartagena may do so.[148] Preachers together with theologians are for him fundamentally servants of the light illumined by the Word of God.[149] Their own words are like spiritual weapons out to vanquish the enemies of the soul,[150] and like the heat of the divine flame in a heart

---

[143] Ibid., p. 94.

[144] *Propugnaculum Catholicum* (1609), Letter of permission from Ludovicus de S. Ioanne Evangelista.

[145] *HCSADM*, (I, Publication approval).

[146] *Praxis Orationis Mentalis* (Coloniae, 1619), Permission for publication. Michael Bihl, s.v. "Friars Minor" in *The Catholic Encyclopedia*, IV (NY, 1913), p. 293, names Cartagena with Alfonso de Castro, Luis de Carvajal, and Pedro de Alcantara as the 16th century's illustrious Spanish Friars Minor theologians and preachers.

[147] Belluco, op. cit., p. 91.

[148] *HCSADM*, lib. XV, hom. III (III, 39b).

[149] Ibid., hom. V (III, 61a).

[150] Ibid., hom. XXI (III, 189a–b).

on fire, they urge men to a knowledge of Christ which leads to eternal life.[151] Cartagena's basic rule of thumb for the preaching apostolate is St. Paul's admonition to Timothy: *"attende tibi, et doctrinae"* (I Tim 4, 16). The preacher must first look to himself; he must lead an exemplary life. With strong words, Cartagena bewails the contrary practise of some preachers.[152] As to *doctrina* or learning, he compares it with salt, which should not be employed excessively, otherwise it becomes counter–productive.[153] For the conversion of the faithful strived for by the preacher is better served by the sanctity of the preacher than by erudition or mere eloquence.[154] Emphatically, he warns against vainglory, the idolatrous thirst for applause and the consequent desire to please the audience.[155] And just as outrightly, he counsels courageous and fearless proclamation of God's Word, if necessary, even against kings.[156] Nor does Cartagena forget points of

---

[151] Ibid., lib. XVIII, hom. ult. (III, 491a).

[152] "...proh dolor, sicut lima limando hebetatur; horologium alios regendo continuis rotarum volutationibus deterioratur; lyra dulcem sonorum concentum auditoribus emittente fides eius atteruntur: ita sane multis accidit concionatoribus, ut dum aliorum vitia reprehendunt, ipsi in eadem prolabantur; et dum aliorum mores componere tentant, ipsi ab incompositis suis moribus nunquam desistant; dumque Evangelicae doctrinae fraeno a peccatis avocant, sibi ad peccandum habenas laxant, quasi alium Deum sibi iudicem futurum credant. Huius conditionis praedicatores non solum Ecclesiae catholicae inutiles, sed nocivi valde sunt. Nam qui vitae integritate, et sanctitatis exemplo non magis quam verbo edocent, Evangelici praedicatores non sunt, sed profanos, et dissolutos, et Dominici gregis non canes, sed infestissimos lupos satius vocitaverim." *HCUCRA*, lib. XV, hom. XV, col. 108–109.

[153] "Secundum vero, ut attendant doctrinae: nam cum haec sit sal, oportet prudenter ea uti. Quippe sicut temperatus salis usus cibum condit, excessivus vero, aut nimius illum corrumpit; simili quoque ratione, si praedicantis doctrina nimio, superfluoque reprehensionis sane abundet, non modo auditoribus non proderit, sed eorum animos potius offendet. Unde existimo, inter plurima, quibus valde similis est animarum debellatio regnorum expugnationi, illud unum praecipuum esse, prudentiam nempe cum labore coniunctam." Ibid., col. 109.

[154] "Et quidem experientia ipsa compertum est, et exploratum satis, in peccatorum obstinatis animis expugnandis maioris momenti semper fuisse concionatorem, sanctitate, et mediocri doctrinae scientia conspicuum, quam nimia eloquentio, inanique dicendi facundia praeditum, quae comicam magis, et historicam, quam Evangelicam dicendi rationem redolet." Ibid.

[155] *HCSADM*, lib. XV, hom. XIX (III, 160b); hom. XXI (III, 194b–195a).

[156] "Velut enim pluvia, necnon et grando non moratur in aere, dum Principes pertranseunt per viam, ne illos offendat, sed indiscriminatim super illos, et abiectissimos quosque homines pari impetu descendit, nec magis purpuram,

technique like voice and volume modulation, and appropriate gestures
to achieve the good of souls.[57]

One other remark is here called for which regards Cartagena's
office as *concionator*, or for that matter as *lector* too, or, in M. de
Castro's unfortunately undocumented assertion, as a procurator of
his Order with the Roman Curia,[158] because it could disprove or at
least threaten Vazquez's theory that Cartagena was perhaps of Jewish
origin, and also Dausquius' light–headed claim that the man was
Moorish. On the question of the candidate's suitability as preacher
or to hold some other office, disqualification may arise by reason of
birth or ancestry. In the papal constitution *Officii nostri* of Clement VII
for the Friars Minor in Spain in 1528, all descendants up to the fourth
generation of Moors, Jews and condemned heretics are declared perpetually unsuited for any office in the Order.[159] Although this papal
document was never promulgated in Spain due to the king's act of
censorship, it was applied by Paul IV in 1559 to all Friars Minor

---

quam saccum suscipit, sed in utrumque aequaliter decidit; ita sane verbum divinum ab evangelico praedicatore effluens indiscriminatim ad Reges, ad Principes,
magistratus, et reliquos diversos hominum status absque tremore, et pavore
dirigi debet. Scio Primates terrae concionatorum increpationem aegre ferre, quia
cum ipsi sint oculi Reipublicae, non secus, ac oculi acrem confricationem moleste
sustinent, et minima quaque paleae laesione offenduntur; ita et ipsi exigua quaque
increpatione exacerbantur. Sed nihilominus prudenter facta reprehensio praeter-
mittenda non est, ut sic admoneantur, ipsos non minus, quam eorum subditos
divinae legi obsequentes esse debere, immo obsequentiores..." *HCUCRA*, lib. XV,
hom. XV, col. 110–111.

[157] Ibid., col. 108.

[158] M. de Castro, art. cit., p. 595.

[159] Belluco, op. cit., pp. 45–46. Although the papal bull could not be promulgated in Spain, more because of politics than because of contrary policies,
a movement to the same effect had been already gathering momentum in the
country. In the later 15th and the earlier 16th centuries, pure ancestry — *limpieza
de sangre* — had gradually become an indispensable condition for membership
in certain Religious Orders, as also in the *Colegios Mayores* at the universities
of Spain. By the middle of the 16th century, the King himself ratified a statute
making purity of ancestry an essential condition for all future appointments to
dignities and prebends. This insistence on purity of blood as a qualification for
office put families of suspicious racial antecedents on the defensive. The well-
known Cartagenas, for example, the family of the *converso* Pablo de Santa Maria,
needed a certificate of *limpieza de sangre* from Philip III in 1604, in order to ward
off any persecution. Cf. Manuel Serrano y Sanz, *Apuntes para una Biblioteca de
Escritores Españoles desde el año 1401 al 1833* (Madrid, 1903), p. 218, and Elliott,
op. cit., pp. 220–224.

throughout the world, and was reaffirmed by Gregory XIII in 1573. It was evidently with reference to this policy that Marchant in his debate with Dausquius challenged the latter's allegation concerning Cartagena's ancestry by pointing out that the Franciscan Order does not accept Moors as members.[160] As we have noted, this manifestation of racial discrimination in the religious Orders in consonance with the time's practise could well undercut the two given opinions regarding Cartagena's origin, but not necessarily, because among the Ultramontane this papal bull was known not to have been always followed. And the fact that the Ultramontane Cartagena was a professor and a preacher in a Cismontane house and in Rome leaves the whole matter open to a variety of conjectures.

F. PAPAL ADVOCATE

A prominent feature of Juan de Cartagena's Franciscan life was his ardent loyalty to the Pope — his Jesuit vow, one might say. He once referred to himself as "most eager to serve the Roman Catholic Church and this Apostolic See." [161] The next chapter will show clearly enough that a great part of his writings was done in the service of the papacy and/or dedicated to the Pope. He wrote an unpublished treatise, for instance, entitled *Homiliae de statu pontificio et cardinalitio* (n.d.), one of whose propositions takes conciliarism directly by the horns:

> Such is the authority of the Roman Pontiff, that in defining truths of the faith he can in no way make error, even if he does it without the Council. On the other hand, although a Council may be legitimately assembled, it can fall into error, unless it looks for the consent or approval of the Highest Pontiff.[162]

But it was during the fight between Paul V and the Republic of Venice that Cartagena demonstrated his indefatigable dedication to the Holy See. When Venice climaxed a policy of increased usurpation of the rights of the Church by subjecting a bishop and an abbot

---

[160] Marchant, op. cit., p. 41. Cf. Dausquius, op. cit., p. 222.

[161] *De Sufficientia et Efficacia Divinae Gratiae*, a manuscript by Cartagena now published in *Verdad y Vida*, 86 (1964) 200.

[162] *Homiliae de Statu Pontificio et Cardinalitio*, hom. 45, f. 699r; quoted by Vazquez, art. cit., p. 273, note 3.

to trial in the secular courts, the Pope reacted in April of 1606 with an interdict of the whole territory and the excommunication of the *Consiglio de pregadi*, which in turn responded with more reprisals against ecclesiastical immunity. Theologians and jurists, among them Bellarmine and Baronius, went to work to support the papal measure and to expose the illegality of the Venetians' behaviour. Newly arrived in Rome, "before the whole Church and in the midst of a most learned people, to whom a certain excellence in doctrine and in the arts is a requirement," as N. Antonio sets Cartagena's Roman surrounding, the *Hispanus* lost no time in offering his services too, thus establishing for himself a reputation of erudition and clear judgment.[163] By the beginning of August of that year, Cartagena presented to the Pope the draft of a first treatise of 14 chapters on the Venetians' total obligation to papal laws. Personally encouraged by the Roman Pontiff to finish the project, Cartagena submitted a few days later the second treatise with 23 chapters.[164] Paul V sent both works to the Dean of the Roman Rota for censorship before publication. The censor took at least a couple of months to go through the manuscripts, declaring the first volume sound in doctrine, but specifying a number of corrections for the second.[165]

---

[163] N. Antonio, op. cit., p. 672; Tejera, op. cit., p. 120, repeats Antonio, adding: "adquiriendose una buena y no común reputación como hombre de claro entendimiento y de vasta erudición."

[164] The manuscripts of both these treatises are in the Vatican Archive, Archivum Arcis, Arm. I–XVIII, vv. 808 & 809: *Tractatus I de Omnimoda Obligatione Venetorum ad Parendum Apostolicis Praecepta a Sanctissimo Domino Nostro Paulo V illis impositis pro Ecclesiastica libertate Venetorum cum Libertate Ecclesiastica ex Diametro Pugnantes.* Both works were dedicated to Pope Paul V. In the dedication of the second tractate, Cartagena recalls how Paul V encouraged him to finish the series, when he presented to the Pope the first volume: "Cum paucis ante hoc diebus Tuae Beatitudini, Sanctissime Pater, offerrem apologeticum tractatum... iussit mihi Tua Beatitudo, ut quod sibi probaretur opus a nobis inceptum, illud in finem perducerem." Quoted by Vazquez, art. cit., p. 274.

[165] The censor Francisco Peña very objectively wrote of the first treatise in an accompanying folio: "Doctrinam tutam continet hic tractatus: sed haec videntur animadvertenda quae facile emendari possunt: primum, abstinendum videretur a frequenti allegatione quorundam recentiorum, et eorum loco substituendi alii ponderosioris auctoritatis. Secundo, emendandae forent mendosae allegationes et videndi doctores in fonte; quoniam alias facile redargueretur auctor vel negligentiae vel falsitatis culpabilis." Regarding the second treatise, the censor judged: "Hic secundus tractatus exacta indiget consideratione non solum ratione doctrinae, sed etiam ratione allegationum. Ratione doctrinae: quia nonnulla

On January 5, 1607, after putting in two more months to rework it, Cartagena presented to the Pope the first treatise, the original 97 pages having grown to 643 and the 14 chapters to 9 books. He promised Paul V to deliver the second "as speedily as I can (God willing), if our pen, not ours, but the pen of the scribe can be fast enough, as this work shows, which was produced in such a short period of hardly 60 days." [166] The promised second volume returned also much enlarged, the original 160 pages now 232 and the 23 chapters now 4 books. The first volume did go into print to join in the fray. [167] But the second did not make it, because on April 21, 1607, an accord was reached among the belligerents and any further polemical writing would have been construed as a *post bellum* provocation.

This second treatise was to be published, later on after Cartagena excised a chapter and retouched the whole, substituting the title *"adversus Ecclesiae iura violantes"* for the original *"adversus Venetos."* [168] In dedicating the book to Paul V, Juan de Cartagena felt assured of the Pope's good pleasure.

> I deliberately pass up entreating Your Beatitude that this work, which in the opinion of important doctors will be of use to the Catholic Church, be kindly received. For considering both the usefulness itself of the work and our other books consecrated

---

asseruntur quae facile ferant correctionem, imo quae sine correctione publicari non debeant, ut in margine notatur, tum pag. 24 et pag. 51 et pag. 68, ubi admittuntur leges principium saecularium circa vim tollendam in causis ecclesiasticis, tum alibi, ubi facile excurrit calamus. Ratione allegationum, magna indiget diligentia, quia auctor theologus multos legistas et canonistas allegat, quos non vidit, ut patet ex eorum dictis. Disputatio de excellentia potestatis Christi cap. 16 et seq. sana est, et bene ad propositum facit, sed quae mendose allegantur, corrigendae sunt."

Peña also noted when the tractates were handed over to him: "Transmisit ad me Franciscum Peniam, de ordine S.D.N. Pauli pp. V, dominus Marcus Antonius Tanus, die 26 augusti 1606." Cf. Vazquez, ibid., pp. 275 & 294–295.

[166] Vatican Archive, Archivum Arcis, Arm. I–XVIII, v. 806.

[167] *Pro Ecclesiastica Libertate, et Potestate Tuenda. Adversus iniustas Venetorum Leges eiusdem Sacrae libertate laesivas...* Tomus Primus (1607). In later dedicating the *HCUCRA* to Paul V, Cartagena would refer to this book: "...cum inter alias sacrae Theologiae divisiones, illa celebris sit in moralem, scholasticam, et positivam, ex singulis his totidem opera tuo clarissimo nomini dicavi: ex Theologiae moralis fonte hausi volumen illud libros novem continens pro Ecclesiastica libertate tuenda..."

[168] *Propugnaculum Catholicorum de Iure Belli Romani Pontificis Adversus Ecclesiae Iura Violantes* (1609).

to your illustrious name and accepted by you happily, I cannot at all doubt that this labor of ours undertaken for the sake of the Catholic Church will be most pleasing to Your Holiness.[169]

Then Cartagena went on in his book to maintain that as the highest monarch of the Christian State, the Pope possesses the supreme authority to declare a just war against any violator of the Church's rights.[170] To pursue such a legitimate warfare, the Roman Pontiff may with clear conscience employ even pagan troops,[171] and his generals may resort to ambushes and deceptions (*"insidiis"*) to the same end.[172] Moreover, Cartagena personally approves of preemptive occupation of enemy possessions, and of the right to levy necessary compensation not just from the guilty parties, but also from a non–guilty citizenry.[173] Ringing like a true "hawk," Cartagena entitles the last chapter of his book with a veritable war–cry: *"Quam utile, et gloriosum sit militare in bello adversus iura Ecclesiae violantes."* [174] No wonder Cartagena was so sure of the papal good pleasure! It goes without saying, that these writtings by Juan de Cartagena did not escape the attention of many a court in the capitals of Europe. They unmistakably projected their author as an unmitigated papist.[175]

---

[169] Ibid., Dedication.

[170] Ibid., p. 27 ff.

[171] Ibid., p. 131 ff.

[172] Ibid., p. 149 ff.

[173] Ibid., p. 193.

[174] Ibid., p. 241. Interestingly, Suárez wrote too at about the same time during the Venice conflict an apologetical treatise *De Immunitate Ecclesiastica* in favor of Paul V. But it was never published, probably because it did not go far enough in giving leeway to papal action. When later Suárez was asked to write a treatise against the King of England, he dilly–dallied, partly due, it seems, to his dissatisfaction that "la repuesta qua habia escrito contra los venecianos" was not published. Cf. Scorraille, op. cit., II, pp. 124–128, and L. Lopetegui, S.J., "La Secretaría de Estado de Paulo V, y la composición del 'Defensio Fide' de Suárez," *Gregorianum*, 27 (1946) 584–596.

[175] Cf. Biografia Eclesiastica Completa, op. cit., p. 464; Jöcher, op. cit., col. 1707; Bayle, op. cit., p. 66: "Jamais homme ne fut plus devoué que lui aux intérets de la cour de Rome, et n'outra davantage les droits des Papes"; and *Diccionario Enciclopedico Hispano–Americano*, op. cit., p. 322: "Adquirió notoriedad por la defensa que hizo de la Santa Sede en las contiendas que ésta tuvo con la República de Venecia." S. Ferrier especially in his *Le Catholique d'Estat, ou Discours politique des alliances du Roy très-Chrestien, contre les calomnies des*

G. WORTHY OF PROMOTION

His unwavering loyalty to the papacy and his industry, in addition to his theological erudition, naturally endeared Juan de Cartagena to Pope Paul V. Wadding wrote of him that he was *"Paulo V summe charus."* [176] We have seen above Cartagena's own acknowledgment of the Pontiff's "many favors" to him.[177] Soon, Paul V was thinking of rewarding him more. On January 31, 1614, the Papal Secretariat of State sent a letter to the Nuncio in Madrid, Antonio Caetani, Archbishop of Capua, wishing that Juan de Cartagena be recommended ...

> ...to the Majesty of the King, to the Lord Duke of Lerma, to the Father Confessor, and to other ministers, so that he may be nominated in case of some vacancy in the Church of Spain proportionate to his person. Our Lord [the Pope] will feel much pleased when he is rewarded, because this Father besides being a natural–born subject of His Majesty has made himself a person eminent in learning, which is shown by his published works as well as in prudence and virtuous life. And I will be much beholden myself, if Your Lordship will be so good as to work for his benefice, as I pray for it.[178]

In the context of the royal *patronato* of the Spanish Church, the Crown had the right to present its own candidate to any bishopric in Spain, and the Pope would then duly appoint the royal nominee. Juan de Cartagena, a professor in the *patronato* convent of San Pietro in Montorio, was no stranger to King Philip III, to whom volume two of the *Homiliae Catholicae* had been dedicated in 1611. That the Nuncio received a directive to get the ears too of the Duke of Lerma, Don Francisco de Sandoval y Rojas, was but a recognition

---

ennemis de son Estat (Paris, 1626[3]) finds Cartagena's claims for the Pope treasonous to the king. See pp. 13 & 199–120.

[176] Wadding, loc. cit.

[177] *HCUCRA*, Dedication. And Cartagena missed no chance to eulogize his patron. Cf. *HCSADM*, lib. XV, hom. XXII (III, 202b–209b), where he says among others, perhaps self–consciously, that the Pope has been generous to deserving men: "praestantes viros absque numero virtute conspicuos, ac literarum peritia insignes, variis honoribus cumulatos, et ad purpuream usque dignitatem evectos."

[178] Vatican Archive, *Nunz. di Spagna*, v. 339, f. 25r: Letter of the Secretary to the Nuncio, January 31, 1614; quoted by Vazquez, art. cit., p. 278.

by Rome of the 17th century political reality in Spain, where the Favourite, the so–called *Privado* or *Valido*, of the king ruled, while the king himself merely reigned. The royal confessor, Luis Aliaga, was also a friend of Cartagena, meriting to have the third volume of the *Homiliae Catholicae* dedicated to him in its Paris edition of 1616, after Cardinal Arrigoni died to whom the book was first dedicated. The Spanish Ambassador to Rome, Francisco Castro, a nephew of the Duke of Lerma, was another intimate of Cartagena. The fourth volume of the *Homiliae Catholicae* in its 1612 edition by Facciotti was dedicated to him.

But three years passed and nothing had happened to procure an ecclesiastical appointment in Spain for Cartagena. So, on March 22, 1617, the Secretary of State, Cardinal Escipión Borghese, once more reminded the Nuncio in Madrid of the previous communication.

> Regarding Father Fray Giovanni Cartagena of the Order of Friars Minor Observant of St. Francis, many things contribute together to make him worthy of a Church in accordance with his quality, to which purpose Our Lord [the Pope] ordered me in the year past to recommend him to Your Lordship, so that the good grace of your office may bring him the nomination of His Majesty.[179]

Presupposing that the Nuncio made the effort, what could have stymied the papal wish on behalf of Cartagena? It could not have been for lack of good connections. On the Spanish side, as we have seen, he had more than a good share of favorable contacts. And on the Roman side, in addition to the Pope's special liking for him, we have already noted that he had dedicated a book to Cardinal Pompeyo Arrigoni and another book was also dedicated around this time to Cardinal Fabrizio Veralli, both of whom were Protectors of the Franciscans. His close friendship with Cardinal Marcello Lante della Rovere was a well–known fact in the Roman circles.[180] All these "Spanish and Roman connections" notwithstanding, Juan de Cartagena was never made a bishop.[181] Were his papalist views seen with

---

[179] Ibid., v. 340, f. 221: Letter of the Secretary to the Nuncio, March 22, 1617; Vazquez, ibid.

[180] Laurus, op. cit., p. 47.

[181] Pedro de Alcántara Martínez, O.F.M., believed Cartagena to be a bishop in his article "La Inmaculada Concepción segun las Doctrinas de Juan de Cartagena y Juan Serrano, O.F.M. (s. XVII)," in *Virgo Immaculata*, Academia Mariana Internationalis (Romae, 1957), p. 209.

misgivings in the Spanish Court? And was it considered for the moment a bad precedence for the royal patronage over the Church in Spain to honor this unsollicited papal recommendation to a bishopric? And, if it were true that Cartagena came from a *converso* family, were objections mounted against his appointment on the ground of the doctrine of *limpieza de sangre?* Or was it simply death that prevented the realization of the Pope's plan for Cartagena?

H. DEATH

In late November, 1617, Juan de Cartagena set out on a journey, which would prove to be his last service to the Holy See. Making the same trip with Cartagena was an English convert to Catholicism, Sir William Cecil, Baron of Roos, who fled from his country just three months before and who was then thinking of becoming a religious.[182] The Count of Gondomar, Diego Sarmiento de Acuña, the Spanish Ambassador to London, was instrumental in the conversion of the man and in fact engineered the Baron's escape to Rome. The Englishman and Cartagena apparently became friends in Rome through the Count of Gondomar, who was an old acquaintance from Cartagena's Valladolid days. At that time Acuña was the chief auditor of the *Cortes* which had then been newly moved to Valladolid. He became too in 1602 the city's *corregidor*, after refusing the governorship of the Philippines.[183] The Count had told the Baron to proceed south to Naples, an Aragonese possession and a Spanish province, for political and financial purposes.[184] Coincidentally, it seems, Cartagena was also headed that way, according to Wadding, *"Pauli iussu."* [185]

At least three bishops were consecrated for Spain during the time that Cartagena's nomination was being recommended. Cf. Patritius Gauchat, O.M.Conv., *Hierarchia Catholica Medii et Recentiores Aevi*, IV (Münster, 1935), p. 383. And there is no indication either that Cartagena might have refused any such intended honor, as suggested by the *Biografía Eclesiastica Completa*, op. cit., p. 465.

[182] Cf. *Documento inéditos para la Historia de España*, ed. Duque de Alba et al., I (Madrid, 1936), p. 79.

[183] Ibid., p. 17. A *corregidor* is a royal official appointed to all cities and principal towns of Castille, with administrative and judicial duties, serving as the essential link between the central and local governments.

[184] Ibid., p. 176.

[185] Wadding, loc. cit.

Why did Paul V send Cartagena to Naples? A contemporary tells us of Cartagena's remarkable friendship with Naples' Viceroy, the Duke of Osuna, "who is so bound to him [Cartagena] with the sweet shackles of virtue, that you simply cannot distinguish which one of the two is more loved and respected by the other." [186] Pope Paul V apparently dispatched Cartagena to Naples to use his influence on the Viceroy. He wanted to reduce the friction there over jurisdictional matters between the King's and the Pope's representatives in the best tradition of the fluctuating feud between the Spanish Crown and the Papacy. More specifically Cartagena would be voicing the Pope's desire that the Viceroy stop warring against the Republic of Venice. To weaken Venice further meant not only Spanish domination in Italy but also a free–hand for the Croatian pirates in the Adriatic. But the Viceroy was intent on resisting the haughty republic.[187]

Apparently the papal emissary was fatally disabled during the trip. On July 10, 1618, Diego de Silva, the Valencian servant accompanying the Baron of Roos, announced to the Count of Gondomar the death of his English master which had just occurred.[188] And in another letter to the Count dated September 26, 1618, from Naples, de Silva lamented the tight financial situation to which he had been reduced "during the sickness of both [the Baron and Cartagena], for Father Cartagena also died of the same infirmity three days before my master." [189] So, the death of Juan de Cartagena must have oc-

---

[186] "Mox Neapoli, ubi Petrum Gironum Ossunae Ducem Proregem... ita sibi virtutum grata compede obvinxerat: ut uter alteri esset carior, venerabiliorque non plane dispiceres." Laurus, loc. cit.

[187] Replying to the Pope's message, the Viceroy justified his stand against the Doge and the Republic with some ironic allusion to the Pope's own previous fight against the Venetians: "desde que llegué a este reino he entendido de diferentes personas la asistencia que venecianos daban al duque de Saboya contra las armas del Rey, mi señor... Lo que suplico a V. Santidad en su nombre, pues han negado la obediencia a V.S., que sin ella ninguno puede ser católico... y traído y pagado herejes de Francia al servizio del duque de Saboya, y de Holanda al suyo..." Vatican Archive, Borghese, IV, v. 38, ff. 51–52; quoted by Vazquez, art. cit., p. 283.

The Duke of Osuna, who was viceroy of Sicily in 1611–1616 and of Naples in 1616–1620, was later recalled in disgrace in 1620 and imprisoned.

[188] Madrid, Academia de la Historia, col. Salazar, ms A–84, f. 74; cited by Vazquez, ibid., p. 284.

[189] Ibid., ff. 221–224.

curred in early July of 1618.[190] He was buried in the chapel of San Jacobo de la Marca in the convent of Santa Maria la Nova. His contemporary humanist Ioannes Baptista Laurus said of Cartagena's premature death: *"Neapolitanus aer culpandus est in hoc."* [191] The almost simultaneous death of the travelling companions was probably caused by some local plague which proved fatal to the visitors. And thus Juan de Cartagena ended his life at the age of 55 during a mission of diplomacy in the service of the Papacy.

---

[190] Wadding, loc. cit., gave 1617 as the year of Cartagena's death. This has been simply taken at its face value by N. Antonio, op. cit., p. 673; J. de San Antonio, loc. cit.; Bayle, loc. cit.; Jöcher, loc. cit.; the *Biografia Eclesiastica Completa*, op. cit., p. 465; Renedo, op. cit., p. 125; Tejera, op. cit., p. 121; the *Diccionario Enciclopedico Hispano–Americano*, loc. cit.; Hurter, loc. cit.; Amann, loc. cit.; Zawart, op. cit., p. 490; Bihl, loc. cit.; E. Allison Peers, *Studies of the Spanish Mystics*, III (London, 1960), p. 214; Stegmüller, art. cit., col. 1067; Schneyer, op. cit., p. 297; and Castro, loc. cit.

[191] Laurus, loc. cit.

CHAPTER TWO

HIS WORKS

If the details in the life of Juan de Cartagena were once shrouded in the unknown, his works and writings in general have fared better and are more certified. In fact Cartagena's name came down in history principally because of his published works. Historians and theologians have made references to, and have with varying thoroughness commented on, his writings. But even here research remains to be done and some clarification can still be made. We shall attempt in this chapter to present as complete a bibliography as possible of Cartagena's works. The full length informative title of the original and annotations about each writing will be given, together with a list of libraries in Western Europe and North America where the writings are known to be available.[1]

I. PUBLISHED WORKS

A. Disputatio Insignis Utilis Valde ac Pernecessaria ad Extirpandum Quoddam Latentis Simoniae Vitium, *hac tempestate nimis frequens, tam in Italia, quam in Hispania, et aliis regionibus. In qua*

---

[1] This bibliography and list of pertinent libraries are based on our own research and on the following works: Vazquez, art. cit.; *Catalogue Général de Livres Imprimés de la Bibliothèque Nationale*, 79 (Paris, 1931) and 194 (Paris, 1966); *The British Museum Catalogue of Printed Books*, 9 (Michigan, 1946); *Bibliotheca Catholica Neerlandica Impressa 1500–1727* (The Hague, 1954); Aimé Trottier, C.S.C., *Essai de Bibliographie sur saint Joseph* (Montreal, 1968, 4th edn); E. Allison Peers, op. cit., pp. 284–285; and Toda y Güell, op. cit.

We would like to take this opportunity to thank the following institutions for their kind cooperation in providing us with pertinent informations: the U.S.A. Library of Congress' National Union Catalog Publication Project, the Koninklijke Bibliotheek at The Hague, the Zentralkatalog der wissenschaftlichen Bibliotheken des Landes Nordrhein–Westfalen in Cologne and in Düsseldorf, the Bayerischer Zentralkatalog in Munich, the Zentralkatalog Baden–Württemberg in Stuttgart, the Hessischer Zentralkatalog in Frankfurt, the Norddeutscher Zentralkatalog in Hamburg, the Niedersächsischer Zentralkatalog in Göttingen, and the Berliner Gesamtkatalog in Berlin, and the two dozens or so individual libraries in the Federal Republic of Germany which have replied to our questionnaire.

diligenter investigatur: Sitne simonia dare pecuniam intercessori pro intercessione facienda alicui Principi ad obtinendum beneficium Ecclesiasticum? Authore R.P.F. Joanne de Carthagena Hispano, ordinis Minorum de Observantia, Concionatore, ac Sacrae Theologiae Praelectore Generali Romae in Regali Conventu S. Petri Montis Aurei. In hac secunda impressione ab eodem authore recognita. Romae, apud Stephanum Paulinum. 1607. *Superiorum authoritate.* In–4. 16 pp.

The first edition of this short treatise was most probably published in Milan a year or so before, as a result of Cartagena's stopover on his way to Rome.[2] The Spanish officials in the Lombardian State had pressed the travelling theologian to take up his pen against the rampant practice of simony. Interestingly, what appears to be a typographical error in the work of Sbaralea has been handed on by Toda y Güell and even by Castro to the present day. They assign to this booklet 1657 as the year of its second edition.[3]

Copies of this work are in:

Rome, Biblioteca Angelica, F.4.17

Biblioteca Nazionale, 34.9.F.15–3 (3 copies)

Vatican, Biblioteca Vaticana, Barberini, F.VIII.75 (2 copies).

B. Pro Ecclesiastica Libertate, et Potestate Tuenda. *Adversus iniustas Venetorum Leges eiusdem Sacrae libertatis laesivas, perniciosque illarum defensorum errores nunc primum renatos, et a Supremo Pontifice Inquisitionis Tribunali consulto Summo Pontifice Paulo V. publico Edicto Romae damnatos. Tomus Primus. Authore R.P.F. Joanne de Carthagena Hispano, ordinis Minorum de Observantia, concionatore Sacrorumque Canonum professore, ac Sacrae Theologiae Praelectore Generali Romae in Regali conventu S. Petri ad Sanctiss. D.N. Paulum V, P.M. Romae, apud Stephanum Paulinum.* 1607. *Superiorum authoritate.* In–4.

No existing copy of this work is known. We know, however, that it is made up of 9 books and that handwritten it amounted to 643 pages.[4] This was the first of the two volumes Cartagena wrote in defense of the papal action against the Republic of Venice in 1606.

---

[2] Cf. above, p. 46.

[3] Hyacinthus Sbaralea, *Supplementum et Castigatio ad Scriptores Trium Ordinum S. Francisci a Waddingo, aliisve descriptos* (Romae, 1921) II, p. 52; Toda y Güell, op. cit., p. 340; and Castro, art. cit., p. 595.

[4] Cf. above, pp. 56–57.

Toda y Güell made two errors in listing this book, claiming that it was published "ex Tipographiae Camerae Apostolicae, 1609." [5]

C. Selectarum Disputationum in Quartum Sententiarum. *To-mus primus in quo de Sacramentis in genere, ac de instrumentali eorum efficientia disserte, et copiose pertractatur. Authore F. Ioanne de Car-thagena Hispano, Ordinis Minorum de Observantia, Sacrae Theologiae Lectore Generali Romae in Conventu S. Petri Montis Aurei. Ad S.D.N. Paulum V, Pontificem Maximum. Romae, apud Stephanum Pauli-num. 1607. Superiorum permissu.* In–4. 397 pp.

The publication approval for this book was given by Andrés Justinianus, O.P., dated November 13, 1608! Apparently, it was to correct the antedated year of publication, that J. de San Antonio changed it to 1609.[6] Huster and Renedo followed suit.[7] Based on his research and lectures as *praelector* in San Pietro in Montorio, this volume was planned by the author to be the first in an unrealized series of four devoted to special questions in theology.[8] The project seemed to have been dogged by difficulties. By late 1608 this first volume was not yet in the hands of the printer, thus giving credence to San Antonio's corrected date of publication. For, in a book of his which came out in early 1609, Cartagena himself made the passing remark : "I shall now leave unmentioned what I think about this matter, referring the reader to our selected discussions of the whole of theology, which God willing will soon be given to the press." [9] In 1611, the publisher assured the readers of Cartagena's *Homiliae Catholicae* that all four volumes of the series were forthcoming.[10]

---

[5] Toda y Güell, op. cit., p. 335.

[6] San Antonio, op. cit., p. 143. This must have misled Stegmüller, art. cit., col. 1067, to list two Roman editions for this work: 1607 and 1609!

[7] Hurter, op. cit., p. 149, and Renedo, op. cit., p. 127.

[8] "Instituti mei non est in hac homilia Theologicis satisfacere difficultatibus, quae in scholis tractantur, quoniam iam de illis peculiares disputationes in meis quaestionibus selectis instituto, quae auxiliante Deo super universam Theologiam, quatuor voluminibus divisam, in lucem proferentur." *HCUCRA*, lib. IV, hom. VIII, col. 49. Cartagena expected to deal with special questions spanning the whole of theology. In this first volume he got only as far as commenting on the 4th book of the Sentences of Peter Lombard, and only on the preliminary questions of sacramental theology at that.

[9] Ibid., lib. VIII, hom. IV, col. 31.

[10] "Deum disputationes miscellaneas de arcanis sacrae Theologiae, tam scholasticae quam moralis, in quatuor volumina divisum (sic). Haec nempe omnia

A 1618 edition of this work published in Venice is included in the bibliographies by Antonio, Tejera, *Biografia Eclesiastica Completa*, Amann, and Castro.[11]

Copies of this book are available in:

Madrid, Biblioteca Nacional, 6–i, 46

Paris, Bibliothèque Nationale, D.8242

Rome, Biblioteca Angelica, O.13.18

Biblioteca Nazionale, 14.17.E.17.

D. HOMILIAE CATHOLICAE

1. *Tomus primus. Homiliae Catholicae in Universa Christianae Religionis Arcana Cunctis Divini Verbi, Praeconibus Utiles Valde, Atque Pernecessariae in Libros Sexdecim Divisae. Ad S.D.N. Paulum V. Pont. Max. Auctore P.F. Ioanne Carthagena Hispano ordinis Minorum de Observantia, olim apud Salmanticenses Sacrae Theologiae professore, et nunc Romae de mandato Sanctissimi Lectore generali in Regali conventu Sancti Petri montis aurei. De facultate Superiorum. Romae, ex officina Alphonsi Ciaconi.* 1609. In–folio. 194 homilies in 16 books, with numerated columns. Tables and indexes.

The title page of this volume is bordered by a figure of Christ and pictures of Franciscan Saints, with the image of Paul V in the center. The approval for publication given by Luis de San Juan Evangelista was dated March 28, 1609, and the papal letter of special privilege to the publisher December 6, 1608. The preliminary leaves give the dedication to Pope Paul V, plus an introduction by the author. The certification by the delegated censor, Marcellus Baldassinus, is without date. Being the subject of the present study, these volumes of the *Homiliae Catholicae* will be described more fully in the next chapter.

Copies of this first volume are in:

London, British Museum, 3553.e. and C.66.b.3

Rome, Antonianum, G.8–c.17a

Biblioteca Nazionale, 8.14.N.1

---

docte et ornate felicissimum auctoris ingenium effudit, quae ab eodem impetrata, in lucem dabo." *HCSADM* (I, Publisher's Note). In the Cologne edition of 1613, this note is found at the back of the volume.

[11] N. Antonio, op. cit., p. 673; Tejera, op. cit., p. 121; *Biografia Eclesiastica Completa*, op. cit., p. 465; Amann, art. cit., p. 754; Castro, loc. cit.

Salamanca, Biblioteca Universitaria
Trier, Priesterseminar Bibliothek, L.966
Vienna, Österreichische Nationalbibliothek, 21.N.34.

2. *Tomus secundus. Ad catholic. potentiss. Regem Philip. III.*
Homiliae Catholicae de Sacris Arcanis Deiparae Mariae et Ioseph.
Auctore P.F. Ioanne de Carthagena Hispano Ord. Minorum de Obser-
vantia, Sacrae Theologiae Lectore generali Romae de mandato Sanctis-
simi, in Regali Conventu S. Petri in Monte Aureo. Cum quadruplici
Indice atque privilegio et Superiorum Facultate. Romae, apud Bartho-
lomaeum Zannettum. 1611. In–folio. 720 pp.

On the engraved frontispiece there is a baroque altar to Mary
with the Child Jesus in her arms and Joseph beside her. Publication
approval was by Arcángel de Mesina, given on May 12, 1611. A dedication to King Philip III. A letter of privilege by Paul V to the
publisher, dated November 5, 1611. A note by the author to his
reader, and another by the publisher. This volume was certified by
the censor, Placidus Philingerius, on June 4, 1611.

Copies of this second volume are in:
Lisbon, Biblioteca Nacional
Rome, Biblioteca Angelica, P.7.7
    Antonianum, Dep. 1, GR 69–2
    Biblioteca Nazionale, 204.18.F.8
Vatican, Biblioteca Vaticana, Barb., V.11.32
Washington DC, Holy Name College Library

3. *Tomus tertius. F. Ioan. de Carthagena Hispani celeberrimi*
Theologi ex Ordine Min. de Observan. insignis Provincitiae Immacula-
tae Conceptionis Homiliae Catholicae de Sacris Arcanis Deiparae et
Iosephi. Ad Illustrissimum Arigonium. Romae escudebat Bartholo-
maeus Zannetti. 1614. In–folio. 724 pp.

The same frontispiece engraving as in the previous volume.
The publication approval was the same as in the preceding work.
Certification by Ioannes Franciscus Palumbrus, delegated censor,
dated July 20, 1614. Dedication to Cardinal Arrigoni. A note from
the publisher to the reader.

Copies of this third volume are in:
Madrid, Biblioteca Nacional, G–i, 605
Rome, Biblioteca Angelica, P.7.8
    Antonianum, Dep. 1, GR 69–3
    Biblioteca Nazionale, 8.14.N.3 (2 copies)

Vatican, Biblioteca Vaticana, R.I. 11.899
Washington DC, Holy Name College Library

4. *Tomus quartus. F. Ioan. de Carthagena Hispani celeberrimi Theologi ex Ordine Min. de Observan. insignis Provincitiae Immaculatae Conceptionis Homiliae Catholicae de Sacris Arcanis Deiparae et Iosephi. Ad Rmum. P.F. Antonium de Treja Vicarium Generalem totius ordinis Seraphici P.N.S. Francisci. Romae, escudebat Iacobus Mascardi.* 1616. In–folio. 1160 columns of text. Indexes.

The same frontispiece engraving as the previous two volumes. Publication approval by Pedro Jover, dated February 10, 1616. Certification by the delegated censor, Nicolaus Rodulphus, O.P., on January 22, 1616. Papal privilege for the publisher given on August 26, 1615. Dedication to Antonio de Trejo.

Copies of this fourth and last volume of the series are in:

Rome, Biblioteca Angelica, P.7.9

Antonianum, Dep. 1, GR 69–4

Biblioteca Nazionale, 8.14.N.4

Washington DC, Holy Name College Library

5. *Subsequent Editions of the Homiliae Catholicae.* In 1611, the Roman publisher Zannetti claimed that "...when the first volume of the *Homiliae* was issued a few months ago, within a short time one thousand copies were scooped up by the libraries. Already they are being reprinted in Germany and France..." [12] Indeed, bibliographers list various editions; but just how often, when and where the *Homiliae Catholicae* were reprinted, nobody seems to be complete. We shall take the term "edition" in the more inclusive and general sense of reprint, with or without alteration, which will be noted on occasion. Also, for the sake of clarity, we shall distinguish here the first volume, the *Homiliae Catholicae in Universa Christianae Religionis Arcana* (HCUCRA), which is essentially Christological, from the other three volumes, the *Homiliae Catholicae de Sacris Arcanis Deiparae Mariae et Ioseph* (HCSADM), which are primarily Mariological. Hence, although in a particular edition all four volumes might have been published as a set or in a series, they will be listed separately according to the above twofold classification, with the explanatory remark as to which was published with which. As will be seen, some

---

[12] *HCSADM* (I, Publisher's Note).

publishers themselves have treated the first volume of the *Homiliae Catholicae* as basically different from the rest. Or as the author himself said, the second volume of the set is "*Mariani huius operis primum volumen.*" [13]

a) HOMILIAE CATHOLICAE IN UNIVERSA CHRISTIANAE RELIGIONIS AR-
   CANA

   1) Roman editions:
   a. The publisher Facciotti must have put out his own edition of the first volume early in 1611. In his 1612 edition, he mentioned the fact that he had already reprinted this same work.[14] And the above quotation from Zannetti seems to be alluding to an edition of the volume during the first half of 1611. There is however no known copy of this early edition, although Castro has it in his list.[15]
   b. The 1612 edition by Guilelmus Facciotti is entitled *Homiliae Catholicae de Sacris Arcanis Christianae Religionis ad Christum Dominum Spectantibus, ab eodem auctore in hac quinta editione novissime locupletatae. Ad Excellentissimum D.D. Franciscum de Castro.* In-folio. 1,678 columns of text.
   The permission to publish this edition was given by Juan de Hierro, dated August 20, 1612. The title has been modified to bring out more specifically the book's Christological content. In this edition eight new *homiliae* were incorporated, thus giving the total of 202 homilies. Likewise it is to be noted that this edition is already the fifth. Including the claim that the book came out in Venice in 1609, four editions are more or less accounted for. And Zannetti's 1611 report that Germany and France were also reprinting it would mean more than five editions in less than four years. On the other hand, it could be true also that not all the projected foreign publications of the volume related by Zannetti were successfully executed or finished by the time this 1612 edition came out.
   Copies of this Facciotti edition are in:
   El Escorial, Real Biblioteca del Escorial [16]

---

[13] Ibid., (I, Author's Introduction).
[14] "...recusimus et nos idem opus." *HCUCRA* (Romae, 1612), Publisher's Note.
[15] Castro, loc. cit.
[16] This item by Allison Peers, op. cit., p. 284, is also verified by Renedo, op. cit., p. 125.

Paris, Bibliothèque Nationale, D.3105
Rome, Biblioteca Angelica, P.7.6
    Antonianum, Dep. 1, GR 69–1
Vatican, Biblioteca Vaticana, Barb., V.11.31
Salamanca, Biblioteca Universitaria
Vienna, Öster. Nationalbibliothek, 22.C.5

Castro surprisingly considers this Roman edition of 1612 to be a completely different work of Cartagena and even claims two editions of it.[17]

c. A 1614 edition in Rome of this volume has also been filed by Castro.[18] But nobody else besides him makes this affirmation.

2) Venetian editions:

a. Sbaralea mentions a 1609 edition in Venice of this book, supposedly by the publisher Patricio Castruccio.[19] And Facciotti himself gave some backing to this assertion, when he said in 1612 that "it was by no means to be wondered at, that printers both in Venice and in Cologne have gladly labored in cutting the types for this work." [20]

b. Another edition "cum additionibus magni momenti post quintam editionem Romanam" was published in Venice in 1614 by Jacobus de Franciscus, wrote Sbaralea.[21]

3) Cologne editions:

Although Facciotti mentioned in 1612 that printers in Cologne had also set the *HCUCRA* in type, and although Zannetti claimed even a year earlier in 1611 that the book was being reprinted in Germany, we know of no German edition of the work dating so early.

a. The earliest edition we have from Cologne came out in 1614: *Homiliae Catholicae in Universa Christianae Religionis Arcana in libros XVI divisa. Coloniae Agrippinae, sumptibus Bernardi Gualteri.* In–4. 1, 176 pp.

---

[17] Castro, loc. cit. The only basis for such a claim could be the little change in the wordings of the title and the specification that the book has been added to by the author. Both of these factors are true too of the 1614 edition in Venice. Hence its "second edition"? Schneyer, loc. cit., makes the same mistake.

[18] Castro, loc. cit.

[19] Sbaralea, op. cit., p. 51.

[20] *HCUCRA* (Romae, 1612), Publisher's Note.

[21] Sbaralea, loc. cit.

The publisher dedicated this edition to the Archbishop–Elect of Cologne, Ioannes Cholinus, in a letter dated April 4, 1614.

Copies of this edition are in:

Cologne, Erzbischöfliche Diözesanbibliothek, Past f 287
Munich, Bayerische Staatsbibliothek, 4° Hom. 347/1
Neresheim, Bibliothek der Benediktinerabtei, H 251
Neuburg, Staatlische Bibliothek, 4° Theol. Pr.21
Regensburg, Fürstlich Thurn und Taxissche Hofbibliothek, Ma.798
Rottenburg, Diözesanbibliothek, Dz 7177
Trier, Stadtbibliothek, L III 25

b. Gualterius put out another edition four years later in 1618. In–8. 1406 pp.

Copies of this book are in:

Eichstätt, Staats– und Seminarbibliothek, SB VII 802
Latrobe (Pennsylvania), Saint Vincent College and Archabbey
Soest, Stadtarchiv und Wissenschaftliche Stadtbibliothek, IV Ff.10.2a
Vienna, Priesterseminar Bibliothek, K/26/P/g
Walberberg, Bibliothek St. Albert, 5/6
Xanthen, Stiftsbibliothek, 2282

c. Another Cologne edition, also by Gualterius, came out in 1626. "*Editio postrema, recognita ac emendata.*" In–4. 848 pp. Theophilus Georgi tells us that this volume was selling at 16 Groschen a copy during his time.[22]

Copies of this are in:

Eichstätt, Staats– und Seminarbibliothek, B VII 199
Marburg, Universitätsbibliothek, XIXe B 1450^b
Xanten, Stiftsbibliothek, 2280 C

d. Yet another edition printed in Cologne was done by Johann Kinchius in 1641. 848 pp.

A copy is in:

Cologne, Erzbischöfliche Diözesanbibliothek, Ad 19

4) Paris editions:

Zannetti alluded to an early publication of the *HCUCRA* in France. The earliest French edition we know of, however, came out in 1613.

---

[22] Theophilus Georgi, *Europäisches Bücher–Lexikon* (Leipzig, 1742), p. 260.

a. *Homiliae Catholicae in Universa Christianae Religionis Arcana. Editio ultima. Lutetiae Parisiorum, sumptibus D. de La Nouë.* 1613. In–folio. 1,304 columns of text.

Is this edition claiming to be the last or the latest in Paris, meaning that at least one, if not more, earlier edition of this volume had already been published there? Or is it merely advertising that it is the latest reprinting anywhere?

Anyway, copies of this 1613 edition are in:

Brussels, Bibliothèque Royale Albert 1er, V.B.1940

Paris, Bibliothèque Nationale, D.1850 (1)

b. H. Drouart put out too an "editio ultima" in Paris in 1613. In–folio, 1, 303 pp. A copy of this edition used to be in 's–Bosch, Holland, in the library of the Capuchin Fathers.[23]

---

[23] Recently, for the purpose of stream–lining their libraries and saving from unnecessary duplications, the Dutch Franciscans had auctioned off some of their book collections. Some books by Juan de Cartagena belonged to these collections. Below is a list of these works and the former Franciscan libraries they belonged to. Their present whereabouts are not known.

1) *HCUCRA:*

Paris, by Drouart, in 1613
  's Hertogenbosch, Bibliotheek van de Paters Capucijnen, 252
Cologne, by Bualterius, in 1614
  's–Bosch, Bibliotheek Capucijnen, 252
  Maastricht, Bibliotheek van het Minderbroedersklooster
Cologne, by Gualterius, in 1618
  Maastricht, Bibliotheek van het Minderbroedersklooster, Vak 11 171
Antwerp, by Keerberg, in 1622
  Maastricht, Vak 70 No. 406
Cologne, by Gualterius, in 1626
  's–Bosch, 252
  Maastricht, Vak 76 No. 148
  Alverna, Bibliotheek van het Minderbroedersklooster

2) *HCSADM:*

Cologne, by Gualterius, in 1613–1616
  's–Bosch, 252.8
  Maastricht, Vak 76 No. 283–4 (two volumes only)
  Alverna
Antwerp, by Keerberg, in 1622
  Maastricht, Vak 70 No. 407
  's–Bosch, 252.8
Paris, by Fovet, in 1624–1625
  Maastricht

c. Another "Editio ultima ab authore recognita, apud Michae-
lem Sonnium" was published in Paris in 1616. In–folio. 1,329 columns.
Copies of this are in:

    Cologne, Universitätsbibliothek, GB IV 7975
    El Escorial, Real Biblioteca del Escorial
    Leiden, Universiteitsbibliotheek
    London, British Museum, 3835 f.
    Madrid, Biblioteca Nacional, 3–74761
    Valladolid, Colegio de Agustinos Filipinos
    Xanten, Stiftsbibliothek, an 2072

Castro again lists this edition as a distinct work by Cartagena.[24]

d. Drouart seems to have published another edition in 1616,
in–folio.

A copy is in:

    London, British Museum, 3835.f.3

e. Yet another "editio ultima" by another publisher in Paris
came out in 1620, "apud Reginaldum Chaudiere. Cum Privilegio
Regis." In–folio. 1,304 colums.

Toda y Güell says a copy of it is in:

    Barcelona, Biblioteca Universitaria [25]

f. A. Trottier refers to a 1620 edition by Chaffelet.[26]

g. Still another "editio ultima" came out in 1623, in–folio.

A copy is in:

    Amsterdam, Universiteitsbibliotheek

5) Antwerp edition:

As the first in a set of three volumes, *De Religionis Christianae
Arcanis Homiliae Sacrae cum Catholicae, tum Morales. Tomus I.
De SS. Trinitate et Christo Salvatore* was published by Joannes Keer-

---

    Cologne, by Gualterius, in 1625
       's–Bosch, 252
       Maastricht, Vak 76 No. 147 & Vak 7 No. 34
3) *PRAXIS ORATIONIS MENTALIS:*
    Cologne by Gualterius, in 1618
       's–Bosch, 248.4
    [24] Castro, art. cit., p. 596.
    [25] Toda y Güell, op. cit., p. 337, where he also describes it.
    [26] Trottier, op. cit., n. 3748.

berg in 1622 in Antwerp. *Editio postrema, ab auctore recognita.* In-
folio. 520 pp.

Copies of this edition are in:
Den Haag, Koninklijke Bibliotheek, 522 B 1
Eichstätt, Staats– und Seminarbibliothek, B VII 198
Leeuwarden, Provinciale Bibliotheek, R.K. 1107
Nijmegen, Universiteitsbibliotheek, D.125 f.308.3
    Berchmanianum
Paris, Bibliothèque Nationale, D.3115
Passau, Staatlische Bibliothek
Regensburg, Staatlische Bibliothek, 2° Homil. 61
Rome, Antonianum, Dep. 11, GR 22
Xanten, Stiftsbibliothek, 2071

6) Naples edition:

In 1866, more than 250 years after the original Roman edition
of the *Homiliae Catholicae*, the *HCUCRA* was published once more.
This *"editio prima neapolitana"* came out in two parts: *Homiliae
Catholicae de Sacris Arcanis ad SS. Trinitatem, et Christum Dominum
Spectantibus. Ex Typographaeo dicto del Tasso.* In–folio. 472 and 427 pp.
respectively. The first part contains the first 9 books of the original
edition, while the second has books 10 to 16. This edition came out
last as Volume IV/1 and Volume IV/2 of the whole series.[27]

Copies of this late edition are in:
Montréal, Centre de recherche et de documentation de l'Ora-
    toire Saint–Joseph
Rome, Antonianum, G 1–a 1 O–11
Washington DC, Library of the Catholic University of Amer-
    ica, BT 1005 C32 1859 Holy Name College Library

b) Homiliae catholicae de sacris arcanis Deiparae Mariae et
Ioseph

1) Roman edition:

All three volumes of the *HCSADM* are said to have been reprinted in Rome in 1624, according to F. Stegmüller.[28]

---

[27] Cf. Toda y Güell, op. cit., p. 340. Attilio Pagliaini, *Catalogo Generale
della Libreria Italiana dall'anno 1847 a tutto il 1899*, I (Milano, 1901), p. 443, includes
this edition.

[28] Stegmüller, art. cit., col. 1068. The claim by Castro, loc. cit., that at least

2) Venetian edition:

Toda y Güell describes a 1612 edition in Venice of the set's first volume *"apud Iacobum de Franciscis."* In–4. 769 pp. The Council of Venice gave the license for this publication on December 23, 1611. And a copy of it is reported by Toda y Güell to be in the Capuchin Library in Sarriá.[29]

3) Cologne editions:

a. In 1613 the first volume of the *HCSADM* was reprinted by Bernardus Gualterius in Cologne. In–4. 846 pp. The publisher included in it a letter of dedication to Hubertus Germus, Abbot of St. Trudo, dated March 9, 1613.[30]

The second volume appeared in 1615, with 800 pp. and dedicated by the same publisher to the Abbot of Gerode in Eichsfeld on March 13, 1615.

The third volume, *"Operum Tomus IV"*, was published in 1616. 725 pp. It was dedicated by Gualterius to Henricus Spichermagel, Abbot of St. Pantaleon, on September 5, 1616.

The *HCUCRA* volume of this series came out in 1614.

Copies of the three *HCSADM* volumes are in:

> Eichstätt, Staats– und Seminarbibliothek, B VII 385 (only the third volume)
>
> Latrobe (Pennsylvania), Saint Vincent College and Archabbey
>
> Marburg, Universitätsbibliothek, XIXe B 1450 (only the first two volumes)
>
> Montréal, Centre de recherche et documentation de l'Oratoire Saint–Joseph (only the second volume)

---

the *HCSADM* I came out in Rome in 1609 is hard to conceive of, inasmuch as the original edition first appeared in 1611.

[29] Toda y Güell, op. cit., p. 337.

[30] Vazquez, "Nuevo documento de Fr. Juan de Cartagena O.F.M. sobre las controversias 'de auxiliis'," *Antonianum*, 40 (1965) 321, having found in the *Catalogue Général de Livres Imprimés de la Bibliothèque Nationale*, 79, op. cit., an entry on the 1613 Cologne edition of the *HCSADM*, falsely concludes that this volume was the Tomus II, thereby presupposing the earlier publication of Tomus I, as alluded to by both Zannetti in 1611 and Facciotti in 1612. However, the Cologne publisher Gualterius, without naming the 1613 volume as Tomus I, designated its two following volumes as Tomus II and Tomus III respectively. In other words, the *HCUCRA* was considered as a distinctly separate publication. The earliest reprinting in Cologne of the *HCUCRA* seems to be the 1614 edition. Gualterius himself never made mention of any earlier Cologne edition of the book.

Munich, Bayerische Staatsbibliothek, 4° Hom. 347/2,3,4 and
4° Hom. 346/1,2,3 (2 sets)

Münster, Universitätsbibliothek, 1E 539 (only the first volume)

Neresheim, Bibliothek der Benediktinerabtei, H 251 (the second volume only)

Neuburg, Staatl. Bibliothek, 4° Theol. Pr. 17

Oosterhout, Bibliotheek van het klooster St. Catharina–dal

Paris, Bibliothèque Nationale, D.8241 (only the first volume)

Regenburg, Fürst. Thurn u. Taxissche Hofbibliothek, Ma.798a
and Ma.887 (only the first two volumes)

Rottenburg, Diözesanbibliothek, Dz 7175 and 7176 (the last two volumes only)

Soest, Stadtarchiv u. Wissenschaftliche Stadtbibliothek, IV
Ff.10.2 (the first volume only)

Trier, Stadtbibliothek, L III 26, 27, 28

Utrecht, Universiteitsbiblotheek, N° 246–8

Vienna, Öster. Nationalbibliothek, 61.181–B (only the third volume)

Xanten, Stiftsbibliothek, 2285 A–B–C

b. In 1616, as the last volume of the above–mentioned series was published, Gualterius started to put out yet another edition in–8, which was completed in 1619.[31] The *HCUCRA* part of this set was published in 1618, as was the second volume of the *HCSADM*.

Available copies of this edition are in:

Antwerp, Bibliotheek van het Ruusbroec–Gennotschap

Cologne, Erzbischöfliche Diözesanbibliothek, Past X 296 (the second volume only)

Eichstätt, Staats– u. Seminarbibliothek, SB VII 800–801 (the last two volumes only)

Oosterhout, Bibliotheek van het klooster St. Catharina–dal

Walberberg, Bibliothek St. Albert (the third volume only)

Xanten, Stiftsbibliothek, 2285 D (the second volume only)

c. Once more in 1625, Gualterius came out with another Cologne edition, this time in two volumes. "Ultima editio correctior et auctior."

---

[31] That Thomas Hyde listed Volumes I and II of the *HCSADM* with the years 1613 and 1618 as their years of publication in Cologne, obviously means that he had in Oxford Volume I of one edition and a Volume II of a later edition. See his *Catalogus Impressorum Librorum Bibliothecae Bolejanae in Academia Oxoniensi* (Oxonii, 1674), p. 143.

In–4. The second and third volumes of the set were bound into one book of two parts with different paginations, 535 and 478 pages respectively, while the first volume has 561 pages. The 1626 edition of the *HCUCRA* was part of this series.

Copies are in:

    Eichstätt, Staats– u. Seminarbibliothek, B VII 382–4 and
        B VII 201

    Marburg, Universitätsbibliothek, XIXe B 1450ᵇ

    Neresheim, Bibliothek der Benediktinerabtei, H 855

    Nijmegen, Albertinum, 104.a.3 (the last volume only)

    Passau, Staatl. Bibliothek (the first volume only)

    Trier, Priesterseminar Bibliothek, L 945 (the second volume
        only)

    Xanten, Stiftsbibliothek, 2280A

    d. Kinchius put out too the *HCSADM* in 1641, the first volume bound together with the *HCUCRA* and the other two together.

A copy of the first volume with 561 pages is in:

    Cologne, Erzbischöfliche Diözesanbibliothek, Ad 19

4) Paris editions:

a. As continuation of the 1613 Parisian edition of the *HCUCRA*, Sonnius published from 1614 to 1616 the three volumes of the *HCSADM*, in–folio.

Copies of this set are in:

    Brussels, Bibliothèque Royale, V.B., 1940

    Paris, Bibliothèque Nationale, D.1850 (2–4)

    Vienna, Öster. Nationalbibliothek, 7.P.5

    Xanten, Stiftsbibliothek, 2072

b. Almost right on the heels of the previous edition, the same publisher started to put out still another series in 1616 with the publication of the *HCUCRA* as "Editio ultima ab authore recognita," in–folio. The *HCSADM* set was completed in 1618. 966, 922 and 902 pages respectively. And the second volume is newly dedicated to Luis Aliaga.[32]

---

[32] Renedo describes these volumes, which he also claims to have seen in the library of El Escorial. Op. cit., pp. 125-126. However, Allison Peers, who made research in the same library later, apparently did not find them.

    Castro, loc. cit., refers to two different editions of the *HCSADM* in Paris in 1616. Evidently he is talking of the last volume of the 1614–1616 edition and of the first volume of the 1616–1618 edition.

Copies of this Parisian edition are in:

Cologne, Universitätsbibliothek, GB IV 9185

Leiden, Universiteitsbibliotheek (the last two volumes only bound together)

London, British Museum, 3853.f.3

Louvain, Bibliothèque de l'Université de Louvain, B 17938

Salamanca, Biblioteca Universitaria

Valladolid, Colegio Mayor de Santa Cruz

The alleged 1618 three–volume edition in Paris mentioned by San Antonio and also listed by Sbaralea and Stegmüller is none other than this 1616–1618 reprinting.[33]

c. As part of the four–volume set edited by H. Drouart, the *HCSADM* came out once more in Paris in 1616–1618. In–folio.

A copy is in:

London, British Museum, 3835.f.3

d. Reginald Chaudière's "editio ultima" in 1620 had the *HCSADM* in two volumes, in–folio. The first volume has 966 pages.[34]

A copy of this edition is in:

Pommersfelden, Schönberneche Bibliothek, X 123–124.

e. A. Trottier lists a 1620 edition in Paris by Chaffelet in 3 volumes.[35]

f. Trottier mentions also a 1624 Parisian edition by Petit–Pas.[36] And he says that a copy of at least one volume is in:

Montréal, Centre de recherche et de documentation de l'Oratoire Saint–Joseph

g. The three volumes of the *HCSADM* came out too in 1625, in–folio, by R. Fovet. The *HCUCRA* volume appeared in 1623.

A copy is in:

Amsterdam, Universiteitsbibliotheek

T. Georgi listed also this edition of 1625.[37]

h. And L. Ceyssens referred to a 1644 edition in Paris.[38]

---

[33] San Antonio, loc. cit.; Sbaralea, loc. cit.; and Stegmüller, loc. cit.

Martinus Lipinius lists too this 1618 volume in his *Bibliotheca Realis Theologia*, II (Francofurti ad Moenum, 1685), pp. 125b & 37a. So does Trottier, op. cit., n. 3747.

[34] Described by Renedo, op. cit., p. 126. He claims too to have seen a copy of it in Madrid's Biblioteca Nacional. We could not find it there.

[35] Trottier, op. cit., n. 3748.

[36] Ibid., n. 3750.

[37] Georgi, loc. cit.

5) Antwerp edition:

The *HCSADM* volumes of the Antwerp *"Editio postrema"* in 1622 by J. Keerberg came out in two volumes, in–folio, 536 and 445 pages respectively. This edition carried the publication approval by Laurentius Beyerlinck, dated July 10, 1616. According to Wadding, this Antwerp edition was the most widely used of the different editions of the *Homiliae Catholicae* at that time.[39]

Copies of this set are in:

> Den Haag, Koninklijke Bibliotheek, 522 B 1 (bound together with the *HCUCRA*)
> Kaldenkirchen, Klosterbibliothek (one volume only)
> Leeuwarden, Provinciale Bibliotheek, R.K. 1072
> Madrid, Biblioteca Nacional, 2/7447–8 and 6–i, 290
> Nijmegen, Universiteitsbibliotheek, D.125 f.308.3
> Paris, Bibliothèque Nationale, D.3115 and D.625
> Passau, Staatl. Bibliothek
> Regensburg, Staatl. Bibliothek, 2° Homil. 61 (second volume only)
> Rome, Antonianum, Dep. 11, GR 22

6) Naples edition:

The *"editio prima neapolitana"* began in 1859 in an inverted order.[40] Volume I contains the first seven books of the *Homiliae Catholicae de Sacris Arcanis Deiparae Mariae et D. Iosephi Eiusdem Sponsi*. In–folio. 574 pp. *Ex typographia Iosue Vernieri*. 1859. Permission from the General Council of Public Instruction of Naples, dated July 3, 1858.

Volume II has books 8 to 14. 543 pp. *Ex typographaeo dicto del Tasso*. This publisher handled the rest of the series. Volume III, books 15 to 19, plus a 127–page appendix: *"De diversis titulis marianis promptuarium praeconibus laudum B.M.V. perutile. Auctore Ra-*

---

[38] Lucianus Ceyssens, O.F.M., "Fulgence Bottens, OFM, ses difficultés relatives aux 'Scintillae Seraphicae' (1673–1674)," *Franciscana*, 19 (1964) 45, footnote 59.

[39] Wadding, op. cit., p. 198. Lipinius, op. cit., p. 37a, refers to a 1628 Antwerp edition of the *Homiliae Catholicae*. Could this be just a typographical error?

[40] This is described by Toda y Güell, op. cit., pp. 339–340. This place is as good as any to mention that Castro, loc. cit., pulls yet another surprise by listing a 1620 edition in Florence of the *HCSADM*. Could he have been misled by the "sub signo scuti Florentiae" in the title–page of Chaudière's 1620 Paris edition?

phaele Coppola Presb. Neap. Praelato Protonotario Apostolico ad instar participantium, in almo Neapolitano Theologorum Collegio S. Theologiae Magistro." 476 pp. As earlier observed this series closes up with two volumes of the *HCUCRA*.

Copies of this set are in:

Montréal, Centre de recherche et de documentation de l'Oratoire Saint–Joseph

Rome, Antonianum, G 1–a 1 0–11

Washington DC, Library of the Catholic University of America, BT 1005 C32 1859; Holy Name College Library

E. Propugnaculum Catholicum de Iure Belli Romani Pontificis Adversus Ecclesiae Iura Violantes. *Tam Theologis, quam Iurisperitis, pro–futurum valde. In libros quatuor divisum. Auctore P.F. Ioanne de Carthagena Ord. Min. de Obs. Sac. Theol. Lectore Generali de mandato Sanctissimi, in Regali Conventu S. Petri Montis aurei. Ad S.D.N. Paulum Quintum Pontif. Max. Romae, ex typographia Rev. Camerae Apostolicae. 1609. Authoritate Superiorum.* In–8.[41] 244 pp. Indexes.

The permission for publication was given by Luis de San Juan Evangelista in 1609. Certification by the censor Victor Capoleonus, dated June 22, 1609.

Copies of this book are in:

Lübeck, Stadtbibliothek, 8° 8003

Madrid, Biblioteca Nacional, 3–13218

Paris, Bibliothèque Nationale, E.4620

Rome, Biblioteca Angelica, MM 9 51

Biblioteca Nazionale, 8.27.A.33 (4 copies)

Salamanca, Biblioteca Universitaria

Vatican, Biblioteca Vaticana, Barb., HH.1.106

F. Zwanzig Schöner Ausführlicher Concept, über der glorwürdigsten himmel Königin Mariae, hochheiliges Lobgesang: das Magnificat genandt. *Erstlich von P.F. Ioanne Carthagena Hispano, Franciscaner Ordens der Observantz SS. Theologiae Lectore Generali: aus Befelch Päpst... in Deutsche Sprache ubersezt durch P.F. Thobiam Hendschelium.* Ingolstadt, 1617. In–4. 404 pp.

---

[41] Wadding, loc. cit.; San Antonio, loc. cit.; and Tejera, loc. cit., have all described this book to have come out in–4.

The original of this German translation is the 6th book of the *HCSADM*'s first volume: "*De Sacris Arcanis Visitationis B. Virginis, ac de Celeberrimo, quod in Illa Cecinit Cantico.*" This book's first eight homilies are excluded. The translator, the Franciscan guardian of the convent of Saint Jerome in Vienna, expressed his goal in the title–page. He wanted to make the work available to a wider public. "*An jetzt aber nicht allein allen Catholischen Predigern und Seelsorgern zu Verfassung uber aus schöne Predigen, sondern auch allen Ordens Geistlichen und Weltlichen Standspersonen zu sonderlicher Lehr, herzigtlichen Trost und Andacht.*" The translation was dedicated to H. Casparo, Abbot of the Benedictine Abbey of Mölct.

Copies of this German work are in:

Eichstätt, Staats– u. Seminarbibliothek, SB I 927 and B VII 386 (two copies)

Munich, Bayerische Staatsbibliothek, 4° Hom. 345

Soest, Stadtarchiv und Wisseschaftliche Stadtbibliothek, IV Gg.11.18

Washington DC, Holy Name College Library

G. Praxis Orationis Mentalis ad Faciliorem Eius Usum Reddendum. *Omnibus et singulis statibus accommodatissima: In libros V distributa. Authore F. Io de Carthagena, Hispano, Sacrae Theologiae Generali Lectori emerito, Ordinis Min. de Observantia, Immaculatae Conceptionis Provintiae Alumni. Cum Privilegiis, ac Superiorum permissu. Venetiis, apud Iacobum de Franciscis. 1618. In–4. 261 pp.* Indexes.

An engraved frontispiece with the sign of peace. Dedicated to Cardinal Fabrizio Veralli. Publication approval by Emmanuel da Vila, given on February 14, 1617. Certification by the censor Pedro Jover, dated March 10, 1617. Allison Peers wrote about this spiritual book: "As Cartagena became a Franciscan, one might have hoped for an interesting dissertation, but in fact one finds only the dullest of text–books." [42]

---

[42] Allison Peers, op. cit., p. 214. He also claimed a 1613 Cologne edition of this work meaning that the 1618 publication was just a later reprint. A copy, he said, is in the University Library of Barcelona. A little caution is here in order. For Peers died before this third volume of his *Studies of the Spanish Mystics* could be published. His bibliographies especially were only later compiled from his notes.

Copies of this work are in:
Antwerp, Bibliotheek van het Ruusbroec–Genootschap
Barcelona, Biblioteca Universitaria
London, British Museum, 697.f.30 (an imperfect copy with
 pages missing)
Rome, Biblioteca Nazionale, 8.35.021 ; 42.6.J.14–3 ; and 8.31.
 C.20
Salamanca, Biblioteca Universitaria
Vienna, Öster. Nationalbibliothek, 20.T.4

1) Cologne's B. Gualterius also published this book in the same
year, 1618, in–12. 668 pp.
Copies of this Cologne edition are in:
Cologne, Universitätsbibliothek, GB IV 5781
Neuburg, Staatl. Bibliothek, 4° Theol. Pr. 512
Paris, Bibliothèque Nationale, D.39419
Regensburg, Staatl. Bibliothek, Cas. 107
Vienna, Öster. Nationalbibliothek, 15.608–A

2) Moreover, the *Bibliotheca Catholica Neerlandia Impressa
1500–1727* lists a later 1620 edition of this same work in Cologne,
and locates a copy in:
Heeswijk, Bibliotheek van de Norbertijnenabdij [43]

H. De Sacra Antiquitate Ordinis B. Mariae de Monte Carmelo
Tractatus Duo, Quorum Primus Originem et Laudes Eius Re-
censet: Alter Quorumdam Sequius Sentientium Obiectiones
Refellit. *Authore R.P.F. Ioanne de Carthagena Ord. Minorum de
Observantia. Antwerpiae, apud Gulielmum a Tongris, ad insigne Gry-
phis.* 1620. In–8. 148 pp.

The publication approval for this posthumous book was given
by Laurentius Beyerlinck, on October 16, 1619. It included an exhor-
tation to the sons of Carmel, and a Horacian parody in praise of the
Order. Actually this volume is more of a reprint than a completely
new work.[44] It is made up of the 4 homilies in the 17th book of the

---

[43] *Bibliotheca Catholica Neerlandica*, op. cit., n. 6778.

[44] Interestingly, Wadding, loc. cit., mentioned that this work remained
unpublished, while Antonio, loc. cit., noted that he himself had never seen it. The
Catalogus Bibliothecae Bunauianae, III–1 (Lipsiae, 1755), p. 506b, has an entry
on it.

HCSADM's last volume. As the publisher himself explained: "Inasmuch as this dissertation seemed to come to the hands of so few, because it is inserted in the volumes of bigger works, we thought it good to put it out in this separate booklet for the convenience and use of more people and to give to you what the author produced originally for you." [45]

Copies of this book are in:
    Coimbra, Biblioteca Universitaria
    Cologne, Universitätsbibliothek, WB II³ 246
    Paris, Bibliothèque Nationale, H.10588
    Rome, Biblioteca Nazionale, 10.4.B.20 and 10.5.B.16
    Tübingen, Bibliothek des Wilhelmsstifts

1) This work was translated the following year into Dutch: *Bewys des Outheyts der Orden Vande H. Moeder Godts Maria des Berghs Carmell*, by Gaspar Rinckens, O. Carm., in Antwerp, 1621. In–12. 290 pp. [46]

Copies of this Dutch publication are in:
    Antwerp, Bibliotheek van het Ruusbroec–Genootschap [47]
    Münster, Universitätsbibliothek, 47:9772

2) Then came the first Spanish translation of the same: *Dos Tratados de la sagrada Antiguedad del Orden de la bienaventurada Virgen Maria del Monte Carmelo*. Sevilla, 1623. In–8. 111 pp. This translation was done by Gerónimo Pancorvo, published with the approval of Juan Serrano de Vargas y Urena, and dedicated to Diego Salvador, Carmelite Provincial of Andalucia.

Copies of this Spanish translation are in:
    Lisbon, Biblioteca Nacional
    Madrid, Biblioteca Nacional, 3–14081 and 3–61690

3) Also in 1623, a second Spanish translation came out in Madrid, done by Manuel Roman, and incorporated in his volume: *Elucida-*

---

    [45] *De Sacra Antiquitate*, Publisher's Note.

    [46] By the turn of the 20th century, this book was considered rare in Holland and was priced at 2 Florins. Cf. Burgersdijk & Niermans, *Théologie et philosophie. Catalogue de livres anciens et modernes* (Leyde, 1900), n. 2718, p. 108.

    [47] *Bibliotheca Catholica Neerlandica*, op. cit., n. 6925. Reference is there made to I. Rosier, O. Carm., *Biographisch in bibliographisch overzicht van de vroomheid in de Nederlandse Carmel* (Tielt, 1950).

ciones varias sobre dos tratados de la sagrada antiguedad de la Orden de N.S. del Monte Carmelo: colegidas de graves padres y doctores.[48] 190 pp.

A copy is still in:

Madrid, Biblioteca Nacional, 7/12810

4) More than twenty years after its first compilation from the *HCSADM*, the *De Sacra Antiquitate* became once more a part of a bigger volume containing the works of Aubert Le Mire and of Johann von Trittenheim. The anthology was entitled: *De Ortu et Progressu ac Viris Illustribus Ordinis Gloriosissimae Dei Genitricis Semper Virginis Mariae, de Monte Carmelo Tractatus Ioannis Trithemii Abbatis Spanheimensis, Auberti Mirai Bruxellensis, et Ioannis de Carthagena Ord. Minorum de Observantia. Accedit catalogus illustrium scriptorum ejusdem ordinis, cum aliis quibusdam opusculis. Coloniae Agrippinae, sumptibus Jodocum Kalchoven,*[49] 1643. *Cum gratia et privilegio S. Caes. Maiest.* In–8. 414 pp. Pages 239 to 368 give Cartagena's treatise.

Copies of the compilation are in:

Augsburg, Staats– und Stadtbibliothek, Th o
Cologne, Universitätsbibliothek, GB IV 2221
Den Haag, Koninklijke Bibliotheek, 1122 D6
London, British Museum, 296. q. 22
Paris, Bibliothèque Nationale, H.10589
Rome, Biblioteca Angelica, T 11.31
Vatican, Biblioteca Vaticana, Barb., H.VI.153

5) Cerreto, Amann, Stegmüller and Castro include in their bibliographies a 1645 Cologne edition, in–8, of the *De Sacra Antiquitate.*[50]

---

[48] C. Pastor Perez, *Bibliografia Madrileña*, III (Madrid, 1907), p. 243, mistakenly claims that this translation by the Franciscan M. Roman was the first edition ever of Cartagena's manuscript.

[49] Jodocus Kalckhoven took ownership in 1641 of the printing press of Bernhard Walter or Gualterius, the publisher of Cartagena's works in Cologne. Gualterius himself was a Dutchman who married into the big Cologne publishing family of Maternus Cholinus. Cf. Joseph Benzing, *Buchdruckerlexikon des 16. Jahrhunderts* (Frankfrut am Main, 1952), p. 97.

[50] Cerreto, op. cit., p. 260; Amann, loc. cit.; Stegmüller, loc. cit.; and Castro, loc. cit. Sbaralea, however, op. cit., p. 52, does not think there was such an edition.

I. Conciones Quadragesimales in Sacrosancta Evangelia, in Quibus Celebriores Fidei et Morum Materiae Resolutae Continentur, cum SS. Patrum Expositionibus, Piis Meditationibus, Crebris Reprehensionibus et Exemplis ex Evangelio Collectis. *Parisiis, apud Joannem Petit–Pas.* 1632. In–8. 888 pp.

This collection was gleaned together from the *Homiliae Catholicae*'s Gospel commentaries corresponding to the 44 pericopes used from the *"Feria Quarta Cinerum"* to the *"Feria III hebdomadae sanctae."* An unknown Friar Minor of the Observance did the compilation.

A copy is in:

Paris, Bibliothèque Nationale, D.39418 [51]

J. De Sufficientia et Efficacia Divinae Gratiae. Edited by Vazquez from the manuscript 196, ff. 472–484 of the Biblioteca literaria of the University of Salamanca. *Verdad y Vida,* 86 (1964) 200–219.

Dedicated to Paul V, its probable date could be October of 1605. Cartagena is here answering actual questions proposed to the Congregation *de auxiliis* for the November 29, 1605, session.[52] To the principal question whether God moves the human will with the divine efficacious grace *"non solum interius suadendo, invitando, excitando, aut aliter moraliter attrahendo, sed etiam vere et active proprie, salva tamen humana libertate,"* Cartagena gives his answer in his third assertion: *"Antequam convertatur peccator, non solum trahit illum Deus moraliter alliciendo, suadendo, invitando, sed etiam praemovendo physice eius voluntatem."* [53] This clear–cut espousal of the Bañezian doctrine of *praemotio physica* leaves no doubt as to the author's stand against Molinism.

K. Regulae Quaedam Proponuntur Apprime Necessariae Valdeque Utiles ad Definiendam Veritatem Praesentis Controversiae de Efficacia Divinae Gratiae. Edited by Vazquez from the manuscript found in the Dominicans' General Archive in Rome,

---

[51] Sbaralea, ibid., notes that the *Catalogus Librorum Omnium Facultatum* (Lugduni, 1656), p. 107, of the office of Philippe Borde, Laurence Armand and Claude Rigaud includes this work by Cartagena.

[52] Cf. Vazquez, "Tres inéditos de Fray Juan de Cartagena sobre las controversias 'de auxiliis'," *Verdad y Vida,* 86 (1964) 197.

[53] Ibid., p. 206.

Santa Sabina, XIV, vol. 259, ff. 4r–8r. *Verdad y Vida*, ibid., pp. 220–227.

The original copy of this short treatise was sent to Paul V and is now in the Vatican Archive, Borghese I, vol. 388–399, ff. 102–106b. It was probably written during the first months of 1606, when the discussions *de auxilis* were drawing to an end and attention was turned to what could be defined.

L. REFERUNTUR VARIA TESTIMONIA SCHOLASTICORUM DOCTORUM IN FAVOREM SENTENTIAE ASSERENTIS OMNES ACTUS LIBEROS HUMANAE VOLUNTATIS PRAEDEFINIRI ET PRAEDETERMINARI A EFFICACI ET ABSOLUTA VOLUNTATE. Edited by Vazquez from the manuscript in Santa Sabina, XIV, vol. 259, ff. 1r–3r. *Verdad y Vida*, ibid., pp. 227–231.

Cartagena sent this paper to Tomás de Lemos, O.P., his friend who was handling the Dominican case against Molinism. Lemos must have asked the Franciscan theologian to provide him with a list of Scholastic doctors in favor of some physical premotion, in preparation for the session of the Congregation on February 22, 1606, which was to be devoted to an examination of the Scholastics' teaching on the matter. In his speech on that day, Lemos actually used the material given him by Cartagena.[54]

M. CANONES... AD RADICITUS EXTIRPANDAM OMNEM DOCTRINAM PELAGIANUM ERROREM REDOLENTEM. Edited by Vazquez from the manuscript found in the Vatican Archive, Borghese I, vol. 388–399, f. 100. *Antonianum*, 40 (1965) 324–325.

These twelve anathemas were sent to Pope Paul V, in effect a summation of Cartagena's anti–Molinism. These *canones* were apparently composed during the last quarter of 1607, when the Pope was still waiting for some definitive resolution of the controversy.[55] The dissolution of the Congregation did not stop the discussion. And it seems that the Pope had later asked some theologians not directly involved with the proceedings to write down their own opinions. Cartagena's first canon is indicative: *"Si quis dixerit peccatorem, qui convertitur, non praemoveri a Deo ad actum conversionis physice, sed tantum moraliter: anathema sit."*

---

[54] Ibid., pp. 198–199.
[55] Cf. Vazquez, "Nuevo documento de Fr. Juan de Cartagena...," art. cit., pp. 322–324.

II. MANUSCRIPTS

A. QUAESTIO 88° DE VOTO A REVERENDO PATRE IOANNE DE CARTA-
GENA E SOCIETATE JESU [crossed out and above it added: ORDINIS
MINORUM OBSERVANTIAE] THEOLOGIAE, SALMANTICAE IN COLLEGIO
SOCIETATIS JESU [crossed out] PUBLICE PROFESSORE. In–4. Bound
in parchment with 164 sheets of text.

This manuscript deals with the 88th question of the *Secunda
Secundae*, and according to the plan of the author the whole matter
of *de voto* would be discussed in 8 disputations. It goes only as far as
the sixth disputation, however, probably because Cartagena had to
give up his theology professorship in Salamanca before the course
could be completed. This manuscript is found in Rome in the Archive
of San Isidoro, ms. I/III.[56]

B. DE SUFFICIENTIA ET EFFICACIA DIVINORUM AUXILIORUM.

This manuscript is in the Biblioteca literaria of the University
of Salamanca, ms. 196, f. 472. Cartagena himself had made a reference
to this work in a dedication to Paul V: "...I have written a whole
volume on the sufficiency and efficacy of the divine graces, which
work, Most Holy Father, we have rightly consecrated to Your Beatitude." [57] He must have written it sometime during the second half
of 1605, probably following Paul V's election to the papacy. The
subsequent discussions by the Congregation *de auxiliis* could have
made this manuscript partly absolete; that was why Cartagena never
published it.

C. HOMILIAE DE STATU PONTIFICIO ET CARDINALITIO. In–folio. 816 ff.
49 homilies.

This manuscript is kept in Rome in the Archive of San Isidoro,
ms. 2/50. It must have been written later than 1609, because in his
book published then, the *Propugnaculum Catholicum*, Cartagena wrote:
"...it must be demonstrated that the Roman Pontiff is the supreme
head of the Catholic Church, so that no one on earth, not even a general council legitimately assembled, is superior to him (as I shall
most throughly discuss elsewhere)..." [58] The Library of Lyon, Cod.

---

[56] Vazquez, "Fr. Juan de Cartagena...," art. cit., pp. 297–298.

[57] *De Sufficientia et Efficacia Divinae Gratiae*, in *Verdad y Vida*, 86 (1964) 200.

[58] *Propugnaculum Catholicum de Iure Belli Romani Pontificis* (1609), p. 30.

357 (formerly 285), has this catalogue entry: "By Juan de Cartagena, Friar Minor of the Regular Observance, two books on the papal state and on the cardinalate, in which he considers learnedly and seriously the special arguments that pertain to both states, catalogued now for the first time, having been identified by Rev. Fr. Luke Wadding, of the same Order, professor of theology in Rome," ms. s. XVII, 471 ff.[59]

D. Responsio ad Interrogationem super Dispensatione pro Matrimonio Roderici Henriquez, Subdiaconi, cum Anna Henriquez, eius nepote ex fratre, et Sorore Viventis Almirantis Castellae. *San Pietro in Montorio*. September 15, 1613.

This letter is supposedly in Rome in the Biblioteca Casanatense, ms. 2107, ff. 267–284.[60] The library staff, however, could not locate it, when asked.

E. Carta a Felipe III en favor de la Inmaculada Concepción: Philippo Tertio Regi Catholico, Acerrimo Christianae Religionis Propugnatori, Hispaniarum et Indiarum Supremo Monarchae, Fr. Ioannes de Cartagena Aeternam Felicitatem Precatur. c. 1616.

The Archive of San Isidoro in Rome has this letter, ms. 2/39, ff. 432–435. The historical background for this letter was the royal effort to incite Rome to define solemnly the doctrine of the Immaculate Conception.

F. Pro Opinione Pia. c. 1616.

This manuscript is found in Madrid, Biblioteca Nacional, ms. 461, ff. 244–258v.[61] It was directed to the Pope, apparently in conjunction with the previous letter in favor of the Immaculate Concep-

---

[59] Cf. *Catalogue général des bibliothèques publiques de France, Départments,* 30 (Paris, 1900), p. 83. B. Millet, O.F.M., reports, however, that he did not find this manuscript in Lyon. See his article, "Guide to Material for a Biography of Fr. Luke Wadding," in *Father Luke Wadding: Commemorative Volume* (Dublin, 1957), pp. 235–236. The manuscript in San Isidoro in Rome, explains Vazquez, art. cit., p. 299, was probably the basis of a copy sent to Lyon. Wadding himself, op. cit., p. 198, said of this work: "nondum prodiit."

[60] Cf. Sbaralea, loc. cit.

[61] Cf. M. Castro, "Manuscriptos franciscanos en la Biblioteca Nacional de Madrid," *Archivo Ibero–Americano,* 19 (1959) 596.

tion. Vazquez gives this manuscript another designation: *Catholicum Propugnaculum Immaculatae Conceptionis*, according to the wordings of the manuscript itself.[62] The Immaculate Conception was obviously considered at that time only an opinion.

G. The publisher Zannetti in his oft–cited note in the 1611 edition of the *HCSADM* I, referred to other manuscripts about which we know nothing more. He planned to put out Cartagena's "...work on the mysteries of the Gospel teaching, distributed in two volumes; then the work on the mysteries of the saints, who are honored by the Catholic Church with a special feast; and the selected disputations about dialectical, philosophical and metaphysical topics; finally, the miscellaneous disputations about the mysteries of sacred theology, both scholastic and moral, divided into four volumes." [63] It could be that Juan de Cartagena began these projected books, as was the case with the *Selectarum Disputationum*, but was unable to finish them.

III. ALLEGED WORKS

A. Tractatus de Praedestinatione et Reprobatione Angelorum et Hominum. *Romae, apud Vincentium Accoltum.* 1581. Dedicated to Gregory XIII.

This book, oft attributed to Juan de Cartagena,[64] was actually written by Francisco de Cartagena, a priest of the Diocese of Salamanca and a Magister of theology in the last half of the 16th century.[65]

---

[62] Vazquez, art. cit., p. 300.

[63] *HCSADM* (I, Publisher's Note).

[64] San Antonio, loc. cit., listed this book as Cartagena's and available in Biblioteca Slusiana. Cerreto, loc. cit., Hurter, loc. cit., Tejera, loc. cit., Renedo, op. cit., p. 127, and Toda y Guell, loc. cit., all did the same. The Biblioteca Casanatense in Rome catalogues this book, Banc. H. 172, under the name of Juan de Cartagena. And Vazquez himself was at first uncertain as the authorship of this work became questionable. Only later did he definitely exclude it from Cartagena's bibliography.

[65] Sbaralea, loc. cit., rightly notes that this work was by Francisco de Cartagena. Copies of it are in: Madrid, Biblioteca Nacional, R 26305; Rome, Biblioteca Angelica, P 3, 28; and Vienna, Öster. Nationalbibliothek, 7.M.31. Cf. also Jöcher, op. cit., col. 1707.

B. Disputatio Insignis contra Latentem Usuram ad Paulum V.

N. Antonio first made the claim that this unpublished manuscript was also Cartagena's.[66] It seems to be a confusion with the *Disputatio Insignis... ad Extirpandum Quoddam Latentis Simoniae Vitium.*

C. Disputatio in Universa Christianae Religionis Arcana.

This book by Cartagena was supposed to have been published in Rome by A. Ciacconi in 1609.[67] Sbaralea–Accurti thinks that this alleged work is none other than the first volume of the *Homiliae Catholicae*, which was put out by the same publisher in the same year.[68]

D. De Vita Christi Domini ac de Gestis Sanctorum Medita-tiones.

Could this be the projected work *"De Arcanis Sanctorum"* mentioned by Zanetti? San Antonio noted that the *relación* of the Province of the Immaculate Conception referred to this book by Cartagena.[69] Vazquez doubts the credibility of this record. Moreover, it mentions a life of Mary, not a life of Christ.[70] Cartagena hinted to the readers of his *Homiliae Catholicae* that he would be treating certain matters more extensively in a book *"De Sacris Arcanis Sanctorum Ecclesiae Catholicae."* [71]

---

[66] Antonio, loc. cit.; San Antonio, loc. cit.; Sbaralea, op. cit., p. 51; Tejera, loc. cit.; and Cerreto, op. cit., p. 261, said the same.

[67] This is asserted by Wadding, loc. cit.; Antonio, loc. cit.; Jöcher, op. cit., col. 1708; Hurter, loc. cit.; *Biografia Eclesiastica Completa*, loc. cit.; Amann, loc. cit.; and Cerreto, loc. cit.

[68] "...procul dubio nihil aliud sunt quam Homiliarum catholicorum tomus primus supra notatus." Sbaralea, loc. cit. On the other hand, San Antonio, loc. cit., Renedo, loc. cit., and Castro, loc. cit., even list two editions (1601 and 1609) of this alleged work.

[69] San Antonio, loc. cit., writes: "...ex relatione laudatae Provinciae Conceptionis, nisi idem sit cum suo 'de oratione tractatu'." Cerreto, loc. cit., simply repeats San Antonio. Sbaralea, loc. cit., however, makes the following observation about the treatise on prayer: "Non videtur potuisse inscribi 'De vita Christi Domini, ac de gestis sanctorum meditationes,' quum nec *meditationes* contineat nec *de gestis Sanctorum* aliquid habeat."

[70] Vazquez, art. cit., p. 301.

[71] *HCSADM*, lib. III, hom. VI (I, 281a).

CHAPTER THREE

THE HOMILIAE CATHOLICAE

What preserved the name of Juan de Cartagena for posterity is, more than anything else, his four volume collection of the *Homiliae Catholicae*. These volumes constitute his major work, published during a period of eight years in the maturity of his career as a theology professor. They establish his name as a theologian especially in the field of Mariology, where Stegmüller thinks they have exerted a great influence.[1] Cartagena's humanist contemporary, Ioannes Baptista Laurus, must have been echoing a popular sentiment, when he said that "we cherish... the books of the man." [2] Indeed Wadding could report of the *Homiliae Catholicae* that "they were so well liked by everyone, there had to be many editions." [3] Reprinted and reedited at least a dozen times in six major European cities, the volumes have the distinction of having been republished more than 240 years after the original came out. Parts of the work have in addition been reprinted eight different times not just in the original Latin, but also in translations into Spanish, German and Dutch.

It is the purpose of this present chapter to take a closer look at the *Homiliae Catholicae*, at its contents, its intentions, make–up and structure, and at the various influences which contributed to its composition. The explorations of this chapter will be exhaustive only to the extent sufficient to provide the necessary background for the following Part II on Cartagena's Mariological teachings. We shall sample particularly the first book of the *HCSADM*, which in its methods and characteristics is typical of the whole work.

---

[1] Stegmüller, op. cit., col. 1068.

[2] "Fovemus... Libros Viri." Laurus, op. cit., p. 46.

[3] "Adeo omnibus placuerunt, ut multas fieri oportuerit editiones." Wadding, op. cit., p. 198.

I. CONTENTS

A. HOMILIAE CATHOLICAE IN UNIVERSA CHRISTIANAE RELIGIONIS ARCANA

This 1609 opening volume of the series is essentially a Christology. Its 1612 edition by Facciotti brings this out by adding to the title: *ad Christum Dominum Spectantibus*.[4] For, of the volume's original 194 *homiliae* 183 are devoted to the mysteries of Christ, and only the first 11 to the Trinitarian mystery as an introduction to the main body.

Its 16 books cover the following matter according to the arrangement of the first Roman edition. The additions Cartagena later made will be duly noted. Book 1 with its 11 homilies in 72 columns is entitled *De Altissimo Trinitatis Arcano*. Following this introductory book comes the rest of the volume concentrated on Christ. Book 2 is *De Ineffabili Incarnationis Verbi Divini Arcano*, with 120 columns of 13 homilies. Book 3, *De Duplici Christi Redemptoris Nostri Nativitate*, 12 homilies, 94 columns. Book 4, *De Circumcisione Christi*, 8 homilies, 56 columns. Book 5, *De Sanctissimi Nominis Iesu Excellentia*, 11 homilies, 64 columns. Book 6, *De Felicissima Christi Epiphania*, 9 homilies 68 columns. In the 1612 edition, two more homilies were inserted into this book as the 5th and 6th respectively. Book 7, *De Baptismo a Christo Domino Suscepto*, 4 homilies, 44 columns. Book 8, *De Gloriosa Christi Domini Transfiguratione*, 13 homilies, 116 columns. Later another homily was added here as the 11th. Book 9, *De Augustissimo ac Ineffabili Eucharistiae Sacramento*, 29 homilies, 222 columns. A new 22nd homily was also added here, thus bringing the total to 30. Book 10, *De Acerba Christi Domini Salvatoris Nostri Passione*, 27 homilies, 256 columns. Three homilies as the 15th, 16th and 17th were inserted in 1612. Book 11, *De Septem Verbis Christi Domini*, 15 homilies, 172 columns. Book 12, *De Arcanis in Vulnere Lateris Christi Latentibus*, 2 homilies, 16 columns. Book 13, *De Honorifica Christi Domini Sepultura*, only 1 homily in 14 columns. Book 14, *De Triumphante Christi Domini Resurrectione*, 13 homilies, 88 columns. A 14th homily rounded out this book in 1612. Book 15, *De Admirabili Christi Domini Ascensione*, 15 homilies, 118 columns. And Book 16, *De Portentosa Missiones Spiritus Sancti*, has 11 homi-

---

[4] Cf. above, p. 73.

lies in 80 columns. This last book brackets off Cartagena's Christology with a little on Pneumatology and Ecclesiology.

The homilies in this in folio volume average 8.2 columns of text each, i.e. around 3,800 words. The shortest homily has only 3 columns, while the longest goes on for 53 columns or 24,300 words, as is the case with homily 15 of Book 11.

B. Homiliae Catholicae de Sacris Arcanis Deiparae Mariae et Ioseph

The next three volumnes, first published in 1611, 1614 and 1616 respectively, give Juan de Cartagena's Mariology. Together they make up 19 books encompassing the mysteries of Mary's life, with a total of 2,371 pages in the Cologne edition of 1613–1616. These volumes will be the basis of Part II's doctrinal analysis of certain salient points in the Mariology of the author. As in the previous section, it suffices here to present an overall view of their contents.

1. *Tomus primus.* The seven books of this volume span the time from Mary's conception to her giving birth to Christ. The 19 homilies of Book 1 treat *De Sacris Arcanis Aeternae Praedestinationis, ac Immaculatae Conceptionis Deiparae Virginis Mariae.* Book 2 is *De S. A. Felissimi Ortus B.V.M.*, with 14 homilies. Book 3's 6 homilies are *De S. A. Praesentationis B. Virginis in Templo.* Book 4, with 13 homilies, *De S. A. Desponsationis B. V., necnon de Eximiis Laudibus Dilectissimi eius Sponsi Ioseph.* Book 5, *De S. A. Angelicae Annunciationis, et Christi Conceptionis in Utero Virgineo,* 20 homilies. Book 6, with 28 homilies, *De S. A. Visitationis B. V., ac de Celeberrimo, quod in illa Cecinit, Cantico.* And Book 7 covers *De Explicatione Partus Deiparae Mariae, ac de Perpetua, et nunquam Violata Integerrima eius Virginitate* in 13 homilies.

The 116 homilies of this first in quarto volume average 7.2 pages each, i.e. around 3,800 words each just like in the *HCUCRA*. It is from Book 6 that T. Hendeschel translated the *Zwanzig schöner ausführlicher Concept.* [5]

2. *Tomus secundus.* The mysteries from Mary's purification in the temple up to her assumption and coronation in heaven are the

---

[5] Cf. above, pp. 88–89.

topics of the seven books of this second volume. Book 8, therefore, has the heading *De S. A. Purificationis B. Virginis, et Praesentationis Christi Domini in Templo* for its 16 homilies. The 11 homilies of Book 9 are on the *Fuga Christi Domini, Mariae, et Iosephi in Aegyptum*. Book 10, *De S. A. B. V. Amittentis Iesum in Templo*, 15 homilies. Book 11, with 13 homilies, *De S. A. B. V. Conversionem Aquae in Vinum a Filio Suo Postulantis in Nuptiis Canae*. Book 12, 11 homilies, *De S. A. B. V. Passionem, et Mortem Christi Domini Plangentis*. Book 13, 7 homilies, *De S. A. B. V. in Morte, Sepultura, et Resurrectione eius Latentibus*. And Book 14's 27 homilies has *De S. A. B. V. in eius Assumptione, et Coronatione Latentibus*.

These 100 homilies average 8 pages each, i.e. around 500 words more per homily than the previous volume.

3. *Tomus tertius*. This last volume is no longer about the mysteries of Mary's life, but is rather concerned with Mariology in the believers' religious life, with Marian cult in other words. Completing then the two foregoing volumes, the five books of this tome are broken up in the following way: Book 15 deals with the *Festum ad Nives* in 22 homilies, Book 16 with its 10 homilies handles the *S. A. Deiparae V. in Sacerrimo eius Rosario Latentibus*, Book 17 *De S. A. Deiparae Mariae de Monte Carmelo* in 4 homilies, Book 18 in 15 homilies *De S. A. Cultus et Devotionis erga Deiparam Virginem ac D. Iosephum eius Sponsum*, and finally Book 19 *De Mirandis Deiparae Virginis tam in Gratiam, quam in Vindictam*. This last book is composed of 238 sections narrating wonders attributed to Mary.

Book 17 is the original of the posthumously published *De Sacra Antiquitate*, also translated into Dutch and twice into Spanish, and later included in the anthology: *De Ortu et Progressu... Ordinis Gloriosissimae Dei Genitricis... de Monte Carmelo*.[6]

II. CHARACTERISTICS

A. "Pro Cibandis Fidelibus"

In his letter dedicating the *HCUCRA* to Pope Paul V, Juan de Cartagena states the objective of his book:

---

[6] Cf. above, pp. 91 & 93.

The most important reason for the present work is, since it strives for this goal, to open the most secret mysteries of the Catholic faith, labored at with enormous and unimaginable effort, as the rich material of the homilies will easily show...[7]

He wanted to unfold the mysteries of the faith, the *universa arcana religionis Christianae*, as the original title announces. And the reason is already there in the initial sentence of the same letter. Cartagena considers himself to be contributing into the Church's granary what he has been toiling at *"pro cibandis fidelibus"* — for the nourishment of the faithful.[8] The pastoral orientation of the entire endeavor is foremost as the author envisions what he hopes to accomplish by the writing of the *Homiliae Catholicae:*

> ...so that I may be of use, who otherwise cannot be of much service to the universal Church by means of the spoken word, and so that I, who cannot with my own mouth report to all the faithful the mysteries of the Incarnate Word, may through the mouths of all the preachers to whom these writings will undoubtedly be valuable, unfold and announce to all the inestimable riches of Christ, and to the extent that I can, help the interest of the common good of the Christian society.[9]

And the practical moral aim of preaching, which Cartagena intends to serve by composing his *Homiliae Catholicae*, he himself describes in saying that Christ sent preachers of the Gospel into the world, in order that they may conquer the world with the Gospel teachings, eradicate vices, foster virtues, and lead to paradise those who were formerly cursed.[10] On another occasion he pictures the work of a

---

[7] "Argumentum praesentis operis gravissimum omnium est, cum ad hunc scopum tendat, ut abditissima fidei catholicae arcana aperiat, a me ingenti, et incredibili labore elucubrata, ut facile indicabit copiosa seges homiliarum..." *HCUCRA,* Dedication.

[8] "Quae per annos ferme vigintiquinque (Beatissime Pater) continuis lucubrationibus elaboravi pro cibandis fidelibus... incipio nunc sub apostolicis tuis auspiciis in Dominicum horreum Ecclesiae catholicae... feliciter inferre." Ibid.

[9] Ibid. The same pastoral zeal urged him to publish his *Praxis Orationis Mentalis.* Cf. its Dedication.

[10] "Christus Dominus mittit in mundum Evangelii praecones, qui Evangelicae doctrinae armis illum debellent, humani generis hostem abigant, vitia eradicent, peccata extirpent, virtutes plantent, ac tandem mundum alioquin immundum mundent, et qui antea execrandus, infernus erat, in amoenum paradisum convertant." Ibid., lib. XV, hom. XV, col. 106.

preacher as speaking to his time and trying to lead everyone to the knowledge of the true God.[11]

From his own statement of intention and from his understanding of the goal of preaching, it is unmistakable that Cartagena had before him a very pastoral and practical objective. Through his *Homiliae* he wished to preach, so to say, vicariously through other preachers using his books, and thereby help in spreading the message of the Gospel and in promoting Christian life. Thus he admits the difference between the *Homiliae Catholicae* on one hand and on the other his *Selectarum Disputationum in Quartum Sententiarum.* If the first is intended to be a practical aid for preachers, the second is a work for technical theological refinements.[12] Consequently, in talking, for instance, about predestination and damnation, Cartagena points out in the *Homiliae Catholicae,* "I direct my speech not to fawn the intellect with the subtlety of deep reasoning, but rather to inform the will and to curb evil habits." [13] For, such subtlety and hair–splitting are more suited to scholastic disputations than to the resolution of common difficulties taxing the mind of believers.[14] He always has an eye for the special point of view of a preacher trying to guide the faith of the people. He entitles, for example, a homily: *"Permultis Moralibus Rationibus Concionatorio Muneri Aptissimis Illibatem Deiparae Mariae Conceptione, non Parum Stabilimus."* [15] Whenever he can, he addresses himself directly to the realities of Christian living. Treating of Mary's consecration to God by her parents, for instance,

---

[11] Itidem veri praedicatores de sursum illuminantur, suo tempore loquuntur, et ad verum Deum cognoscendum, quoscumque convertere conantur." *HCSADM,* lib. XVIII, hom. ult. (III, 491a).

[12] "Instituti mei non est in hac homiliae Theologicis satisfacere difficultatibus, quae in scholis tractantur, quoniam iam de illis peculiares disputationes in meis quaestionibus selectis instituto, quae auxiliante Deo super universam Theologiam, quatuor voluminibus divisam, in lucem proferentur: et ideo tantummodo nunc eas perstringam, quae divini Verbi concionatoribus aptiores esse videbuntur." *HCUCRA,* lib. IV, hom. VIII, col. 49.

[13] Ibid., lib. VIII, hom. IV, col. 24.

[14] "Verum, quia scholasticis disputationi, quam suggesto aptior est huiusmodi tractatio, omittam modo quid circa haec sentiam, ad selectas nostras disputationes universae Theologiae lectorem mittentis... Nunc eo contentus ero, ut communi difficultati, quae multorum fidelium mentes defatigare solet, satisfaciam." Ibid., col. 31.

[15] *HCSADM,* lib. I, hom. XVIII (I, 92b). See also, ibid., hom. IV (I, 19) and lib. II, hom. XI (I, 198).

Cartagena does not miss the chance to remind parents in general to bring up their sons and daughters religiously. And he points out that correct education begins already in infancy and childhood, otherwise it might be too late. Don't spare the rod, he adds.[16] Likewise he chides the parents who hinder their children from entering the religious life, or who let go only those mentally dull or physically deformed.[17] After the example of Joseph's careful deliberation upon finding out about Mary's pregnancy, he recalls the necessity of examining first before passing judgment. He especially warns against rash judgment.[18] And from Mary's prudent questioning regarding the how of the Incarnation, Cartagena proceeds to admonish young girls to be prudent especially with regards the promises of men. One can ask of a suitor, for instance, "How will your parents of renowned rank accept that you marry a lowly maid?" Alas, he says, he has seen many naive girls take as true the false promises of men and thus lose their virtue.[19] And when he deems it imperative to go into details about scholastic niceties over the Immaculate Conception, to cite an example, thus seeming to exceed the bounds of a preacher's purpose, Cartagena does so with a clear warning that they are not to be used in sermons, and that they are given more for the theological background of the users of his book.[20]

The *Homiliae Catholicae* therefore were intended to be a sort of

---

[16] Ibid., lib. III, hom. II (I, 253a–254b).

[17] Ibid., (254b–256b).

[18] Ibid., lib. IV, hom. X (I, 352a–b).

[19] Ibid., lib. V, hom. XI (I, 460a).

[20] "Ideo licet alioquin Concionatori muneris limites transilire videar, ne hanc de Immaculata Virginis conceptione tractationem, mutilam, et truncam, sed quantum a me praestari possit, omnibus numeris absolutam Ecclesiae Catholicae redderem, cui pro hac veritate definienda non parum aliquando illam profuturam spero, operae precium duxi omnibusque, tam ab auctoritate, quam a ratione peti possunt respondere, eisque plene satisfacere, satius iudicans argumenta modesto responso diluere, quam inutili silentio praeterire. Illud tamen verbi divini praecones salubriter admonemus, ne in concionibus Scholastica hac disputatione utantur, nisi velint, et in alienam messem falcem mittere, et salubra Pontificum decreta id prohibentia ausu temerario violare, quare illis, non ut concionatoribus, sed quatenus Theologis Scholasticis haec damus." Ibid., lib. VII, hom. XV (I, 811b–812a). Cf. ibid., lib. VII, hom. XIII (I, 802b).

Thus Cartagena, to ascertain that pure speculation remains marked out in his work, customarily refers to such materials under the rubric of *"Scholastica,"* as a description of some homilies. Cf. ibid., lib. VII, hom. XV (I, 811a) and hom. XVI (I, 840a).

reference–book for preachers. It offers materials for sermons about the mysteries of the life of Christ and of the lives of Mary and of Joseph. Cartagena covers his topics *per longum et per latum*, and professionally as a theologian, hence their deep dogmatic quality, but always with the preachers in mind and also the faithful in their actual spiritual needs. It could very well be that many of the ideas offered in these four volumes had actually been used by their author in his more than 12 years of preaching apostolate. But he certainly is not marketing here pre–fabricated sermons, that can be delivered as they are or have been delivered as they are.

That Cartagena's *Homiliae Catholicae* were taken by his contemporaries as books for preachers and for the faithful in general is oft shown by the letters or notes accompanying the volumes. Arcángel Mesina, Minister General of the Franciscans, in allowing the publication of *HCSADM* I & II in 1611 considered them "advantageous to the preachers of the Divine Word and to the rest of the faithful." [21] The publisher himself saw the work to be for the wonderful use of preachers.[22] The censor Franciscus Palumbus described the *HCSADM* II to be opening "most abundant springs to all who are thirsty: preachers, theologians and devotees of the Virgin." [23] Another censor for the last volume termed it as "a most rich treasury for the preachers of the Word of God." [24] Wadding himself classified the *Homiliae* with the following words: "These four volumes possess rich erudition, easy in style but thoroughly expounded, collected and conveniently ordered for sacred preachers." [25]

The above words by Wadding capture the essence and purpose of the *Homiliae Catholicae*. Juan de Cartagena composed these four volumes as a sourcebook for the use of preachers, offering not ready-made sermons but rather abundant materials presented compositely in the systematic exposition of the topics under consideration. Most popular compilations to help preachers were in the form of *distinctiones* or *dictionarius*, i.e. more encyclopedic in order, giving under a

---

[21] "...praecipimus cum merito salutaris obedientiae... divini Verbi praedicatoribus quam maxime, ac cunctis fidelibus multum utilitatis allaturum." *HCSADM* (I, Permission for publication).

[22] "...opus vero hoc mirum in modum utile Concionatoribus..." Ibid. (I, Publisher's Note).

[23] Ibid. (II, Censor's Note).

[24] Ibid., (III, Censor's Note).

[25] Wadding, loc. cit.

topical word pertinent biblical citations, patristic quotations, obser-
vations, moralizings. Cartagena conceived of his *Homiliae Catholicae*
as a specialized source–book structured along the line of the history
of salvation. His expositions and deliberations therefore move con-
secutively from the mystery of Christ's eternal procession to his
Incarnation, his life on earth, his death and resurrection. Likewise,
we have homilies successively treating Mary's predestination, her
conception, the annunciation, etc., up to her coronation in heaven.
Within this framework of salvation history, Cartagena gathers and
orders materials from the Bible with commentaries, teachings of the
Fathers and of the theologians, and sundry items to explain the
mysteries of the faith.

B. "Ex Theologiae Positivae Thesauris"

Although the volumes of the *Homiliae Catholicae* were intended
and taken to be of a pastoral nature, they contain so much theological
material and reflection, that some commentators have tended to
view them as more than just a *homilético* or books for preachers.[26]
Vazquez would like to translate *homilia* in this case to mean *tractatus*
or *enarratio*.[27] Cartagena's "homilies" then would be really theological
treatises or essays, as Vazquez points out, *"ex Theologiae positivae
Thesauris,"* which are Cartagena's own words.[28] Stegmüller, in
agreement, terms them *Abhandlungen*.[29] To be sure, the *Homiliae*
of Cartagena are more like essays or treatises than sermons. Indeed,
they are not actual homilies, but material–books to aid preachers in
preparing their sermons. Vazquez seems to be implying that because
Cartagena's *homiliae* are very theological, they could not be just for
preaching, notwithstanding their avowed practical and pastoral
purpose.[30]

Juan de Cartagena's admission, referred to by Vazquez, that
his *Homiliae Catholicae* belong to the field of positive theology has
more to it than first meets the eyes. Cartagena was a child of his

---

[26] "...es más un tratado teológico que homilético." Angel Uribe, O.F.M.,
"La Inmaculata en la literatura franciscano–española," *Archivo ibero–americano*,
15 (1955) 248.

[27] Vazquez, "Fr. Juan de Cartagena...," art. cit., pp. 270–271.

[28] *HCUCRA*, Dedication.

[29] Stegmüller, op. cit., col. 1068.

[30] Vazquez, loc. cit.

time, product of Jesuit training. Positive theology was for him a name that stood for the ideals of the movement to harness in the service of the faith what humanism could offer. It means the systematic reaching back behind scholasticism to the sources of faith. Cartagena's own words to Pope Paul – describing the *HCUCRA* are very indicative of his whole approach, succinctly summarized by the phrase *"ex Theologiae positivae Thesauris."* The author himself indicates what is to be found in his *homiliae:*

> There are in them manifold expositions of many difficult passages of Sacred Scripture, not a few versions of the same citation..., and the various teachings of the holy Fathers, of the sacred Pontiffs and of the Councils... both in order to present difficult mysteries of the Catholic faith and to set in order the habits of men.[31]

John Major, professor in Paris, seems to be the first to have used the expression positive theology in his Commentary on the Sentences (1509).[32] The term came to be employed in distinction to scholastic theology or a purely speculative theology. It connoted the study or the preaching of the Bible and of the Fathers. It meant a return to the sources of faith with a strong practical, pastoral and kerygmatic orientation. The emphasis on Holy Scripture and the Fathers manifests humanist influence. In fact, for a time *cátedra de positivo* stood for the professorial chair in Scripture.[33] The pastoral note came from the time's reform and observance movement and from the new consciousness ushered in by the Catholic Reformation.

St. Ignatius of Loyola typified this new consciousness and this openness to the ideals of humanism. For very pastoral and practical reasons one was to go back to the sources of faith. In the 11th rule

---

[31] *HCUCRA*, Dedication.

[32] Cf. R. Garcia Villoslada, S.J., "Un teólogo olvidado, Juan Mair," *Estudios Eclesiasticos*, 45 (1936) 96–109. See also M. Andres Martin, *Historia de la Teologia en España*, op. cit., p. 64.

[33] Gregorio de Valencia's, S.J. († 1603), description of positive theology underlines this close connection to Sacred Scripture: "Positiva enim theologia dicitur quatenus occupatur potissimum in explicando ipso Scripturae sacrae sensu, ad eumque eliciendum, tum aliis adminiculis, tum praecipue auctoritate sanctorum Patrum utitur. Quo ipso quasi principia firma aliarum conclusionum theologicarum ponit: et ideo positiva videtur dicta, quia scilicet ponit atque statuit ex Scriptura principia theologiae firma." *Commentarii Theologici* (Ingolstadt, 1591), disp. I, q. 1, punct. 1.

of his famous *"recte sentire in Ecclesia,"* which Ignatius wrote while studying in Paris in 1534, he said:

> Praise both the positive and the scholastic teaching. For just as the positive teachers like St. Jerome, St. Augustine, St. Gregory and others are more suited to move the affections to love God our Lord in everything and to serve Him, so also are the scholastics like St. Thomas, St. Bonaventure, the Master of the Sentences and others more suited to define or explain to our times the things necessary for salvation and to fight and expose all errors and falsehoods. Since the scholastic doctors belong to the modern times, they not only make good use of the correct understanding of Sacred Scripture and of positive and holy doctors, but they also find help, enlightened and illuminated by divine grace, in the Councils, the Canons and Constitutions of our holy Mother the Church.[34]

The pastoral concern is unmistakable, and the harmonization of the positive and the scholastic typical. This distinction between positive and scholastic theology and at the same time their desired coordination stand out too in the Constitution of the Society of Jesus. We read for example that theology, both scholastic and positive, can help attain the goal of Jesuit work in education, i.e. the use of learning for the knowledge and love of God and for one's salvation.[35] Ignatius was an advocate of the return to the sources of revelation and to tradition, but not at the expense of scholastic theology, as Erasmus would have it.[36] Rather he saw scholastic theology too as founded on Scripture, the Fathers, the Councils and the teaching of the Church, as Francisco de Vitoria and Melchior Cano had in fact envisioned, and which "marriage" actually triggered the revitalization of theology in the time of the Catholic Reformation. And it was such a unifying theology that characterized the Society of Jesus from the beginning.

---

[34] This is the first version of the *Regulae* as given by Pedri Leturia, S.J., "Sentido verdadero en la Iglesia militante," *Gregorianum*, 23 (1942) 166–167. Cf. Ignatius von Loyola, *Geistliche Übungen*, hrsg. Emmerich Raitz v. Frentz, S.J. (Freiburg i. Br., 1951 – 11 edn), pp. 184–185. In this eleventh rule Ignatius saw the internal danger in the Church with Erasmus' brand of humanism which would reject all Scholasticism.

Re the distinction between the Jesuits' understanding of positive theology as an approach and that of M. Cano, e.g., as a function, see M.–J. Congar, "Théologie" in *DThC*, 15 (Paris, 1946) col. 426–430.

[35] *Constitutiones Societatis Iesu*, P. IV, c. 5 & 12. See also P. IV, c. 14.

[36] D. Erasmus, *Enchiridion Militis Christianae*, nn. 245–246.

It was this understanding of theology which Juan de Cartagena had imbibed as a theology student and as a young Jesuit professor of theology. And this approach he retained even later. He saw theology not just as an exercise in speculation but as a search for the truths of faith *"pro cibandis fidelibus,"* as we have seen him express what he considered to be the ultimate aim of his own theological studies and labors. Positive theology especially, under whose light he wrote his *Homiliae Catholicae*, distinguishes itself from scholastic theology precisely on the ground that it does not simply cerebrate and theorize but teaches from the sources for the purpose of Christian life. Ignatius pictured it as moving the affections to love and serve God in everything. Cartagena in his own description of his work claims to present the mysteries of the faith *and* to set in order the life of a believer. Positive theology was understood to be a study of the sources of our faith with a definitely pastoral dimension. Cartagena indeed wanted some sort of a *homilético* to aid preachers of the Word and vicariously to enable him to preach the riches of the Gospel to as many people as possible. For this goal he collected and orchestrated pertinent passages from Holy Scripture, the corresponding explanations, the teachings of the Fathers, the words of theologians, the testimonies of history and literature, etc. in a synthesis of theological erudition. That his principal goal was pastoral, precisely because he was writing from the viewpoint of positive theology, does not in any way imply that his *Homiliae Catholicae* should be for that reason less theological. And that his work is permeated with theological science does not disprove either that his objective was pastoral. It was the genius of positive theology that the dichotomy between scientific theologizing and pastoral care had been removed. In his *Homiliae Catholicae* we encounter Juan de Cartagena as a pastoral theologian. As a professor of scholastic theology he worked no less professionally in trying to share with the faithful and more immediately with other preachers the fruits of his labor.

The employment of positive theology for preaching, a not uncommon method towards the end of the 16th and in the beginning of the 17th centuries, is superbly portrayed in the following dialogue from *Viaje a Turquía*, a literary piece attributed to Andrés de Laguna:

> Juan – Does this theology (of St. Thomas, Scotus and Gabriel)
> seem bad to you?

Pedro — Certainly not, on the contrary very holy and very good.
But for myself I am content with that of Christ, which
is the New Testament, and secondly with positive theology, especially for preaching.

Juan — Don't they know these?

Pedro — I don't know. At least, they don't show it in the pulpit.

Juan — How do you know that?

Pedro — I'll just say this: all the sermons delivered in Spain...
are so scholastic, that you could not hear anything else
from the pulpit except "St. Thomas says... in distinction
143... in questione 26... of article 62... in answer to that
objection... Scotus holds the contrary opinion on such
and such a question... Alexander of Hales, Nicholas of
Lira, John Major, Cajetan say this and that..." These
things are little liked by the people and I believe that
there are not many who think they understand.

Juan — Well, what would you want?

Pedro — That they do not talk there of any other doctrine except
the Gospel, and something of Chrysostom, Augustine,
Ambrose, Jerome — who wrote about the Gospel. The
rest, leave them for students taking up the course.

Mata — In this I am of the mind of Pedro Urdimalas, that all
sermons are as he says, and he is right.

Juan — Do you hold the theologians of Spain for so stupid, that
they have forgotten the New Testament and its commentators?

Mata — I well think that they have forgotten. For what reason,
I do not know.[37]

C. Biblical

Juan de Cartagena, in the spirit of his time and of his particular
training, tried to make up for such a widely felt neglect of Sacred
Scripture in the ministry of preaching, evident in the above–cited
dialogue. He wrote his *Homiliae Catholicae* under the rubric of positive theology, which of necessity is basically biblical. It is remarkable
how all the four volumes of the set are structured along the developments of Gospel events. A glance at the table of contents, as we

---

[37] *Viaje de Turquía*, quoted by Marcel Bataillon, *Erasme et l'Espagne* (Paris, 1937), p. 729. Cf. pp. 712–735. This Spanish literary work had traditionally
been attributed to Cristóbal de Villalón. Dedicated to Philip II, it remained in
manuscript form until it was edited by Manuel Serrano y Sanz, *Autobiografías
y memorias* (Madrid, 1905), pp. 1–149. The above quotation is on p. 86 of this first
edition.

have done in the first part of this chapter, attests to this biblical orientation. Mary's life, every step of it from her predestination to her coronation in heaven, is traced from the words of the Bible. Just how Cartagena built up such a biblical foundation for the Marian mysteries will be a main concern of Part II. We are for the moment merely interested with the sheer bulk of scriptural recourse.

Suffice it here to note, for instance, that in the first volume of the *HCSADM* only 16 homilies out of 116 in 7 books are not *ex professo* by their very titles directly biblical in their immediate concern. And of the 100 homilies that are immediately scriptural, 67 are principally explanations of passages from Scripture, containing in their very headings words like: *"elucidantur verba illa...," "ostenditur... in eadem Verba," "ex divinis oraculis aggredimur," "varia sacrae Scripturae loca... explicantur."* To take a particular book, *Liber V* on the mysteries of the Annunciation and of Christ's conception in Mary's womb, 16 of its 20 homilies are directly occupied with elucidations of some *"verba"* from Scripture. Another example is the next book, *Liber VI* on the Visitation, of whose 28 homilies only 2 are not direct interpretations and explanations of some words from the Gospel account.

Regarding biblical quotations, sprinkled generously in the homilies, an idea of their density can perhaps be gathered from the fact that the 19 homilies of *Liber I* on Mary's predestination and Immaculate Conception have as many as 622 direct quotations or references to the Bible. This means an average of 32 biblical quotations or citations per homily. In this sample of the first book alone, the most cited books of Scripture are the following:

Psalms	– 86	times
Genesis	– 76	»
Songs of Songs	– 61	»
Ecclesiasticus	– 40	»
Exodus	– 29	»
John	– 22	»
Luke	– 21	»
Isaiah	– 21	»
Proverbs	– 21	»
Matthew	– 19	»
Revelation	– 18	»
Corinthians	– 18	»
Job	– 17	»
Kings	– 16	»

Judith	— 13	»
Jeremiah	— 13	»
Samuel	— 11	»
Romans	— 10	»

Also cited less than 10 times each are: Acts, Chronicles, Daniel, Deuteronomy, Esther, Ephesians, Ezekiel, Ezra, Galatians, Habakkuk, Haggai, Hebrews, Hosea, James, Joshua, Jude, Judges, Leviticus, Macabees, Malachi, Mark, Numbers, Peter, Philippians, Ruth, Timothy, Titus, Wisdom, and Zechariah.

This topical concentration on the Bible, in Cartagena's own words, this *"quamplurium locorum difficilium sacrae Scripturae multiplex expositio,"* [38] is all in consonance with the "rediscovery" of sacred Scripture for pastoral and theological purposes. The humanists called for a return to the sources of revelation, and the alert theologians heard them. The reformers had fallen back on the sole authority of Scripture, and there they had to be met. The faithful needed the nourishment of the Word of God, and the pastorally minded strove to present the Word to them.

D. PATRISTIC

Together with the return to Scripture during the 16th century theological renewal was a concurrent rediscovery of the patristic writers, a return to those early commentators of the faith. Cartagena reflects this interest by his notable use of the writings from the first centuries of Christianity. The Fathers, he says, did not have the difficulty he has in talking about and giving praise to Mary.[39] In fact, he attributes to them a special authority, almost some sort of infallibility, applying to them Christ's words that they would not be speaking by themselves, but that it would be the Holy Spirit speaking in them.[40] That is why at the very outset of his work Cartagena considers it imperative to call upon the Holy Spirit for guidance and to

---

[38] Cf. *HCUCRA*, Dedication.

[39] *HCSADM*, lib. I, hom. I (I, 3a).

[40] "Illud sane non leve, imo irrefragabile argumentum esse arbitror adversus haereticos, quod omnes Sancti Patres... quos inficiari velle summa temeritas... maxime Christo Domino ad illos dicente: 'Non enim estis vos qui loquimini, sed spiritus patris vestri, qui loquitur in vobis' (Mt 10, 20)." Ibid., lib. VII, hom. XII (I, 787b–788a).

look for illumination from these holy Fathers who are like bright stars shining in faith and never knowing any setting.[41]

Cartagena quotes from and refers to patristic writers no less than 230 times in the first book of the *HCSADM*. In these 19 homilies, each of which averages around 12 patristic citations, 50 early Christian writers in all have been called upon. They are:

Abdias of Babylon (c. 620)	– 2 times
St. Ambrose († 397)	– 15 »
St. Anastasius Sinaites († 700)	– 2 »
St. Andreas Cretensis († 740)	– 2 »
Apelles (c. 150)	– once
Aratus († c. 550)	– »
Arnobius the Younger (c. 450)	– »
St. Athanasius the Great († 373)	– 3 times
St. Augustine († 430)	– 46 »
St. Avitus Alcinus Ecdicius († 518)	– once
St. Basil the Great († 379)	– 3 times
Bl. Bede the Venerable († 735)	– 4 »
Chrysippus of Cappadocia († 479)	– once
St. Cyprian († 258)	– 5 times
St. Cyril of Alexandria († 444)	– 7 »
Diodorus († c. 394)	– once
Dionysius the Areopagite (c. 500)	– 8 times
St. Ephraem of Syria († 373)	– 2 »
Epiphanius of Salamis († 403)	– 8 »
St. Eucherius († c. 450)	– 2 »
Eusebius of Caesarea († 339)	– once
Firmianus Lactantius (c. 250)	– 2 times
Gennadius I († c. 471)	– 2 »
Germanus I († 733)	– 3 »
St. Gregory the Great († 604)	– 9 »
St. Gregory of Nazianzen († 390)	– once
St. Gregory of Nyssa († 394)	– 3 times
St. Hilarius of Poitiers († 367)	– 2 »
St. Ildephonsus of Toledo († 367)	– 3 »
St. Irenaeus († c. 202)	– 5 »
St. Isidore of Sevilla († 633)	– 10 »

---

[41] "Idem nobis, qui inscrutabilium arcanorum Deiparae Mariae vastissimum mare ingressi sumus, agendum est; primo placidus nobis ille spiritus implorandus, de quo Psalmista: 'Spiritus (inquit) tuus bonus deducet me in terram rectam' (Ps 142, 10); deinde Sancti Doctores pia mente, ac vigilantibus oculis lustrandi sunt, qui tanquam arcturi nunquam occidentis lucida sydera stabili fide semper fixi steterunt, et lucem fidei fundentes, erroris occasum nescierunt..." Ibid., lib. I, hom. I (I, 5a).

St. Jerome († 420)	– 21	»
St. John Chrysostom († 407)	– 4	»
St. John Damascene († c. 750)	– 13	»
St. Justin († c. 165)	– once	
St. Leo the Great († 461)	–	»
St. Maximus of Turin († c. 420)	–	»
St. Methodius († c. 311)	–	»
Origen († c. 254)	– 3	times
Paulus Orosius († c. 418)	– once	
St. Peter Chrysologus († 450)	–	»
Philoxenus of Mabbug († 523)	–	»
St. Pierius of Alexandria († 312)	–	»
Procopius Gazensis († 528)	–	»
Sedulius (c. 400)	– 2	times
St. Sophronius of Jerusalem († 638)	– once	
St. Symmachus († 514)	– 2	times
Tertullian († 220)	– 5	»
Theodoret († 466)	– 4	»
Theodosius (c. 520)	– once	

Sts. Augustine, Jerome and Ambrose head the list in the frequency their authority is cited.

E. ECLECTIC

If Cartagena is decidedly patristic, he is also overwhelmingly eclectic in his attitude toward theologians of the Middle Ages. He refuses to be narrowly identified with any one school of thought. As he once wrote to Pope Paul V, "Not because I am a Friar Minor shall I be perpetually following Scotus, nor shall I always be contending with St. Thomas, whose teaching we accept and respect." [42]

---

[42] *HCUCRA*, Dedication.

Incidentally, as a Friar Minor, Cartagena was to some extent compelled to adhere to Duns Scotus. The Ultramontane Constitutions adopted in Toledo in 1583 and the Cismontane Constitutions adopted during the General Chapter in Valladolid in 1593 by the Observance both stipulated that all professors of theology should explain and concentrate on the teachings of Duns Scotus. The 1593 Constitutions, for example, says: "Caeterum, quia concertatio scholastica inter doctorem subtilem et alios exorta, nec inutilis, nec nocua, sed omnino utilis et proficua et Ecclesiae et Religioni nostrae semper fuit, cum ingenia maxime acuat, scholas nutriat et veritati diligentius investigandae vias aperiendo, veritatem ipsam dilucidet; idcirco universis studiorum huiusmodi lectoribus praecipimus ut litteram Scoti solum et non alios auctores ex professo explicare conentur; ut materias prolixas omnino relinquant, ut tempore lectionibus audiendis

Otherwise, it would be the passion to fight (which Cartagena says, *"a me longe abesse cupio"*) rather than the desire to investigate the truth that reigns. Like a diligent bee gathering nectar in the garden of theology, Cartagena pictures himself making straight for the flowers of correct teaching whether they be of Thomas or of Scotus or of somebody else.[43] Once more he typifies in this regard the open-ended approach of the early Jesuits, who accepted the teachings which had the best reasons for them irrespective of their origin.[44] Cartagena remained above the unfortunate parochialism and narrow sympathies of theological schools so rampant at that time. This independence of thought, as we have seen, involved him in the backlash of the *encuentro* between Suárez and Marcos in Salamanca. But the unhappy incident apparently did not discourage him. In his *Homiliae Catholicae* he welcomes anybody who has anything to contribute to the matter at hand. Much like a compiler, he marshals the words of any author, so long as they are of assistance in his aim of nourishing the faithful.

Again, just so that we can sample him, let us take a look at the first book of the *HCSADM* in the light of his extensive references to other theologians. We shall group these authors into those belonging more or less to the Middle Ages and early Renaissance and the second group into the *"Moderniores theologi"* – to use Cartagena's term for his contemporaries and the more recent writers.[45]

---

praescripto, generalem totius ecclesiasticae disciplinae cognitionem studentes comparare possunt, qui tractu temporis fusionem postea per se ipsos theologiae scientiam assequi poterunt, prout multorum, qui hanc formam servantes, doctissimi evaserunt, clarissima nobis exempla extant...

Lectores vero theologi quatuor annorum spatio, cursum unum absolvere conentur, quo tempore quatuor Sententiarum Scoti libros, quoad fieri possit, interpretatri curent..." *Statuta, Constitutiones et Decreta Generalia Familiae Cismontanae Ordinis S. Francisci de Observantia, ex decreto generalis Capituli Vallisoletani a. 1593 celebrati, restituta,* c. V (Placentiae, 1596), pp. 94–95; quoted by Michael Brlek, O.F.M., "Legislatio O.F.M. circa Doctorem Immaculatae Conceptionis," in *Virgo Immaculata,* VII–3 (Romae, 1957), p. 194.

[43] "His ergo Pater Beatissime Sancti Augustini vestigiis insistens instar sedulae apis ex Theologiae amoenissimis hortis puriores (ni fallor) verarum opinionum flores diligenter decerpsi. Sive illos Angelicus Thomas, sive subtilis Scotus, sive alius quivis veritatis amator severit, quod ut praestitisse videar faxit Deus ut mihi edere licuerit de illo Isaiae butyro melle mixto, ut sciens reprobare malum, bonum elegerim." *Selectarum Disputationum in Quartum Sententiarum,* Dedication.

[44] Cf. Inauen, art. cit., pp. 227–228.

[45] Cf. e.g. *HCSADM,* lib. V, hom. VII (I, 423a–b).

1. *Older Writers:*

Adamus of St. Victor († 1192)	– 2 times
Alanus ab Insulis, OCist († 1202)	– 2 »
St. Albert the Great, OP († 1280)	– 4 »
Alexander of Hales, OFM († 1245)	– 5 »
St. Anselm of Canterbury († 1109)	– 14 »
Antonius de Butrio († 1408)	– once
Archidiaconus or Guido de Baysio († 1373)	– »
Arnaldus Amalrici, OCist († 1225)	– »
St. Bernard of Clairvaux, OSB († 1153)	– 30 times
St. Bernardine of Sienna, OFM († 1444)	– 6 »
St. Bonaventure, OFM († 1274)	– 2 »
St. Bruno of Segni, OSB († 1123)	– once
Conradus of Erbach, OCist († 1399)	– »
Durandus de S. Porciano, OP († 1334)	– 2 times
Franciscus de Maironis, OFM († c. 1328)	– 4 »
Fulbertus of Chartres († 1028)	– once
Gerardus of Bologna, OCarm († 1317)	– »
Gilbertus of Poitiers († 1154)	– »
Gulielmus Varro, OFM († 1270)	– »
Henricus de Gandavo or Gent († 1293)	– 2 times
Honorius Augustodunensis or Autun (c. 1100)	– 3 »
Hugo of St.–Cher, OP († 1263)	– 5 »
Innocent II († 1143)	– once
Innocent III († 1216)	– »
Ioannes de Basilea, OESA († 1392)	– »
Ioannes Charlier Gerson († 1429)	– »
Ioannes Duns Scotus, OFM († 1308)	– 3 times
Ioannes Pico or Peckham, OFM († 1292)	– once
Ioannes de San Gimigniano, OP († c. 1300)	– »
Ioannes Taulerus, OP († 1361)	– »
Ivo Carnotensis († 1116)	– »
Bl. Jacobus a Voragine, OP († 1298)	– 2 times
Kallistos Xanthopulos Nicaephorus († c. 1335)	– once
Marsilius of Inghen († 1396)	– »
Moses Barcepha († 903)	– »
Nicholas of Lyra, OFM († 1349)	– 4 times
Panormitanus or Nicholas of Tudeschic, OSB († 1445)	– once
Petrus de Aquilla « Scotellus », OFM († 1361)	– »
Petrus Aureolus, OFM († 1322)	– »
Petrus Comestor († c. 1179)	– 2 times
Petrus Hispanus († 1277)	– once
Petrus Lombardus († 1160)	– 5 times
Rabbanus Maurus, OSB († 856)	– once
Remigius of Florence, OP († 1319)	– »
Richard Armachanus († c. 1360)	– »
Richard Mediavilla, OFM († c. 1302)	– »

Richard of St. Victor († 1173)	– 3 times
Robert Holcot, OP († 1349)	– once
Rupert von Deutz, OSB († c. 1129)	– 8 times
Simeon Metaphrastes († c. 1000)	– once
St. Thomas Aquinas, OP († 1274)	– 25 times
Thomas de Argentina, OSA († 1357)	– once
Ubertino da Casale, OFM († c. 1317)	– »
St. Vincent Ferrer († 1419)	– »
Vitalis de Furno, OFM († 1327)	– »
Walafrid Strabo, OSB († 849)	– »
William Ockham, OFM († 1347)	– »

2. *"Moderniores Theologi"*:

Abulensis or Alfonso Tostado de Madrigal	– 7 times
Albert Pigge or Pighius († 1542)	– once
Alfonso de Castro, OFM († 1558)	– »
Alfonso Salmeron, SJ († 1585)	– »
Ambrosius Catharinus, OP († 1553)	– 4 times
Andres de Vega, OFM († 1549)	– once
Angelus de Pas, OFM († 1596)	– once
St. Antonio di ser Niccolo di Pierozzo de Forciglioni, OP († 1459)	– 3 times
Antonio de Cordoba, OFM († 1578)	– 2 »
Antonius Honcala († c. 1553)	– once
Bl. Baptista Mantuanus, OCarm († 1516)	– »
Benedictus Pererius, SJ († 1610)	– 3 times
Bernardinus de Busto, OFM († 1500)	– 2 »
Caesar Baronius († 1607)	– once
Cajetan de Vio, OP († 1534)	– 5 times
Cornelius Jansenius the Elder († 1576)	– once
Diego de Corvarruvias y Leyva († 1577)	– »
Bl. Dionysius de Kartäuser († 1471)	– »
Emanuel Viguerius, OFMConv († 1516)	– »
Francisco de Suárez, SJ († 1619)	– 4 times
Francisco de Toledo, SJ († 1596)	– once
Franciscus Venetus, OFM († 1540)	– »
François Feuardent, OFM († 1610)	– »
François Vatablus († 1547)	– 4 times
Friedrich Nausea († 1552)	– once
Gabriel Biel († 1495)	– »
Gulielmus Hamerus, OP († c. 1564)	– »
Ioannes Raulinus, OSB († 1515)	– »
Ioannes Viguerius, OP († 1550)	– »
Jacob Peres de Valentia, OESA († 1490)	– 4 times
Jacques Almain († 1515)	– once
Jodocus Clichtoveus († 1543)	– »

Johann Driedro († 1535)	– 2 times
Johann Trithemius, OSB († 1516)	– once
St. John Fisher or Roffensis († 1535)	– »
Juan de Pineda, SJ († 1637)	– 3 times
St. Laurentius Iustinianus († 1455)	– 5 »
Luis de Carvajal, OFM († 1552)	– once
Luis Molina, SJ († 1600)	– »
Luigi Lippomani († 1559)	– »
Martinus del Rio, SJ († 1608)	– »
Navarrus or Martin de Azpilcueta, OESA († 1586)	– »
Nicholas of Cusa († 1464)	– »
Pelbartus Ladislai von Temesvar, OFM († 1504)	– 2 times
Petrus Canisius, SJ († 1597)	– 5 »
Petrus Galatinus, OFM († 1540)	– 7 »
Petrus Tartaretus († 1500)	– once
Petrus Thyraeus, SJ († 1601)	– »
St. Robert Bellarmine, SJ († 1621)	– 3 times
Santes Pagnino, OP († 1541)	– 4 »
Tomas Malvenda, OP († 1628)	– once
Vincentius Cartari (c. 1550)	– »

These 109 authors cited 269 times altogether in the first book of the
HCSADM mean that each homily has the average of more than 13
such citations. St. Bernard of Clairvaux tops the long line–up, followed by St. Thomas Aquinas, in the number of times they have been
cited in the 19 homilies.

F. ECCLESIAL

In his *Homiliae Catholicae* Cartagena tries as much as possible
to present the words and speculations of theologians together with
and under the measure of the *magisterium* of the Church. Here one
can feel the effort to follow the Ignatian *"sentire in Ecclesia."* It is
part and parcel of positive theology that the pronouncement of the
Popes and the documents of the Councils are taken into consideration.
The Council of Trent, for instance, is cited no less than 14 times in the
Liber primus alone. The ordinary *Magisterium* too makes an entry
into the references, for example, St. Innocent I's († 417) letter to
the Synod of Numedian bishops in Mileve summoned in 416 by
St. Augustine against Pelagius, the decree of the Synod of Clermont–
Ferrand, and the decretal of Sixtus IV († 1484) on Marian cult.[46]

---

[46] Ibid., lib. I, hom. XIX (I, 118 & 101a–103b); lib. I, hom. XIV (I, 73a).

In addition, Cartagena loves to quote under the designation *"Ecclesia"* liturgical texts from the Mass, the Divine Office and religious hymns.[47] He does so no less than 10 times in the first book of the *HCSADM*.

G. HUMANISTIC

The 15th and 16th centuries' return to the sources of revelation was prepared by the renaissance of the Graeco–Roman spirit. This fresh recourse to the cultural heritage of antiquity, which marked Cartagena during his years of formation, affects too the program of the *Homiliae Catholicae*. In the dedication of the *HCUCRA*, Cartagena presents his work as containing not only biblical expositions and the teachings of the Fathers, of the sacred Pontiffs and of the Councils, but also the erudition *"ex ethnicis, et profanis auctoribus,"* which he is appropriating for a Christian purpose and thus in a way reclaiming from unjust possessors.[48]

In the first book of the *HCSADM*, the profane authors of antiquity referred to are:

Aristotle	— 5 times
Bias, a Greek philosopher	— once
Cicero	— 2 times
Aulus Gelli, a Latin grammarian	— once
Horace	— »
Hesiod	— »
Hippocrates	— »
Josephus	— »
Juvenal, poet–satirist	— »
Martial, epigrammatist	— »
Ovid	— 4 times
Pedanios Dioscorides	— 2 »
Palladius Rutilius Taurus (c. 450)	— once
Pitagus	— once
Philon of Alexandria	— »

---

[47] Ibid., lib. I, hom. II (I, 8a); hom. III (I, 14b); hom. VI (I, 32a); hom. VII (I, 35b); hom. XII (I, 64a & b).

[48] "...adest enim in eis... ex ethnicis, et profanis auctoribus, tamquam ab iniustis possessoribus (ut ait Augustinus) multiplex eruditionis supellex arrepta..." *HCUCRA*, Dedication. The reference to St. Augustine is c. 2 of *Doctrina Christiana*, paulo ante finem. Cartagena himself repeats this view of the right of appropriation. Cf. *HCSADM*, lib. VII, hom. III (I, 739b).

Pliny the Elder	– 10 times
Plutarch	– 3 »
Socrates	– once
Suetonius, Roman poet	– »
Thales of Miles, philosopher	– »
Virgil Maro	– 3 times

The other secular authors of later period whose names appeared in the *Liber primus* are:

Andrea Alciat († 1550), humanist	– once
Bartolo of Sassoferrato († 1357), jurist	– »
Ludovicus Coelius Richerius Rhodiginus († 1520), philosopher	– »
Chleogolus	– »
Gervasius of Tibury († c. 1220), jurist	– »
Fabritius Dateranus	– »
Marianus Socini Senis († 1467), humanist & jurist	– »

Besides citing civil laws, Cartagena quotes Spanish idioms and adages, giving national color to the *Homiliae Catholicae*, so to speak.[49]

III. SOURCES

The above–mentioned general characteristics of Juan de Cartagena's major work are better seen in context with the sources and books he utilized in composing his homilies. As already remarked, we do not intend to be exhaustive. A complete study of Cartagena's quotations and sources would involve much more research, which for our purpose is not really that necessary. The Fathers, theologians, commentators, homilists, humanists, poets, satirists, philosophers, lawyers, historians, chroniclers, and hosts of other medieval and clas-

---

[49] Ibid., lib. IV, hom. XI (I, 359b), where St. Joseph's fatherhood, pictured in the Psalmist's words, "Sede a dextris meis" said to the son, is expressed "perlepide" by a Spanish poet:

"Y estando à la mesa vuestra,
Pudistes decir al hyjo?
Para darle de amor muestra,
Hyjo, sientate a mi diestra."

Cf. also lib. I, hom. VI (I, 30b); hom. IV (I, 20a & 21b); hom. XI (I, 56a); lib. V, hom. XII (I, 467a); hom. VII (I, 418b).

sical writers jostle each other in Cartagena's pages. We want an overall picture of them, not a study in detail.

Did Cartagena have the almost 200 authors he cites in the first book of the *HCSADM* actually before him as he wrote his *Homiliae Catholicae?* And how about the many more other writers subsequently to appear in the pages of his volumes? This is a question of fact, which we cannot categorically answer because we lack detailed knowledge of his library or of the libraries he had access to. But Cartagena does give us some hints as to his actual and first–hand sources. The more recent books, for example, which were published during his time and therefore almost surely available to him, are cited with exactness, sometimes even with the year of the publication and the place of the particular edition, although Cartagena typical of his age often does not give the page nor the complete title of his source. At times he provides only the name of the author. His references to older and ancient writings especially are done in this way, taken most probably second–hand from source–books and collections of *auctoritates, exempla, narrationes, rationes,* etc., which were very popular and widely used.[50]

A. BIBLE COMMENTARIES

The very framework of the *Homiliae Catholicae* based as it is on the development of biblical events and the consequent centering on Sacred Scripture lead one to expect that Cartagena's primary source would be biblical commentaries and concordances. He quotes at length from the commentaries of Sts. Augustine, Jerome, Ambrose, Basil, Gregory and others. More immediate to him were the newer works of Salmeron, Pineda, Abulensis, Alanus, Honcala, Toledo, Hamerus, Nicholas of Lyra and Pagnino. And it seems that Cartagena had most of these commentators at hand as he worked on his homilies. The library of San Pietro in Montorio, being a house of studies, must have been furnished with a decent supply of contemporary books.

As we know, the oldest biblical concordances were primarily intended as homiletic aids, sifting and arranging biblical passages for the use of preachers. Such for instance was the *Collectarium Bibliae* (Cologne, 1513) of John Pecham, OFM, which was also known as the *Collectarium Divinarum Sententiarum.* Peter Aureolus put out

---

[50] Cf. Zawart, op. cit., pp. 355–369, and Schneyer, op. cit., pp. 178–184.

his own popular *Breviarium Bibliorum* or *Compendium Literalis Sensus Bibliae* (Strasburg, 1500), enjoying many reprintings as late as the 1613 edition in Paris. In this class also were Vitalis de Furno's *Speculum Morale Totius Sacrae Scripturae* (1513) and Petrus Bechorius' *Reductorium Moralizationum super Universam Bibliam* (1477) and his *Dictionarius seu Repertorium pro Praedicantibus* (1489). Cartagena was familiar with, and referred to, the works of these authors.[51] He must have had available to him also the widely circulated *Biblia Pauperum* alleged to be St. Bonaventure's as late as 1596. It was by the Dominican Nicholas Hanapis († 1291), who also published the much used *Virtutum Vitiorumque Exempla* (1477), a topical Bible concordance.

For commentaries properly so–called, Cartagena's list is headed by the venerable *Glossa Ordinaria* (the 1559 Lyon edition), which he cites 7 times in the *Liber primus*, making the appropriate distinctions when he is referring to the *"marginalis"* or to the *"interlinearis"* glosses.[52] Then there are the *Postilla* (from *"post illa verba"*), i.e. explanations of biblical texts or books. Cartagena frequently refers to Nicholas of Lyra's *Postilla litteralis*, as he does to John Pecham's *Postilla in Cantica Canticorum*.[53] He also cites Honorius of Autun's commentary on the Song of Songs.[54] Of later date were other commentaries Cartagena likewise utilizes: Cornilius Jansenius the Elder's *Concordia Evangelica*,[55] Alanus de Rupe's *Cantica Canticorum*,[56] Antonio Honcala's Genesis commentary,[57] Gulielmus Hamerus' *Commentationes in Genesim*,[58] Santiago Perez de Valencia's *In CL Psalmos Expositio*,[59] Santes Pagnino's *Isagoge ad Sacras Lit-*

---

[51] Cf. e.g., *HCSADM*, Lib. I, hom. XIX (I, 121a); lib. V, hom. XIII (I, 474a & 476b); hom. XIV (I, 480a); lib. VI, hom. XI (I, 699b–700a). On the works of these men, see F. Stegmüller, *Repertorium Biblicum*, IV, 6425 ff, 6415 ff; V, 8309 ff.

[52] Ibid., lib. I, hom. XIX (I, 110b, 114b & 124a).

[53] Ibid., lib. I, hom. VIII (I, 39a); hom. XIII (I, 68a); hom. XV (I, 81b & 82b). Cf. Stegmüller, op. cit., IV, 5827–5994.

[54] Ibid., lib. I, hom. IX (I, 43b); hom. XVI (I, 86a); hom. XIX (I, 123b). Cf. Stegmüller, op. cit., III, 3566–79.

[55] Lib. I, hom. XV (I, 81a); lib. VI, hom. XIII (I, 609b & 613b); hom. XV (I, 625b).

[56] Lib. I, hom. IX (I, 43b); hom. XV (I, 80b).

[57] Lib. I, hom. XV (I, 81a).

[58] Ibid.

[59] Lib. I, hom. XIX (I, 100a & 108a). Cf. Stegmüller, op. cit., III, 3982–6.

teras et ad Mysticos S. Scripturae Sensus,[60] François Vatablus' commentaries and *Adnotationes* or *Scholia in VT*,[61] and Pelbartus Ladislai's commentaries.[62] Contemporary to Cartagena were the comprehensive commentaries by his former co–religious Alfonso Salmeron,[63] Juan de Maldonado,[64] Francisco de Toledo,[65] Benedictus Pererius,[66] and Juan de Pineda,[67] all of whom he quotes. Cartagena could have availed himself too of the manuscript Gospel commentaries of Angelus de Pas, who lived and passed away in San Pietro in Montorio.[68] His jesuit friend, Martinus del Rio, must have been of some assistance with his work, *In Canticum Canticorum Salomonis Commentarius Litteralis, et Catena mystica* (1604).

In his use of biblical texts, the author at times resorts to the various readings, although he gives preference to the Vulgate version in the spirit of the Council of Trent.[69] When necessary, he compares the merits of the different readings and also turns to the Hebrew and Greek texts. For this he employed Cisneros' *Complutensis* and Pagnino's *Thesaurus Linguae Sanctae*.[70]

B. THEOLOGICAL REFERENCES

Among the many theologians, both old and contemporary, whom Cartagena quotes and refers to, there are naturally some on whom his interest and with whom his relationship go further than just a passing citation. We prescind now from his dependence on the theological giants like St. Thomas, Scotus and Suarez, which shall be self–evident in Part II. More interesting for the moment is Cartagena's recourse to the relatively lesser luminaries of his time. A couple of books espe-

---

[60] Lib. I, hom. XI (I, 58a); hom. XIII (I, 65b); hom. XIV (I, 73a).

[61] Lib. I, hom. XI (I, 58a); hom. XIII (I, 70b); hom. XIV (I, 73a); lib. VI, hom. XV (I, 625a).

[62] Cf. lib. I, hom. XIX (I, 106a & 123a). Cf. Stegmüller, IV, 6371, 1 ff.

[63] Lib. I, hom. XIX (I, 123b).

[64] Lib. VI, hom. XV (I, 625a).

[65] Lib. I, hom. XIX (I, 123b).

[66] Lib. I, hom. XIII (I, 68b); hom. XV (I, 78b & 81a).

[67] Lib. I, hom. XIII (I, 67b & 68b); hom. XV (I, 81a).

[68] Cartagena refers to Angelo de Pas as "insignis noster." Lib. I, hom. XIX (I, 121b). Cf. Wadding, op. cit., pp. 23–25.

[69] *HCUCRA*, Dedication. Cf. S. Muñoz Iglesias, "El decreto tridentino sobre la Vulgata...," *Estudios Bibl.*, 5 (1946) 137–169.

[70] *HCSADM*, lib. I, hom. XV (I, 81b); hom. XIV (I, 73a).

cially, which he seems to have highly regarded, are Petrus Galatinus'
De Arcanis Catholicae Veritatis (1518) and Luis de Carvajal's *Declamatio Expostulatoria pro Inmaculata Conceptionis*, which first came out
in Sevilla in 1533. The work of Galatinus most probably influenced
the very title of the *Homiliae Catholicae*.[71] Cartagena repeatedly
quotes from both of these fellow Franciscans. Once he cites Carvajal
in a long verbatim quotation, even specifying the edition he is using
as that of Paris, 1541.[72] But he also copies lengthily from Carvajal
without even a mention, as for example in the first four sections of
the 19th homily in *Liber primus*.[73] It is surprising that Cartagena
should subscribe to this form of plagiarism, even if it was widely
practised then. Other authors who could have provided him with
materials for his Mariology were: Juan de Pineda, who wrote in 1603
his *Immaculata Beatae Virginis Conceptio ex Sacrae Scripturae Prae-
cipuis Textibus Deducta et Comprobata* and Martinus del Rio in his
*Florida Mariana sive de Laudibus Sacratissimae Virginis Deiparae
Panegyrici XIII* (1598).[74]

C. OTHER SOURCES

Cartagena's numerous other references and citations of older
theologians, patristic writers, Church documents and literature from
antiquity would be partly explained by the time's available source–
books. One such work he has explicitly cited is John Viguerius' *In-*

---

[71] Dausquius' snide comment on the title of Cartagena's *Homiliae Catholicae* was: "Ista incuriosa curiositate victus Cartagena volumina ista, quibus
orbis cymbalum audire meruit (an etiam voluit?) inscribit 'de religionis Christianae arcanis'. Quae scilicet – 'Arcano quodcumque volumine Moses' clausit, et de
'Arcanis Catholicae veritatis' quaecumque Galatinus compilavit, veritate diligentia, immanitate superavit Cartagena. Ideo non trivialem aliquam doctrinam sparsit
in vulgus: sed arcanam, abstrusam, reconditam in arculis maternis, dum inibi
sanctificati sunt tanto numero puelli ex eius opinamento." *Sancti Josephi Sanctificatio extra Uterum, seu Binoctium adversus F. Marchantii Inanias*, pp. 116–117.

[72] Lib. I, hom. XIV (I, 116a–117a). For his quotations of Galatinus, see
Lib. I, hom. V (I, 26a); hom. VII (I, 36a); hom. X (I, 48b); lib. V, hom. XIV
(I, 481b); lib. VI, hom. II (I, 537b); hom. XVII (I, 644a). Cf. A. Kleinhans, OFM,
"De Vita et Operibus Petri Galatini, OFM," *Antonianum*, 1 (1926) 145–178,
327–356.

[73] Cf. Pius Sagues, O.F.M., "Doctrina de Immaculata B.V. Mariae Conceptione apud P. Ludovicum de Carvajal, OFM († 1552)," *Antonianum*, 28 (1943)
247, footnote 2.

[74] Lib. I, hom. I (I, 5b).

stitutiones ad Naturalem ac Christianam Philosophiam, maxime vero ad scholasticam theologiam, sacrarum litterarum universaliumque conciliorum auctoritate, et doctorum ecclesiasticorum praesertim D. Thomae Aquinatis eruditione confirmatae, omnibusque animarum curam gerentibus admodum necessariae (1549).[75] The avowed pastoral objective characterized too the many oft–reprinted encyclopedic books of Middle Ages conceived of to help preachers. They were not Bible concordances but scrapbooks giving a potpourri of excerpts with an abundance of interpretations and moralizings. Such were the following works which certainly would be in a Franciscan library : Thomas of Pavia's († c. 1280) famous *Distinctiones Bovis,* an immense repertoire of alphabetically arranged subjects enriched with mystical, allegorical and moral commentaries plus quotations from the Bible, the Fathers, philosophers and profane authors; Nicholas of Byard's (c. 1261) popular *Dictionarius Pauperum;* Mauritius Anglicus or Hibernicus's (c. 1250) *Distinctiones Sacrae Scripturae;* and John of Wales' († 1303) *Breviloquium de Quatuor Virtutibus Cardinalibus Antiquorum Philosophorum et Principum* (1498), his *Communiloquium sive Summa Collationum Dictus ad Omne Hominum Genus* (1472), and especially his *Expositio seu Moralitates Fabularum Ovidii* (1509), which explains Ovid's Metamorphoses in a Christian manner and which could have been a main source of Cartagena's many quotations from and "Christianizings" of Ovid. John of Wales, long before the Renaissance, gave an impulse to the moral interpretation of Greek and Roman history and mythology. All of these above–mentioned compilers were Franciscans.

Specifically as patristic concordances for the use of preachers, we have Bl. Walter of Bruges' († 1307) *Excerpta ex Sanctis Patribus: Augustino, Gregorio, Hieronymo, etc.* and Thomas Hibernicus or Palmeranus' († 1296) *Manipulus Florum* (1483), whose 1606 Cologne edition carried the title *Flores Doctorum pene Omnium tam Graecorum tam Latinorum, qui tum in theologia quam in philosophia hactenus claruerunt.* A highly esteemed compilation of the Fathers which Cartagena uses in Thomas Beauxamis or Bellamicus', OCarm († 1589), *Commentariorum in Evangelicam Harmoniam ex Antiquis Eclesiae Patribus congestorum... tomi duo* (1582).[76]

And aside from the many collections of sermons that were avail-

---

[75] Lib. I, hom. V (I, 26a); hom. XIX (I, 123a).
[76] Lib. VI, hom. XV (I, 624b–625a); hom. XIX (I, 661b).

able, Cartagena's other main source for materials came from example books.[77] He availed himself, for example, of a *Compendium Mendicantium*, probably of Marianus of Florence's *Compendium Chronicorum OFM*,[78] of the *Margarita Confessorum*,[79] of the *Thesaurus Catholicus* (Coloniae, 1599),[80] and of the *Lexicon Theologicum*.[81] But these were actually general reference books. More of the genre of example books compiled for preachers were Holcot's *Moralitates* (c. 1334),[82] Jacobus a Voragine's *Legenda Aurea Sanctorum* (c. 1264), Antonius Rampegolus' († c. 1424) *Figurae Bibliorum* and the anonymous *Speculum Exemplorum Magnum* (c. 1480) edited in 1607 by John Major, S.J. For illustrations from profane history, Cartagena could have used too the *Gesta Romanorum Moralisata*.

A special type of example book comes from natural history, the so-called emblematic books. Like most preachers of his time and particularly of the Middle Ages, Cartagena turned to irrational creation for illustrations and symbolizations. In Part III of this study, we shall analyze more the background of this method from the point of view of scriptural interpretation. Suffice it here to note that Cartagena, for example, has a homily entitled: *"Eadem Paradisi Metaphoram Prosequitur: ostendentes, quam apte beatissima Virgo in sua Conceptione se comparavit insignioribus arboribus, quae in illo consitae erant, ut Cedro, Cypresso, Cinnamomo, Ficui, Malogranato, et Palmae."* [83] The snake in Paradise is naturally a classic instance for emblematic moralizing,[84] as is the dove from the arch of Noah,[85] and many precious stones.[86] Source books for this are numerous: e.g. John a San Gimigniano's *Summa de Exemplis et Similitudinis Rerum*, Bartholomaeus Anglicus' (c. 1250) *Liber de Proprietatibus Re-*

---

[77] Cf. J.-Th. Wetter, *L'exemplum dans la littérature religieuse et didactique du moyen age* (Paris–Toulouse, 1927).

[78] Lib. I, hom. XIX (I, 101b, 106a & 123a).

[79] Lib. XVIII, hom. ult. (III, 493b & 487b).

[80] Lib. I, hom. XIX (I, 111a).

[81] Lib. XVIII, hom. ult. (III, 493b).

[82] Cf. B. Smalley, "Robert Holcot," *Archivum Fratrum Praedicatorum,* 26 (1956) 25–26.

[83] Lib. I, hom. XVI (I, 82b–89b). Cf. lib. I, hom. VIII (I, 42a–b).

[84] Lib. I, hom. III (I, 19a–b); hom. V (I, 26b–27a).

[85] Lib. I, hom. VII (I, 35b–36a).

[86] Lib. I, hom. VI (I, 32b–33a & 36b).

rum, and Petrus Berchorius' *Inductorium vel Reductorium Morale de Proprietatibus Rerum*.[87] He could have used too a manuscript copy of the Franciscan theologian Servasanctus' *Liber de Exemplis Naturalibus*.[88] Cartagena's citations of Pedanios Dioscorides, for instance, are probably second–hand from Bartholomaeus Anglicus or Vincent of Beauvais' († c. 1264) *Speculum Naturale*, both of whom copied much from Pedanios' *Materia Medica*.[89]

IV. EXCURSUS: CARTAGENA'S JOSEPHOLOGY

As we noted earlier in Chapter I Juan de Cartagena got involved posthumously in a controversy over St. Joseph. We would like to say more about this controversy and about Cartagena's teaching on St. Joseph. The aim of this excursus is merely to shed more light on an interesting development in the history of Juan de Cartagena's works and teachings.

The very title of Cartagena's major work includes St. Joseph: *Homiliae Catholicae de Sacris Arcanis Deiparae Mariae et Ioseph*. It is only in one book out of 19, however, that he treats of St. Joseph *ex professo*, i.e. in *Liber quartus*, which is *De Sacris Arcanis Desponsationis Beatae Virginis; necnon de eximiis laudibus dilectissimi eius sponsi Ioseph*. All 13 homilies of this book are either totally or partially concerned with Mary's spouse.[90] The penultimate book, the 18th, has the title: *De Sacris Arcanis Cultus et Devotionis erga Deiparam Virginem ac D. Josephum eius Sponsum*, but it is only in the last two homilies out of 15 that St. Joseph enters the discussion.

---

[87] On San Gimigniano, see Antoine Dondaine, O.P., "La vie et les oeuvres de Jean de San Gimigniano," *Archivum Fratrum Praedicatorum*, 9 (1939) 128–183, esp. pp. 157–164 about the *De Exemplis et Similitudinis Rerum*.

[88] Cf. Martin Grabmann, "Der Liber de exemplis naturalibus des Franziskanertheologen Servasanctus," *Franziskaner Studien*, 7 (1920) 85–117.

[89] Lib. I, hom. XVI (I, 86a & 88a).

[90] Cartagena's homilies on St. Joseph have been included in the anthology of J. C. Vives y Tutó, OFMCap, *Summula Iosephina* (Roma, 1907). See also E. del Sdo Corazon, OCD, "La paternidad josefina en los escritores españoles de los siglos XVI y XVII," *Estudios Josefinos*, 6 (1952) 152–178; *idem*, "Razón de prioridad y preeminencia entre el matrimonio y la paternidad de S. José, segun Juan de Cartagena y Fray Melchor Prieto, O.M.," *ibid.*, 13 (1959) 62–90.

A. Main Teachings

1. *The man.* Cartagena points out that at the time of his marriage with Mary, Joseph could hardly have been as he is traditionally pictured: a very old man.[91] Joseph was taken by the people afterwards to be the father of Jesus, hence he must still be young enough to be a normal father. A senile old man fathering the son of a very young girl would have been a source of scandal. To have earned a living for his family as a carpenter, and to have made those trips to Bethlehem and to Egypt back and forth, Joseph must have been strong and young and not a superannuated *"grandaevus."* He was probably in his forties at the time he took Mary as his wife.

Joseph's geneology given in the first chapter of St. Matthew is also Mary's, because as customary among the Jews the man takes his wife from the same branch and tribe as his.[92] Jacob was Joseph's natural father, and Heli (Lk 3, 23) his legal father.[93] The suggestion that Joseph might have already been married before taking Mary as as a widower is rejected by Cartagena. It is against his virginity and total commitment to the Holy Family.[94] In regards to the death of Joseph, the author is inclined to accept the opinion that he lived to about the time that Jesus was baptized in the Jordan.[95] He rose again together with the other Saints at Christ's own resurrection,[96] and is rightly second only to Mary in heaven in nearness to Christ.[97]

2. *The espousal.* Cartagena holds that Joseph was truly married to Mary, notwithstanding the contrary opinion of some Fathers. To reconcile this seeming discrepancy, he makes a distinction. They were truly married, as is clear from the Gospel words that he was "the husband of Mary" (Mt 1, 16), from the angel's assurance to Joseph not to be afraid to take Mary as his wife (Mt 1, 20), from the account that "Joseph set out together with Mary, his betrothed, who was with child" (Lk 2, 5), and from the remark that Mary was found to be with child "before they came to live together" (Mt 1, 18), meaning

---

[91] Lib. IV, hom. I (I, 289b–290a).
[92] Lib. II, hom. I (I, 125a–b). Cf. lib. XVIII, hom. ult. (III, 504a–505b).
[93] Lib. IV, hom. III (I, 295a).
[94] Ibid., (I, 297b–298a).
[95] Ibid., (I, 300b–301a); lib. XVIII, hom. ult. (III, 517b–518b).
[51] Lib. IV, hom. III (I, 303a); lib. XVIII, hom. ult. (III, 520a).
[97] Ibid., (III, 520b–522b).

that they could live publicly together because they were legally married.[98] But they did not have a consummated marriage. Admittedly the Fathers who denied a true marriage between Mary and Joseph were actually denying only what is termed a consummated marriage. For Cartagena the Tridentine distinction between *ratum* and *consummatum* dissolves the difficulty. The union of Mary and Joseph was ratified by mutual consent but not consummated by any sexual union.[99] Thus was Mary's virginity safeguarded, while still being really Joseph's wife. And likewise her reputation was protected and Jesus' legitimacy assured.[100]

Regarding the non–consummation of the union, Cartagena theorizes that perhaps before their espousal Joseph and Mary made an agreement not to ask the *debitum* from one another.[101] The *domnium* and *potestas* remained, only the *usus* was given up. Cartagena, however, finds St. Thomas' idea more likely that Mary somehow learned through some revelation from God that her husband–to–be would never demand carnal union with her and so entered marriage with Joseph certain that her virginity would be preserved.[102]

3. *Joseph's sanctification.* In discussing the character of Joseph, Cartagena quotes and makes his own the words of John Charlier Gerson († 1429) delivered in a sermon during the Council of Constance:

> Just as it was fitting that the Virgin should be endowed with the highest purity, so also was it fitting that she should have a husband equally most pure in his own way, who would remain a virgin with the perpetual virgin. Both were illustrious by their royal lineage. Both received sanctification while still in the womb; Mary full of grace was never touched by the stain, Joseph filled with grace overcame all mortal sin.[103]

---

[98] Lib. IV, hom. I (I, 286b).

[99] Ibid., (I, 286b–287a).

[100] Lib. XVIII, hom. ult. (III, 506a–507a).

[101] Lib. IV, hom. I (I, 287b).

[102] Thomas Aquinas, *Summa theol.*, III, q. 29, art. 1 ad 1.

[103] *Sermo de Nativitate Mariae*, quoted by Cartagena, lib. IV, hom. III (I, 296b). Cf. P. Glorieux's edition of Gerson, *Oeuvres complètes*, V (Paris, 1963), p. 353; and Paul Arendt, *Die Predigten des konstanzer Konzils* (Freiburg i. Br., 1933), pp. 101 & 103. Jöcher, op. cit., col. 1708, cites this doctrine of sanctification and also that of St. Joseph's martyrdom as examples of Cartagena's "wunderliche Lehr-Sätze."

As Cartagena explicitly points out, this teaching about St. Joseph's sanctification while still in his mother's womb is not of his own making but came from the mind of the former Chancellor of Paris.[104] Jacob de Valentia († 1490) and Johannes Eck († 1543) have also propounded the same doctrine.[105]

The argument for holding that St. Joseph had been sanctified in the womb is *a fortiori*. If the prophet Jeremiah and St. John the Baptist were sanctified in the womb, how much more St. Joseph. The two were made holy in the womb, in order to preach about Christ and to baptize and point him out. It is not unreasonable that he who would be feeding the most sacred body of Christ for many years and who would be caring for him should also be sanctified even in his mother's womb.[106] Actually, to believe in this special sanctification of St. Joseph is not that unusual, considering that many other Saints are held by some authors to have been sanctified in the womb, e.g. Sts. James the Lesser, Nicholas, Dominic, Asella, George, Paul and even Moses and Samson.[107] And these are believed to have been sanctified either because of their future dignity or because of their particular relationship with Christ. Joseph, whom the Holy Spirit canonized in the New Testament as a "just man" (Mt 1, 19) and who was so intimate with Christ, is certainly more apt to have been made holy.[108] It is moreover held by the author that in St. Joseph concupiscence and all evil inclinations had been either extinguished or muted.[109]

---

[104] "...non ex parte meo, sed ex mente insigni illius Cancellarii Parisiensis." Lib. IV, hom. III (I, 296b). When later Marchant in defending Cartagena argued that the man was simply relying on the teaching of Gerson, Dausquius gave it back to him straight, op. cit., p. 117: "Inutilis, et intuta evasio! Nunquam credam seu vivus, seu mortuus Cartagenam a tumulo surrexisse, ut secretam in aurem Marchantio ogganniret se ex aliorum sententia, non de sua, hoc posuisse. Alienis enim sensibus suos corroboravit: ergo alienam sententiam pro sua dedit."

[105] Jacob de Valentia, *Cantica Virginis*, and Johannes Eck, *Sermo de S. Ioseph*, cited by Cartagena, lib. IV, hom. III (I, 296b). See also lib. XVIII, hom. ult. (III, 487b).

[106] Lib. IV, hom. III (I, 296b–297a); lib. XVIII, hom. ult. (III, 488a).

[107] Lib. IV, hom. III (I, 297a–b).

[108] "Gravissimi Auctores constanter affirmant, Beatum Iosephum fuisse sanctificatum in utero materno... Idque mihi persuadeo verissimum, quia omnis sanctificatio in utero fuit, aut propter sanctificati excellentem dignitatem futuram, aut quia ad Christum Sanctum Sanctorum speciali ratione ordinabatur: utrumque autem in nostro Ioseph excelluit..." Lib. XVIII, ho . ult. (III, 487a).

[109] Ibid., (III, 488a–489a).

4. *Joseph's martyrdom.* Another thesis of Cartagena about St. Joseph concerns his singular martyrdom. Like Mary, he was a martyr too, and their *"carnifix"* was none other than Jesus.[110] Mary suffered the passion of Christ; Joseph suffered his conception. That terrific, uninterrupted anguish Joseph underwent as Mary became pregnant is termed by the author, a *"zelotypia."* Joseph's heart was torn by the deepest pain and agony, as he felt the pangs of his pure love for his wife and of his self–conscious unworthiness to be the husband of the Mother of God. The thought of having to separate from her tortured him, especially since he suffered all this alone within himself.[111] And if, as some would claim, Joseph suspected Mary of adultery, the resulting perplexity because he was also convinced of her sanctity would have been no less mortifying.[112] In fact, Joseph's whole life as the husband of Mary was a prolonged martyrdom, a series of sorrows: the trip to Bethlehem and finding there no better place for Mary; Simeon's prophesy; the circumcision; the flight to Egypt; the return to Judea with the threat from Archelaeus; losing Jesus in Jerusalem; and his labor to the end to provide for the Holy Family.[113]

5. *Joseph's dignity.* The fact that Joseph was the husband of the Mother of God is the basis of the great honor due to him. This dignity is like a principle whence Joseph's sanctity excelling other Saints is founded.[114] Having been chosen by God for the honor to be the husband of Mary and the father of Jesus, Joseph would have been endowed by God with all the gifts and graces necessary for the execution of his functions.[115] Just as God selected the best woman to be Jesus' mother, so was it proper that the best man be chosen to be her husband. Joseph's role in salvation history lies therefore in his cooperation with Mary in her privilege as the mother of the sa-

---

[110] Lib. IV, hom. III (I, 298b).

[111] Ibid., (I, 299a–b).

[112] Ibid., (I, 299b). Cf. hom. X (I, 343b–355b); lib. XVIII, hom. ult. (III, 497b–498b).

[113] Lib. IV, hom. III (I, 299b–300a).

[114] Ibid., hom. VIII (I, 328b). Cf. also lib. XVIII, hom. ult. (III, 497b–498b).

[115] Lib. IV, hom. VIII (I, 329a–b). On Joseph's place in salvation history, cf. K. Rahner, " 'Nimm das Kind und seine Mutter.' Zur Verehrung des hl. Josef," *Geist u. Leben*, 30 (1957) 14–22.

vior. Unlike Adam and Eve, Joseph and Mary gave us the Life of
the world: she conceived and gave birth to Christ, he nourished and
protected him.[116] In fact, Joseph could also be called the "spiritual"
father of Christ, because in his heart and mind he in a way conceived Christ and fostered him.[117]

Joseph's dignity is further enhanced by Mary's most pure love
for him and by his close contact with her.[118] And in his intimate
relationship with Christ himself, Joseph approaches even the most
sublime dignity of the Mother of God. The grace of the hypostatic
union is most perfect in the humanity of Christ united to his divine
nature, then in Mary who bore and gave birth to the Word Incarnate,
and thirdly in Joseph who fed, brought up and protected the God–
Man.[119] Joseph might be the least in this regard, but *infimum supremi* surpasses *supremum infimi*. Thus in ministering to Christ's
natural body, he surpasses in grace even the function of the Apostles
which is for Christ's mystical body. Cartagena exclaims,

> The more I contemplate the heavenly gifts with which the
> boundless generosity of Christ the Lord has enriched Joseph,
> the legitimate husband of his Mother and his legal father, the more
> am I seized by admiration and the more am I inclined to the opin-
> ion, that he must be put above all worshipers in heaven with the
> exception of Mary.[120]

B. THE CONTROVERSY

1. *The exchange.* The whole affair started with another ex–
Jesuit, Claudius Dausquius, a canon of Tournai.[121] In 1627, he

---

[116] "Ac tandem sicut Adam, et Eva mortem peccati in posteros omnes trans-
funderant, ita Maria, et Ioseph vitam in universum Orbem terrarum intulerunt,
illa concipiendo, et pariendo auctorem vitae Christum Dominum, hic vero eundem
infantem nutriendo, fovendo, et ab Herodis tyrannida liberando." Lib. XVIII,
hom. ult. (III, 510a).

[117] Ibid., (III, 315b–316a).

[118] Lib. IV, hom. VIII (I, 330a–331a). Cf. lib. XVIII, hom. ult. (III, 514b).

[119] Lib. IV, hom. VIII (I, 334a).

[120] Ibid., hom. IX (I, 337a).

[121] Dausquius was born in Saint–Omer in 1566, joined the Society of Jesus
in 1585 and left it 25 years later. He first established his name as a philologist
with the publication of an annotated Latin translation of the homilies of St. Basil.
He died in 1644. Cf. Sommervogel, op. cit., II, 1842–1843; and the *Biographie
Nationale de Belgique* (Bruxelles, 1873), IV, 698–702.

published in Paris a book, *Sancti Pauli Apostoli Sanctitudo in Utero, extra, in Solo, in Caelo Lib. III Decertata.* The work denies St. Paul's sanctification in the womb and in the process rejects the opinion that the privilege is attributable to other Saints, including St. Joseph. Thus was Juan de Cartagena's name dragged in, being a proponent of St. Joseph's "uterine sanctification," as we have just seen. Dausquius spared no punches in assaulting the deceased Franciscan. Another devotee of St. Joseph and a partisan Friar Minor took up the challenge. Pierre Marchant, a prolific writer who had held high offices in his Order,[122] answered the attack against Cartagena with a book of his own, *Sanctificatio S. Iosephi Sponsi Virginis, Nutritii Jesu, in Utero Asserta, pro R.P.F. Joanne Carthagena Ordinis S. Francisci olim in Academia Salmanticensi professore, et in urbe de mandato Sanctissimi Generali lectore contra R.D. Claudii Dausquii Tornacensis Canonici Calumnias*, published in Bruges in 1630. Quick to reply, Dausquius lost no time in coming out with his second book dedicated to Pope Urban VIII: *Sancti Josephi Sanctificatio extra Uterum, seu Binoctium adversus F. Marchantii Inianias... Item Aplysiarum FF. Minorum Audomarensium Spongia*, Lyon, 1631. The book's second part, the *Spongia*, in itself a separate work, was directed against another booklet, *Institution de la sodalité du bienheureux S. Joseph érigée en l'église des frères mineurs de l'observance de Saint–Omer.* Dausquius has widened his target and was shooting at the Friars Minor as a group. Marchant's riposte betrays the quickened phase of the debate. His *Factus Dies Illustrans Sponsi Mariae, Nutritii Jesu Gratiosam Sanctificationem in Utero, ab eo quem Pater Sanctificavit et Misit in Mundum, contra R.D. Cl. Dausquii... Binoctium* was published in Ghent in 1631. At the same time a new edition of his *Sanctificatio S. Josephi* came out. At this juncture the Congregation of the Index stepped in and published on March 19, 1633, a condemnation of Marchant's first book placing it on the Index of Prohibited Books.[123]

2. *The points at issue.* Marchant had a double objective in debating with Dausquius, i.e. to uphold the doctrine of St. Joseph's

---

[122] Marchant was born near Liège in 1585 and died in 1661. He became provincial, definitor general, and commissary general over the provinces of Germany, Belgium, Holland, England and Ireland. Cf. *DThC*, s.v. "Marchant, Pierre (1585–1661)," by Edouard d'Alençon, IX, 2004–2006.

[123] Cf. *Biographie Nationale de Belgique* (Paris, 1926), XIII, 451–452.

sanctification in the womb and to defend Juan de Cartagena against Dausquius' withering assault. The latter's method and tactic were a mixture of good theology and of personal invectives, of logic and of uninhibited sarcasm. Marchant in general managed to acquit himself, if not doctrinally, at least for his gentlemanly self–restraint.

In his *Spongia*, Dausquius points out that prior to Gerson and his faction the idea about St. Joseph being sanctified in the womb was unknown. In the same breath he continues with a not too subtle swipe at Cartagena, "Then some sermon books, I do not know which, spread it rapidly around as if by a fickle rabble out for novelty and with a desire for fame, presenting to the hearer as real fruit what really is a cockle. Sublime theology does not matter much to twaddle–retailers."[124] The philologist in Dausquius is unmistakable and he is wielding his pen like a sword! The popularity of the *Homiliae Catholicae*, as attested by Wadding, meant the rapid spreading of the doctrine regarding St. Joseph's special sanctification. It must have goaded Dausquius in his private war against any maximalism with St. Joseph. As a group, the Franciscans were moreover known as promoters of the devotion to the saint, especially St. Bernardine of Sienna and Bernardine de Busto.[125]

But it was with his *Binoctium* that Dausquius tried to demolish systematically the thesis of Gerson and Cartagena. In chapter XVII with the heading: "*Cartagena scripturae laevus interpres*," he begins by twitting Marchant for getting excited over his earlier charge that Cartagena (Marchant's "*personatus patronus*," according to Dausquius) had distorted the Scripture with reckless temerity. Lecturing Marchant, he goes on, " Your task is to show how Cartagena had appropriately marshalled the scriptural *loci* and how he had soundly interpreted them. But you do no such thing, nor can you do it. As it is your aim to defend Cartagena, it is mine to expose to the world how he abused Sacred Scripture." [126] And going to particulars, Dausquius singles out the instances Cartagena presented in his homilies as examples of sanctification in the womb. Cartagena accepts the opinion that Jeremiah (1, 5) was sanctified in the womb of his mother.[127] Dausquius reasons to the contrary that here is not a case

---

[124] *Spongia*, pp. 47–48.

[125] Cf. lib. XVIII, hom. ult. (III, 490b; 488a & 493b).

[126] *Sancti Josephi Sanctificatio... seu Binoctium*, p. 82. Bayle, op. cit., p. 67, went to some length to comment on this critique by Dausquius.

[127] Lib. IV, hom. III (I, 296b).

of sanctification from sin.[128] Cartagena deduces St. Paul's sanctification in the womb from the words in Gal. 1, 15: "God... has especially chosen me while still in my mother's womb." [129] His first book, Dausquius says, has conclusively dealt with this matter, so much so that Marchant has been reduced to silence. He also implies heresy on the part of Cartagena, if he meant that Paul never sinned,[130] — which Cartagena really never said. Cartagena likewise cited Gen. 28, 15: "I will keep you safe wherever you go" to claim that Jacob had been sanctified too in the womb.[131] Dausquius rightly makes the reminder that God said these words to a grown–up Jacob.[132] It has been also interpreted from Judges 13, 5: "...the boy shall be God's nazirite from his mother's womb" that Samson was made holy in his mother's womb.[133] Dausquius counters that it is merely being said that Samson would be dedicated to God from his very infancy, otherwise the patriarch Joseph, who was also thus dedicated (Gen. 49, 29 & Deut. 33, 16), would have been sanctified too in the womb.[134] Dausquius concludes that Cartagena and his lackey Marchant violate the prohibition by the Council of Trent against distorting Scripture with strange interpretations from the Fathers.[135] Our own analysis of Cartagena's use of Sacred Scripture is in Part III of this study.

From Cartagena's words: *"Iosephum Dei Genetricis Sponsum pie credamus in utero sanctificatum, cum et idem singulare privilegium de aliis multis sanctis a gravissimis auctoribus creditum fuerit,"* Dausquius notes, that the repetition of *"credamus"* and *"creditum"* betrays the whole thing to be empty "credulity" described as pious, a sandy and ruinous foundation for any teaching.[136] With rash facility Dausquius cries "Of what use is the blood of Christ, if St. Joseph were sanctified in the womb because of a privilege of special love?" — forgetting that Cartagena himself said that such a privilege is due to St. Joseph's

---

[128] *Binoctium*, p. 83.
[129] Lib. IV, hom. III (I, 297a).
[130] *Binoctium*, loc. cit.
[131] Lib. IV, hom. III (I, 297a–b).
[132] *Binoctium*, p. 84.
[133] Lib. IV, hom. III (I, 297b).
[134] *Binoctium*, loc. cit.
[135] "At Concilium Tridentinum vetat Scripturam interpretatione a veterum Patrum scitis, ac sensibus aliena dehonestari. Fecit Cartagena, et eius pedisequus Marchantius." Ibid.
[136] Ibid., pp. 82–83. The reference is to Cartagena's lib. IV, hom. III (I, 297a).

special relation to Christ and therefore is due to Christ's grace.[137] Dausquius also makes the blanket charge that Gerson, Cartagena and Marchant smack of Pelagianism,[138] but without proving it. The teaching itself of sanctification in the womb for St. Joseph earns from Dausquius the note: *"ventosa, futilis, nulla recta, solidave ratione fulta."* [139]

To Marchant's remark that this teaching together with Cartagena's works has been approved by ecclesiastical censors, Dausquius retorts that the censors had merely glanced over, rather than critically examined, many things "in that most verbose vastness of Cartagena's volumes (only one other writer in the whole generation yielded to such a loquacity)." [140] Besides, Suarez himself has said of it, that this teaching could hardly be taught and believed in, "being contrary to the general canons of Scripture, and without having any convincing reason for it, or the great authority of the Church, or the approval of the Fathers." [141]

---

[137] *Binoctium*, p. 8.

[138] Ibid., pp. 9 & 13.

[139] Ibid., p. 108. Dausquius accuses Cartagena of "propudiosae adsertiones, coniecturae vanae, dubitationes infirmae" (p. 119), "sexcentas" of which can be found by anyone who reads him critically and dares to write his "Verriculum" (pp. 123-124).

[140] Ibid., p. 109.

[141] Suarez, III, q. 29, a. 2 sect. 2, quoted by Dausquius, op. cit., pp. 260–261.

PART TWO

THEMES IN CARTAGENA'S MARIOLOGY AND HIS USE OF SCRIPTURAL ARGUMENT

Having seen the life and works of Juan de Cartagena according to currently available information, we shall in this next part consider his teachings on the Blessed Virgin Mary as contained and expounded in his volumes of Marian homilies. We shall do so, not intending to make a compendium of everything the man ever wrote about her, but rather making a selection of his thoughts and examining them under one special aspect of particular interest to modern Mariology, namely, the way he bases these reflections on Sacred Scripture or, more exactly, the way he tries to bring Scripture into play in connection with these teachings. So far we have encountered only peripheral glimpses of Cartagena's mind. We now want to look deeper into it.

Partly due to ecumenism and partly because of the biblical movement, theologians today are striving harder than ever to assess objectively what Sacred Scripture affirms of Mary. The development of Catholic faith about her has been a bone of contention among theologians of various hues and/or denominations. Almost universal among the separated brethren is the claim that the Catholic dogmas of the Immaculate Conception and of the Assumption have no solid foundation in Scripture, that the proofs for these teachings have been forced out of the Sacred Books.[1] Even within Catholic theology

---

[1] Cf. F. W. Künneth, "Maria im Glaubenszeugnis der Kirche Evangelisch–Lutherischer Reformation," in *Maria in Sacra Scriptura*, VI (Romae, 1967), pp. 5–13; W. Cole, "Scripture and the Current Understanding of Mary among American Protestants," ibid., pp. 95–161; A. Braundenburg, "De mariologia ac cultu Mariae apud protestantes," in *De Mariologia et Oecumenismo* (Romae, 1962), pp. 479–516. Typical perhaps of the Protestant reaction to the two Marian dogmas of the Immaculate Conception and of the Assumption as far as Scripture is concerned are the words of Oxford's John N. D. Kelly, commenting on Vatican II's Constitution on the Church. While admitting the document's very good points,

nowadays there is a certain polarization over the question of Mary's
virginity in relation to Scripture.[2] These are some instances of the
more prominent issues in Mariology's present self–examination. But
they give us a frame of reference in studying the thoughts of Juan
de Cartagena. Moreover, he has treated the three principal Marian
doctrines of the Immaculate Conception, the Virginity and the
Assumption into heaven rather extensively in his *Homiliae Catholicae*,
so that investigating them and their presuppositions should provide
us with an adequate picture of his main Mariological positions and
tendencies. We plan therefore to present Cartagena's teachings on
the three above doctrines and to consider at the same time the
scriptural accompaniment he provides. Our interest is theological
and historical. There is no intention of resolving any conflict then
or now. We simply want to study and understand what the man
taught and wrote, and thereby to appreciate more properly our
own Mariology in the light of one of its forerunners.

Each of the three following chapters will first be concerned with
Cartagena's systematic teachings, and then with his use of Sacred
Scripture in support of them. We believe that understanding his
method of bringing Sacred Scripture into the deliberations of
his *Homiliae Catholicae* will explain Juan de Cartagena to us more
than anything else. Likewise, it should give us the chance to see
how warranted or not was the early charge that he was a *"scripturae
laevus interpres."* [3]

---

he could not help but note that "Trotzdem bestätigt die Konstitution die Unbefleckte Empfängnis und die leibliche Aufnahme der Jungfrau in den Himmel
und beruft sich dabei (wie man traurig feststellt) auf Kirchenväter späteren
Datums und zweifelhafter Autorität... jeder Hinweis darauf, daß sie eine einzi-
gartige und privilegierte Stellung inne hat, in ihrer Empfängnis oder in bezug auf
ihre jetzige Stellung unter den Heiligen Gottes, scheint ihnen [den Anglikanern]
weder aus der Schrift noch aus der richtig verstandenen Tradition beweisbar zu
sein." "Die Konstitution vom anglikanischen Standpunkt aus gesehen," in *De
Ecclesia*, II, ed. by G. Barauna (Freiburg, 1966), p. 528.

Incidentally, the series *Maria in Sacra Scriptura* (Romae, 1967) in its six
volumes of the papers given at the International Marian Congress of 1965 held
at Santo Domingo, Dominican Republic, is one of the major Catholic efforts to
evaluate anew the biblical data on Mary.

[2] Cf. Raymond E. Brown, "The Virginal Conception of Jesus," *Theological
Studies*, 33 (1972) 3–34; and *Zum Thema Jungfrauengeburt*, hrsg. K. Suso Frank
et al. (Stuttgart, 1970), which provide a good overview of the present discussion
with regard to Mary's virginity.

[3] Cf. above, p. 150.

CHAPTER FOUR

THE IMMACULATE CONCEPTION

Historically, the development in the consciousness of the Church of the doctrine on the absolute sinlessness of Mary was antedated by the earlier conviction that she conceived and gave birth to Christ virginally. And even within the stream of this line of development the realization that Mary is free from original sin came only afterwards as an expansion of the thesis regarding her holiness. We shall start, nonetheless, with the doctrine of the Immaculate Conception, as Juan de Cartagena did in the *HCSADM*, whose initial book is *"De Sacris Arcanis Aeternae Praedestinationis, ac Immaculatae Conceptionis Deiparae Virginis Mariae."* For the Immaculate Conception, Cartagena observes, is truly the beginning in any contemplation of the mysteries of Mary.[4]

I. SYSTEMATIC TEACHING

A. The Nature of The Immaculate Conception

1. *A brief historical background.* Before we go into Cartagena's effort to explain the doctrine of the Immaculate Conception systematically, i.e. as a teaching in harmony with other articles of faith, we have to situate him within the historical development of the doctrine. As already remarked, the question of Mary's freedom from original sin was only a later ramification of the earlier discussion about the sinlessness of her life.[5] The Pelagian controversy, which spotlighted original sin, gave rise to the corollary question whether Mary, believed to be perfectly holy, was free too from original sin. St. Augustine held that like any other human being she was born with the *"conditio nascendi,"* having been conceived in *"concupiscentia,"*

---

[4] "...si mysteria beatae Virginis contemplemur, sicut Assumptio gloriosa in coelum fuit eorum finis, et corona, ita et principia extitere immaculata eius conceptio, ac sancta eius Nativitas." *HCSADM*, lib. I, hom. VIII (I, 41b).

[5] Cf. A. Müller, "Maria," *LThK*, VII, pp. 28–29, on the historical discussion concerning Mary's sinlessness.

which effects the transmission of original sin.[6] With the exception of
the opposite opinion by St. Andrew of Crete,[7] the above teaching
of the Bishop of Hippo prevailed from the 5th to the 12th century,
with St. Anselm teaching that Mary sinned too in Adam as everybody
else.[8] In his letter of 1138 to the Canons of Lyon, St. Bernard chided
them for introducing there the Feast of the Conception of Mary,
which the Church ignores, reason disavows, and tradition disapproves.[9]

But it was precisely the liturgical feast celebrating the mystery
of Mary's conception that in spreading and gaining popularity gave
cause for another look at the whole question. Eadmer, Anselm's
close associate, came out openly advocating Mary's Immaculate
Conception in response to Bernard's negative stand.[10] In no time a
full–blown controversy was churning among the great Scholastics.
Peter Lombard, Alexander of Hales, Bonaventure, Albert the Great
and Thomas Aquinas espoused the common maculist teaching of the
day, which maintained, however, that Mary was entirely cleansed
from original sin before she became the Mother of Christ.[11] The Angelic Doctor formulated the argument against the Immaculate Conception thus, "If the soul of the Blessed Virgin had never been defiled
by original sin, this would derogate from the dignity of Christ as
Redeemer of all mankind." [12] William of Ware, Raymond of Lull
and Duns Scotus defended the immaculist position. Scotus produced
the novel solution of pre–redemption: while remaining a subject
to the universal law of original sin, Mary nonetheless was never af-
fected by it thanks to Christ's foreseen merits. This decisive twist

---

[6] Augustine, *Contra secundum Iuliani Responsionem Imperfectum Opus* 4,
122 (PL 45, 1417–1418) and 6, 22 (PL 45, 1553). For the contrary interpretation
of St. Augustine, see Ildefons Maria Dietz, OESA, "Ist die hl. Jungfrau nach
Augustinus 'Immaculata ab initio',", in *Virgo Immaculata*, IV (Romae, 1955),
pp. 61–112.

[7] Andreas of Creta, *Hom. I in Nativitate B. Mariae* (PG 97, 813C–816A).

[8] Anselm, *Cur Deus Homo*, 16 (*PL* 158, 416).

[9] Bernard, *Epistola 174: Ad Canonicos Lugdunenses de Conceptione S. Mariae*, n. 7 (*PL* 182, 335).

[10] Eadmer, *Tractatus de Conceptione Sanctae Mariae* (PL 159, 301–318,
esp. 304–306). Cf. Godfried Geenen, OP, "Eadmer, le premier théologien de l'Immaculée Conception," in *Virgo Immaculata*, V. pp. 90–115.

[11] Cf. X. Le Bachelet, "Immaculée Conception, IV. dans l'Eglise latine
après le Concile d'Ephèse," *DThC*, VII, col. 979–1218.

[12] Thomas Aquinas, *Summa Theol.*, III, q. 27, art. 2 ad 2.

to the problem was followed by a long and spirited debate between the Dominicans and the Franciscans.

Pope Sixtus IV, recognizing the growing general conviction of the faithful on the subject, forbade in 1483 the antagonists and the protagonists from branding each other as heretics.[13] This first pontifical intervention was favorable in a negative manner. It inspired the Council of Trent in 1546 to declare that it was not the intention of the Council to include the Virgin Mary in its decree on the universality of original sin.[14]

It was at this juncture, when the *pia sententia* was definitely gaining official sanction, although the discussion among the maculists and the immaculists was still going strong, that Juan de Cartagena entered the scene. He himself wrote that, notwithstanding the bitter opposition of its enemies, experience shows the teaching of the Immaculate Conception to be daily gaining strength and winning the adherence of the faithful and of the Church.[15] Cartagena personally experienced the more positive step taken by his friend Pope Paul V, who in mid–1617 prohibited altogether any attack against the teaching.[16] The following year, King Philip III pressed further and through his special delegation to the Holy See petitioned for a dogmatic definition of the doctrine.[17] The development of faith concerning Mary's freedom from original sin culminated years later in its definition by Pius IX on December 8, 1854 with the Bull *Ineffabilis Deus*.[18]

---

[13] *DS* 1425 f. Cf. Cherubinus Sericoli, OFM, "Ordo Franciscalis et Romanorum Pontificum Acta de Immaculata BMV Conceptione," in *Virgo Immaculata*, II, pp. 129–130.

[14] *DS* 1516. Cf. Sericoli, op. cit., pp. 131–132.

[15] "...si assertio immaculatam Virginis conceptionem astruens falsa fuisset opinio, aut humanum consilium, firmisque fundamentis non inniteretur, certe, tot fortissimis oppugnatoribus acriter illam labefactare conantibus, iam devicta, ac superata penitus corruisset; at, cum e contra certe accidat, experientia ipsa comprobante, ut in dies nova incrementa suscipiat, ac tenacius quotidie fidelium etiam doctissimorum mentibus inhaerescat, et Ecclesia Catholica magis, ac magis in illam propendeat..." Lib. I, hom. IV (I, 19b–20a).

[16] Sericoli, op. cit., pp. 133–134.

[17] Cf. Luke Wadding, *Legatio Philippi III et IV Catholicorum Hispaniae Regum ad SS. DD. NN. Paulum PP. V et Gregorium XV de Definienda Controversia Immaculatae Conceptionis B. Virginis Mariae per Illum et Revmum D.F. Antonium de Trejo Episc. Carthag. et ex Ordine Minorum* (Lovanii, 1624).

[18] *DS* 2803: "Declaramus, pronuntiamus et definimus doctrinam, quae tenet,

2. *Original sin and its transmission.* A fundamental preliminary
to the understanding of the Immaculate Conception is what original
sin means. Characteristically, Cartagena replies in a Scotistic way.
In creating man, God bestowed upon him a supernatural gift, called
original justice, which raised him to the supernatural order. Together
with this sanctifying grace were preternatural gifts inclining man towards God and keeping his body in subjection to the soul. The loss
of original innocence constitutes original sin; the formal element of
it thus is the deprivation of the original justice which is normally
due to man.[19]

Adam received original justice for himself and his descendants.
They should have received it as a natural inheritance. Its transmission was conditioned by a pact that created Adam not just the natural
but also the moral head of mankind. As our moral head the transmission to us of original justice depended upon his decision, so that his
decision became our own. When therefore Adam lost original justice,
we also lost it through him and in him, by an act virtually ours.[20]
Original sin, then, or the deprivation of original justice, is transmitted

---

beatissimam Virginem Mariam in primo instanti suae conceptionis fuisse singulari
omnipotentis Dei gratia et privilegio, intuitu meritorum Christi Jesu Salvatoris
humani generis, ab omni originalis culpae labe praeservatam immunem, esse a
Deo revelatam atque idcirco ab omnibus fidelibus firmiter constanterque creden-
dam." Cf. Vatican II, *Const. on the Church*, n. 56.

[19] "...peccatum originale non est privatio justitiae originalis materialiter
sumptae, prout erat quidam habitus, sed formaliter prout causabat rectitudinem
rationis, et subiectionem in ordine ad Deum..." Lib. VII, hom. XV (I, 827a).
Cf. Scotus, *Opus Oxoniense (Ordinatio)*, II, d. 32, n. 7: Vives edition, XIII, 310–311.

[20] "...Si ille [Adam] non pecasset, iustitia originalis omnibus eius posteris
absque exceptione donaretur, ita et carentia illius, ob peccatum primi parentis,
eos omnes tetigit..." Lib. I, hom. IV (I, 26a).

"Adam fuit constitutus a Deo caput suae posteritatis tam naturale, quam
morale: naturale quidem, quia omnes posteri ab eo erant per naturalem generationem propagandi: morale vero, quia in illius deliberatione constituit Deus tam
pro se, quam pro filiis suis permanentiam in statu innocentiae, vel culpabilem illius
amissionem. Unde in voluntate Adae moraliter constituit Deus voluntates omnium
posterorum: ex quo fit, ut ipso transgrediente divinum praeceptum, omnes in illo
transgressores facti sint; quoad sufficientiam quidem antequam generarentur;
quoad efficaciam vero, quando actu geniti sunt: tunc enim actu contrahunt peccatum ipsum originale, quod licet non fuerit voluntarium actu proprio, et formali,
vere tamen quasi virtualiter, et interpretative, in actu primi parentis, quatenus
in eius voluntate, ut in capite morali, omnium voluntates continebantur, et omnes
in illo unum erant." Lib. I, hom. IV (I, 20b). Cf. Scotus, *Opus Ox.*, II, d. 32, n. 15:
Vives, XIII, 318.

to us through natural propagation. But original sin is not some permanent corruption of our nature transmitted by an infected seed, or some physical taint communicated to the soul, an inherited concupiscence, as many Scholastics following Augustine affirmed.[21] If original sin involved an infected condition communicated through natural generation, it would present a difficulty to Mary's freedom from it, inasmuch as she physically descended from Adam. Hence, Scotus, following Anselm, denied that original sin means a physical corruption of our nature.[22] Original sin is a moral disordinateness, the absence of primordial justice and of the concomitant integrity moderating and harmonizing the whole man.

3. *The Immaculate Conception and preservative redemption.* The Immaculate Conception is essentially Mary's exemption from the consequence of Adam's sin. She has been granted the privilege of being preserved from original sin and having sanctifying grace bestowed upon her from the very first moment of her conception.[23] Duns Scotus' crucial distinction of *redemptio praeservativa* resolved the old quandary associated with the Pauline teaching that "sin entered the world through one man, and through sin death, and thus death has spread through the whole human race because everyone has sinned" (Rom 5, 12).[24] The objection, which was for a long time insurmountable, that the universal need of redemption precludes anybody's being exempted from original sin, was laid to rest by the admission that Mary too needed redemption and that her prerogative

---

[21] "...conceptio ex semine infecto, aut contactus animae cum carne infecta, non est causa formalis peccati originalis..." Lib. VII, hom. XV (I, 827a). Cf. ibid. (I, 826a–b).

On the teaching of Augustine that original sin is virtually found in the infected human body, see A. Michel, "Justice originelle, problème théologique," *DThC*, VIII, 2031–3.

[22] Scotus, *Opus Ox.*, III, d. 3, n. 18: Balić edition in *Ioannis Duns Scoti Theologiae Marianae Elementa* (Sibenici, 1933), p. 27. Cf. Michel, art. cit., 2033–2034. See also Anselm, *De Conceptu Virginali*, c. 3 (PL 158, 436).

[23] "Licet tamen B. Virgo, quia erat in Adamo, sicut caeteri, tanquam in radice, ac principio suo, naturali, et morali, peccato originali infici debebat, ob divinae tamen gratiae illam praeservantis mirabile antidotum, neutiquam infecta fuit." Lib. I, hom. V (I, 26b).

[24] Scotus, *Opus Ox.*, III, d. 3, n. 14: Balić, 35. Cf. C. Balić, "De significatione interventus Scoti in historia dogmatis I.C.," in *Virgo Immaculata*, VII-1, pp. 74–95.

lies in the fact that she was pre–redeemed. Mary is a daughter of Adam and therefore is subject to original sin and in need of redemption just like any other of his descendants. According to the distinction employed by Cartagena, Mary was a sinner *antecedenter*, i.e. she had by birth what should have made her contract original sin.[25] She did not escape the universal law which establishes that by reason of human generation everyone is born without original justice. But she was never a sinner *consequenter*, because although she had what was *ad sufficientiam* to contract original sin, this transmission of sin never took place *ad efficaciam* due to the grace of God preserving her from it.[26]

In the Schoolmen's mediate animation views, the body must be properly organized prior to the induction of the soul. The human individual begins at the point of animation. Denying the maculist

---

[25] "Ille dicitur peccator, et mortem incurrisse antecedenter, qui in suis proximis causis habuit omnia sufficientia, et requisita ad peccandum, sive ad incurrendam mortem peccati. Ille vero dicitur consequenter peccator, et mortuus, qui de facto peccatum contraxit; primo ergo modo concedi potest, quod Beata Virgo peccavit antecedenter, quia quatenus fuit propagata ex commixtione maris, et foeminae, habuit sufficientiam causam ad contrahendum peccatum originale, et hoc est, fuisse peccatricem, et mortuam antecedenter; sed inde non licet inferre; Virgo Maria antecedenter contraxit originale peccatum, ergo de facto contraxit..." Lib. VII, hom. XV (I, 815a–b). Cf. Lib. I, hom. XIX (I, 118a–b). Scotus used a similar distinction. Cf. *Opus Ox.*, II, d. 32, nn. 9 & 10: Vives, XIII, 313.

[26] "...quod de contractione debiti, et peccati originalis, possumus loqui, vel quoad sufficientiam, vel quoad efficaciam... sicut ergo non omnes vivificati sunt quoad efficaciam, ut patet de infidelibus, sed solum quoad sufficientiam, ita etiam verificatur, quod in Adam omnes mortui sunt, et quod omnes debitum peccati originalis contraxerunt, quoad sufficientiam, quoad efficaciam vero, omnes qui gratia Christi non praeveniuntur; Beata autem Virgo quia praeventa fuit, contraxit debitum illud quoad sufficientiam, quia peccatum Adam, ut peccatum capitis sufficiens erat, ut in eam, tanquam in membrum refunderetur; quoad efficaciam vero nullum reipsa contraxit, in se ex divinae gratiae munere illam praeservantis..." Lib. VII, hom. XV (I, 827b).

"...peccatum originale non est privatio justitiae originalis materialiter sumptae, prout quidem habitus, sed formaliter, prout causabat rectitudinem rationis, et subiectionem in ordine ad Deum; haec autem rectitudo etiam tribuitur per gratiam: unde licet B. Virgo, quantum est ea vi suae propagationis, fuerit concepta obnoxia privationi praedictae rectitudinis, de facto vero non fuit concepta cum tali privatione, sed cum gratia, quae illam impedivit." Ibid. (I, 827a–b).

Cartagena employs yet another distinction: "...solus Christus immunis fuit a peccato originali principaliter, sed beatissima Virgo minus principaliter; Christus de iure, Beata autem Virgo de facto, non de iure." Lib. I, hom. XIX (I, 118b).

contention that there must have been two successive states in the soul of Mary by which she was at one time in need of sanctification and at another time sanctified, Cartagena holds that there was no moment during and following her animation when Mary was ever with sin. In the order of our ideas, various states could be made out at the moment of animation: the moment of the union of the body and soul, the moment of the emergence of Mary's person without any moral connotation, i.e. neither with sin nor with grace, and the moment when she has grace through God's intervention.[27] But these stages are *signa rationis* and do not indicate real segments of time. They show rather a twofold relation in Mary at the first instant of her existence: that of a daughter of Adam because of which she is subject to the common law; and the other, that of God's privileged one, exempted from the consequences of the common law.

The foreseen merits of Christ's sacrifice preserved and redeemed

---

[27] "Ad hanc obiectionem respondeo, admittendo tertium membrum praefatae divisionis, nimirum quod sanctificatio fuit in ipsa animatione; nam in instanti temporis praedictae animationis considerantur plura instantia naturae: In primo est ipsa informatio, et unio animae, et corporis: In secundo instanti ex unione, et informatione resultat persona Virginis, quae vere est filia Adae secundum seminalem propagationem; et sic consideratur Virgo sine peccato, et sine gratia; in tertio vero instanti, seu signo rationis, habuit gratiam, habitura tamen peccatum, si sibi dimitteretur, et a Deo non praeveniretur... in illo primo instanti naturae, seu signo rationis, in quo Virgo intelligitur Adae filia per abstractionem praecisivam, quae est sine mendacio, intelligitur non intellecta gratia et iustitia: Nec obstat obiicere: ergo intelligitur non habens gratiam, nec iustitiam; negandam enim est consequentia; nam in consequenti est praecisio, et divisio cum mendacio, ut, cum considero in homine rationalitatem tantum per abstractionem, tunc non considero in illo animalitatem, non tamen inde recte infertur: ergo considero hominem non habentem animalitatem: Et cum rursus obiicis; in illo instanti Virgo non intelligitur iusta, et sancta; ergo intelligitur, iniusta, et peccatrix: Nego consequentiam; sicut non sequitur: In hac mensa non est papyrus, alba; ergo est papyrus non alba: Dico igitur, quo esse personale Virginis praecedit omne esse morale illius, nec proxime capax gratiae, neque peccati, in sequenti vero instanti, quando secundum legem ordinariam habitura erat, peccatum habuit de facto gratiam praeservantem illam ab omni labe peccati ex meritis Christi Domini praevisi." Lib. VII, hom. XV (I, 838b–839a). Cf. Scotus, *Opus Ox.*, III, d. 3, n. 14: Balić, 34. It was with this distinction between the priority in the order of nature and priority in the order of ideas or in the logical order that Scotus was able to break the deadlock as to whether Mary was sanctified before or after or a little after the infusion of her soul into her body. He restated the problem thus: Could Mary have been redeemed *"primo instanti conceptionis?"*

Mary from original sin.[28] The privilege of her Immaculate Conception
did not derogate from the dignity of Christ, the universal redeemer.
In fact, redeeming her by preservation is a more perfect way of redemption.[29] Preventing an offense is a more perfect form of mediation than reconciling after the offense. To be preserved from original
sin, Mary actually needed much more of the grace of God.[30] For preserving her from sin in view of Christ's foreseen merits implies a far
greater grace, just as it means a far greater perfection of redemption.

In comparison with the rest of mankind, Mary was redeemed
by Christ in a manner all her own. He offered himself to the Father,
in order to attain the remission of our sins; he died for Mary, in order
to keep from her all sin and to endow her with all graces.[31] And from

---

[28] See the last sentence of the above quotation from Cartagena. And:
"Constanter asserimus, – quod licet peccatum primi parentis ob rationes dictas,
habuerit sufficientiam ad maculandum beatam Virginem, sicut et reliquos posteros
Adae, re tamen ipsa non habuit efficaciam inferendi ei maculam aliquam: quia
filius Dei praevidens illam ipsius matrem futuram, divina sua gratia, ne inficere-
tur, illam praemunivit." Lib. I, hom. IV, (I, 21a).

[29] "...cum Christus Dominus esset humani generis Redemptor perfectissimus... ad eundem pertinebat, ut aliquod, ut minimum individuum naturae praeservaret a peccato originali; tum quia ille est perfectissimus redemptor, cui non
deficit praestantissimus modus redimendi, sicut et medicandi; at praestantissimus
modus est per praeservationem..." Lib. I, hom. XVIII (I, 95b).

"...excellentior modus medicandi, est praeservare a morbo, quam ab illo
sanare... Beata autem Virgo, nisi specialiter praeservaretur, exposita esset periculo incidendi in varia peccata... et ideo indiguit Christo Domino, ut medico praeservante." Lib. VII, hom. XV (I, 834b). Cf. Lib. I, hom. XVII (I, 91a).

Scotus' own words about the matter are: "...ex hoc quod Filius Dei fuit
redemptor universalis, sequitur quod fuit perfectissimus mediator: ergo habuit
perfectissimum modum mediandi, quem potuit habere respectu excellentissimae
personae sub ipso. Sed actus perfectissimus praeservat ab omni peccato, quia
nullus perfecte placat pro aliquo nisi praeveniat offensam, si posset; sed si culpa
aliquando inesset, non ita perfecte placasset Christus, sicut si praevenisset offensam, quia perfectius placet ille, si praeveniat ne alius umquam offendat, quam
si post offensam quod alius remittat." *Reportatio*, III, d. 3, n. 5: Balić, 48.

[30] "Solum enim ostendit Virginem indiguisse magis hac gratia Dei, et ideo
maiori misericordia fuisse praeventem, et aliquid magis concedendum esse Matri,
quam servis." Lib. I, hom. XVIII (I, 98a). Cf. Scotus, *Opus Ox.*, III, d. 3, n. 14:
Balić, 35. See also Edward Schillebeeckx, *Mary, Mother of the Redemption* (London, 1964), pp. 67–70.

[31] "...respondeo, Christum Dominum obtulisse Deo Patri seipsum in sacrificium pro beata Virgine, et pro nobis; sed diversa intentione, quia in ordine ad
nos intendebat remissionem peccatorum, in ordine vero ad beatam Virginem
gratiarum, et coelestium donorum copiam." Lib. VII, hom. XV (I, 834a).

the point of view of redemption *per modum emptionis*, Mary was also ransomed by Christ, but not because there was positively any sin found in her as in our case, but simply because having been sold out to the devil in Adam she had in the order of nature no claim on God's grace.[32] Her justification then lies in the fact that in the state of nature she did not have original justice and from this state Christ raised her to the state of grace and justice. It is not essential to justification that the one to be redeemed be positively in a state of injustice or sin; it suffices that he be without original justice.[33] The satisfaction that Christ did for her was to free her from the debt of sin, extinguishing in her the necessity of contracting sin.[34] And this brings us to another important element in Mary's privilege of being immaculately conceived.

4. *Debitum contrahendi peccatum originale.* By the end of the 16th century the main weight of the controversy about the Immaculate Conception had shifted to the finer issue of the *debitum*, from the question of the possibility to the question of the mode and manner. The terminology was introduced by Cajetan to distinguish between

---

[32] "...quod B. Virginem esse alienatam a Deo, potest sumi dupliciter, uno modo positive per peccatum ei inherens, et sic nunquam fuit alienata; alio modo negative, quatenus pro aliquo priori poterat intelligi non pertinere ad Deum iure gratiae, scilicet pro illo priori, quo esse naturae processit in illa ad esse gratiae; concedo item, omnes fuisse venditos in Adam, sed inde non efficitur, B. Virginem fuisse venditam in seipsa, sed in Adam solum; et haec duo sufficiunt, ut in toto rigore dicatur empta per sanguinem Christi, neque aliquod aliud genus alienationis requiritur ad praedictam emptionem..." Lib. VII, hom. XV (I, 833a–b).

[33] "Item ad illud de iustificatione, respondeo, ad rationem essentialem iustificationis solum requiri, quod de non iusto fiat iustus, itaque non opus est, ad rationem iustificationis, ut terminus a quo illius sit positiva iniustitia subiecti, a quo recedat, sed sufficit negativa; Beata autem Virgo de non iusta negative pro priori naturae, quo esse naturale illius praecessit infusionem gratiae, facta est iusta per infusionem illius; quod autem de facto, quotquot iustificantur, recedant ab iniustitia, est mere per accidens ad rationem iustificationis, sicut per accidens est ad id, quod dealbatur, quod prius fuerit nigrum; nam motus dealbationis non exigebat nigredinem pro termino a quo sed solam negationem albedinis in subiecto dealbando." Lib. VII, hom. XV (I, 833b). The author understands mediation in the same manner. Cf. ibid. (I, 834a).

[34] "...ad illud vero de satisfactione, respondeo, satisfactionem esse pro debito, beata autem Virgo debitum habuit in se, vel in Adam contrahendi peccatum originale, et Christus Dominus obtulit satisfactionem pro hoc debito; liberans illam de solutione illius..." Lib. VII, hom. XV (I, 833a).

original sin and the debt of original sin or the necessity of contracting it, but subdistinctions have proliferated to such an extent, that the *lis de verbo* is still going on today.[35] At the time of Juan de Cartagena, the initial insistence by most theologians on the *debitum* in Mary was already counting its days. A definite maximalism with regards to her was evolving. Cartagena himself must have followed with interest the developments in Toledo, where in 1615 a group of Franciscan theologians defended the thesis that Mary did not contract even the debt of original sin. Denounced before the Inquisition, the Friars Minor were vindicated; they were told the thesis could be upheld.[36] This opinion eventually reigned during the 17th century up to the 18th, only to fade away again.

At the turning point of the controversy was the question: from what would Mary have been redeemed, if she were conceived without sin at all? Like a pivot in the whole discussion is the concept of *debitum*. It explains how she was also a "sinner" in need of redemption, hence specifying whence she was saved, and how she belonged to the fallen human race, yet without contracting original sin. What we have seen of Cartagena's teaching shows the question of debt to be part and parcel of his Mariology. He defines it as the necessity of contracting the guilt of the offense of our foreparent, or the impotence to avoid being contaminated by it.[37] The debt is a penalty, not itself a guilt; it is the penalty that man left by himself cannot help but contract sin.[38] Because she is a daughter of Adam, Mary falls

---

[35] Cf. "Disputatio circa debitum peccati in B.V. Maria," in *Virgo Immaculata*, XI, pp. 456–499; and Pacific Hug, OFM, "The Modern Challenge against the Franciscan Tradition as having taught an Immaculate Conception Incompatible with Redemption," ibid., pp. 365–413.

[36] On this development, see Pedro de Alcantara, "La Redención Preservativa y el Débito Remoto," *Salmanticensis*, 1 (1954) 301–327.

[37] "...huiusmodi debitum formaliter loquendo nihil aliud est quam infirmitas, vel impotentia vitandi contractionem culpae, seu necessitas contrahendi illam inducta per voluntatem Primi Parentis..." Lib. VII, hom. XVI (I, 845b).

Pedro de Alcantara rather negatively writes of Cartagena on the question: "Primeramente no presenta en sitio alguno la definición del débito, mas la supuesta en el desarrollo de su doctrina..." "La Inmaculada concepcion segun las doctrinas de Juan de Cartagena..." in *Virgo Immaculata*, p. 217.

[38] "...debitum contrahendi peccatum originale poena est, non culpa, alioquin prius natura, quam quis haberet peccatum originale, praehaberet aliud genus culpae; cum debitum contrahendi culpam originalem, praeintelligatur ad actualem contractionem illius..." Lib. VII, hom. XV (I, 827b).

also under the common law, by which in view of our first parent's sin she should be born deprived of original justice. The force of this law applies to her. But the law never went into effect in her case due to God's intervention, by which she was preserved from incurring the guilt.[39] It is from the certainty of inheriting original sin, if she were left to herself, that Christ saved and redeemed her.[40] And Mary had this *debitum* in herself (*debitum proximum*, in later terminology) and not just in Adam (*debitum remotum*), as some would claim; for she was in herself redeemed by Christ and not in Adam.[41] Cartagena is fully aware of the opinion holding that Mary did not even have the debt to contract original sin and that she was exempted from the general law itself.[42] But he finds the position of Suárez more compelling, that Mary herself had the *debitum* and that it was the prevention of it from taking full effect which constitutes her preservation from sin by God's grace.[43] We shall see below more of this question in connection with Mary's predestination.

---

[39] "Ab hac tamen communi lege omnipotentia Dei Matrem suam excipere dignata est: In instanti enim Conceptionis, in quo, iuxta legem latam originalis macula inesse debebat, impedita fuit per infusionem gratiae, quae peccatum nullum abstulit, sed vetuit, ne inesset." Lib. I, hom. XIV (I, 72b). Cf. Lib. I, hom. IV (I, 21a); hom. VI (I, 30a-b); hom. VIII (I, 42a); Lib. VII, hom. XV (I, 827a-b).

[40] "...duplicem esse modum redemptionis, quorum primus supponit captivitatem; secundus, et perfectior supponit tantum debitum incurrendi captivitatem; Beata ergo Virgo ex vi peccati primi Parentis supposito pacto Dei, licet actu non fuerit sub peccati originalis captivitate, habuit tamen debitum incurrendi illam, et quia de facto praeservata fuit, ex meritis Christi, ne incideret in talem captivitatem, ideo absolute, et simpliciter fuit redempta per Christum." Lib. VII, hom. XV (I, 828a). Cf. Lib. I, hom. XVII (I, 90a).

[41] "Genus hoc debiti constituebat illam captivam non solum in Adamo, sed in seipsam, quia debitum illud erat quaedam obligatio moralis propria ipsius Virginis; omnia autem obligatio est quoddam genus captivitatis, et ideo indiguit redemptione non solum in Adamo, sed in seipsa." Lib. VII, hom. XV (I, 828b). Cf. Lib. VII, hom. XVI (I, 844b).

At this time and during the Alcalá–Toledo debates, the distinction between *debitum proximum* and *debitum remotum* was not operative yet. Cf. Alejandro de Villalmonte, OFM, "La Inmaculada y el Debito del Peccado," *Verdad y Vida*, XII (1954), esp. pp. 57–58 & 60, where Cartagena is cited to exemplify this period.

[42] See Lib. I, hom. V (I, 25a–26a). Cartagena also says that such an exemption of Mary from the *debitum* itself is not impossible for God. Cf. Lib. I, hom. XVIII (I, 93a).

[43] "Mirabili, ac salutifera illa confectione aquae, et sanguinis ex latere eius

B. Reasons for The Immaculate Conception

In the development of faith in the mystery of Mary's Immaculate Conception, the centuries–old opposition against it was principally on account of the absence of any explicit scriptural testimony for the doctrine. Moreover, St. Paul's unmistakable teaching that all men sinned and that Christ redeemed all men seemed to deny completely any such privilege of being immaculately conceived. As we

---

in Cruce fluentis, velut probatissima theriaca, ab aeterno praevisam, futuram Matrem suam inunxit, atque hac ratione illam praeservavit, non a debito contrahendi maculam originalem, sed ab actuali huius maculae contractione." Lib. I, hom. V (I, 27a). On the opinion of Suárez, cf. Jose Bover, SJ, "Posición de Suárez en la controversia concepcionista," in *Virgo Immaculata*, XI, pp. 276–277.

Pedro de Alcantara, art. cit., p. 219, makes it sound that Cartagena takes no position regarding this controversy. It is most surprising too that Alcantara, ibid., pp. 219–220, fails to take Cartagena in context and sees the following words as a denial of the *debitum* in Mary: "...non dissimiliter in proposito, cum mors peccati originalis ex Adamo primo parente ortum habuerit, omnibus eius filiis per naturalem propagationem ab ipso descendentibus, mors illa imputatur, tanquam praevaricationis in ipso capite contentis; at Beata Virgo apertissime probat sibi non imputandam esse mortem peccati, quia antequam essent abyssi originalis culpae, etiam in aeterna permissione, permittente omnes ab Adam naturali via propagatos inci, iam ipsa in mente Dei concepta, et in divina voluntate praeordinata erat: atque hinc est, quod licet in profundo illo abysso ac profluvio originalis peccati submersi fuerint omnes ab Adamo progeniti... beatissima vero Genitrix ex speciali Filii sui beneficio, in conceptione sua submergi non potuit." Lib. I, hom. II (I, 14a). Cartagena is here clearly saying that the *guilt* of original sin, the death *de facto* inherited by all the other descendants of Adam, cannot be imputed to Mary because of special grace. The author is not concerned here at all about the *debitum*, but simply with the question whether Mary had original sin or not.

Cartagena's attitude on the matter is explicit. After explaining the teaching of Catharinus and Galatinus — that Mary could have been exempted from the pact with Adam and therefore would be without any debt at all — he goes on to say: "Verum licet omnia praedicta parte praecedenti quandam veritatis speciem prae se ferre videantur; *solidiorem* tamen doctrinam alii (ut sibi visum est) amplectentes asserunt nihil prorsus derogare immaculatae Virginis Conceptioni, nec eximat eius puritati ac sanctitati, quod in Adamo peccaverit et debitum incurrendi peccatum originale in illo, imo et in se ipsa contraxerit, quia hoc non est ipsam pro aliquo instanti etiam rationis in se habuisse maculam peccati, sed solum primum eius Parentem pecasse, in quo tanquam in capite, naturali et morali ipsa continebatur." Lib. VII, hom. XVI (I, 844b). Italics added.

Alcantara refers to Lib. I, hom. V (I, 25a–28b) as showing Cartagena's "ambiguity." The homily is devoted to expounding the two opinions: with or without the *debitum* for Mary. Two columns are given to explain the *sine debito*

have seen, the deadlock was only broken by Scotus' subtle distinction of pre–redemption. That explains *how* Mary has been redeemed and yet conceived immaculately. The *why*, the theological reasons, consequently crystallized into more coherence and credibility. Cartagena has quoted from Pseudo–Augustine regarding a similar situation about Mary's assumption into heaven, on which Sacred Scripture is also silent. In such a case he implies, theological reasons gain importance. The truth itself becomes the authority, and without it no authority is valid.[44] Let us investigate then Cartagena's presentation of the reasons clarifying the mystery of the Immaculate Conception.

1. *Mary's predestination*. First of all, Cartagena frames his theological reasoning for the mystery within the context of Mary's predestination. In the so–called Golden Age of Franciscan Mariology following the Council of Trent and extending up to the beginning of the 18th century, the teaching concerning her predestination was one of the dominant themes. She is seen as included in the primacy of Christ's own predestination. Duns Scotus above all refined the thesis that Christ, the God–Man, was predestined first and absolutely in the divine plan of creation; Christ would have become man, even if Adam had not sinned. It would be tantamount to making Christ's

---

position, and five to the *cum debito* side. Cartagena demonstrably keeps his distance from the first by prominently repeating *"inquiunt"*. In propounding the second view, on the other hand, he slips into the first person. Moreover, he unmistakably expresses his personal position in favor of the latter in Lib. VII, hom. XVI (I, 845b–846a).

Pedro de Alcantara is to repeat this misinterpretation of Cartagena's teaching in his article "La corredencion y el débito según los teólogos salmantinos," in *Virgo Inmaculata*, XI, p. 251, in the footnote. Making the same mistake is Jean–Fr. Bonnefoy, OFM, "Marie indemne de toute tache du péché originel," ibid. ,p. 27. But it seems that this misreading of Cartagena started rather early. Bonaventura Belluti, OFMConv. († 1676), in his book *Disputationes de Incarnatione Dominica ad Mentem Doctoris Subtilis* (Catanae, 1645), p. 275, also claimed that Cartagena among others taught Mary's exemption not just from original sin, but also from the debt to contract it. Cf. Luigi Macali, OFMConv., "La Dottrina dell'Immacolata nei Grandi Scotisti OFMConv. dei Secoli XVI–XIX," in *Virgo Immaculata*, VII–2, p. 67.

[44] "Ubi Scriptura divina nihil de illa commemorat; inquirendum est, quid conveniat rationi; fiatque ipsa ratio, auctoritas, sine qua nec est, nec valet auctoritas." Pseudo–Augustinus, *De Assumptione Beatae Mariae Virginis*, c. 2 (PL 40, 1144), quoted by Cartagena in Lib. I, hom. XVIII (I, 92b). The author's citation differs somewhat from the wording of Migne's edition.

divine predestination to glory dependent upon Adam and his foreseen
fall into sin, if we were to assert that Christ's only purpose in the
incarnation were the redemption of the human race.[45] Besides, such
an assumption would not be in accord with the theological principle
that in the intention of God the worthier objective takes precedence
over lesser goals.[46] The Subtle Doctor himself, however, had not
worked out a Mariological corollary to this primacy of Christ's predestination. But his followers did. John of Bassoly († 1347) and Francis of Mayron († 1328), for example, both claimed that Christ's
predestination includes that of his mother. For even if Adam had
not sinned, she would have still been the predestined Mother of God,
just as Christ would have still become a man, even if there had been
no fall.[47]

Cartagena likewise holds Mary's primary predestination to glory
as the Mother of Christ.[48] Christ is the first of the predestined; the

---

[45] "...sed non propter illam solam [redemptionem] videtur Deus praedesti-
nasse illam animam ad tantam gloriam, cum illa redemptio sive gloria animae
redimendae non sit tantum bonum, quantum est illa gloria animae Christi; nec
est verisimile tam summum bonum in entibus esse tantum occasionatum propter
minus bonum solum, nec est verisimile ipsum prius praeordinasse Adam ad tantum
bonum quam Christum, quod tamen sequeretur. Immo et absurdius ulterius sequeretur, scilicet quod praedestinando Adam ad gloriam, prius praevidisset ipsum
casurum in peccatum quam praedestinasset Christum ad gloriam, si praedestinatio
illius animae tantum esset pro redemptione aliorum." Scotus, *Opus Ox.*, III, d. 3:
Balić, 6–7. Cf. Meinolf Mückshoff, OFMCap., "Die mariologische Prädestination
im Denken der franziskanischen Theologie," *Franziskanische Studien*, 39 (1957)
346–356.

[46] "...universaliter enim ordinate volens prius videtur velle hoc quod est
fini propinquius, et ita sicut prius vult gloriam alicui quam gratiam, ita etiam
inter praedestinatos, quibus vult gloriam, ordinate prius videtur velle gloriam illi,
quem vult esse proximum fini, et ita huic animae prius vult gloriam quam alicui
alteri animae velit gloriam, et prius cuilibet alteri gloriam et gratiam quam prae-
videat illi opposita istorum habiturum [i.e. peccatum et damnationem]." Scotus,
Opus Ox., loc. cit.: Balić, 5. For a modern critique of the thesis on Mary's predestination, see A. Müller, "Marias Stellung und Mitwirkung im Christusereignis,"
in *Mysterium Salutis*, III–2 (Einsiedeln, 1969), pp. 422–426. See also M. J. Nicolas, "De transcendentia Matris Dei," in *Maria et Ecclesia*, II (Romae, 1959),
pp. 73–87.

[47] Cf. Mückshoff, op. cit., pp. 435–437. Suárez holds Mary's absolute predestination, *De Mysteriis Vitae Christi*, disp. I, s. 3, n. 2 & 4; III, 2, 1–5, 8: Vives, XIX.

[48] "Ratio etiam idipsum confirmat: Nam, cum Deus decrevit filium suum
ex Beata Virgine futurum esse hominem, consequens erat, nihil immediatius prae-

second is Mary.[49] In fact, the two are inseparable, inasmuch as mother
and son are co–relative: the preordination of the son means at the
same time preordaining the mother.[50] By reason of this immediacy,
as the Mother of God, Mary's relation to Christ touches the order of
the hypostatic union.[51] The Incarnation is so intrinsically linked up
with the divine motherhood, that Mary similar to the human nature
of Christ shares too the grace of the Word Incarnate. "She approaches
Christ both in the order of nature and in the order of grace." [52]
Thus she surpasses the predestination of any other creature *"prioritate rationis et dignitatis."* [53]

On the basis of her special predestination, Cartagena then
proceeds to reason to Mary's Immaculate Conception.[54] He does so

---

destinare, quam Matrem ex cuius thalamo tamquam sponsus processurus erat."
Lib. I, hom. II (I, 7b). Cf. Vat. II, *Const. on the Church*, n. 61.

Juan Serrano, OFM († 1637), in his book *De Immaculata Prorsusque Pura
Sanctissimae semperque Virginis Genitricis Dei Mariae Conceptione* (Neapoli,
1635), lib. IV, c. 10, p. 490, practically repeats Cartagena in this: "...quod Deus
decrevit Verbum divinum futurum hominem, nihil videatur immediatius prae-
destinasse post Christus, quam matrem ex cuius utero purissimo tamquam sponsus
procederet de thalamo suo." Quoted by Mückshoff, op. cit., p. 481.

[49] "Inter hos ergo praedestinatos Christus Dominus... primum locum obtinet... Secundum vero sanctissima eius Genitrix, quos divina omnipotentia adeo
exaltare dignata est, ut ille ad divinae, et increatae filiationis celsitudinem, haec
ad Dei Matris culmen pertingeret." Lib. I, hom. II (I, 7a).

[50] "...cum Mater, et Filius relativa sint, mutuo se respicientia, non poterat
praeordinari filius, non praeordinando simul et matrem." Lib. I, hom. II (I,
8a). Juan de Serrano closely reechoes here Cartagena; cf. Mückshoff, op. cit., p. 482.

[51] "...quia dignitas Matris Dei adeo praecellens est, ut suo modo pertineat
ad ordinem unionis hypostaticae naturae humanae cum Verbo divino, cum Ma-
ternitate haec ita illam intrinsice respiciat, et ab ea dependeat, ut omnino repug-
net, esse Matrem Dei unione hypostatica deficiente." Lib. I, hom. II (I, 7b–8a).
Again, the Spanish Observant, Juan Serrano, is here dependent on Cartagena.
Cf. P. Alcantara, art. cit., p. 252, and Mückshoff, op. cit., p. 481.

The idea that Mary belongs to the same order of the hypostatic union as
the humanity of Christ is rather widespread during the time of Cartagena. Bernardine of Sienna taught it too. Cf. Mückshoff, ibid., p. 448. See Nicolas, art. cit.

[52] "...cum Mater Dei sit, quae magis accedit ad Christum, tam in esse naturae, quam gratiae... non est, cur dubitemus, praedestinationem Virginis fuisse
immediatam praedestinationi Christi." Lib. I, hom. II, (I, 8a).

[53] "In eo tamen beatissimae Virginis singularis electio, cuiusque purae creaturae praedestinationem valde excelluit, quod licet absque propriis meritis fuerit,
prioritate tamen rationis, et dignitatis longo intervallo reliquas superavit." Lib. I,
hom. II (I, 6b).

[54] The initial book of the *HCSADM* is significantly entitled: "De sacris

on two counts: her predestination as the Mother of God and as Christ's
coadiutrix.

2. *Mother of God.* For Juan de Cartagena the fact that Mary
is the natural Mother of God is the principle and the source of all
her graces and prerogatives.[55] And if the evangelists are silent about
her praises, they have anyway already said everything in principle
in stating that Jesus was born of her. For in this one verity is contained all her infinite honors.[56] From this Mariological principle of
Mary as the Mother of God the author sees the reason why she has
been immaculately conceived. It is but fitting and proper that the
predestined woman through whom God would be taking flesh in
becoming man should be most pure and holy, worthy of her exalted
function and preserved from original sin.[57] She surpasses by the

---

arcanis aeternae praedestinationis, ac immaculatae conceptionis Deiparae Virginis Mariae." And the book's second homily, following the introductory one, goes
by the heading: "Ostenditur Beatissimam Virginem inter omnes puras Creaturas
primum, ac principem locum tenere in divina praedestinatione, ex quo illibata
eius Conceptio comprobatur..." Lib. I, hom. II, (I, 5b–6a).

[55] "...ita titulus ille augustissimus (*Matris Dei naturalis*) *principium* est,
et *origo*, ex quo prudenter inferimus, praeclarissima gratiarum munera Virgini
fuisse donata." Lib. I, hom. III (I, 15a). Italics added.

[56] "Mirantur non pauci, Evangelistas omnes beatissimae Virginis ortum,
mortem, et in coelum Assumptionem, et alia similia silentio praeteriisse... Verum
id divino consilio factum, non est ambigendum, quia huiusmodi silentium plenius
et cumulatius quam quaecumque foecundissima dicendi facultas B. Virginis stu-
pendam excellentiam commendat... specialia Virginis praeconia Evangelistae
siluere, contenti dixisse, quod ex ea natus fuerit Iesus, quod infinita in se claudit
praeconia." Lib. II, hom. II (I, 133b–134a).

Alfonso Salmeron had said something similar: "...satis potest dici scriptum
quodcumque privilegium Virginis in eo quod vocat eam Matrem Christi." *Commentarium in Evangelia et Actus Apostolorum*, XI, (Coloniae, 1604), tr. 37, pp.
303b–304a.

[57] "Cum igitur beatissima Virgo fuit electa a Deo ad praestantissimum et
excellentissimum omnium Matris Dei officium: ipsa enim tribuit Verbo divino
carnem et sanguinem ut ex ea Deus homo fieret, consequens est, copiosissime ei
praestitisse omnem sufficientiam et idoneitatem ad tantum munus recte geren-
dum. Unde, si Ioannem Baptistam, quia Praecursorem adventus sui in carne praee-
legerat, in utero materno sanctificavit; eam, quam praedestinavit in Matrem, suae
carnis genetricem, nonne par erat, ut excellentiore sanctificationis genere (cuiusmodi est peccati originalis praeservatio) illam donaret? Ut enim *decuit*, naturam,
quam Creator sibi hypostatice uniebat, omni divinorum charismatum genere ple-
nissimam esse; ita, et *decebat, quam Virginem in matrem elegit, coelestibus donis
repleri.*" Lib. I, hom. III (I, 15a). Italics added.

grace of her maternal dignity all the angels and even Adam in the state of original justice; it stands to reason that Mary was created too in grace and enjoys God's sanctification from the first moment of her conception.[58] And, insofar as a son shares in any honor or dishonor of his parents, divine wisdom chose for Christ a mother without any stain whatsoever.[59] The underlying line of reasoning in all this is evidently the Scotistic *"potuit–decuit–ergo–fecit"* argumentation foreshadowed by St. Anselm's words: "It was appropriate, that the Virgin should be endowed with that purity, any greater than which below God is inconceivable." [60]

If on the strength of her motherhood the Fathers attributed so many privileges to Mary, like her immunity from actual sin and the incorruptibility of her body, a conclusion to be drawn *a fortiori* (i.e., based on Scotus' solution of pre–redemption) is that on the fundament of her same motherhood she is exempt from original sin. Around the 8th century, for example, Pseudo–Augustine reasoned that corruption of the body would be unworthy of Mary's dignity, and that it is to her maternal honor to be preserved from any such bodily degradation.[61] Cartagena leads on, "If Augustine judges that putre-

---

[58] "Habet enim hoc, hierarchicus ordo... ut inferiorum perfectiones, ac virtutes sint in superioribus praestantiori modo repositae. Unde, cum intra latitudinem, et ambitum ordinis puras creatuas, consequens est perfectiones tam Angelorum, quam hominum excellentiori modo in ea reperiri. Constat autem, non solum Angelos, sed et primos nostros parentes in gratia fuisse creatos, ita ut simul Deus in eis esset condens naturam, et largiens gratiam; satis ergo rationi consonum est, ut dicamus beatam Virginem ab instanti suae Conceptionis gratam Deo extitisse." Lib. I, hom. III (I, 15a). Cf. Suárez, op. cit., IV, 1, 4 & XVIII, 2, 2–4, 6. Cf. Vat. II, *Const. on the Church*, n. 53.

[59] "Quia ergo si B. Virgo originalis culpae labe fuisset deturpata, adhuc sanctificata, peccati illa infamia remansisset, ob quam semper de ea posset dici, semel in peccatum fuisse prolapsam, et inimicam Dei, et odio habitam illi; ideo ad sapientissimam Dei providentiam spectabat, ut quam in matrem elegerat, a peccati originalis macula omnino praeservaret. Si enim nullus sanae mentis, cui fingeremus optionem dari, ut matrem sibi eligeret, minime alicuius infamiae nota inquinatam acciperet: ut quid, increatam Dei sapientiam, matrem sibi elegisse putabimus originalis peccati litura deformatam, cum Angelis, et primis parentibus puriorem assumere facile potuerit?" Lib. I, hom. III (I, 15b).

[60] Anselm, *De Conceptu Virginali*, c. 18 (*PL* 158, 451), quoted too by Scotus, *Opus Ox.*, III, q. 1: Balić, 20. At the same time Scotus referred to the similar basic attitude of Augustine: "Cum de peccatis agitur de Maria nullam volo habere quaestionem." *De Natura et Gratia*, c. 36, n. 42 (*PL* 44, 267).

[61] "Si dicimus, eam mortis vinculo teneri; resolutam in communem putredinem, vermem, et itinerem, deliberandum est, si tantae sanctitati conveniat,

faction of the body does not become the blessed Virgin, I should say, to be logical, that it does not become her to have contracted in her soul the putrefaction of original sin." [62] And, "if the preservation of the body from putrefaction redounds to her maternal honor, the preservation of the soul from the corruption of original sin contributes much more to the same honor." [63] As Pseudo–Augustine himself in his defense of the Assumption concluded: it is more repugnant to conceive of Mary's soul corrupted by original sin than of her body putrefying.[64]

The divine motherhood, which for St. Thomas provides the basis why Mary is eminent in grace and immune from any venial sin,[65] becomes then for the proponents of the Immaculate Conception the ground for her exemption from original sin itself. Because of her divine motherhood Mary is endowed with all the graces from the first moment of her existence.

3. *Christ's coadiutrix.* In historical perspectives, Cartagena belonged to the period when the bold term *corredemptrix* for Mary had not yet found favor. Bernardine of Sienna († 1444), Bernardine of Busti († 1500) — and the source of both of them, Ubertino da Casale († c. 1317) —, and Pelbartus of Temesvar († 1504) all spoke of her as *reparatrix* and *adiutrix* in her cooperation in the work of redemp-

---

et tantae aulae Dei praerogativae..." And "Nunquid non pertinet ad dignitatem Domini, Matris suae servare honorem...? ...qui in vita prae caeteris illam gratia conceptus sui honoravit: pium est credere, singulari salvatione, etiam et in morte, et speciali gratia honorasse; poterit enim a putredine, et a pulvere alienam facere, qui ex ea nascens, potuit eam Virginem relinquere; putredo enim, et vermis opprobrium est humanae conditionis, a quo opprobrio cum Iesus sit alienus, natura Mariae excipitur, quam de ea suscepisse probatur; Caro enim Iesus, est caro Mariae..." Pseudo–Augustinus, *De Assumptione Beatae Mariae Virginis,* c. 5 (*PL* 40, 1145); quoted by Cartagena, Lib. I, hom. XVIII (I, 95a).

[62] Lib. I, hom. XVIII (I, 95a).

[63] Ibid.

[64] "Illud sanctissimum corpus, de quo Christus carnem assumpsit ,et divinam naturam humanae univit, non amittens, quod erat, sed assumens, quod non erat, ut Verbum Caro, hoc est, Deus, homo fieret, escam vermibus traditum sentire non valeo, dicere pertimescit, quod corpus Virginis putredine inquinetur, quanto magis horrere debet, quod originalis peccati putredine eius anima inficiatur?" Pseudo–Augustinus, op. cit., c. 6 (*PL* 40, 1146); quoted by the author, Lib. I, hom. XVIII (I, 95a–b).

[65] Aquinas, *Summa Theol.,* III, q. 27, art. 4.

tion.[66] Angelus Volpi († 1647) was the first Franciscan to attribute the title of *corredemptrix* to Mary.[67] Between these two stages of development was a period of trying to clarify how and why Mary can also be a *redemptrix*. It was during this time that Cartagena, as one of the very first, drew the consequence that Mary's predestination with Christ entails also her cooperation in his work of redemption.

Mary's predestination before all other creatures manifests in the mind of the author that she is foreseen not only as the mother of Christ but also as his *coadiutrix* in the redemptive work, which fact when analyzed signifies too her Immaculate Conception.[68] The author, typical of the time, strongly leans on the patristic teaching on Adam and Eve's prefiguration of Christ and Mary.[69] Just as Eve was the helper of Adam in the carnal generation of men, so is Mary,

---

[66] Cf. Balić, "Die Corredemptrixfrage innerhalb der franziskanischen Theologie," *Franziskanische Studien*, 39 (1957) 238–244.

[67] Ibid., pp. 247–249.

[68] "Porro, si ex alio capite beatissimae Virginis praedestinationem contemplemur, quatenus scilicet electa, et praedestinata fuit, non solum ut mater Christi foret, sed ut coadiutrix eius esset, et comes individua in redemptione, et reparatione generis humani, haud difficile est, illibatam eius conceptionem inde deprehendere." Lib. I, hom. III (I, 15b–16a).

Petrus Correa, OFM (f. 1615), holding the same, just repeated Cartagena: "E se por outra consideramos a predestinaçao da Virgen, he a saber em quanto escolhida nao sò para May de Deos, man para quem seu modo fosse unica ajudadora e reparaçao immaculada." *Triumphos Ecclesiasticos*, p. I, disc. 8, concept. 8 (Olissipone, 1617), p. 171a; quoted by Wenceslaus Sebastian, OFM, *De B. Virgine Maria Universali Gratiarum Mediatrice* (Romae, 1952), p. 48, nota 40.

[69] "Quod ut altius repetamus, supponere oportet, quod sicut iuxta communem, et receptissimam Patrum sententiam, primus parens Adam Christum Dominum praefiguravit, ita et Eva eius uxor B. Virginis typum ad vivum gessit." Lib. I, hom. III (I, 16a).

"Sicut enim decrevit Deus primum parentem Adamum generis humani caput constituere, eique sociam Evam adhibuit ex dormientis ipsius latere formatam; ita ad reparandum Genus humanum, et, ut in mundo esset caput alterius propagationis spiritualis, non ex sanguinis, neque ex voluntate carnis, sed ex Deo, et eius divino spiritu Christum praedestinavit: quem ob id Paulus secundum et novum Adamum (I Cor 15, 45) crebro appellat: ex cuius latere dormientis in Cruce eduxit hanc secundam Evam, id est, Matrem viventium, per gratiam. Unde sicut Eva secunda post Adam procreata fuit, ita et Maria immediate post Christum secundo loco praedestinata fuit." Lib. I, hom. II (I, 7a). Cf. Lib. I, hom. III (I, 17b).

This Eve–Mary typology is one of the earliest theological reflections about Mary in the post–apostolic times. As early as the 2nd cent. Justinus' *Dialogue with Trypho*, c. 100 (*PG* 6, 709–712) develops this antithesis. Cf. A. Müller, *Ecclesia–Maria* (Freiburg, ²1955), pp. 48–53.

the Second Eve, the helper of Christ, the New Adam, in the *recapitu-latio* of mankind, in setting mankind free from the boundage of sin.[70] But Mary's role in the economy of salvation seen in terms of the Eve–typology is not simply a prefiguration but more specifically an anti-thesis. In the words of Irenaeus quoted by Cartagena, Eve by her disobedience became the cause of death for the human race; Mary by her obedience became in the *recircumlatio* of mankind the cause of life and liberation.[71] "Hence just as Eve was the principle of our fall, so Mary appeared as the source and origin of our salvation." [72]

How is Mary *reparatrix* of the world and the *socia Christi* in saving the human race? [73] First of all, the correct understanding of her participation in the work of salvation can only be gotten in the context of Christ's unique role as redeemer. Considering that the teaching of the Immaculate Conception has been till lately vehemently opposed on the ground that it derogates from the dignity of Christ's work of redemption, it is not surprising that Cartagena goes out of his way to stress the singularity of Christ as savior. Christ alone saved mankind from sin.[74] Mary is involved only *participative*, cooperating

---

[70] "...opinor Evam B. Virginis typum gessisse, quod sicut illa data fuit Adae in adiutricem, ad temporalem filiorum generationem... ita, et Christo Do-mino data fuit beatissima Virgo in coadiutricem ad spiritualem filiorum sobolem procreandam, et humanum genus a diabolica captivitate redimendum." Lib. I, hom. III (I, 16b). Correa, op. cit., p. 172a, repeated these words of Cartagena; cf. Sebastian, op. cit., p. 122, n. 38.

"...infero... Christo, ut principali auctori; Virgini, ut minus principali [opus redemptionis attribui]: sicut peccatum originale principaliter Adae, minus prin-cipaliter Evae adscribi solet." Lib. I, hom. III (I, 17a).

[71] "Quemadmodum illa virum quidem habens Adam virgo tamen adhuc exsistens, inobediens facta et sibi et universo generi humano causa facta et mortis, sic et Maria habens praedestinatum virum, et tamen Virgo, obediens et sibi ut universo generi humano causa ἐπελεύσεται, καί δύναμις ὑψιστον ἐπισκιλςει αὐτην facta est salutis." Irenaeus *Contra haereses*, III, c. 22 (*PG* 7, 958b); quoted by the author in a somewhat abbreviated form in Lib. XII, hom. XI (II, 507b). Cf. Müller, op. cit., pp. 57–59, and D. Unger, OFMCap., "S. Irenaei doctrina de Maria, socia Iesu in recapitulatione," in *Maria et Ecclesia*, IV (Romae, 1959), pp. 67–140. Cf. Vat. II, *Const. on the Church*, n. 56.

[72] Lib. V, hom. IV (I, 402b).

[73] "Non semel legi apud illos [sanctos Patres et gravissimos doctores] Beatam Virginem fuisse coadiutricem, et cooperatricem Christi ad redemptionem generis humani: immo, et causam nostrae salutis, necnon et reparatricem Mundi..." Lib. XII, hom. XI (II, 507b). Cf. Lib. I, hom. III (I, 15b).

[74] "Non tamen ipsa redemit, sed Christus solus." Lib. XII, hom. XI (II, 510b). Cf. Lib. XII, hom. VIII (II, 487b).

but not herself redeeming, and joining in but neither *per modum effi- cientiae* nor *de condigno*, but only *de congruo*.[75] Although herself *redempta*, it is definitely appropriate that Mary participates in the work of saving mankind. But there is no proportionality at all between

---

[75] "...nemo Catholicus negabit in Beatam Virginem excellentius convenire, esse salvatricem, in eodem sensu scilicet participative, cum perfectius quam Apostoli cooperata fuerit ad salutem humani generis consequendam." Lib. XII, hom. XI (II, 510a).

"Audiant etiam magnum discrimen esse (in quo nonnulli sunt decepti) inter cooperari ad redemptionem generis humani, et redimere ipse genus humanum... B. Virgo cooperata fuerit ad redemptionem generis humani... meritis suis de congruo..." Lib. XII, hom. XI (II, 510b).

"...licet B. Virgo cooperata fuerit ad redemptionem generis humani, non solum meritis suis de congruo, et precibus, sed et praebendo Redemptori corpus et sanguinem, quo redemit nos: non tamen ipsa redemit, sed Christis solus... Solum advertere oportet, ut recte adnotavit Franciscus Suarez tomo 2. in tertiam partem disputatione 23. sect. 1. quod Haeretici illi... in eo errore erant ut putarent Beatam Virginem fuisse praecipuam salutis nostrae causam, vel per modum efficientiae, et redemptionis aut meriti de condigno; quod constat adversari, et pugnare cum fide Catholica, a quo errore longe abest sententia Sanctorum Patrum, dum B. Virginem unanimi consensu contestantur coadiutricem, et cooperatricem cum Christo ad reparationem, et salutem generis humani. Sicut certum enim est, secundum fidem Catholicam, Adamum extitisse totalem causam perditionis generis humani; ita ut si ipse non pecasset quantumcumque Aeva inobediens fuisset, genus humanum non periret: et nihilominus unanimus est omnia Catholicorum consensus et vox, Evam multum cooperatam fuisse ad perditionem generis humani, et ideo magis novercam quam matrem appellandam: sic etiam licet certum sit, secundum Fidem Catholicam, Christum solum fuisse redemptorem generis humani, id nihil prorsus obstat, quominus B.V. Evae ex diametro opposita multum cooperata fuerit ad redemptionem generis humani." Ibid. (II, 510b–511a).

Juan de Cartagena is understandably cautious in talking about Mary as participating in the work of salvation. He specifies exactly the limitation of her part, and his own favorite term for her is *coadiutrix*, which he uses in the title of the first book's third homily: "Praedestinatam fuisse Beatam Virginem in Matrem Christi Domini, et coadiutricem illius ad redemptionem Generis humani; priscorum Patrum monumentis ostenditur..." (I, 14a). Two years later after the publication of *HCSADM* I in putting out the second volume of his Marian homilies (1614), Cartagena returns to the subject in the 12th book's last homily, which we have just extensively quoted, with the heading: "Quo pacto Beata Virgo Cruci astans humanae generi multum profuerit: et qua ratione intelligendi sint Sancti Patres, palam asserentes, illam cooperatam fuisse ad redemptionem generis humani, cum tamen certum sit secundum fidem Catholicam, solum Christum Dominum suo sanguine nos redemisse, luculenter enucleatur." (II, 506b). Following the detailed explanations, Cartagena pointedly states, apparently in response to some people who might have misread the words of his earlier volume: "Quare quae in hoc genere argumenti dixi supra lib. 1. hom. 3. non aliter intelligi desidero,

her merits and the work of salvation.[76] Nothing on her part could
have changed the complete gratuity of redemption.

And it is on her divine motherhood that Mary's role in the salvation of man is founded. Her functions as mother and *coadiutrix*
are interdependent, one emanating from the other as from a principle. She has something to do with our redemption mediately or
remotely in that the external circumstance of Christ's birth was determined by her cooperation. While agreeing with Bonaventure's
and Aquinas' opinion that Mary deserved only *de congruo* or with
some appropriateness the dignity of being the Mother of God,[77]
Cartagena nevertheless thinks that *not improbably* she merited also
de condigno or worthily to conceive Christ, presupposing that the
Incarnation has been already decreed.[78] Only she and not any other

----

quam secundum sensum, quo illa intellexerunt S. Patres a me hic et ibi relati;
nec non gravissimi Theologi me citati. Haec Catholicis damus." (II, 511a).

In view of the above clarifications by the author, it is surprising that Balić
judges Cartagena's position unclear as to whether Mary is *causa efficiens* or not
of redemption! Cf. Balić, "Die Corredemptrixfrage...," art. cit., p. 272.

[76] "Itaque tam ex sacra Scriptura, quam ex Patrum et antiquorum Doctorum testimoniis: immo ex ipsa nominis Mariae significatione colligimus, praelec-
tam fuisse a Deo, in coadiutricem Christi opus redemptionis; non quia solus
ipse non sufficeret, sed quia *consentaneum erat*, ut ait Irenaeus, 'ut sicut per foeminam Adamum seducentem mundus fuerat perditus, per foeminam Christo in-
servientem restauraretur' (*Contra haereses*, III, c. 22: *PG* VII, 958b), quod et
D. Bernardus his dulcissimis verbis pereleganter dixit: 'Ad restaurationem humani generis sufficere poterat solus Christus, sicut omnis sufficientia nostra ex
ipso est, sed bonum non erat nobis, hominem esse solum: congruum magis erat,
ut adesset nostra reparationi sexus uterque, quorum corruptioni neuter defuisset'
(*Sermo de dominica infra octavam assumptionis B.V. Mariae: PL* 183, 429C)."
Lib. I, hom. III (I, 17b–18a).

[77] "Merito condigni non potuit mereri concipere Filium Dei, pro eo quod
hoc excedit omne meritum. Sive enim dicamus Deum fieri hominem, sive dicamus
mulierem fieri Matrem Dei, utrumque est supra statum qui debetur creaturae;
et ideo tam hoc quam illud fuit benignitatis et gratiae." Bonaventure, *In 3 dist. 4*,
q. 2, art. 2: Quaracchi edn., III, 107.

"Beata Virgo non meruit incarnationem; sed praesupposita incarnatione
meruitque per eam fieret; non quidem merito condigni, sed merito congrui."
Aquinas, *In 3 dist. 4*, q. 3, art. 1 ad 6. Cf. *Summa Theol.*, III, q. 2, art. 11 corp.
& ad 3.

[78] "Quamvis autem non improbabiliter Abulensis [Alfonso Tostado de Ma-
drigal], Gabriel [Biel], et Maior [Ioannes, † 1550] in ea fuerint sententia, ut putarent, B. Virginem ea suppositione incarnationis a Deo iam praedefinitae meruisse
de condigno, ut potius ex ipsa, quam ex quacumque alia foemina Verbum divinum
carnem assumeret, Angelici tamen Doctoris S. Thomae, ac Seraphici doctoris

woman would have been chosen to be the Mother of God. This position is later to prevail among theologians. Too, Mary's cooperation in the objective redemption of mankind consists in providing our Savior with the body and blood with which we were redeemed.[79] It is through the fruit of her womb that "sinners are reconciled with God and joined to their Creator in a new bond of friendship." [80]

S. Bonaventurae doctrinae magis consentiens, B. Virginem assero de congruo meruisse, ut Dei genetricis dignitatem obtineret." Lib. V, hom. XVIII (I, 519b).

Cartagena's attitude towards the nominalist thesis, benign in context of the time's raging controversy on the issue, reflects Suárez's own position that, "Non est improbabile meruisse etíam de condigno esse Matrem Dei." *Quaestio 18*, dico 4, n. 14: ed. by J. de Aldana, SJ, "Quaestio 18, Utrum B. Virgo meruerit de condigno esse Mater Dei," *Archivo Teologico Granadino*, 25 (1962) 234. This 1585 position of Suárez became a bit toned down five years later, when he said of the traditional thesis that it is "magis probabilis et simpliciter vera," although the nominalist position is "non... omnino aliena a modo loquendi Patrum et eam tenent auctores graves non sine probabili coniectura." *Commentaria et Disputationes in III. Partem D. Thomae*, q. 2, art. 11, disp. 10, sect. 7, nn. 6 & 9. Cf. Aldama, "El mérito condigno de la maternidad divina de Nuestra Senora en la teología de los s. XVI–XVII," *Archivo Teologico Granadino*, 25 (1962) 179–224. Cartagena himself favorably quotes Suárez who teaches that Mary merited the Incarnation only *de congruo:* "Tandem ut alios omittam, Franciscus Suarez... postquam dixerat B. Virginem ad nostram salutem cooperatam fuisse, id explicat tribus modis, in haec verba: 'Primo merendo de congruo incarnationem secundo orando, et petendo, et quamdiu fuit in vita, de congruo merendo nobis salutem: tertio concipiendo Christum nostrae salutis Authorem...' *(Comment. et Disp. in III. Partem*, q. 38, art. 4, disp. 10, sect. 1, n. 4: Vives, XIV, 330)." Lib. XII, hom. XI (II, 512a). In the light of the Scotistic teaching that Christ was absolutely predestined to glory, the complete gratuity of the Incarnation even as far as Mary's merits are concerned would be more logical. Duns Scotus wrote: "Posset dici quod in universis operibus Dei non fuit aliquod opus mere gratiae nisi sola incarnatio Filii Dei, et hoc si ad illam nulla merita praecesserunt, quod utique verum est in ordinatione divina de illa incarnatione. Quia si tempore conceptionis praecesserunt aliqua merita Mariae, tamen non erant bona absolute respectu incarnationis, sed forte accelerationis..." *Opus Ox.*, IV, d. 2, n. 11: Vives, XVII, 248. Carried, however, by the maximalizing tendency of the time, the Franciscan position on the matter would reach its classic expression in Carlos de Moral's († 1731) opinion that Mary merited mankind's objective redemption *de condigno*. Cf. Sebastian, op. cit., pp. 133–154.

[79] "...B. Virgo cooperata fuerit ad redemptionem generis humani, non solum meritis suis de congruo, et precibus, sed et praebendo Redemptoris corpus et sanguinem, quo redemit nos." Lib. XII, hom. XI (II, 510b).

"Cum ergo Deipara Virgo suo modo redemptrix fuerit, precium sanguinis filio suo tribuens, quo nos ipse redemit..." Lib. I, hom. III (I, 18a).

[80] Lib. XIV, hom. III (II, 576b).

Mary's "proximate" cooperation has been based by Cartagena
first of all on her suffering with Christ on Calvary. As she stood there
afflicted to the depths of her being, she took upon herself the pains
for our sake, and thus gave birth to us spiritually.[81] In a way she is
then the mother of all the living, given to Christ like a second Eve
for the spiritual generation of mankind.[82] She interceded and prayed
for us, for our reconciliation with God, identifying herself in a spiritual martyrdom with her Son and his self–offering, as she lived the
cross in deepest *compassio* with him.[83]

---

[81] "Sicut enim Christus nos genuit verbo veritatis ad esse gratiae spirituale,
in cruce patiendo; ita et Beata Virgo Maria nos genuit, et peperit in maximis
doloribus filio compatiendo, poenas immensas pro nobis patienti." Lib. XV, hom.
XVII (II, 147a).

[82] "...opinor Evam B. Virginis typum gessisse, quod sicut illa data fuit
Adae in adiutricem, ad temporalem filiorum generationem... ita, et Christo Domino data fuit beatissima Virgo in coadiutricem ad spiritualem filiorum sobolem
procreandam, et humanum genus a diabolica captivitate redimendum." Lib. I,
hom. III (I, 16b).

"Hinc rursus Patres apertissime etiam in eam assertionem conspirant, ut
B. Virgo una cum Christo Domino magnam filiorum spiritualium sobolem procrea-
verit, praesertim tamen D. Augustinus libro de sanctissima Trinitate, ca. 7.
ut refert Canisius lib. 1. de Deipara, c. 1. adstruit Mariam corporalem simul et
spiritualem Christi matrem esse, quia non modo caput ipsum et Salvatorem totius mystici corporis enixa est, sed et spiritu matrem se membrorum Christi prae-
buit, ut fideles in Ecclesia nascerentur." Lib. XII, hom. XI (II, 509b). See Lib.
XV, hom. XVII (III, 144b–150a), which entire homily discusses how Mary is
"Mater omnium viventium." Cf. Vat. II, *Const. on the Church*, n. 62.

[83] "Beata autem Virgo in mundum veniens, cuncta composuit, e potestate
diabolica precibus suis peccatores eruens, et creatori suo illos reconcilians." Lib. I,
hom. III (I, 16b). "Beata autem Virgo, tum propter summam cum Christo coniunctionem, tum quia simul cum illo constanter perseverabat in suae fidei, et amoris
reddendo testimonio simul cum ipso patiebatur, et consequenter simul cum Christo martyr effecta est." Lib. XII, hom. VI (II, 478a). "...ita etiam voluit Dominus,
et ordinavit quod in ligno sanctae Crucis vir, et mulier licet diversimode offerent
sacrificium pro illius peccati expiatione; ita ut ille secundum carnem moreretur,
ista vero secundum spiritum; Christus carnem, et Maria spiritum immolaret, quamvis solius Christi passione, et morte redempti sumus, et iustificati, non Mariae
compassione, quae alioquin suspiriis, et precibus suis Christo in Cruce iacente,
iuxta Crucem stans nostram salutem sollicite curavit." Lib. XII, hom. VIII
(II, 487b–488a). Cf. Lib. XII, hom. XI (II, 507a).

Salmeron, who uses the term *corredemptrix* for Mary, has a lengthy treatment of Mary's *compassio* on Calvary. Certain of Cartagena's ideas are traceable
here, although one feels that the author has been rather selective. See Salmeron's
Commentaria in Evang., op. cit., X (1604), tr. 41 & 51, p. 423b ff. & p. 337b ff.;

And her intercession for mankind was not just during her lifetime in this world, but always and even now, in the distribution of the fruits of redemption, in our subjective redemption. What we receive from God are communicated to us through her mediation.[84] This role of Mary as our heavenly advocate and distributor of grace springs also from her divine motherhood. (We shall enlarge on this later in the consideration of her glorification in heaven in the chapter on the Assumption.) By reason of her maternal intimacy with Christ, she is supreme in dignity among pure creatures and possesses a special access to the benefits won by Christ's sacrifice. The underlying reason for all her prerogatives perdures and was ended neither by Christ's death nor hers. Mary remains the Mother of God and retains that unique right to her Son's benefits.[85] Moreover, Christ has handed over to her the function of being our intercessor, as he was hanging on the cross.[86]

III (1602), tr. 9, p. 72b ff.; VI (1602), tr. 6, p. 30b ff. Cf. also Melquiades Andrés, "La compasion de la Virgen al pie de la Cruz, deducida de su triple gracia, según Salmeron," *Estudios Marianos*, 3 (1946) 359–388.

[84] "Et ex alia parte Sancti Patres late a me supra citati, relatis eorum testimoniis, luculenter doceant quaecumque beneficia divinitus descendunt a Patre luminum, per Virginis preces, et intercessionum communicari..." Lib. XIV, hom. XVIII (II, 70b). Cf. Lib. XII, hom. XI (II, 510a).

[85] "...illud omnino certum est, beatam Virginem ratione huius maternitatis excellentissimum quendam, ac supremum dignitatis gradum inter puras creaturas attigisse, propter singularissimam, quam cum Deo habuit, coniunctionem: necnon etiam certum est, ratione eiusdem maternitatis, ius habuisse ad bona omnia filii sui, superioritatemque quandam supra Christum obtinuisse, qualem habere decebat matrem respectu sui naturalis filii: quod genus supremae auctoritatis, utpote supra Deum, adhuc in patria viget in Virgine, quia praeter quam quod attinet ad matris dignitatem, morali modo consideratam certissimum est eam perseverare in Deipara, neque umquam fuisse imminutam; quia licet in triduo mortis Christi non esset hic homo, quem B. Virgo genuerat, vere tamen erat ille, quem genuit, hoc est, filius Dei, habens unitas sibi partes illius humanitatis, quas ex Virgine accepit; praeter hoc (inquam) existimo beatam Virginem actu habere eandem realem relationem maternitatis, quam generando Christum sibi acquisivit; licet enim in morte sua illam amitteret, in resurrectione tamen eam recuperavit, ut sic ex omni parte perfecta esset eius resurrectio, dum non solum resurgeret ea, quae fuerat Christi mater, sed etiam formaliter in quantum mater." Lib. V, hom. XVIII (I, 519b–520a).

[86] "Caeterum, ut hoc *Advocatae* munus, quo Beata Virgo fungitur in Coelo, pro nobis incessanter intercedens, variisque beneficiis nos frequenter cumulans, altius repetamus, praesupponere oportet officium hoc *Advocatae*, iniunctum fuisse Virgini a filio suo, dum aliquo Crucis penderet. Etenim clementissimus Iesus eo

The foregoing consideration concerning Mary's cooperating role in the salvation of mankind provides Cartagena another justification theologically supporting the doctrine of her Immaculate Conception. Christ's helper in saving man from sin should be herself free from all sin.[87]

4. *Some clarifications.* We have already remarked above how strong in the Franciscan theology of the time was the thesis that Mary actually did not even have any *debitum contrahendi peccatum originale.* If she is absolutely predestined with Christ, then she transcends the Adamitic line and is over and beyond the common law necessitating all men to inherit original sin.[88] But Cartagena does not go Franciscan all the way on this point.[89] He believes Mary to be indeed

---

tempore, quo acrius iustitia, et misericordia inter se dimicabant cum illa a latere suo tot fautores haberet, quot vulnera Christo inflicta, quot iniurias ei illatas, quot blasphemias in eum prolatas, quot dolores tandem et cruciatus, quibus supra modum angebatur. Quae omnia vindictam de peccatoribus enixe a Deo postulabant, ut adversus totum hunc iustitiae exercitum misericordia praevaleret; voluit Dominus matrem suam munere advocatricis fungentem, misericordiae partes agere, ne peccatores penitus perirent. Unde proximus morti illos omnes Ioanni Virgini commendans, dixit ei: *Mulier ecce filius tuus.* Quam commendationem arbitror piisimum Iesum consulto usque ad illud mortis tempus distulisse, quia sciebat ea, quae in puncto mortis alicui commendantur, libentius suscipi, et tenacius memoriae impressa retineri..." Lib. XIV, hom. XVI (II, 684a–b).

[87] "Cum ergo Deipara Virgo suo modo nostra redemtrix fuerit... consequens est, ab omni originali alienissima fuisse; sicut enim (ut ait Paulus) de Christo redemptore loquens: 'Talis decebat nobis esset Pontifex, sanctus, et excelsior coelis factus' (Heb 7, 26); sic etiam, Virginem, Christi coadiutricem, et sociam in reparatione generis humani oportebat et coelo ipso puriorem esse." Lib. I, hom. III (I, 18a).

[88] Juan de Segovia, OFM († 1458), for example, who greatly influenced the Council of Basel's decree on the Immaculate Conception, taught that Mary does not belong to the Adamitic order at all but to the *ordo hypostaticus* and is therefore not included in the law concerning original sin. Cf. Mückshoff, op. cit., pp. 453–457. And Cartagena's great contemporary, St. Lawrence of Brindisi, OFMCap. († 1619), preached something similar in his concept of Christ with Mary on the tip of the pyramid of being, as *radix humanitatis,* full of grace and beyond sinfulness. Cf. Mückshoff, ibid., pp. 466–467, 474–475. Angelus Volpi, OFM († 1646) defended the same thesis. Cf. Mückshoff, ibid., p. 478.

[89] Gabriele Roschini, OSM, misinterprets Cartagena in this regard, writing that: "Coloro — gli scotisti — i quali ammettono la predestinazione di Cristo e di Maria SS. indipendentemente dal peccato originale (di modo che senza di esso il Verbo si sarebbe incarnato ugualmente), logicamente ne deducono l'esenzione di Maria SS. dal debito del peccato, poiché predestinata madre di Dio prima

included in Christ's absolute predestination. However, she remains a true daughter of Adam, on account of which she had in fact the *debitum* in herself and not just remotely in him. Cartagena opted for this solution in maintaining that Mary too was redeemed by Christ.

The question comes up: if Mary was indeed pre–redeemed through Christ's foreseen merits, how could she have been absolutely predestined with her Son independently of Adam's fall into sin? In rejecting the Thomistic view and in defending the Scotistic thesis on Christ's, and Mary's, absolute predestination, while maintaining that Mary was saved from the *debitum*, how could this be possible without a prior vision of Adam's sin and the sin of all his descendants, which would mean that Mary herself was among those seen in need of redemption? Some contemporaries of Cartagena saw the way out of this corner in Molina's *scientia media*, which explains how God could preordain Christ's coming into the world as a redeemer and, consequent to it, Mary's preservation from sin through Christ's foreseen merits, even before any absolute prevision of Adam's fall.[90] The *futuritio* of Christ's coming and his foreseen merits, even prior to any sin, embraces too Mary's pre–redemption through his merits. But Cartagena finds it better to explain the difficulty differently along the line of Scotus' distinction between the order of nature or time and the order of ideas. The predestination of Christ and Mary's preservation from sin are more together than separate. The divine decree that Christ would come as redeemer has priority over Mary's foreseen innocence inasmuch as it is the formal cause of her preservation from all sin. In turn, Mary's privilege of i n n o c e n c e is also only *secundum quid* prior to the divine decree concerning her preservation from original sin in that it is the material cause for it.[91]

---

ancora della previsione — a nostro modo di intendere — del peccato. Ne è esempio tipico il Minorita P. Giovanni da Cartagena il quale scrisse: 'Beatissima vero Genitrix, ex speciali Filii sui beneficio, in conceptione sua submergi non potuit, ipsa dicente: *Nondum erant abyssi* peccati originalis, et *ego iam concepta eram* in mente Dei.' (Lib. I, hom. II: I, 12b)." "Il problema del 'debitum peccati' in Maria Santissima," in *Virgo Immaculata*, XI, p. 345.

[90] Cf. Pedro de Alcantara, OFM, "La redención de Maria y los meritos de Cristo," *Estudios Franciscanos*, 55 (1954) 195–254.

[91] "Primo dicendo, quod sicut in rebus naturalibus stat, aliqua duo se mutuo excedere, in diverso simpliciter, sed secundum quid, ita praevisio carnetiae peccati originalis in Virgine, et praedestinatio Christi, seu Decretum de Adventu illius in carne passibili mutuo se excedunt in diverso genere causae; nam praedicta visio est prior illo Decreto in genere causae materialis; praedestinatio

Or, breaking it up in the order of ideas, in the first instant God sees the fall of Adam; in the second instant all his descendants inheriting the debt to contract original sin; in the third, or perhaps even in the second, God decrees Christ's coming into the world as redeemer; and in the third (or fourth) instant, God sees all men incurring the sin, with the exception of Mary who is preserved in view of Christ's foreseen passion.[92] However, these stages or instants are nothing but a logical partition to distinguish mentally certain elements in God's plan which in themselves do not imply any real priorities.

5. *Definibilis*. Juan de Cartagena holds the doctrine of the Immaculate Conception as *vera*, though not for sure as *de fide*. The devotion of the universal Church, which celebrates the feast of Mary's conception, shows the doctrine to be true.[93] And he finds two reasons why God allows the mystery to remain until then without the defi-

---

vero est prior illa quasi in genere causae formalis; Et si obicias, in illo priori, quo praevidetur peccatum ante Decretum de Adventu Christi in carne passibili, quod Virgo videatur sine contractione peccati originalis, est effectus Passionis Christi, et redemptionis illius; ergo, nec pro illo priori potuit videri sine peccato, absque eo, quod simpliciter, et absolute praecesserit praedestinatio, seu Decretum de Adventu Christi in ratione medici, et Redemptoris per Passionem suam. Respondeo, aliud esse, quod pro illo priori, quo in Virgine praecedit visio carentiae peccati originalis, non sit praedictum Decretum de Christo, ut medico, et Redemptore, aliud vero, quod pro illo priori non intelligatur tale Decretum, primum est falsum, secundum tamen verum." Lib. VII, hom. XV (I, 830a–b).

[92] "Secundo respondeo, instantia rationis in hunc modum coordinanda esse, ut prius Deus videat Adam peccantem, deinde in secundo instanti ex peccato illius, tanquam ex causa, omnes futuros eius posteros, contrahere debitum incurrendi peccatum originale; in 3. instanti, vel etiam in eodem secundo fuit decretum de Adventu Christi in carne passibili, in remedium peccati generis humani, ...infalibiliter futurum erat illos esse maculandos, et sic immediate post hoc providit de remedio tanti mali, per decretum Adventus Christi... prius Deus vidit peccatum Adae, quam reliquorum; et sic pro illo priori non vidit posteros in peccato, nec sine illo per praeservationem, sed cum capacitate ad utrumque; et sic etiam visa est virgo pro illo priori; in 3. tandem, seu 4. signo vidit Deus posteros Adae incurrere peccatum originale, Beatam vero Virginem praeservari ex meritis Christi iam praevisis, etc." Lib. VII, hom. XV (I, 830b).

[93] "Universalis Ecclesiae cultus, quae celeberrimum festum Conceptionis celebrat, non obscure ostendit Ecclesiam Catholicam hanc sententiam tanquam veram, licet non certam de fide, approbare... Temerarium autem esset asserere, Ecclesiam in celebratione festi errare, et Indulgentias concedere assertoribus alicuius erroris: unde, si Ecclesia id celebrat, videtur id omnino esse verum, quia ipsa non celebrat, nec Indulgentias concedit sub conditione." Lib. I, hom. XIX (I, 103b).

nition of faith by the Apostolic See. The first is to avoid the possible consequence that the simple people, upon learning that Mary did not contract original sin, might jump to the conclusion that she is a Goddess.[94] The second reason why the teaching on the Immaculate Conception is still only on the controverted level of a theological opinion is so that its defenders may the more diligently take up the cause and more deeply study the mystery and thus bring out more the glories of Mary.[95] But Cartagena foresees the time, when the doctrine would be taken as *de fide*.[96] In the meantime, the differences in opinion should result in fuller knowledge about Mary.

---

[94] "Quod adeo verum est, ut quamvis Deus perplura alia obscurissima arcana Ecclesiae suae manifestaverit, immaculatae tamen conceptionis Matris suae mysterium occultaverit, nolens hanc veritatem a Sede Apostolica tanquam catholicam fidei assertionem definiri, cuius divinae dispositionis, utpote secretissimae causas investigare licet difficile admodum sit, eas tamen quae nobis occurrit, in medium producere non erubescam. Prima sit, quod... nonnulli fuerunt, qui tantum honoris B. Virgini detulere, ut eam tanquam veram Deam colerent... quia ergo non pauci indes homines, si exploratum habuisset, beatissimam Virginem non contraxisse peccatum originale, facile deciperentur, illam Deum esse putantes, ideo noluit Deus eos certos facere de hac veritate." Lib. I, hom. IV (I, 23b–24a).

[95] "Secundam, eamque certissimam causam arbitror, quod ea propter sub opinionis involucris latitet, ut tanto solertius, ac diligentius propugnatores immaculatae Conceptionis ad eam ab omni labe vindicandam animum appellerent... Unde contigisse arbitror, quod quemadmodum in rebus naturalibus per antiparistatim contraria contrariis augentur, ita per involuntariam quandam antiparistatim illibatam Virginis Conceptionem oppugnantes magis ac magis illam elucidant, dum, vel omnia illorum tela in eos retorquentur, vel nullius roboris esse ostenduntur..." Lib. I, hom. IV (I, 24a–b).

In a later homily, Cartagena returns to this subject in connection with the temple of Solomon, which should prefigure Mary's Immaculate Conception. He pitches for unanimity in teaching the mystery. But the "clouds" of diverse opinions are in accordance with God's will. He goes on: "Addit etiam sacer textus verba alia (2 Chronicles 5, 13), quae singulari mysterio non vacant: nam loquentes de nebula, et caligine operiente templum, molestam fuisse sacerdotum oculis illorum, quorum officium erat clangere tubis: itaque maiestate Dei ingrediente illud templum, sacerdotum oculos nebula prohibebat videre gloriam eius ibi corruscantem, non tamen impediebat ore tuba canere ad celebrandam solemnitatem illam; non secus in celebri hoc immaculatae conceptionis festo vult quidem Dominus oculos humani intellectus non curiose illud aspicere, aut humano discursu illud scrutaris; unde noluit infallibilis definitionis Ecclesiae lumine illud clarere, sed quod sub opinionum nebula velut velamine lateret; cupit tamen, eique gratissimum est ut omnes sacerdotes tubis clangant, hoc est, unanimes ore et opere celebrent aedificationem mystici huius templi Dei, quae est immaculata Virginis Conceptio." Lib. I, hom. XII (I, 60b).

[96] "Dicendi ergo finem facio verbis illis Danielis. 'Tu autem Daniel claude

II. SCRIPTURAL ELUCIDATIONS

The "silence" of Sacred Scripture on the matter of Mary's Immaculate Conception is seemingly so obvious, that from the earliest time when the question in the form of her sinlessness was being posed, the answer tended to be only negative. In addition, certain scriptural texts explicitly teach what appears to be doctrines essentially contrary to the Marian proposition. Thus, for instance, when Origen touched on the subject of Mary's holiness, he believed her to have sinned also, because Christ is the savior of all and therefore of her too.[97] This line of reasoning held sway up to the time of the great Scholastics. St. Paul's words that: "As one man's fall brought condemnation on everyone, so the good act of one man brings everyone life and makes them justified" (Rom 5, 18), and again that: "there is only one mediator between God and mankind... Christ Jesus, who sacrificed himself as a ransom for them all" (I Tim 2, 5-6), seem to preclude totally the exemption of anyone from original sin. Thomas Aquinas saw the case of Mary not to be different.[98] And even with regard to the modified thesis the Angelic Doctor accepted, namely that Mary was sanctified in the womb following her animation, he carefully noted that no explicit testimony for this opinion can be found in Sacred Scripture.[99]

Juan de Cartagena himself could only claim that Scripture *"non obscure indicat"* Mary's freedom from all stain of sin.[100] And signi-

---

sermones, et signa librorum, usque ad tempus statutum, plurimi pertransibunt, et multiplex erit scientia' (Dan 12, 4): ac si diceret: Nondum advenit tempus praefinitum, ut veritas haec tanquam de fide referetur; interim tamen, dum clausa est, dum sub opinionum velamine latet, multiplex erit scientia, hoc est (ut ait ibi Glossa interlinearis) 'diversi diversa opinabuntur.' " Lib. I, hom. IV (I, 24b). Cartagena will give the same theological note for the doctrine on the Assumption. On Bellarmine's contrary opinion, cf. H. Graef, *Maria, eine Geschichte der Lehre u. Verehrung* (Freiburg, 1964), p. 338.

[97] Origen, *Homilia in Lucam*, XVII (*PG* 13, 1845-6).

[98] Aquinas, *Summa Theol.*, III, q. 27, art. 2.

[99] "...quamvis sanctificatio Beatae Virginis in utero expresse in Scripturis veteris et novi Testamenti non legatur; tamen pro certo haberi potest ex his quae ibi leguntur." Thomas Aquinas, *Commentarium in Libros Sententiarum*, Dist. III, q. 1, sol. 3, ad 3. Cf. Petrus G. Duncker, OP, "Auctoritas S. Scripturae et Praevia Sanctificatio B. V. Mariae iuxta S. Thomam," in *Virgo Immaculata*, VI, pp. 92-102.

[100] "...ad Sacram Scripturam, quae (ut nos probavimus) non obscure in-

ficantly towards the end of the *Liber primus* of the *HCSADM*, establishing Mary's predestination and her Immaculate Conception, Cartagena rounds up his scriptural presentation with the careful distinction that *"Christian piety* adequately brings out from the sacred books the Virgin's Immaculate Conception."[101] He asserts nonetheless that "no testimonies clearer than these, with which we establish the Immaculate Conception, are to be found in the sacred words." [102]

We now want to see the biblical texts and their interpretations presented in Cartagena's Marian homilies in support of Mary's Immaculate Conception. We have entitled this section as "Scriptural Elucidations," since, as has been observed, no explicit texts from Sacred Scripture can be summoned to demonstrate the mystery of the Immaculate Conception; whatever scriptural texts are given can only serve the purpose of indicating and elucidating the teaching. First to be laid out will be the scriptural passages Cartagena dealt with at some length and in which he is mainly concerned with the principal concept or idea contained in the text. Secondly, we shall line up some figures, images and metaphors Cartagena has woven together from the Bible into a tapestry spelling for him the Immaculate Conception of Mary. The overall evaluation of his use of Sacred Scripture will be given in Part III of this study. Let it be already noted here, however, that we think it is beside the point to try to compare Cartagena's "exegesis" point by point in every instance with modern biblical interpretation. A brief glance at his manner of interpretation will be sufficient to show that his art belongs altogether to another cast of thought, which is best taken as it is, in order to be appreciated and understood, as we shall later attempt to do.

A. Principal Biblical Passages

1. *Proverbs 8, 22–24.* The second homily of the *HCSADM*'s first book, following the introductory homily on the difficulties and inherent limitations entailed in any effort to explain the mysteries of Mary, sets out to show with and from Mary's predestination her untainted conception. This is to be accomplished through an examination of

---

dicat beatam Virginem ab omni penitus macula peccati alienam." Lib. VII, hom. XV (I, 824b).

[101] Lib. I, hom. XIX (I, 100b).
[102] Ibid. (I, 101a).

the very first scriptural passage Cartagena puts forward for that
purpose, Proverbs 8, 22–24: "The Lord possessed me in the beginning
of his ways. From everlasting I was firmly set, before he had made
anything from the beginning. And from of old, before the earth was
made, when there were no depths, I was already brought forth." [103]
The passage belongs to the culmination of the Book of Proverbs'
teaching on wisdom, where she pictures herself as a cherished companion of God in creation. Cartagena concurs with the interpretation that sees the person of Christ, the uncreated Wisdom, in this
wisdom of the Old Testament.[104] However, he maintains that the
passage can be understood too as referring to Mary, following the
example of the Church which has adopted this text in her liturgical
celebration.[105] For sure, what fits a giant will hardly be exactly to
the size of one of lesser stature. And if these words of Proverbs are
to be taken as speaking literally of the Word Incarnate, they can
only refer to Mary in another sense, i.e. according to the *sensus*

---

[103] The title of the homily is: "Ostenditur, Beatissimam Virginem inter
omnes puras Creaturas primum, ac principem locum tenere in divina praedestinatione, ex quo illibata eius Conceptio comprobatur in illa verba: Dominus possedit me..." Lib. I, hom. II (I, 5b–6a). Cartagena prefaces his actual treatment of
this text with the words: "Sed pergo iam proposita Ecclesiastici verba, quae
idipsum mirifice illustrant, elucidare, ex quibus immaculata Virginis Conceptio
non parum corroborabitur." Ibid. (I, 8a).

[104] Without naming names, he rejects the position of some "Doctores
Salmanticenses" who teach this is simply *sapientia* as *directiva actionum*. He prefers the interpretation, for example, of St. Thomas, *Summa Theol.*, I, q. 41, art.
3, ad 4.

It is interesting to note that it was precisely in view of this New Testament
tradition of applying the doctrine of wisdom to the person of Christ, that St.
Jerome, as mentioned by Cartagena, Lib. I, hom. II (I, 8b), adopted the word
possedit instead of *creavit*, in order to forestall Arius' teaching that the Word,
Wisdom, was a created being. Cartagena makes much out of this word *possedit*.

[105] "Verumtamen in sensu mystico proposita verba apte satis intelligi de
sanctissima Deipara Maria, Ecclesiae Catholicae Romanae Authoritas nos docet,
dum non semel ei illa accomodans Virginem introducit ea loquentem, quod non
parum arbitror tantae Virginis excellentiam commendare." Ibid. (I, 9a).

In the old Mass of the Immaculate Conception (December 8) this passage
from the Book of Proverbs was given as a reading, so also in the Masses of the
Nativity of the Blessed Virgin Mary (September 8) and of the Blessed Virgin Mary
of the Rosary (October 7). It used too to be a lesson in the Divine Office for the
Apparition of our Lady of Lourdes (February 11) and for the Common of the
Blessed Virgin Mary.

mysticus, based on something infinite that is common somehow to both of them, namely their eternal predestination.[106]

Applied to Mary, the first of the mysteries (*"sacramenta"*) hidden in these words is her statement: *"Dominus* — not *Deus* — *possedit me."* As the Lord with absolute dominion over her from the very beginning, God would have the power to dispense her from the universal law of contracting the stain of original sin. Moreover, Mary would not be even for a second under the diabolic power due to original sin, simply because she could not be under two masters at the same time. Clearly, then, Mary lived under the dominion of God, the *Dominus*, from the very moment of her conception.[107] The verb *possedit* gives the same idea with more precision. God may have dominion and ownership over all the blessed, but the actual possession of some of them may pass on to the devil, when they fall into mortal sin. Such is the case with every human being born in original sin; they are under the dominion of the demon and also in his actual possession. Mary on the contrary has always been in the possession of God, since she has never been stained by original sin.[108] The inter-

---

[106] "Nam quis quaeso non mirabitur, ut, quae secundum sensum literalem de increata sapientia, aut Verbo incarnato intelliguntur, Beatae Virgini in sensu mystico facile adaptentur? Sane vestis magno Giganti apta, statura pusillis congruere minime potest: cum ergo, quae de infinita Dei sapientia dicuntur de Beata Virginis etiam verificentur; necesse est illam ex infinitate filii infinitam quandam dignitatem mutuasse, indeque est, ut utrique (licet in diverso sensu) verba illa plane conveniat." And "Cum ergo sapientia Incarnata dicatur initium operum Dei, et id nequeat intelligi secundum exequutionem, necessario est intelligendum secundum praedefinitionem aeternam." Lib. I, hom. II (I, 9a).

[107] " 'Dominus possedit me,' et non, 'Deus possedit me': nam, cum in Conceptione Beatae Virginis Creator generis humani, tanquam absolutus Dominus nullo positivo iure adstrictus se gessisset, in universali lege de contrahenda labe peccati originalis cum Beata Virgine dispensans... Aliter etiam idipsum explicare possumus, ut dixerit: 'Dominus', ad significandum Deum a principio suae conceptionis perfectum illius dominium habuisse, atque adeo per peccatum originale diabolico dominio nec per momentum subiacuisse. Cum enim idem non possit a duobus dominis sub aspecto dominio possideri... consequens est, quod cum Beata Virgo a principio suae Conceptionis sub Dei dominio extiterit, peccati originalis labe, quae sub diaboli dominio animam constituit, omnino caruerit." Ibid. (I, 9a–10a).

[108] "Haec igitur est mira excellentia Beatissimae Virginis super omnes praedestinatos, quod quamvis Deus eorum omnium semper dominium habuerit, et proprietatem, non tamen semper possessionem, quia toto tempore, quo fuerunt labe peccati originalis infecti, Daemon habuit eorum possessionem. Beatissimae

pretation of the same words for the uncreated Wisdom, that the possession means the Son's eternal union with the Father and vice versa
the Father's eternal union with the Son, is seen by Cartagena to be
in accord too in the mystical sense with his own adaptation of the
text to Mary. Applied to her, such meaning of possession connotes
her predestination to divine motherhood and consequently her preor-
dained conception without original sin. "Such possession means that
in the divine plan the son was always in the mother and the mother
in the son; hence Mary was never, not even for a moment, deprived
of God's grace and was ever envisaged as the one to give birth to
the author of life and of grace." [109]

The Lord possessed her "*in initio viarum suarum.*" Among the
various interpretations of this phrase is the opinion that the ways
here denote the divine processions of the Son and of the Spirit, and
that therefore to be possessed by God in the beginning of his ways
is to say that from the eternity of the trinitarian processions Mary
has been predestined to be in God's possession through grace from
the moment of her conception, so that there simply was no possibility
of her being taken over by the devil through original sin.[110] To be
noted is St. Thomas Aquinas' fine exposition of the same words and
the remarkable manner with which it illustrates too the Immaculate
Conception. He said that *viarum* can be understood to mean the way
of mercy and the way of justice, as it is sung in Psalm 24, 10: "*Universa via Domini misericordia, et veritas.*" Mercy is named first; it
preceeds justice, that is why it is the beginning of the ways of the
Lord. In the case of Mary, it means that God acting out of mercy
took possession of her from the moment of her conception. He acted
on mercy and not on justice; otherwise, based on justice alone or above
all it would have been the devil of original sin who should have laid
claim on her.[111]

---

autem Virginis, quia nulla umquam macula peccati infecta fuit, semper, et pro
omni instanti Deus habuit dominium, proprietatem, et possessionem." Ibid.
(I, 10a).

[109] Ibid. (I, 10b).

[110] "Alii curiose opinantur, nomine *viarum* denotari divinas processiones
Filii, et Spiritus sancti; ...cum ergo (inquiunt) Beata Virgo dicit; possessam fuisse
a Deo in initio viarum suarum, significare voluit, ab aeternitate, in qua Filiis,
et Spiritus sanctus fuere producti, ipsam esse praedestinatam ad hoc, ut ab instanti suae conceptionis ita possideretur a Deo per gratiam, ut nullus pateret
aditus diabolicae possessioni per maculam originalem." Ibid. (I, 11a).

[111] "...Deus misericordiae suae innitentem, non iustitiae, ab instanti suae

"*Ab aeterno ordinata sum*" connotes not just Mary's eternal pre-destination but also her original integrity, the orderly disposition of her appetites and the harmony between her body and soul.[112] "*Ex antiquis*'" signifies that God combined in Mary all that is beautiful found in her ancient predecessors, in the angels and the Patriarchs.[113] Or taking "*ex antiquis*" to mean the three divine persons of the Trinity, inasmuch as the one and triune God is called also "*antiquus dierum*' (Dan 10, 12), it says that the three divine persons in a sin-gular manner poured out gifts upon Mary from their appropriated attributes.[114]

Proceeding to the rest of the passage, Cartagena next interprets: "*Nondum erant abyssi, et ego iam concepta eram.*" It is not sufficient, he says, to assert that Mary was conceived in the divine mind for all eternity (i.e. "*ab aeterno ordinata sum*"), because so is every crea-ture conceived and not just she. But certainly in election and in the gifts and grace conferred by God, Mary surpassed all other creatures.

Conceptionis illam possedisse; nam si instanti, et non misericordia uti voluisset, non ab ipso, sed ab hoste peccati originalis a principio possideri incepisset." Ibid. (I, 11b–12a).

[112] "Cum ergo Beata Virgo ait: 'ab aeterno ordinata sum': supposuit in se fuisse partes inaequales, ac dispares, animam scilicet, et corpus, rationem supe-riorem, et appetitum sensitivum; has tamen partes ita bene inter se dispositas, et sibi cohaerentes habuisse, ut neutra contra aliam unquam conspirarit, nec enim corpus rebellionem tentavit adversus animam, nec sensualis appetitus rationi unquam restitit. Tali quidem ordine decebat Dei genitricem ordinatam fuisse, quae regulatissimum (ut ita dicam) ipsum ordinem mundo, ad illum regulan-dum paritura erat." Ibid. (I, 11b).

[113] " 'Ex antiquis', non parum Beatae Virginis commendat excellentiam: sicut enim excellentes pictores solent antiqua exemplaria observare, ut ad eorum inspectionem, quae pulchriora sunt, seligentes, pulcherrimam ipsi imaginem ef-forment: ita Deus Angelos, ac veteres Patriarchas, qui antiquitate temporis re-liquos praecellunt, ab aeterno contemplans, pulchriora ex eis selegit, ut in Beatam Virginem omnia illa simul conferret, et pulcherrimam omnium imaginem illam effingeret." Ibid.

[114] "Vel certe, cum (sacra Scriptura id attestante) Deus trinus, et unus vo-cetur, 'antiquus dierum', non incongrue dicemus, per verba illa: 'ex antiquis' significari singulas divinas Personas ex appropriatis sibi attributis singulares quas-dam nulli creaturae in eo gradu unquam communicandas perfectiones, Virgini liberaliter donandas praedefinivisse: Pater virtutem, et potentiam ad generan-dum Deum; Filius, sapientiam, qua velut sapientissima magistra instar Deborae, quae Filiis Israel responsa dabat, ipsa praeesset Ecclesiae; Spiritus sanctus fer-ventem adeo amorem, ut ardentissimos quosque Seraphinos longe superaret." Ibid.

If the Ark of Noah or the Temple of Solomon took so long to pre-
pare, it could not have been shorter for Mary, the future Ark of the
true Noah and the living Temple of the Incarnate God.[115] Indeed it
was from all eternity, when the *abyssi* were not yet. In this instance,
abyssus is to be understood as a derivative, the absence of *byssus*,
of lustre or whiteness. Aptly then is *a–byssus* seen as sin, which de-
prives the soul of the lustre of grace. In the light of this signification,
Mary clearly claims that sin's death cannot be imputed to her, because she has been conceived in the mind of God even before any
sin was existent. Although all the descendants and progenies of Adam
went down into the abyss of original sin, Mary by a special grace of
her Son was not pulled down too in her conception, having been
predestined by God even before sin was.[116]

Thus, Juan de Cartagena thinks Mary's Immaculate Conception
can also be indicated in Sacred Scripture. It is an exposition of biblical words along the so–called mystical sense. It is not literal ; the
methodology does not measure up to the strict *Wissenschaft* of today's biblical studies. But Cartagena considers it appropriate for his
purpose in writing his *Homiliae Catholicae*, i.e. "*pro cibandis fidelibus.*" Let us go on with the rest of the scriptural "testimony" presented by the author.

2. *Song of Songs 4,7*. The ninth homily begins with Mary's ut-
terance of the Bride's opening words in the first poem of the Song of
Songs 1,5 : "I am black but lovely, daughters of Jerusalem, like the
tents of Kedar, like the pavilions of Solomon." Addressed to those

---

[115] Cf. Lib. I, hom. II (I, 13b).

[116] "Celebris ille Archidiaconus, in cap. nonne 37. distinct. docet: Abyssum
dici ab A, quod est sine, et 'Byssus', quod genus quoddam lini candidissimi significat: unde ait; idem esse Abyssum, quod sine Bysso, seu, sine candore: hoc supposito, apte quidem per 'Abyssum' intelligitur peccatum, quod candore divinae
gratiae animam privat... B. Virgo apertissime probat, sibi non importandam esse
mortem peccati, quia antequam essent abyssi originalis culpae, etiam in aeterna
permissione, permittente omnes ab Adam naturali via propagatos infici, iam ipsa
in mente Dei concepta, et in divina voluntate praeordinata erat: atque hinc est,
quod licet in profundo illo abysso, ac profluvio originalis peccati submersi fuerint
omnes ab Adamo progeniti, de quibus in sensu mystico intelligi possunt verba illa
Exodi: 'Submersi sunt in Mari rubro, Abyssi operuerunt eos, descenderunt in
profundum quasi lapis': Beatissima vero Genetrix ex speciali filii sui beneficio,
in Conceptione sua submergi non potuit: ipsa dicente: 'Nondum erant Abyssi'
peccati originalis, 'et ego iam concepta eram' in mente Dei..." Ibid. (I, 13b–14a).

who are stained by original sin, these words correct their mistaken presumption that she was also blackened by sin. In her case "black is beautiful," since her beauty is much like the hidden, interior beauty of the tents of Kedar and the pavilions of Solomon. For, although she was born like any other man and therefore would seem to have contracted too the same stain of original sin with which everyman is born, Mary is interiorly adorned with the glories of divine grace and was never for a moment infected by sin.[117] She is "black" only because she belongs integrally to the fallen human race. The following words of the poem convey the same thought of hidden beauty underneath a misleading surface: "Take no notice of my swarthiness, it is the sun that has burnt me" (1, 6). Notwithstanding all appearances, she has been preserved from the incursion of sin by the divine rays of the sun of justice and hence colored with the darkish tinge of charity.[118]

The Bridegroom's own words (4, 7) are of the like intent: "You are wholly beautiful, my love, and there is no blemish in you." Even if this passage has been commonly interpreted as referring to the Church, at least to the Church Triumphant, it has been understood too as speaking of Mary, who is without any blemish of sin whatsoever. Cartagena finds it intriguing that the Holy Spirit, inspiring the sacred writer, said first that Mary is beautiful, *"Pulchra es amica mea,"* and then that she is without blemish of sin, *"et macula non est in te."*

---

[117] "Licet nigra sim apud vos, qui me peccati originalis nigredine deturpatam fuisse putatis, sed vestra vos fallit opinio, quia formosa, et pulchra sum, sed pulchritudine instar tabernaculum cedar, et pellium Salomonis, quae licet extrinsecus tamen miram pulchritudinem abscondebant: non secus ego, licet per communem generis humani propagationem progenita fuerim, et hac ratione maculam contraxisse videar, intrinsecus tamen illius propagationis labe, quae omnes inficere solet, nec per momentum temporis infecta, sed miris divinae gratiae splendoribus illustrata fui." Lib. I, hom. IX (I, 43a).

Cartagena cites among others the Song of Songs' commentaries by Alanus ab Insulis (*PL* 210, 51–110), Honorius Augustodunensis (*PL* 172, 347–496), and Rupert von Deutz (*PL* 168, 873–962). On the Marian interpretation of the Song of Songs, see Helmut Riedlinger, "Maria–Kirche in den marianischen Hohenliedskommentaren des Mittelalters," in *Maria et Ecclesia*, III (Roma, 1959), pp. 241–289; and J. Beumer, "Die marianische Deutung des Hohen Liedes in der Frühscholastik," *Zeitschrift für katholische Theologie*, 76 (1954) 411–439.

[118] "Quamvis obnoxia sim peccato originali, sicut et reliqui omnes, atque ex hac parte fusca appaream propter debitum contrahendi hoc peccati genus, verutamen ex divina solis iustitiae irradiatione ab eo praeservata, et purpureo claritatis habitu colorata sum, 'quia decoloravit me sol.'" Ibid. (I, 43a–b).

She is so completely beautiful, that there is not even a venial sin in her. And if no venial sin, much less the greater deformity of original sin.[119]

This spiritual beauty of Mary has been foreshadowed by the physical beauties of Rebecca, Rachel and Judith.[120] And the Holy Spirit knowing the inadequacy of any one creature to picture the beauty of Mary, compares her to a veritable litany of beautiful things: to the beauty of the moon (Song of Songs 6, 9), of the sun (Song of Songs 6, 9), of the stars (Numbers 24, 17), of a heavily fortified and impregnable stronghold (Song of Songs 7, 5), of a ship driven by a good wind (Proverbs 31, 14), of a bowl made with consummate skill (Song of Songs 7, 3), of a fountain and of a well giving forth most clear water (Song of Songs 4, 15), of a vine (Ecclesiasticus 24, 23), of a nard (Song of Songs 1, 12), of a lily (Song of Songs 2, 2), of a rose (Ecclesiasticus 24, 18), of a big heap of wheat (Song of Songs 7, 2), etc.[121] The beauty of Mary is such, in other words, that she is devoid of the slightest moral imperfection. And this perfect image, coming from the hand of the divine painter, bears the title: *Tota pulchra es, amica mea*, as if to say that no perfection due to the Mother of God is found lacking in her.[122] The author returns in another homily to this idea of God as an artist in the world studio who created an unblemished picture, Mary. God made this most beautiful image in the moment of her conception, and it is unthinkable that she ever lacked grace even for an instant.[123]

---

[119] "...quod beata Virgo omni peccato veniali semper caruerit, quod minus commaculat animam, congrue satis infertur, etiam caruisse originali, quod deformius inficit illam: si enim Matrem Dei levis culpa, multo magis gravis, et mortifera, cuiusmodi est peccatum originale." Ibid. (I, 44b).

[120] Cf. Ibid. (I, 44b–45a).

[121] Cf. Ibid. (I, 45a–46a).

[122] "Sola beatissima Virgo omnes puras creaturas in eo valde praecellit, quod pulchritudo eius adeo est omnibus numeris absoluta, ut minimae etiam moralis imperfectionis maculae poenitus sit expers... pulcherrima haec imago beatae Virginis... perfecta adeo ex manibus supremi pictoris prodivit, ut hanc ei subscriptionem apposuerit: 'Tota pulchra es, amica mea'; ac si diceret: nihil perfectionis Genitrici Dei debitae in te desideratur." Ibid. (I, 46b–47a).

[123] "Hanc pulcherrimam imaginem Deus in die Conceptionis in theatrum mundi producit, ut ab omnibus inspiciatur. Absit ergo, ut quispiam defectum aliquam ipsi attribuat, aut illi gratiam, vel uno tantum temporis momento defuisse affirmet. Maxime cum artifex omnium peritissimus, laudet illam dicens: 'Tota pulchra es amica mea, et macula non est in te.' Eamque prae omnibus

3. *Song of Songs 6, 9.* Juan de Cartagena suggests in his eleventh homily that we, as "Catholic astrologers," explore the auspices surrounding the conception of Mary. There is the passage from the Book of Revelation to begin with: "Now a great sign appeared in heaven: a woman, adorned with the sun, standing on the moon, and with the twelve stars on her head for a crown" (12, 1). For Cartagena this text serves as a bridge to the more pregnant passage of the Song of Songs. This description of Mary enveloped in light from head to foot signifies, the author asserts, that from beginning to end she is shining brightly with the splendor of grace. And in rapt admiration of her the angels exclaim: "Who is this arising like the dawn, fair as the moon, resplendent as the sun, terrible as an army in array?" (Song of Songs 6, 9).[124]

First, she is compared to the *dawn*, which starts to light up and increases in brightness until it is joined to the burning sun. Similarly Mary at the point of her conception began to shine forth with the light of divine grace and climbed up to the light of day, the apex of brightness, when she was joined with Christ, the sun of justice she bore.[125] As Psalm 45, 5 has it: "at crack of dawn God helps her." That is, at the crack of dawn, at the moment of her conception, God freed and preserved her from the stain of original sin.[126] At her conception therefore a new light rose up, that by the grace of God broke through the darkness normally surrounding human conception blemished by sin. The words of St. John's Prologue apply here: "*Et lux in tenebris lucet, et tenebrae eam non comprehenderunt.*" Thus as in

---

aliis tanti faciat, ut licet ceterae omnes imagines obscurentur peccati litura, hanc tamen omnino incolumen esse voluerit." Lib. I, hom. X (I, 52a).

[124] "Ecce describit Virginem a capite usque ad pedes undique perlucidam, ac fulgentem, ut significet, a principio usque ad finem gratiae splendore semper coruscasse; cuius tam singularis excellentiae admiratione rapti Angeli dixerunt: 'Quae est ista, quae progreditur, quasi aurora consurgens, pulchra, ut luna, electa, ut sol, terribilis, ut castrorum acies ordinata?'" Lib. I, hom. XI (I, 54b). Cf. Lib. V, hom. XVI (I, 496a).

[125] "...sic immaculata Virgo in puncto, ut concepta fuit, coepit divinae gratiae luce clarere, et in hac claritate in dies succrescens, tandem cum sole iustitiae Christo Domino in coelesti beatitudine mirae gloriae decorata fulgoribus fuit coniuncta." Ibid.

[126] "Atque huc faciunt verba illa Davidica: 'Adiuvabit eam Deus mane diluculo'... ut adiuvaret Virginem, non solum mane surrexit, sed 'mane diluculo' eam praeliberans, et preservans in puncto Conceptionis suae a macula culpae originalis." Ibid. (I, 54b–55a).

the creation of the world, God created the light and finding it good he separated the light from darkness. In like manner in creating Mary, God gave her at the moment of her conception the light of divine grace, which God found so pleasing that he separated Mary forever from the darkness of sin.[127] That is why it can be said of her: "God will not be moved from her midst" (Psalm 45, 6), which means that God dwells in her permanently and has never left her due to original sin or any mortal sin, nor has God been ever "moved" in her because of a venial sin.[128]

Secondly, Mary is likened to the *moon*, which from its very inception has been reflecting the light of the sun and which consequently has never known darkness. Mary from the moment of her conception has likewise been illuminated with the light of the sun of justice, and has never known the darkness of original sin.[129]

Not satisfied with comparing her to the dawn and to the moon, the angels next match her with the *sun*. Why so? First of all, Mary is likened to the sun, in order to bring out the fact that the prerogative of her Immaculate Conception as prefigured by the dawn and the moon is hers alone and uniquely, just as the light of the sun is alone its own. Also, such a gradation in light, so to say, from the dawn to the moon to the sun will forestall any hasty conclusion that Mary is a god. That could easily have been the case, had she been likened to the sun only, says Cartagena in the same tone with which he finds justification why the doctrine of her Immaculate Conception

---

[127] "Hoc est, in medio tenebrarum Conceptionis, ubi nemo unquam vidit lucem, nova haec divinae gratiae lux emicuit; huicque factum est, ut tenebrae caliginosae noctis peccati originalis eam comprehendere non potuerint... Sic Deus in constructione beatissimae Virginis, hoc est, in eius conceptione, primum quod effecit, fuit lux divinae gratiae, quam Virgini inesse tantopere Deus sibi complacuit, ut illam a tenebris peccati divisam semper permanere voluerit." Ibid. (I, 55a).

[128] "Si ergo summa infoelicitas est, recessus Dei ab anima, foelicissima sors beatae Virgini contigit, in qua semper Deus inhabitavit, et in qua permanenter adeo pedem fixit, ut non solum non recederet ab ea per peccatum originale, aut mortale, sed neque commoveretur levi aliquo veniali, Davide dicente: 'Deus in medio eius non commovebitur'." Ibid. (I, 55b).

[129] "...sicut luna in primo instanti suae creationis fulgentissimis solis radiis coepit irradiari, ita sacratissima Virgo in puncto suae Conceptionis, solis iustitiae clarissimo lumine illam irradiante, coepit divinis fulgoribus coruscare. Unde sicut luna in sui creatione tenebras nescivit; ita et Virgo in sua Conceptione peccati originalis caliginem ignoravit." Ibid. (I, 56a).

is still not solemnly defined.[130] Furthermore, it can be said that like
the sun which is midway among the planets (Cartagena obviously
rejects Copernican astronomy), Mary has a position midway between
God and the angels. If she is however superior to the angels, then
she could not have had original sin, since the angels never had it.[131]

The question which remains is why is she next pictured as an
army in battle array? The images of the dawn, the moon and the sun
do not exactly jibe with that of an *acies castrorum*. The author
thinks that these similes are really not that foreign to one another.
For, just as nothing is more beautiful during the day than the sun,
so also nothing is more beautiful in battle than an army in array.[132]
And as St. Paul observed: "It is not against human enemies that
we have to struggle, but against the Sovereignties and the Powers
who originate the darkness in this world" (Ephesians 6, 12). In this
warfare against darkness — returning to a favorite image of Cartagena — Mary is the sun and the moon assisting us, as Gedeon was
assisted by the sun and the moon to victory. Mary is like a terrifying
army scattering the forces of darkness.[133] Cartagena drives his point
home:

---

[130] "Respondeo primo, solis comparationem addidisse, ut significarent in
hac immaculatae Conceptionis praerogativa per auroram, et lunam praesignifi-
cata, solam et unicam instar solis inter puras creaturas beatam Virginem extitisse... Secondo respondeo, id consulto effecisse, ne, si tantum Virginem soli com-
parassent, quae supremum habet lucem, et cuius nullum decrementum, aut
augmentum esse noscitur, Deus esse credetur. Unde ut puram creaturam esse
faterentur, compararunt illam primo aurorae, quae minus lucida, deinde lunae,
quae lucidior est, ac tandem soli, qui reliqua omnia claritate superat. Haec enim
mutabilitas per incrementum lucis, et per verbum illud, 'progreditur', significata,
quae Deo minime competere potest..." Ibid. (I, 57b–58a). Cf. above, p. 177.

[131] "Denique Soli apte Virginem comparari ex eo non obscure liquet, quod,
quia medius est inter planetas, ita ut super se habebat tres, et infra totidem alios,
sic beata Virgo in excellentia et puritate ita medium locum tenet inter Deum,
et Angelos, ut, si de Personis loquamur, super se solum habeat tres divinas Personas, quae sunt praecipue planetae, ex quorum influentia tota mundi machina
pendet; infra se vero habet tres alios planetas, scilicet Hierarchiam Angelicam,
omnes Angelos in se comprehendentem. Si ergo in puritate medium locum tenet
Beata Virgo inter Deum, et Angelos, et consequenter caruisse omni labe peccati
tam actualis, quam originalis, cum etiam Angeli ea poenitus caruerit..." Ibid.
(I, 58a).

[132] "...sicut nihil est pulchrius in die, quam sol, nec pulchrius in nocte,
quam luna, ita in bello pulchrius nihil, quam castrorum acies bene ordinata."
Ibid. (I, 58b).

[133] "...puto Angelos alludere ad solem, et lunam, qui tempore Gedeonis

If therefore the Blessed Virgin is like a terrifying army in defending the faithful, how much more terrible against the devil must she have been in her own defense, when at the moment of her conception the devil attempted to overcome and lead her to slavery? [134]

Moreover, it is to be noted that Mary is likened to an army *bene ordinata*. A well–ordered army should have its front and its rear properly protected, its *antiguardia* and *retroguardia*, as they say in Italian. It was exactly so with Mary, because at her conception, i.e. her *antiguardia*, she did not suffer the corruption of original sin, and at her death, i.e. her *retroguardia*, she did not return back to dust.[135] As a terrifying army entering the world against the devil, it is inconceivable that Mary appeared already a captive of the enemy through original sin! [136]

4. *Psalm 8,4 2.* We turn now to other passages employed by Cartagena, but which are dealt with more in passing than in homily–long development. Cartagena in discussing Mary's predestination sees her preservation from original sin indicated in the words of the psalmist: "You blessed, Lord, your land," i.e. with the benediction of sanctifying grace. For, just as the first Adam was formed out of

---

cursum suum cohibentes steterunt, ut milites Gedeonis hostes suos expugnare possent. Unde gloriosa illa victoria non tam fuit Gedeonis, quam solis, et lunae, cum eorum auxilio illam tulerit. Cum ergo fideles continuum bellum gerant adversus Principes tenebrarum, iuxta illud Divi Pauli: 'Non est nobis colluctatio adversus carnem, et sanguinem, sed adversus Principes, et Potestates tenebrarum harum,' sitque etiam per quam manifestum, nihil magis opponi tenebris, quam lucem solis, et lunae, recte beata Virgo, quae ad pugnam illam eos vehementer adiuvat, soli, et lunae merito comparatur." Ibid.

[134] Ibid. (I, 59a).

[135] "Ordo autem Exercitus in eo praecipue attenditur, ut principium, et finis illius, quod vulgari sermone Italice dicitur: 'L'antiguardia, et retroguardia', undique clausi sint, ut hostis nulla ratione possit illum irrumpere, alioquin confundet ordinem, et facile tota militum acies vincetur. Beatissima igitur Virgo fuit velut acies castrorum recte ordinata, quia nec in fine, nec in principio suae Conceptionis, quae fuit velut 'antiguardia', nec in fine suae mortis, quae se habuit velut 'retroguardia', aditus ullus unquam Doemoni patuit, et ideo nec animae eius in Conceptione corruptione peccati originalis, nec corpus in morte conversionem in pulverem sustinuit." Ibid.

[136] "...si, velut exercitus armatus, et Diabolo terribilis, ac formidabilis ingreditur mundum, manifestum est, non ingredi velut captivam Doemonis. Hanc enim captivitatem peccatum originale inducit." Ibid. (I, 59b).

the pure earth which had not yet been condemned, so also did Christ the Second Adam come from Mary as from a land uncontaminated by original sin. God's blessing is a preservative from and not only cure of the captivity by the devil, as is expressed further by the same passage: "You prevented the captivity of Jacob." The word *"avertisti"* is used instead of *"abstulisti,"* to signify clearly that the slavery of original sin had been hindered from affecting Mary. Her preservation from it is distinctive of her sanctification, because the same psalm in talking of the sanctification of others uses the "curative" terms: *"remisisti iniquitatem plebis tuae"* and *"operuisti omnia peccata eorum"* (Psalm 84, 3).[137]

5. *Genesis 3, 15.* Concerning Mary's role in the work of redemption, Cartagena admits that some would rather water down the teaching. But he believes to be able to support it with scriptural testimonies among others.[138] The doctrine is obviously indicated, he says, in the words of the Book of Genesis: *"Inimicitias ponam inter te, et mulierem, et inter semen tuum, et semen illius; ipsa conteret caput tuum."* Although in the original Hebrew the equivalent of *ipsum,* instead of the Vulgate's *ipsa,* is found as designated to crush the snake's head, the very diversity of the readings is ground enough for the author

---

[137] "...sicut terra illa, ex qua productus fuit Adam, nulli unquam maledictioni obnoxia fuerat; ita, et B. Virgo, ex qua secundus prodiit Adam, nulli originalis peccati maledictio subiacuerat... Quod eapropter in spiritu praevidens Regius Vates arbitror dixisse: 'Benedixisti Domine terram tuam,' benedictione, inquam, divinae gratiae animam sanctificantis. Ne autem quispiam putaret, ipsum loqui de benedictione sanctificationis post contractum peccatum originale, continuo subiunxit: benedictionem illam fuisse praeservativam, ne in Daemonis captivitatem veniret: 'avertisti captivitatem Iacob'; non dixit: 'abstulisti' captivitatem, quasi iam illam incurrisset; sed 'avertisti', ut palam significaret originalis peccati servitutem propulasse, et beatam Virginem prohibitam, seu impeditam fuisse, ne in illam incideret. Unde notanter loquens in eodem Psalmo de sanctificatione aliorum, non dixit: 'Avertisti captivitatem', sed, 'Remisisti iniquitatem plebis tuae, operuisti omnia peccata eorum': quo dispari loquendi genere, non obscure docuit David, hoc fuisse discrimen inter sanctificationem Virginis, et aliorum, quod illius praeservativa, horum sanativa extiterit." Lib. I, hom. III (I, 16a–b).

[138] "...Christo Domino data fuit beatissima Virgo in coadiutricem ad spiritualem filiorum sobolem procreandam, et humanum genus a diabolica captivitate redimendum, quam veritatem, tametsi nonnulli inficiari tentaverint, sacras nihilominus scripturae testimoniis, et veterum Patrum monumentis confirmare adnitar." Ibid. (I, 16b).

to see that Mary has indeed a part in redemption, though a minor one, since Christ plays the principal role.[139] She is the *ipsa* who would contribute in crushing the devil.

This participation by Mary is contained also in the passage: *"Cum eo eram componens"* (Proverbs 8, 27). Before her conception everything was in disorder due to the sin of man. With her coming, however, order sets in, in that she reconciles men to their Creator and through her prayers saves sinners from the power of the evil one.[140]

A consequence of the above, that Mary would tread on the head of the snake, is the reality of her Immaculate Conception. The devil's head is none other than original sin, which Mary at her conception treaded upon. It was then either his head or her head, which would have meant that she were conceived under the domination of the enemy.[141]

---

[139] "Idipsum magis adhuc perspicue, et distinctus indicant verba illa Genes. 1. 'Inimicitias ponam inter te, et mulierem, et inter semen tuum, et semen illius; ipsa conteret caput tuum'; ex quo loco non obscure patet opus redemptionis Virgini suo modo attribui; licet enim in Hebraeo legatur: 'Ipsum' scilicet, semen 'conteret caput tuum', hoc est Christus, qui redemit nos ab originali... tamen non 'ipse', sed 'ipsa'... legit nostra vulgata: ex qua versionum diversitate infero, iuxta unam interpretationem Christo, iuxta alteram Virgini opus redemptionis attribui; Christo, ut principali auctori; Virgini, ut minus principali: sicut peccatum originale principaliter Adae, minus principaliter Evae adscribi solet." Ibid. (I, 16b–17a).

This interpretation of the passage by Cartagena as referring (too) to Mary is noted by Tiburtius Gallus, *Interpretatio Mariologica Protoevangelii Posttridentina*, op. cit., pp. 111–112.

[140] "Id enim sibi volunt (ni fallor) verba illa Proverbium: 'Cum eo eram cuncta componens.' Sane ante conceptionem Virginis, cuncta erant incomposita, propter enormia hominum scelera, quibus divinam iram irritaverant: B. autem Virgo in mundum veniens, cuncta composuit, e potestate diabolica precibus suis peccatores eruens, et creatori suo illos reconcilians." Ibid. (I, 16b).

[141] "... 'ipsa conteret caput tuum.' His quidem non obscure mihi persuadeo, immaculatam Virginis Conceptionem aperte comprobari. Cum enim serpens de Eva victoriam reportaverit, constat verba illa de B. Virgine caput serpentis conterente, intelligenda esse... at tanta fuit Virgini divinitus data fortitudo in Conceptione sua, ut hoc Diaboli caput, peccatum scilicet originale, penitus conteret; quod sane si secus accidisset, potius Diabolus Virginis caput contrivisset, eius Conceptionem maculans, quae caput fuit, et principium curriculi totius eius vitae." Ibid. (I, 18a–b).

6. *Luke 1, 28.* If the progenies of Adam should all be born with the debt to contract original sin, Mary is free of such debt, because the angel's greeting to her: *"Ave gratia plena"* shows that she has received as dowry a plenitude of grace, which liberates her from such obligations.[142] With originality, Cartagena sees in this fact that Mary is full of grace sufficient reason both for her Immaculate Conception and her Assumption into heaven, as we shall discuss later. That Mary is immune from any *debitum* is indicated too by the words of the psalmist: *"Adstitit regina a dextris tuis in vestitu deaurato circumdata varietate"* (Psalm 44, 11). From the first moment of her conception, Mary has been standing at the right hand of God, and she is dressed with the gold of grace and wrapped in the richness of all virtues.[143] Also, the queen is ordinarily accoutered similar to the king or the spouse. In that case Mary would have the same dress as her Son. So, it is unthinkable that she was ever covered with the shame of original sin.[144] More appropriately is she vested with the vesture of justice and sanctity through the merits of her Son.[145]

---

[142] "...certum est, plurima debita ob Adae peccatum humanum genus contraxisse: at B. Virgo, cum acceperit gratiam in dotem, Angelo dicente: 'Ave gratia plena', in hac dote protegenda est, et liberanda a solutione debitorum, ad quam alii tenentur... si lex dicat: omnes ex Adam originem ducentes, in peccato fore concipiendos; dotem, et arram suam dicet esse gratiae plenitudinem, atque adeo ab hoc communi debito reipsa solvendo, immunem esse." Lib. I, hom. IV (I, 21b–22a).

[143] "Praeviderat Regius Vates hanc Marianam praerogativam, ac singularem excellentiam, cum dixit: 'Adstitit regina a dextris tuis in vestitu deaurato circumdata varietate', statim in primo conceptionis instanti Regina nostra a dextris Dei, extitit, nunquam nec puncto quidem temporis astitit a sinistris, tunc vestitum induit gratiae deauratum; tunc circumdedit eam omnium virtutum varietas." Ibid. (I, 22a).

[144] "Cum igitur B. Virgo induatur eodem genere vestimenti, quo filius, hoc est, luce; sicut enim 'ipse est amictus lumine sicut vestimento' (Ps 103, 2), ita, et ipsa amicta sole, ut vidit Ioannes; 'Mulier amicta sole, et luna sub pedibus suis' (Apoc 12, 1), et sicut Christus induitur varietate, ut Isaias dixit: 'his omnibus, velut ornamento vestieris' (Isai 49, 18); eadem, et ipsa vestitur, ut ait David: 'in vestitu deaurato circumdata varietate,' manifestum inde relinquitur, turpi illa peccati originalis veste minime fuisse indutam..." Ibid. (I, 22a–b).

[145] "Unde sicut vestimentum Christi Domini fuit iustitia, et sanctitas, hoc eodem vestimenti genere beatissima Virgo ex meritis filii sui induta semper fuit." Ibid. (I, 23a).

B. Biblical Images, Types and Metaphors

1. *Temple*. Among the many biblical types, images and figures used by Juan de Cartagena in his exposition of the mystery of the Immaculate Conception, the metaphor of the temple is dwelt upon longer and more fully than all the others. His metaphor or figure—oriented approach in this regard leads him to gather scriptural texts laden with images which can be made to prefigure Mary. Thus, from the metaphorical perspective of a temple her Immaculate Conception receives an elucidation. "The glory of the Lord filled the Temple of God" (2 Chronicles 5, 14) starts us off, therefore, in a consideration of the glory which enveloped the house of God. Mary too has been overwhelmingly endowed with glorious gifts, that we rightly celebrate.[146] The temple of Solomon was built when he had peace and was waging no war nor suffering any calamity (1 Kings 5, 18). In like manner, the holy temple of Mary started to be built at the time of her conception with no attack from the devil, whom God had disposed of, so that he could not infect her with the virus of original sin.[147] So, this most sacred temple was built on firm and solid foundation, "founded on the holy mountains" (Psalm 87, 1). The obvious way of interpreting these *montibus sanctis* is by taking them to mean the holy saints of God who were the forerunners of Mary's much greater sanctity. But Cartagena finds more appealing the "higher" interpretation that sees these mountains to signify the power of the Father, the wisdom of the Son and the goodness of the Holy Spirit. He makes the application in following terms:

---

[146] The first book's 12th homily is entitled: "Sub metaphora Templi, et Domus Dei varia locis Sacrae Scripturae, multisque animi conceptionibus illustrata, immaculata Virginis Conceptio magis stabilitur." (I, 60a).

Of God's glory filling Mary like the temple the author believes: "Sane cum Deus divinis charismatibus sacrosanctum hoc templum B. Virginis interius, et exterius locupletaverit; ad nos spectat divinis laudibus, et encomiis tam interius, quam exterius immaculatam eius Conceptionem plaudentes celebrare." Ibid. (I, 60b–61a). Cf. Yves Congar, *Das Mysterium des Tempels* (Salzburg, 1960), pp. 244–249.

[147] "Ita sacrosanctum Virginis templum aedificari coepit in eius Conceptione, cum Doemonis occursus non adfuit, quia Dominus ligaverat illum, et os eius concluserat, ne in Virginem, quae futura eius Mater erat, peccati originalis virus evomeret." Ibid. (I, 61a).

Since therefore the Conception of the Virgin, which has such foundations, rests on the power of the Father, surely nobody will disagree that possibly she is free from sin. Since she is also supported by the wisdom of the Son, who will not affirm that it would be wanting of his infinite knowledge and divine mind not to preserve his own mother from original sin, by virtue of the blood of Christ and in view of his merits? And lastly, since the conception of this glorious Virgin is founded on the goodness of the Holy Spirit, it remains that she is a stranger to all sin and therefore had been preserved from the original stain.[148]

That is why she can claim: *"In me gratia omnis viae, et veritatis"* (Ecclesiasticus 24, 17). She has every grace, hence the grace too of preservation from original sin. And the grace is received while on the way and not at the end of this life; it is *gratia viae*. The fact, in addition, that it is the grace of truth confirms that Mary's Immaculate Conception is most true.[149]

With the foundations secured, the builder then raised up various pillars with which this miraculous temple is supported. "She has erected her seven pillars, prepared her wine, laid her table" (Proverbs 9, 1–2). The common patristic interpretation of these pillars takes them to represent the three theological and the four cardinal virtues, or the seven gifts of the Holy Spirit. But what is remarkable is that "she prepared her wine and laid her table." Mary's womb is truly like a sacred workshop where the heavenly bread of Christ's body and the wine of his blood were produced. And just as God does not want leavened bread to be consecrated on the altar, because leaven leads to corruption, so also Christ, in taking his flesh from Mary into the indissoluble hypostatic union, would not have taken it from what is already spoiled by the leaven of sin.[150]

---

[148] Ibid. (I, 61a–b).

[149] "Si ergo 'omnis', gratia praeservationis ab originali ei non defuit. Si 'viae', ergo loquitur de gratia accepta in via, non de ea, quam habet in patria; si tandem, 'veritatis', ergo Virginem in sua conceptione praeservatam fuisse verissimum est." Ibid. (I, 61b). This verse is found only in the Vulgate and some LXX manuscripts.

[150] "...vere uterus virginalis fuit velut sacra quaedam officina, in qua factus est panis coelestis corporis Christi, et vinum sanguinis eius... ex quo inferre licet, quos si Deus velut panem consecrandum in altari absque fermento esse, quia fermentum ad corruptionem tendit, sub quo tamen tamdiu solum delitescit, quamdiu durant species panis, quod modicum temporis est; coniunctum valde

Among other things that we are told about the construction of the temple is that it was built without hammer or any iron tools (1 Kings 6, 7). Opinions abound as to the meaning of this, but Cartagena holds that as regards the Marian temple it indicates that no hammer of sin to strike Mary's head or iron tool of original sin to separate her from God was present or employed even for a moment at her construction or conception.[151] And the words of the psalmist: "Come and see the Lord's works, the astounding things he has done on the earth" (Psalm 46, 8) tell us something else about Mary's special beginning. The Vulgate's *"prodigia super terram"* is given in other versions as *"posuit benedictionem super terram."* This latter translation brings out the contrast between this earth blessed by God and the earth accursed by him to yield brambles and thistles at the beginning of creation following the fall (Genesis 3, 17–18). God blessed this sacred earth of the Virgin at the beginning of her creation, as the words of Ecclesiasticus (1, 9) manifest: "He himself has created her in the Holy Spirit." That is why David could say: "Come and see the astounding things he has done on the earth." [152]

No less revealing about Mary are the words: "The new glory of this Temple is going to surpass the old" (Haggai 2, 9). The author believes that this text could not be talking of Jerusalem's second temple (Ezra 3, 12). It is rather more appropriately understood as speaking of the Blessed Virgin. And the glory of her own temple derives above all from holiness. "Holiness will distinguish your house, Lord, for ever and ever" (Psalm 93, 5). Houses of kings are

---

cum ratione arbitror, ut ad sumendum carnem ex B. Virgine, quae secum indissolubili unionis hypostaticae vinculo unita in aeternum perseveratura erat, non desumeret illam ex materia, quae alicuius peccati fermento corrupta umquam fuisset." Ibid. (I, 62a).

[151] "Certe in magna huius Mariani templi fabrica erigenda audeo dicere, nec malleum, nec ferram fuisse auditam; non malleum peccati, caput Virginis conterentem, quae Diaboli caput contrivit; nec ferram ferream culpae originalis, quae illam a Deo, vel per momentum separaret." Ibid. (I, 62a–b).

[152] "Certe Deus in principio creationis mundi terram maledixit... quae maledictio totam terram adeo inficit... quia ergo Deus e contra a principio creationis huius sacrosanctae terrae B. Virginis illam benedixerat, ut clare verba illa Ecclesiastici indicant: 'Ipse creavit illam in Spiritu sancto, ideo ad hoc prodigium respiciens David, dicebat: 'Venite, et videte, quae posuit prodigia super terram': intueamini rem nunquam visam, et attendite rem inauditam: terram a principio suae creationis, benedictam, et in hac benedictione perpetuo perseverantem..." Ibid. (I, 63a). "In the Holy Spirit" is an obvious addition of the Vulgate.

made renowned by their gold and precious stones. Mary's temple on the other hand is principally ornamented with grace and sanctity.[153] As Ezekiel (43, 12) reported: "This is the charter of the temple: all the surrounding area on top of the mountain is a most holy area." Mary is also such a temple surrounded by holiness, so much so that God symbolized by the sun is like a vestment to this "woman adorned with the sun" (Revelation 12, 1).[154] Furthermore, the glory of Mary as the temple is shown by the fact that God himself is her maker and builder. "It is he who makes her what she is, he, the Most High" (Psalm 87, 5).[155] "Since the majesty and the glory of this temple and sacred house is therefore such, as is abundantly clear from the above, I ask," Cartagena leads on, "who will dare contaminate it with the stain of original sin?"[156]

In another homily the author returns to his metaphor of the temple to reason out to the improbability that Mary as the temple of God could be polluted by sin. If Judas and the others in I Mac-

---

[153] "Denique de hoc sacrosancto templo Virginis existimo intelligi debere verba illa: 'Magna est gloria domus istius novissimae, plusquam primae'; non enim tam apte verificari possunt de templi illo secundo Hierosolymitano, cum hoc fuerit minus gloriosum, quam primum, ut testatur Esdras; aptius ergo intelligenda veniunt de B. Virgine, animato templo, et regia domo Dei, cuius gloriam ex triplici capite deprehendere possumus, primo ex sanctitatis splendore: iuxta illud Davidis: 'Domum tuam Domine decet sanctitudo, in longitudine dierum.' In domibus Regum, ac Principum splendore solent lapides ex iaspide, columnae marmoreae..., at huius sacrosanctae domus universa supellex est charitas, gratia, et sanctitas." Ibid. (I, 63a–b).

[154] "Praeclarissimum omnium huius domus ornamentum, esse sanctitatem, qua undique circumdabatur, ut olim praevidit Ezechiel dicens: 'Ista est lex domus in summitate montis: omnes finis eius, in circuitu, sanctum sanctorum est.' Haec verba solum huic sacrosancto virginis templo, in quo Deus corporaliter inhabitare decreverat, possunt adaptari; ...cum igitur Ezechiel ait: In circuitu Templi esse sancta sanctorum, apte satis arbitramur de beata Virgine intelligi, cuius verum templum, sanctitas undequaque circuit, et circumdat. Immo Deus ipse, qui est sanctus sanctorum per solem significatus, omni ex parte velut vestimentum illam ambit, ut testatur Ioannes, cum vidit beatam Virginem indutam sole: 'Mulier amicta sole.' " Ibid. (I, 63b).

[155] "Caeterum, silentio non praeteribo, quod si inter alia, quae domus, aut templi alicuius gloriam commendant, non infimum locum tenent a peritissimo artifice delineatam, fabrefactam et ad finem usque perductam esse; sane ex hoc capite non parum ostentabitur gloria huius domus, cum Deus ipse supremus omnium opifex eam ab aeterno sua mente praelinearit: ...'ipse fundavit eam Altissimus...' " Ibid. (I, 64b). Cf. Lib. I, hom. X (I, 52b).

[156] Ibid. (I, 65a).

cabees 4, 44–45 destroyed the altar of holocausts because it had been profaned and was no longer suited for the offering to the Lord, much more would have it been intolerable to God, had Mary, his temple, been polluted somehow by the stain of original sin.[157]

2. *Tabernacle*. It is not without merit to think — so Cartagena begins his thirteenth homily of *Liber primus* — that the ancient solemn feast of the Tabernacles foreshadows the Church's own feast in honor of the sanctification of Mary. She is the tabernacle in which for nine months the Host High dwelled corporeally. Mary is prefigured by all the three Tabernacles mentioned in the Bible.

Moses built the first tabernacle in the desert according to a definite model he was given. Mary too as a tabernacle of God was "built" by God himself according to a most beautiful and eternal plan. As she herself has said: *"Ab initio, et ante saecula creata sum"* (Ecclesiasticus 24, 9).[158] Of the tabernacle in the desert it is said: "The glory of the Lord filled the tabernacle" (Exodus 40, 34). Or, as some other versions have it: "The Spirit of God filled it." Similarly, the angel announced to Mary, "The Holy Spirit will come upon you and the power of the Most High will overshadow you" (Luke 1, 35). The Spirit of God descended therefore on her as upon his own tabernacle. And when the Father foretold: "I generated you from the womb before the dawn" (Psalm 110, 3), he was implying that the Son would be borne in a particular womb exclusive to him.[159]

---

[157] "Memoriam dignum est illud, quod refertur I. Machabaeorum, fecisse Iudas: 'Cogitavit,' ait sacer textus, 'de altari holocaustorum, quod prophanatum erat, qui de eo faceret, et incidit illis consilium bonum, ut destruerent illud, ne forte illis esset in opprobrium, quia contaminaverunt illud gentes, et demoliti sunt illud.' Si ergo opprobrium erat Iudae offerri holocausta Deo in altari a gentibus polluto; quanto maius esset Domino, si altare Virginis ipsi consecratum, a Doemone aliquando peccati originalis macula pollutum fuisset." Lib. I, hom. X (I, 52b).

[158] "Refert sacra scriptura, Moysen fecisse olim antiquum illud Tabernaculum ex divino praecepto... sane Deus fabricavit hoc celebre tabernaculum Virginis secundum pulcherrimum exemplar, quod non in monte, sed in mente ab aeterno praehabebat, ut et ipsa praedixit: 'Ab initio, et ante saecula creata sum.' " Lib. I, hom. XIII (I, 65b).

[159] "De deserti Tabernaculo ait sacer textus: 'et gloria Domini implevit illud.' LXX vero vertunt: 'gloria Domini repletum est tabernaculum.'... Paginus: 'Et replevit illud spiritus Dei.' Haec sane multo congruentius in beatam Virginem convenire... Nam praeterquam spiritus Dei, tanquam in eius proprium tabernaculum descenderit, coelesti Paranympho dicente: 'Spiritus sanctus superveniet

The tabernacle built by Solomon was accepted by God with the words: "Now and for the future I have chosen and consecrated this house for my name to be there for ever; my eyes and my heart will be there for ever" (2 Chronicles 7, 16). Solomon sought the best artisans for this tabernacle. The tabernacle that is Mary in comparison was built by the wisdom of God himself. It was to be his own house and royal hall. And with the best care given it during the construction, the first stone in its foundation, i.e. in her conception, was grace, lest, should the foundation be weak, the master of the house might be prevented from staying there.[160] And just as special stones were used by Solomon, in the construction of the tabernacle, Mary too had grace and the various virtues as her materials and ornaments. Her name is truly Maria, the sea (*Mare*) containing in herself all the heavenly graces.[161] And similar to the lamp perpetually burning before the tabernacle, in Mary too is an ever flaming and never dying love. So ardent is this fire of love, it deters the devil and keeps from her all the snares of original sin.[162]

---

te, et virtus Altissimi obumbravit tibi': aeternus Pater filium suum naturalem, quem ex proprio utero generat..." Ibid. (I, 65b–66a).

[160] "At tabernaculum hoc Deiparae Virginis Mariae aeterna Dei sapientia sibi in proprium domicilium, ac regiam aulam extruxit; et ideo maximam adhibuit curam, ut in fundamento illius, quod fuit eius conceptio, primus lapis, qui iaceretur, esset gratia, ne alioquin, si fundamentum defectuosum esset, aedificium ruinam pateretur, aut illius periculo maneret expositum, id enim (ut solet) prohibere, Dominum in eo habitare." Ibid. (I, 66a).

[161] "Narrat sacra Scriptura de illo Salomonis tabernaculo, ac celeberrimo templo, aedificatum fuisse ex lapidibus, iam dolatis, perfectissimeque elaboratis... Id procul dubio egregie mihi delineat immaculatam Virginis Conceptionem, qua prae omnibus aliis sanctis donata fuit... beatam Virginem tanquam excellentissimam imaginem, ac divinum tabernaculum singulari suae omnipotentiae industria non maculam, quam nunquam contraxerat, auferens, aut quidquam imperfectionis, cuius expers semper fuit, adimens, sed gratiam gratiae superaddens, variis charismatum fulcimentis extruxit, ac virtutum splendoribus mirifice perpolivit, et exornavit..." Ibid. (I, 66b).

"...et nomen ipsum (Mariae) non obscure praesefert, quod 'Mare' interpretur, quia sicut (ut habetur in Genesi) congregationes aquarum Dominus vocavit Maria, ita, quia Virgo erat, in quam congregationes gratiarum coelitus confluebant, consulto eam vocavit, 'Mariam,' quod Mare significat." Ibid. (I, 67b).

[162] "Aderat in hoc sacro beatae Virginis tabernaculo ardentissimus, et nunquam deficiens charitatis ignis... dic in sacrosancto Virginis templo ab instanti suae Conceptionis ardentem atque inextinguibilem amoris ignem constituit..." Ibid. (I, 68b). Cf. (I, 69a).

In Lib. I, hom. VII (I, 37a), Cartagena understands the words: "Her lamp

The third tabernacle, which was the one seen by Ezekiel (43, 12), has its surroundings declared by God to be a most holy area. If God cares so much for the surroundings of the tabernacle, would he not care much more for the womb that enclosed his Son, keeping this tabernacle always holy and immaculate? [163]

3. *The Ark of the Covenant.* To hold the tablets of the law, the staff of Aaron and the manna, the ark was made of decay–resistant wood (Exodus 25, 10). Would it not be but fitting that she, who would hold in herself not the tablets of the law but the lawgiver himself, not the manna from heaven but the Son of God himself, not the staff of Aaron but the almighty arm of God — that she should be free body and soul from the corruption of sin? [164] Also, when the water of the Jordan drew back to let the ark of the covenant cross over, it pictured how the water of original sin retreated likewise before this mystical ark of Mary, so that we can correctly ask: "Sea, what makes you run away? Jordan, why stop flowing?" (Psalm 114, 5).[165] And like the old ark bringing disaster to Dagon (1 Samuel 5), this mystical ark armed by divine grace never for a moment allowed the idol of original sin to get close to her.[166]

---

does not go out at night" (Proverbs 31, 18) as meaning that from the moment of her Conception Mary has been an inexstinguishable lamp, a stranger to the night of original sin. He also writes that Mary's love is so ardent, the two cherubim by the Ark cover their faces and their feet out of shame, because their own love looks so tepid in comparison. Cf. Lib. I, hom. XIII (I, 69a).

[163] "Si ergo Deus ita solicitus fuit, ut ea, quae circuirent Tabernaculum, sancta essent, nonne illa, quae circulo sui uteri circumdedit Deum... oportebat, ut sancta semper, et immaculata fuisset? Si enim Deus inanimati Tabernaculi puritatis tam solicitam curam gessit, quanto illa sollicitiorem credendum est gessisse erga custodiam animati tabernaculi Matris suae?" Ibid. (I, 70b–71a).

[164] "...nonne multo convenientibus erat, ut, quae in se continere, ac custodire debebat, non, ut illa tabulas legis, sed legislatorem ipsum; non manna de caelo decidens, sed filium Dei de sinu Patris descendentem; non virgam Aaronis, sed omnipotentis Dei brachium, per quod facta sunt omnia, ex corpore, et anima coalesceret nulla umquam peccati corruptione infectis, aut inficiendis?" Lib. I, hom. VI (I, 31b).

[165] "Legimus apud Iosue, aquas Iordanis hac urbanitate usas fuisse erga sacram testamenti Arcam, ut dum illa pertransiret, impetum sui fluxus reprimentes, retrocederent, quo non obscure arbitror significari aquas peccati originalis ab Adamo per omnes Virginis progenitores defluentes, cum ad hanc mysticam arcam pervenient, minime illam fore invasuras, sed retrocedentes, sicco (ut aiunt) pere liberum ei transitum daturas." Ibid. (I, 31b–32a).

[166] "Quod autem eadem testamenti Arca (ut primo Regum narratur) ferre

4. *The Garden of Paradise.* Unlike the rest of mankind born in the shadows of original sin, Cartagena describes Mary to be "like the Garden of Paradise, conceived and born to the rising sun of justice, illuminating her with the splendor of divine grace which preserved her from the shadows of original sin." [167] But although the beautification of all later, natural gardens is preceeded by the time when they are rough and uncultivated, Mary from the moment of her conception always possessed the beauty of Paradise without thorns and bramble bushes, just as it is written: "God planted a garden in Eden from the beginning" (Genesis 2, 8).[168] In Eden God caused every kind of tree to spring up from the soil, enticing to look at and good to eat, with the tree of life in the middle. In Mary too God effected the growth of all graces and laid in her womb the tree of life.[169] Indeed, while the earthly paradise was irrigated by a river, the new and heavenly paradise is watered by Christ himself, "the river whose streams refresh the city of God" (Psalm 46, 4). Moreover, the Holy Spirit has poured out such an abundance of grace on her, that she really is the *"hortus voluptatis"* to the Son of God.[170] Even the incident following the expulsion of man from the garden of Eden, when cherubs and the flame of a flashing sword were placed in

---

non potuit, ut Dagonis Idolum in altari, in quo ipsa aderat, simul collocaretur, sed illud longe a se expulit, et capite, pedibusque confractis prohibuit, ne in consortio ipsius commoraretur; id apertissime praefiguravit, beatam Virginem, velut mysticam arcam divinae gratiae fortitudine praemunitam, idolum peccati originalis nec per momentum sibi commorari permissuram, sed potius caput, et pedes eius ab ea fore conterendos." Ibid. (I, 32a).

[167] "...beatissima autem Virgo instar Paradisi, concepta, ac nata fuit ad orientem solis iustitiae, divinae gratiae splendore eam irradiantis, qui a culpae originalis tenebris illam praeservavit." Lib. I, hom. XV (I, 76b).

[168] "Ita sane accidit B. Virgini, quae a principio suae conceptionis sub forma Paradisi voluptatis Dei condita fuit, atque adeo absque rusticitate peccati originalis." Ibid. (I, 78b).

[169] "Moyses rursus de paradiso agens, dixit continuere 'omne lignum pulchrum visu, et ad vescendum suave, et lignum vitae in medio paradisi': non secus Deus in amoeno hoc Virginis paradiso, cunctarum produxit germina gratiarum, et exemplaria virtutum; ipsum quoque lignum vitae, Christum Dominum posuit in medio uteris eius..." Ibid. (I, 80a).

[170] "De veteri, et terreno paradiso fluvius egrediebatur ad illum locum voluptatis irrigandum... de isto novo, et coelesti paradiso flumen illud egressum est, de quo legitur: 'Fluminis impetus laetificas civitatem Dei',... flumen hoc Christus est, paradisus vero uterus virgineus, quem Spiritus sanctus tanta gratiarum abundantia perfudit, ut filio Dei fieret 'Hortus voluptatis'..." Ibid. (I, 80a–b).

front of the garden, to guard the way to the tree of life (Genesis 3, 24), prefigures also the woman, who in the moment of her conception closed herself from the first Adam stained by original sin, so that she may be worthy to receive within her the second Adam whose foreseen merits preserved her from all sin. Christ guarded the gate to this virginal enclosure, as it has been said: "This gate will be kept shut by the prince; the prince himself shall sit in there" (Ezekiel 44, 2–3). She has therefore reason to exult as Judith did in triumph over Holofernes: "Long live the Lord, for his angel has guarded me on my way, during my stay and on my return" (Judith 13, 20–21), i.e. divine grace has protected Mary against all kind of sin, in her conception, in the course and at the end of her whole life here on earth. That is why the Bridegroom speaks of her in the following terms: "She is a garden enclosed, my sister, my bride; a garden enclosed, a sealed fountain" (Song of Songs 4, 12). Mary is a garden sealed for God alone and never opened by sin.[171]

5. *The Six Days of Creation.* Cartagena sees too the six days of creation (Genesis 1, 1 – 2, 3) as mirroring the marvel of Mary's Immaculate Conception. Just as on the first day God created heaven and earth, both of which would be joninig forces to produce fruits,

---

[171] After a long discussion of the "historical" interpretation of the above details, Cartagena proceeds: "Qua praemissa literali intelligentia, mysticam, et allegoricam ingrediamur. In eo certe facile detegemus, quam recte paradisus ille beatam Virginem adumbrabit in sua conceptione; sicut enim Paradisus ille admisit in se Adamum innocentem, minime vero recepit Adamum peccatorem, sed longe a se propulsavit; ita beatissima Virgo in puncto suae Conceptionis non admisit Adamum primum peccati originalis labe illam inficientem, sed clausit illi ostium, ut idonea esset ad recipiendum in se secundum Adamum ex praevisis eius meritis illam ab omni macula praeservantem. Angelum enim custodientem Paradisi ostium apparuisse sub specie humana... non obscure significasse mihi persuadeo, filium Dei custodem, ab instanti Conceptionis beatae Virginis, futurum esse, magni consilii Angelum sub specie veri hominis, sicut et ipse sub eadem custos fuit portae virginei claustri, Ezechiele dicente: 'Porta haec clausa erit Principi, Princeps ipse sedebit in ea.' Unde merito ipsa verba illa Iudith contra Holofernem triumphantis sibi usurpans, intonate potest: 'Vivit autem ipse Dominus, quoniam custodivit me Angelus eius, et hinc euntem, et ibi commorantem, et inde huc revertentem', hoc est, adversus omne genus peccati, in Conceptione, in totius vitae decursu, et in fine illius, divina gratia me praemunivit... unde sponsus ait illi: 'Hortus conclusus, soror mea sponsa, hortus conclusus, fons signatus', ecce triplicem clausuram indicat; ut ostendat clausum fuisse hunc coelestem Paradisum triplici peccatorum generi, originali, mortali, et veniali." Ibid. (I, 81b–82a).

so also God created Joachim and Anna, who would be having their blessed fruit in Mary. The meaning of the name Joachim, which is "elevation of God," and of the name Anna, which is "grace," indicates the excellence of their child, who would be raised up in God's grace.[172] The second day's "Let there be light" foreshadows Mary, who like the light has been separated at the very first instant of her conception from the darkness of original sin, so that it can be truly said of her: "and the darkness did not overcome her" (John 1, 5).[173] In addition, as God placed the firmament between the higher and lower waters, so also he placed Mary like a firmament between the blessed in heaven and the pilgrims on earth, sharing with the first the certainty of grace and heavenly joy, with the latter the power to merit and to have compassion.[174] On the third day God said: "Let the water be gathered in one place" — which body of water is called *maria*. In the same manner, this name was given to Mary, because the streams of all graces are pooled together in her.[175] The fourth day's "greater

---

[172] "Argumentum propositum altius repetens, admirandam illam operum sex dierum creationem ad vivum immaculatae Virginis miram excellentiam exprimere, ex eo mihi facile suadeo... certe sicut prima die creavit Deus coelum, et terram, quae pariter ad fructus, quibus utimur, producendos, concursum suum exhibuerunt; sic etiam creavit Ioachim, et Annam, qui maritali affectu ex divina ordinatione coniuncti... fructum benedictum B. Virginis in lucem ediderunt: quorum quidem nomina futurae prolis praecellentiam non obscure indicabant; nam Ioachim, 'elevationem Dei', Anna vero 'gratiam' significat: quasi dicerent: Deus gratia sua eorum prolem elevabit. Elevavit quidem adeo, ut ad dignitatis Matris Dei fastigium illam erigeret." Lib. I, hom. X (I, 48b).

[173] "Secunda die dixit Deus: 'fiat lux', per quam egregie B. Virgo adumbratur: tum quia, sicut ibi sacer textus ait, Deus separavit lucem a caligine tenebrarum; 'et divisit lucem a tenebris'; ita B. Virginem longe adeo separavit a peccatorum tenebris, ut caligine peccati originalis, qua omnes filii Adae in puncto conceptionis suae obscurantur, ipsam nec per momentum involui permitteret, ut non immerito de ea dicere liceat; 'et tenebrae eam non comprehenderunt.'" Ibid. (I, 49a).

[174] "Secunda die posuit firmamentum in medio aquarum superiorum, et inferiorum: non dissimiliter Deus, ut est auctor gratiae, posuit beatam Virginem, tanquam coeleste firmamentum, inter aquas superiores firmas, et immobiles, qui sunt Beati, et aquas labiles, ac fluxui, et mutabilitati obnoxias, eiusmodi sunt viatores: unde sicut medium participat conditionem extremorum, ita beata Virgo cum Beatis fruebatur securitate divinae gratiae, cum Viatoribus merendi virtute, et potestate pollebat: cum Beatis exultatione, et amoris fervore flagrabat, cum Viatoribus cordis compassionem exercebat: cum beatis clarius Moyse, et D. Paulo divinam essentiam non semel vidit, cum Viatoribus vero in dies maiora fidei incrementa suscipiebat." Ibid. (I, 49b–50a).

[175] "Tertia die dixit Deus: 'Congregentur aquae in locum unum', quarum

light" and "lesser light," besides signifying the divine Word and
Christ's human nature in the hypostatic union, the one being the
source of splendor for the other, also point to Christ and Mary,
the latter deriving all her brightness from Christ the sun of justice.[176]
God created on the fifth day the birds and the fishes, whose speed
saves them from being swallowed up by the depths. Similarly, God
created Mary endowed with such a speed that the demons could not
even get near her at the moment of her conception to smear her with
the taint of original sin. Like a fish she could not be overwhelmed
by the water that has pulled down every child of Adam.[177] Finally,
the creation of man on the sixth day as the lord of the rest of creation
compares too with the divine election of Mary as the queen of heaven.[178]

6. *Lily*. Turning to nature for points of comparison and for
properties which can be read as indicative of the mystery of Mary's
Immaculate Conception, Juan de Cartagena next sees in living instances found in Sacred Scripture precisely such "elucidations."
Thus, the words of the Song of Songs 2, 2: "As a lily among the
thistles, so is my love among the maidens" teach us that like a lily
budding among thorns but not touched by them, Mary was born
and grew up among the thistles of original sin. But she has never been

---

congregationem vocavit: Maria. Ad eundem modum B. Virgini divinitus hoc
nomen Maria, impositum fuit, quia gratiarum fluenta in ea erant simul in unum
congreganda." Ibid. (I, 50a).

[176] "Quarta die produxit Deus solem, et lunam; illum 'luminare maius',
hanc, 'luminare minus', appellavit; et merito; quia luna totam suam lucem a
sole mutuat... praeter hoc inquam, luminare illud maius, et luminare minus
Christum, et Mariam praenotarunt, haec enim velut luna a sole iustitiae Christo
totam suam lucem mutuavit." Ibid.

[177] "Quinta die fecit Deus volucres, et pisces: illa incredibili velocitate, hos
tali conditione praeditos, ut vastissimi aquarum gurgites eos suffocare nequeant.
Non dissimiliter Deus beatam Virginem condidit tam singulari velocitate praestan-
tem, ut infestissimi etiam accipitres (Doemones intelligo) in puncto conceptionis
peccati originalis unguibus illam dilaniare tentantes, non solum non comprehen-
derint, sed nec ad illam appropinquare potuerint. Altissimus namque tanto suae
gratiae favore eam praemunivit, ut inter medias propagationis humanae aquas,
quibus omnes filii Adae, cum primum concipiuntur, suffocantur, ipsa instar pi-
scium suffocari non potuerit." Ibid. (I, 50a-b).

[178] "Et sicut sexta die, hominem, quem creavit, constituit dominum reliquorum omnium, sic certe beatam Virginem in Angelorum Dominam, et coelorum Reginam, et universi Imperatricem elegit." Ibid. (I, 50b).

pierced by the thorns, even if she stemmed from ancestors so torn by original sin.[179] Expanding on the image in another direction, the author asserts that the thorns can also be fittingly understood as those thorns in the crown forced on the head of Christ. With them he preserved the lily of Mary from being touched by the devil and from being trampled by the wild beast of sin.[180] Along this idea of being preserved by the thorns, Cartagena draws the connection to the words of Isaiah 41, 19–20: "In the wilderness I will put cedar trees, thistles, myrtles, olives, so that men may see and know, may observe and understand that the hand of Yaweh has done this." The author hears here Christ saying that in the loneliness of his mother at her conception he surrounded her with cedar, thorn–bushes and myrtles, non–decaying trees, to signify that the soul of the Virgin would never be corrupted by sin, while the olive, a symbol of victory, indicates her victory over all sins.[181]

7. *Cinnamon.* Next come the *sacramenta* of the cinnamon tree. "I have exhaled," Mary said, "a perfume like cinnamon and acacia" (Ecclesiasticus 24, 15). First of all, these words shed light on the mystery of her conception, inasmuch as all men conceived in sin carry no sweet fragrance from God but rather a damnable stink. Mary is in other words claiming that the stink of original sin had not infected her. That is why in her stead Moses said: "The Lord smelt the odor

---

[179] "...praesenti argumento satis conveniens est, quia sicut, lilium oritur inter spinas, ab ipso tamen non pungitur; ita B. Virgo, etiamsi in sua Conceptione a progenitoribus peccati spinis confixis oriatur, ipsa tamen, velut coelesti lilium, peccati originalis spina confossa, aut aliqua eius punctura lacerata minime prodiit." Lib. I, hom. VIII (I, 38b).

[180] "Possumus etiam non incongrue per has spinas intelligere eas, quae capiti nostri servatoris affixae fuerunt, quibus suavissimum beatae Virginis lilium praeservavit, ne illud Doemon contrectaret, peccatorumque ferae pedibus conculcarent." Ibid. (I, 39a).

[181] "Cum in Conceptione sua Mater mea sola videatur existere, ita ut nemo ei praestet auxilium, tunc manu mea circumdabo illam cedro, spina, et myrto; quae quidem arbores (ut inquiunt Lira, et Adamus, et alii interpretes) quia incorruptibiles sunt, significant animam Virginis non fore peccato corrumpendam: circumdabo etiam illam oliva, quae signum est victoriae, ut ita Virgo victoriam de omnibus peccatis comparasse declaretur." Ibid.

The author plays on the Vulgate's "solitudinem" to describe Mary as "sola." However, the word "spina," which makes the Isaian passage pertinent, is not found in the more modern versions. The Bible of Jerusalem, for example, has acacia instead.

of sweetness" (Genesis 8, 21). The Hebrew text has *"odorem quietis"* instead of *"odorem suavitatis."* This brings out the fact that God wishing something clean apart from all the stained creatures and seeing Mary conceived without any stain of sin at all found peace in her, the object of his desire.[182] The observation that the cinnamon is so endowed by nature that it thwarts all sorts of corruption and decay points also to the similar gift of Mary, who was so endowed with grace that original sin did not corrupt her.[183] And just as this tree grows in the plains amidst the wildest thorn–bushes and prickly bramble–bushes, so also Mary was conceived by parents who were like thorny bushes with the sharp thorn of original sin. She herself like a cinnamon is without thorn.[184]

Cartagena then turns to Pliny's rich annotations about the cinnamon tree. Book 12, chapter 19 of the *Naturalis historia* has it that the unique bird, the phoenix, was wont to build its nest on this tree and would let no other bird stay there. Moreover, the branches of this special tree could only be cropped by the high priest in sacred vestments and accompanied by various rites, e.g. that the branches might not be cut down before sunrise or after sundown but only in

---

[182] "Ut tamen B. Virgo mirabile suae Conceptionis arcanum amplius explicaret, addidit: 'Quasi cinnamomum, et balsamum aromatizans odorem dedi.' Reliqui omnes, tam viri, quam foeminae, cum in peccato concipiantur, nullum Deo suavem odorem, sed execrandum foetorem mittunt; unde cum B. Virgo dicat in conceptione sua se odoris suavitatem emisisse, consequens est, peccati originalis foetore minime infectam fuisse, quare in figura illius Moyses praedixit: 'Odoratus est Dominus odorem suavitatis'; vel (ut legit Hebraeum originale) 'odorem quietis.' Bene quidam ait, 'odorem quietis,' quia sicut, quando quis desiderans aliquid, et illud non obtinet, inquietum est cor eius, si tamen voti compos evadat, continue eius animus quiescit: non dissimiliter, cum Deus summopere desiderasset mundam aliquam, ac immaculatam Conceptionem (omnes enim erant immundae et infectae) cum primum sacram Virginem absque omni labe peccati conceptam vidit, confestim, velut, qui rem desideratam obtinuisset, animus eius quievit, et ideo ait sacer textus; odoratum fuisse Dominum 'odorem quietis.'" Ibid. (I, 87a–b).

[183] "...ea enim singulari instar cinnamomi, praestitit virtute, ut peccatum originale, quod ex primi hominis corruptione ortum habuit, penitus interimeret." Ibid. (I, 86a).

[184] "Aiunt praeterea cinnamomum, licet in planis gignatur, sed inter asperrimos vepres, et spinosos rubos: non dissimiliter B. Virgo, licet concepta a progenitoribus, qui spinosi vepres fuerant, peccati originalis aculeo puncti, ipsa tamen ex his originem duxit instar cinnamomi absque ulla peccati pungente spina." Ibid. (I, 86a–b).

the light of the day. And of the tree–limbs thus acquired, the first portion was offered to the gods, some were set aside for the priests and a third part was given to the people. All these details correspond to certain points in Mary's life, according to Cartagena. Firstly, the unique creature, the phoenix, refers to Christ, who is unique in his Father as in his mother, and who like the phoenix, which was born and later died in flame, was also born inflamed with the fire of love and died on the cross out of the same fire. This sacred phoenix made its home in the Blessed Virgin as on a cinnamon tree and would not let that plundering bird of prey, the devil, to nest there too. Also, only God and the supreme priest Christ touched her, and under the bright light of divine grace. Likewise the first portion of Mary's life, i.e. her conception, was made holy and had been offered to God.[185] Pliny further reported about an unusual phenomenon he witnessed in a temple: a cinnamon root of great weight, cut and dry on a golden plate and yet oozing a sap which was then made into granules used on the fire in the shrine. Cartagena writes that God allowed this prodigy, in order that even natural things may foreshadow blessed Mary. For she is verily the great root, of whom the Church herself signs: *"Salve radix sancta, ex qua mundo lux est orta."* She is the root whence Christ sprang, hence God took special care of her, nourishing her with the rain of divine grace. She is like a saucer rich in the gold of charity. She has given us Christ and sustains the whole Church

---

[185] "Haec omnia quam apte Virgini congruant, paulatim elucidemus. Imprimis avis illa Phoenix, quae unica est, Christum Dominum refert, tum quia unicus tam Patri, quam Matri suae; tum quia, sicut Phoenix ex igne nascitur, et in igne moritur; ita et Christus igne amoris incensus inter homines nasci voluit, et eiusdem amoris flamma aestuans in cruce obiit. Haec sacra Phoenix in beata Virgine, velut illa in cinnamomo, nidificavit; et sicut illa nullam aliam avem in eodem nido commorari patitur, sic Christus Dominus, rapacem illam avem, Doemonem intelligo, minime inibi unquam inhabitare permisit. Sicut etiam arbor illa non aliis, quam sacris summi sacerdotis manibus contrectari fas erat, nec in ante ortum, vel occasum solis, sed clara eius luce vigente; non dissimiliter sacram hanc cinnamomum beatae Virginis, non Doemonis manus filiorum Adae conceptionem maculantes, sed solius Dei, et summi sacerdotis Christi manus, coelesti divinae gratiae lumine coruscante contigerunt. Atque hinc est, quod sicut prima pars ramorum illius arboris, quae in tres dividi solebat, Deo reservabatur; non secus prima pars totius vitae beatae Virginis, quam constat, Conceptionem eius fuisse, non Doemoni reservata, sed Deo sacrata, et oblata fuit." Ibid. (I, 85b–86a).

"like a conduit from a river, like a watercourse running into a garden" (Ecclesiasticus 24, 30).[186]

8. *Neck*. In addition to lifeless things and instances from the botanical world, Cartagena also finds elucidating images in Sacred Scripture taken from the human level. Thus, "your neck is an ivory tower" (Song of Songs 7, 5) can be aptly understood too of Mary in the mystical sense. Just as the neck is always connected to the head and the head always gives life to the neck, so also Mary is always connected to Christ the head, who never ceases for a moment to impart to her the life of grace. In other words, sin never disconnected this neck from its head.[187] Moreover, she never wore the yoke and the iron chains of the devil. Instead she always has the golden chain of divine love and of graces and virtues. As Habakkuk notes: "You bared its foundations to the neck" (3, 13), as if to say, even if all other parts might be deprived of grace, the neck however and the head are not so, because neither Christ nor Mary has ever been without divine grace.[188]

---

[186] "At voluit Deus hoc prodigium praemittere, ut et res etiam naturales beatissimam Virginem adumbrarent, ipsa quidem est radix illa magni ponderis, quam sancta mater Ecclesia salutat dicens: 'Salve radix sancta, ex qua mundo lux est orta.' Eva radix fuit generis humani, B. vero Virgo radix, unde ortus est Christus. Unde sicut qui arborem fovet, specialem radicis curam habet, et illam colit, illam irrigat, proximam illi terram fodit, ut coelesti pluvia copiosius perfundatur; ita Deus sollicitam curam gessit conceptionis B. Virginis, quae eius radix futura erat, et Mater, atque illam tot divinae gratiae imbribus irrigavit, ac tot coelestibus donis praemunivit, ut peccati originalis vermis ad eam corrodendam minime accedere ausus fuerit: Radix haec in patera inventa fuit, dum aderat in visceribus sacrosanctae Annae matris eius, quae auro charitatis ditissima erat. Quod si radix illa sicca absque illo humore, cuiusdam liquoris guttas emittebat; etiam B. Virgo absque humore virilis seminis Christum parturivit 'fontem aquae vivae'; immo et copiosum fluvium universam Ecclesiam irrigantem, ut ipse testatur: 'ego quasi fluvii Dorix, et sicut aquaeductus exivi de Paradiso.' " Ibid. (I, 86b–87a).

[187] "Comparat enim Virginem collo, quia, sicut collum, nunquam est non coniunctum capiti; nec caput nunquam est non influens vitam in collum; ita sane beata Virgo, nec per momentum extitit non coniuncta capiti suo Christo Domino, neque per momentum caput hoc cessavit vitam gratiae in illam influere; nunquam ergo peccatum divisit collum hoc a capite suo." Lib. I, hom. VIII (I, 38a).

[188] "Collum sane erat beata Virgo, sed collum Doemonis iugo numquam subiectum, nec ferrea illius catena, qua omnes filios Adae, tanquam mancipia devinxerat, oppressum; sed aurea potius divini amoris virtutum distincta, decoratum erat... Audio enim Habacuc dicentem: 'Denudasti fundamentum eius

9. *Esther*. "And Esther won the admiration of all who saw her" (Esther 2, 15). Mary likewise astonishes so many, because she was born of parents who were sinful and yet she is completely without sin. Esther against the common law that no one should appear before the king unsummoned nonetheless went to him and pleaded for her condemned people. Mary too, conceived without sin, appeared before the King in her mother's womb, even if by universal law all descendants of the first men should incur original sin. And just as the king took Esther in his arms to support her, the Son of God took his mother in his hands during her conception to save her from original sin. King Ahasuerus comforted Esther that she would not die, because the law applies to all others but not to her; similarly, Mary was exempted from the universal destiny that all children of Adam should contract original sin.[189] From the law that "all sinned in Adam," Mary was preserved and given an exemption. God was saying to her: "I myself constituted this law, and I of my own accord make you free from it. You would not incur the death of original sin." [190] Enlarging, the author writes that the name Esther means *"abscondita seu elevata in populis, aut praeparata in tempore."* This just suits Mary, who was hidden in the figures of the Old Testament, raised above the choirs of angels, chosen and prepared from all eternity to be

---

usque ad collum': quasi diceret: quamvis cetera omnia membra fuerint gratia denudata, collum tamen, sicut et caput denudatum non est; quia, nec Christus, per caput, nec Maria per collum significati, divina gratia unquam caruere." Ibid. (I, 38a–b).

[189] "...sacra Scriptura Reginae Esther pulchritudinem commendans, ait: 'Erat formosa valde, et incredibili pulchritudine, omnium oculis gratiosa, et amabilis videbatur.' Incredibile videtur multis, quod Maria ex peccatoribus parentibus, ac peccati originalis labe deturpatis, pulchra, et absque macula prodeat... nemo, non vocatus a Rege, ad illum accedere auderet. Esther autem Regina, ut populo Hebraeo, qui ad mortem damnatus erat, libertatem, et veniam a Rege obtineret, non vocata, ingressa fuit ad eum... Non dissimiliter B. Virgo in conceptione sua ait: ingrediar ad Regem coelorum in utero matris meae absque peccato concepta, etiamsi id sit contra universalem mortis legem per peccatum primi parentis inductam... Assuerus ulnis suis tenuis Esther, ne forte timore percita tueret in terram: Filius Dei Matrem suam Reginam nostram manibus suis in conceptione tenuit, ne luto peccati originalis foedaretur." Lib. I, hom. VII (I, 34b–35a).

[190] "...quamvis lex generalis, 'Omnes in Adam peccaverunt', universos filios Adae comprehendat, in B. tamen Virgine, quam Deus praeservavit, exceptionem patitur... illius est, legem abrogare, cuius est eam condere: ego ipse legem hanc statui, ego spontaneus ab ea te liberam feci, minime mortem peccati originalis incurres." Ibid. (I, 35a).

the Mother of God. And just as Esther's beauty very much pleased the king, Ahasuerus, which interpreted signifies *"beatitudo,"* so also Mary "found grace" (Luke 1, 30) with the Son of God, who is objective beatitude itself.[191]

10. *Eve.* Of course, the oldest figure for Mary in Scripture is Eve. "Let us make him a helpmate like him" (Genesis 2, 18). Mary and Eve are like each other not just in nature but also in the grace of original justice and in the absence of the stain of original sin before Eve sinned. And Mary the second Eve is like Christ the second Adam in that both of them are always devoid of sin, one by nature, the other by grace.[192] The two are like the second tablets of stone (Exodus 34, 4) on which Moses had the laws of God. Unlike the first tablets which were broken, thus prefiguring our first parents who sinned, these second ones remained unbroken and whole, just as Christ and Mary were fractured by no sin, but were preserved from the Adamitic shame and are altogether without the imprint of sin.[193]

Such is the privilege of Mary in being immaculately conceived as portrayed and prefigured above in Sacred Scripture,[194] that Car-

---

[191] Lib. I, hom. IX (I, 44b–45a).

[192] "Simile siquidem, non solum in natura, sed etiam in gratia iustitiae originalis, et in carentia ab omni labe peccati. Id sane praefiguravit, secundo Adamo, Christo scilicet Domino, dandam fore in novissimis temporibus secundam Evam, hoc est, beatissimam Virginem, adiutorium simile illi; simile, inquam, in eo, quod sicut Christus omnis peccati expers semper fuit, ita et ipsa nullius culpae particeps umquam fieret; ille quidem per naturam, haec per gratiam; ille ex vi suae conceptionis absque opera virili Spiritu sancto illam supplente; haec ex divino munere, ac caelesti privilegio, naturali propagationi eius minime debito." Lib. I, hom. VII (I, 34b).

[193] "Unde apte mihi videntur praefigurati Christus, et Maria per lapides illos, in quibus Moyses legem Dei exaravit non quidem primos, qui confracti fuere, sed secundos, qui absque ulla ruptione, aut scissura integri permanserunt; illi namque primi primos parentes Adam, et Evam: secundi vero secundos, Christum scilicet, et Mariam eius Matrem adumbrarunt, qui nulla peccati ruptione confracti, sed velut adamantina quadam duritie adea praemuniti fuere, ut peccati characterem in eis imprimere nunquam diabolus potuerit." Ibid.

[194] We have presented above only a sampling of the images and metaphors with which Cartagena enriched his homilies on the Immaculate Conception. In addition he had Mary figured as immaculately conceived in the Davidic City (Lib. I, hom. VI – I, 29a–b), the throne of Solomon (ibid. – I, 32b), the Ark of

tagena thinks it can be said of her: "The Lord guards your coming and your going" (Psalm 121, 8). That is, her coming at her conception enjoyed God's protection, so that she was not infected by original sin.[195] Thus Mary can make her own Judith's words: "Long live the Lord! for his angel has guarded me on my way and during my stay and on my return. The Lord has not allowed his handmaid to be defiled" (Judith 13, 20). The Lord has so guarded her with the divine grace, that she was not defiled by original sin.[196] As Jeremiah observed: "I see a watchful branch" (7, 11). That is Mary who was never put to sleep by sin but remained on the watch. And if other versions have *"Virgam amygdalinam,"* it still signifies the Immaculate Conception, because the almond tree is the first to blossom of all trees, thus aptly typifying Mary who was the first to blossom with grace, being immaculately conceived.[197] And in gratitude for this blessing of God, she could make her own the words of the psalmist: "By this I knew that I enjoyed your favor, because my enemy did not triumph over me. And you took me in because of innocence and set me in your

---

Noah (Lib. I, hom. VII – I, 35b), the abachus (ibid. – I, 36a), the citadel of Jonathan (ibid. – I, 36a–b), the priestly land (ibid. – I, 37a), the yard bought by David (ibid. – I, 36b), the diadem (ibid. – I, 36b–37a), a cedar (Lib. I, hom. XVI – I, 84a), cypress (ibid. – I, 84b–85b), figtree (ibid. – I, 87b–88b), pomegranate (ibid. – I, 88b–89a), palm tree (ibid. – I, 89a), plaits (Lib. I, hom. VIII – I, 39a), feet (ibid. – I, 41a–b), horsemen (ibid. – I, 40a–b), Job's servant (Lib. I, hom. VII – I, 37a), and the good woman (ibid. – I, 37b).

[195] "Alia etiam lex lata erat, ad introitum vitae, ut scilicet, omnes peccato originali inficerentur; desiderans ergo David, ut ab hac etiam liberaretur Deipara Virgo, ita ut in introitu portae Conceptionis, in cuius limine corruebant omnes filii Adae, ipsa singulari Dei protectione custodiretur: ideo dixit 'Dominus custodit introitum tuum.'" Lib. I, hom. VIII (I, 42a).

[196] "Ac si clarius diceret: Gratulor omnipotenti Deo, quod filius eius magni consilii Angelus, divinae suae gratiae munimine ita me protexisti, ut in introitu per Conceptionem, peccati originalis turpitudine non inficeres..." Ibid. This verse from Judith is found only in the Vulgate.

[197] "Huc etiam facere existimo locum Ieremiae: 'Virgam vigilantem ego video': haec est beata Dei genetrix, quae nunquam somno peccati correpta fuit, sed semper vigilavit. Advertere tamen oportet, quod ubi nostra Vulgata legit: 'Virgam vigilantem': alia translatio vertit: 'Virgam amygdalinam,' quae recte praesenti illibatae Conceptionis mysterio quadrat: Tum, quia, sicut amygdalus prius inter omnes arbores germinat, et florescit: sic beata Virgo prius gratia, et charitate floruit, quam reliqui omnes; cum ipsa in sua conceptione sancta, et immaculata extiterit." Ibid. (I, 42b).

presence for ever" (Psalm 41, 11–12). For her enemy the devil failed to triumph over her, since the Lord showed his love for his mother by preserving her from original sin. And she acquired this grace not just for a time but for all eternity.[198]

---

[198] "Ob cuius beneficii largitatem ipsa debitas gratias Deo agens, usurpare sibi poterat verba illa David patris sui: ...Primum opus, quo Deus manifestavit amorem ferventem erga Matrem suam fuit, illam ab originali peccato praeservare, ne Diabolus gloriaretur, sub peccati tyrannico iugo eam habuisse: idque sibi volunt verba illa: 'quoniam non gaudebit inimicus meus super me.' Id autem, quod subit: 'Et confirmasti me in conspectu tuo in aeternum': indicat in Maria repertam fuisse copiosam illam gratiam, quam Adam perdiderat, non quasi mutuo, aut per aliquod temporis spatium datam, sed in aeternum confirmatam." Ibid. (I, 39a–b).

CHAPTER FIVE

PERPETUAL VIRGINITY

As we have already noted at the beginning of the previous chapter, the reflection over Mary's virginal conception of Christ was one of the earliest in the post–Apostolic Church's consciousness about her. The teaching on her virginity developed almost at the same time as the thoughts concerning her parallelism with Eve and her analogy with the Church. Nonetheless we are treating the topic here after considering the mystery of the Immaculate Conception in accordance with Juan de Cartagena's ordering of the Marian mysteries. The author, as has been observed, starts with Mary's predestination and conception and leads on to the incarnation of Christ in her womb.

If during the time of Cartagena and for so many centuries the doctrine of Mary's virginity has been universally taught and accepted, the same tranquillity can hardly be claimed today on the matter. The solid front has cracked in many places. The famous "Dutch Catechism" raised eyebrows by its ambiguity on the factuality of the virginal conception.[1] Some scholars today are inclined to classify this teaching as first given to us in the infancy narratives of Matthew and Luke not as a historico–biological fact, but as a theologoumenon, a historicizing of the truth that Jesus is God's Son and had no human father.[2] Moreover, the old preoccupation with an exclusively or

---

[1] *A New Catechism: Catholic Faith for Adults* (New York, 1967), pp. 74–75. This Dutch Catechism says that the deepest meaning of the article of faith, "born of the virgin Mary" is that "Jesus' birth was not due to the will of a man" – he was born wholly of grace and was *the gift* of God.

The *Acta Apostolicae Sedis*, 60 (1968) 688, reports a Roman directive that the Catechism "must teach equally clearly [with the perpetual virginity of Mary] the doctrine of the virginal birth of Jesus, which is so supremely in accord with the mystery of the incarnation. No further occasion shall be given for denying this truth... retaining only a symbolic meaning [of virginal birth], for instance, that it merely expresses the gift inspired by pure grace that God bestowed upon us in His Son." The Catechism now carries the "correction" as a supplement.

[2] Cf. O. Knoch, "Die Botschaft des Matthäusevangelium über Empfängnis u. Geburt Jesu vor dem Hintergrund der Christusverkündigung des Neuen Testaments," in *Zum Thema Jungfrauengeburt*, op. cit., p. 58; J. Michl, "Die Jungfrauengeburt im Neuen Testament," in *Jungfrauengeburt Gestern und Heute*, hrsg. H. J. Brosch u. J. Hasenfuss (Essen, 1969), p. 183. J. Ratzinger, *Einführung*

predominantly physical understanding of virginity even as it applies
to Mary has been replaced for the most part by a deeper grasp into
its spiritual dimension and consequently liberated from a fundamentally antisexual bias. In the light of these present developments,
a 17th century treatment of the subject becomes historically interesting.

To obtain a comprehensive view of Cartagena's understanding of
the doctrine of Mary's virginity, we shall first try to present systematically his explanation of it and the reasons he has given in its
support. The scriptural testimonies for this mystery as interpreted
in the *Homiliae Catholicae* shall be laid down in the second part of
this chapter. As before, the systematic teaching will first briefly
sketch the historical development of the doctrine.

I. SYSTEMATIC TEACHING

A. THE NATURE OF MARY'S VIRGINITY

1. *A brief historical background.* Juan de Cartagena inherited a
solidly established Catholic doctrine regarding the virginity of Mary,
unlike the still controverted *pia opinio* for her Immaculate Conception.
For as early as the beginning of the 2nd century, Christ's virginal
conception was already being affirmed. Within the context of the
Christological questions of the time, a progressive articulation about
Mary was also taking place. Thus Ignatius of Antioch († 110), with
one eye on the Docetists who denied Christ's true humanity, stressed
the birth from Mary, while with the other eye on the Jews who would
not accept Christ's true divinity, he underlined the fact that Jesus
was conceived from the Holy Spirit by a virgin Mary.[3] The virgin

---

in das Christentum (München DTV, 1971), pp. 197–204, explains that the virginal
conception of which faith speaks in the creed is not a biological fact but an on-
tological one. See W. Kasper's remark on this in *Theologische Revue*, 65 (1969)
183. For theological perspectives in the whole discussion, see K. Rahner, "Dogmatische Bemerkungen zur Jungfrauengeburt," in *Zum Thema Jungfrauengeburt*,
op. cit., pp. 121–158.

[3] Ignatius of Antioch, *Epist. ad Ephesos* 19, 1: J. Fischer, *Die Apostolischen
Väter griechisch und deutsch* (München, 1956), p. 156. On the development of
Patristic Mariology especially with regards the question of Mary's virginity, see

conception was originally a Christological question, not a Mariological one.

Justin the Martyr († c. 165) in pointing out the parallelism between Mary and Eve observed that Mary was a virgin as she received in faith the angel's message, just as Eve was a virgin as she in disobedience took the word of the devil.[4] Irenaeus († c. 202) asserted in turn that the teaching that Christ was born of a virgin, τὴν ἐκ παρθένον γεννησιν, belongs to the faith transmitted by the Apostles,[5] and that in antithesis to Eve, Mary had a man too but yet remained a virgin.[6] By the turn of the century, as the Church acquired a firmer grasp of Revelation's basic contents, her profession of faith already included the article that Jesus Christ was born of the Virgin Mary from the Holy Spirit.[7]

Irenaeus, enlarging on the teaching that Mary conceived Christ virginally, spoke also of his birth as *"mire et inopinate a Deo"* in the sense of a virgin birth.[8] Clement of Alexandria († c. 216) connected too the older belief on the virgin conception with a virgin birth, although he admitted that the masses in their embryonic faith might still hold the contrary, thus giving an indication that the teaching was at first by no means universal.[9] The development and acceptance of the virgin birth "addition" were relatively gradual. Gregory of Nyssa († 394) in his time could already be very explicit and detailed in his teaching that Mary gave birth to Christ also virginally.[10] The doctrine,

---

G. Jouassard, "Marie à travers la Patristique," in *Maria* I (Paris, 1949), pp. 71–157; H. von Campenhausen, *Die Jungfrauengeburt in der Theologie der alten Kirche* (Heidelberg, 1962); and K. Suso Frank, "Geboren aus der Jungfrau Maria," in *Zum Thema Jungfrauengeburt*, op. cit., pp. 91–120.

[4] Justin, *Dialogus cum Tryphone* 100, 2–6 (PG 6, 710). Cf. his *Apologia* I, 46 (PG 6, 426).

[5] Irenaeus, *Adversus Haereses* 1, 10, 1 (PG 7, 550).

[6] Ibid., 5, 19, 1, (PG 7, 1175B) and 3, 22, 4 (PG 7, 959 f.).

[7] Hippolytus, *Traditio Apostolica* (DS 10).

[8] Irenaeus, *Epideixis* or *Demonstratio Apostolicae Praedicationis* 54 (PO 12, 782–3; BKV II, 622). Cf. also *Adv. Haer.* 4, 33, 4 (PG 7, 1074C–1075A) and 3, 21, 4–6 (PG 7, 950–3).

[9] Clement of Alexandria, *Stromata* VII, 16 (PG 9, 929). In addition to the Gnostics, Jewish Christians are known to have rejected the virginal conception of Jesus. Cf. Justin, *Tryphone* 48, 4 (PG 6, 581). Later Origen refers to a sect of Ebionites who denied the same. Cf. his *Contra Celsum* 2, 1 & 5, 61 (GCS 2, 126–7 & 3, 65).

[10] Gregory of Nyssa, *Hom. in Cant. 13* (PG 44, 686).

however, was not held by Tertullian [11] and Origen,[12] who understood
Mary's virginity in the more restricted sense of *virginitas quoad virum*.
For their Christological purpose of defending Christ's true humanity,
they needed to emphasize only that he was born of Mary just like
any other human being, opening the mother's womb. Jerome was of
the same opinion.[13]

But with such proponents as Ephraem,[14] John Chrysostom,[15]
Ambrose,[16] Augustine,[17] and Leo the Great,[18] Mary's virginity both
in conceiving and in giving birth to Christ was a common doctrine
by the middle of the 5th century. Furthermore by then the teaching
that Christ was born of the Virgin Mary had already assumed a yet
third aspect to it. Zeno of Verona († 372) taught that Mary was a
virgin even after conceiving and after giving birth to Christ, and that
she remained also a virgin after the birth.[19] This perpetual virginity
of Mary was defended too by Origen,[20] Ambrose,[21] Basil the Great,[22]
and Jerome,[23] among others. The *Symbolum fidei* of 374 attributed
to St. Epiphanius of Salamis already called Mary the *semper virgo*,

---

[11] Tertullian, *De Carne Christi* 23, 3–4 (CCL 2, 914–915). Tertullian taught
the virgin conception in his *Apologeticum* 21, 14 (CSEL 1, 125) and in *Adv. Iudaeos* 9 (CCL 2, 1364–7). But as a Montanist he denied Mary's perpetual virginity
in his *De Monogamia* 8, 2 (CCL 2, 1239).

[12] Origen, *Hom. in Lc. 14* (Rauer, *Origenes Werke* IX 100, 4 f.). Here Origen
was most probably influenced by Tertullian. Origen taught both the virgin conception, in *Contra Celsum* 1, 28–29 (Rauer I, 79), and the virginity of Mary after
giving birth, in *Comment. in Matthaeum* 10, 17 (GCS, 40, 21–22).

[13] Jerome, *Adv. Helvidium* 17 (PL 23, 201). But he defends Mary's perpetual
virginity, ibid. (PL 23, 211–212).

[14] Ephraem, *Diatessaron* 2, 6 (CSCO 145, 19 f.) and 21, 21 (CSCO, 145, 232).

[15] John Chrysostom, *Hom. in Mt. 5*, 2 (PG 57, 57).

[16] Ambrose, *Epistola Recognovimus* 5–7 (PL 16, 1125 f.).

[17] Augustine, *De Sancta Virginitate* 4, 4 (CSEL 41, 238; PL 40, 398).

[18] Leo the Great, *Ep. ad Flavianum* 2 (DS 291); written in 449, it speaks
of Mary as "salva virginitate concepit."

[19] Zeno of Verona, *Tractatus*, I, 5, 3 & II, 8, 2 (PL 11, 303 & 414–415).
His formulation was the precursor of the classic "virgo ante partum, in partu
et post partum."

[20] Cf. above, footnote 12.

[21] Ambrose, cf. above, footnote 16; *De Institutione Virginis* 5, 35 (PL 16,
314). As the Bishop of Milan wrote, ibid., 5, 36 (PL 16, 328): "By Mary's example
all are summoned to the service [cultus] of virginity."

[22] Basil the Great, *In Sanctam Christi Generationem* 5 (PG 31, 1468B).

[23] Cf. above, footnote 13.

the ἀει παρθένος.[24] Interestingly the *Sitz im Leben* of the new consciousness about Mary's virginity was no longer the Christological controversies. The ascetical movement of the 4th century had appropriated Mary and her virtues as ideal and prototype. Her virginity served well the growing trend towards Christian asceticism and celibacy.

In 553 the Second Council of Constantinople in its second canon demanded assent to the teaching that Christ was born of Mary an ever–virgin.[25] In 649 the Lateran Council specified that the ever–virgin Mary conceived the divine Word by the Holy Spirit without any male seed, gave birth to him *"incorruptibiliter,"* and retained her virginity intact ever after.[26] Nearer to Cartagena's own life–time, in 1555 Pope Pius IV in a papal bull against the anti–Trinitarians and Socinians defended among others the doctrine that Mary remained inviolate in her virginity *"ante partum scilicet, in partu et perpetuo post partum."* [27] Clement VIII confirmed the same constitution in 1603.

Juan de Cartagena could look back therefore to a solid tradition supported by the Magisterium that Mary conceived Christ virginally, gave birth to him without the loss of her virginity, and remained a virgin throughout her life. Hence, unlike the case of the doctrine of the Immaculate Conception, the author was not involved here in any contemporary controversy. Instead of defending any particular thesis against a present threat, Cartagena was more concerned with fully explaining a solidly accepted teaching. And his *adversarii*, when at all, were those of the early centuries.[28]

2. *Mary's vow.* Cartagena understands virginity as a person's total self–consecration to God. It is dying to one's earthly feelings

---

[24] DS 44. Cf. ibid., 46.

[25] DS 422.

[26] DS 503.

[27] DS 1880. On the historico–dogmatic teaching of the Church on the matter, cf. K. Rahner, "Virginitas in Partu," in *Schriften zur Theologie* IV (Einsiedeln, [4]1964), pp. 173–205.

[28] The Reformers maintained Mary's virginity, although later the teaching would be watered down. Luther taught *virginitas in partu, Das Magnificat verdeutschet und ausgelegt,* Weimarer Ausgabe, 7, 549, and in 1543 still defended her divine motherhood and complete virginity, WA, 53, 640–643. Cf. T. Kolbe, *Die symbolischen Bücher der evangelisch–lutherischen Kirche* (Gütersloh, 1912), pp. 299 & 679.

and living for God alone. It is spiritual and bodily integrity preserved perpetually in imitation of the divine holiness.[29] Mary, according to the author, attained to this total oblation of self to God through an early vow of virginity. It came about this way. The parents of Mary made a promise to the effect that they would offer for God's service in the temple their first child, if only their childless marriage would be made fruitful. And so Mary at the age of three was presented by her parents for the temple service.[30] While there in segregation and in service, her desire to please God and to be more acceptable to the heavenly spouse drew her to the decision to consecrate herself completely to God with a religious vow of virginity.[31] She wanted to offer to God not only her fruits, so to say, while retaining the right to the tree, as was the case with virgins temporarily serving in the temple without any religious vow; she wanted to sacrifice the tree itself, giving up all her rights to herself body and soul.[32]

In the perspective of her time, Mary in making the vow of virginity was a true pioneer. Marriage and a lot of children were considered a special blessing. Sterility and spouselessness were looked upon as a big misfortune. And even if there used to be virgins like the vestals, this state was only temporary. It was Mary who was the very first to take a religious vow of perpetual virginity.[33] In this she was the *inventrix* and *vexillifera*, the standard bearer, of virginity. As the author puts it,

> ...unmoved by womanly feeling, unmindful of the world's judgment, unyielding to the feebleness of sex, unaffected by the

---

[29] "In eo etiam praecipue virgines divinae sanctitatis inveniuntur aemulatrices, quod terrenis affectibus morientes, soli Deo vivunt, ac perpetuam mentis, et corporis integritatem perpetuo conservant." Lib. III, hom. V (I, 272a). Cf. ibid. (I, 271a).

[30] Lib. III, hom. II (I, 252a).

[31] Ibid., hom. V (I, 269b). This position is an improvement on Suárez, who holds that Mary made the decision to remain a virgin while still in her mother's womb, since she already had then the use of reason. Cf. his *De Mysteriis Vitae Christi*, op. cit., 6, 1, 3; also, 4, 7 2 f.

A more modern position maintains that Mary made the resolve to remain a virgin following the angel's message to her. Cf. Schilleebeckx, op. cit., pp. 77–80, 84–91.

[32] Lib. III, hom. V (I, 269b–270a). In his typical pre–reformation and overdone style, St. Lawrence of Brindisi, in imitation of St. Bernardine of Sienna, actually spoke of Mary's real marriage with God. Cf. Graef, op. cit., p. 340.

[33] Lib. III, hom. V (I, 268b & 270a). Cf. Lib. VII, hom. IV (I, 744a).

allurements of the flesh, and unhampered by flowering youth, she dedicated to her Creator her virginity to be perpetually kept.[34]

It should be remembered in passing that Cartagena is echoing a Patristic idea born of the ascetical movement, that Mary is the ideal and prototype of virginity and had probably a vow of virginity.[35]

A difficulty crops up in connection with Mary's betrothal to Joseph. If Mary had a religious vow of virginity, how could she have consented to a marriage with him? Some theologians say that the two had a previous understanding that neither of them would demand the *debitum* of marital union from the other, and that it was under such a condition that they contracted marriage. Such an agreement or condition does not militate against the substance of matrimony, since there is a distinction between *dominium* and *usus*. Abstinence from a particular *usus*, in this case the use of the marriage right to sexual relationship, does not negate the *potestas dominii* or the right itself. The author personally leans however toward another explanation advocated by St. Thomas for instance, that on a special impulse from the Holy Spirit or by virtue of a divine revelation to her, Mary consented unconditionally to a marriage with Joseph notwithstanding her vow of virginity, because she knew that he would never ask for any carnal union.[36]

3. *Virgo ante partum.* The conception of Christ is described by Cartagena as the assumption of humanity from Mary by the divine Word.[37] It is the incarnation of the Son of God in her womb. And this mystery took place with her freely given consent and cooperation.[38] However, it is through the efficacy of the Holy Spirit that the formation of Christ's body in her womb happened. She became pregnant in other words by the power of the Holy Spirit,[39] conceiving

---

[34] Lib. III, hom. V (I, 266b–267a).

[35] Cf. Origen, *Comment. in Matth.* 10, 17 (GCS 40, 21–22); Ambrose, *Comment. in Lc.* II, 1–35 (CSEL 32/4, 3–30); Augustine, *De Sancta Virginitate* 4, 4 (PL 40, 398); *Sermo 225*, 2, 2, (PL 38, 1096 f.); Gregory of Nyssa, *Orat. in Diem Nat. Christi* (PG 46, 1140). See Lib. III, hom. V (I, 267a–b).

[36] Lib. IV, hom. I (I, 287b–288a). Cf. *Summa Theol.*, III, q. 29, art. 1, ad 1. On the marriage between Joseph and Mary, see above, pp. 142–143.

[37] Lib. V, hom. XIII (I, 473b); hom. XIV (I, 477a); Lib. VII, hom. IV (I, 743a).

[38] Lib. V, hom. XIII (I, 467a–468b).

[39] Lib. VII, hom. I (I, 728a); hom. II (I, 734b). Cartagena names the Ebio-

"ex vivifico vento Spiritus sancti." [40] The Holy Spirit consequently was the *"activum principium"* of Christ's conception.[41] Mary had a more passive role; her blood was the *"principium materiale"* of the Incarnation.[42] The author does not accept the "modern" opinion that Mary actively contributed to the generation of Christ by means of the female seed.[43]

Knowing no man and without the operation of any male seed,[44] Mary received the divine seed, the *"coelestem rorem Verbi divini,"* [45] into her *"virgineus thalamus."* [46] She therefore conceived Christ *"salva virginitate,"* without any detriment to her integrity.[47] It was both a supernatural and a natural conception.[48] It was a real human generation of Christ by Mary through the power of the Holy Spirit, so that she is truly Christ's mother who shared with him her substance.[49]

In terms of medieval biology, Cartagena explains Mary's physical

---

nites, "primi et praecipui Marianae Virginitatis hostes," Corinthus and Carpocrates as adversaries who claimed that Joseph was Christ's real father. Ibid., hom. XIII (I, 802b).

[40] Lib. VII, hom. III (I, 739a). In Lib. V, hom. XX (I, 526b) the author has the similar expression: "Divino eius spiramine afflata."

[41] Lib. V, hom. XIV (I, 481b). The Holy Spirit is not called the father of Christ, although Christ's conception is especially attributed to him, inasmuch as he did not share with Christ his substance which is the essence of fatherhood. Lib. V, hom. XII (I, 466a–467b). Cf. *Summa Theol.*, III, q. 32, art. 3.

[42] Lib. V, hom. XIV, (I, 481b).

[43] Ibid., hom. XVII (I, 508a). Cartagena follows St. Thomas' "sententia probabilissima" that women do not actively cooperate in the actual generation of a child. Cf. Lib. VII, hom. XIII (I, 808b).

[44] Lib. IV, hom. XI (I, 355b); Lib. V, hom. XIV (I, 481a); hom. XVI (I, 494a); hom. XVIII (I, 514b); Lib. VI, hom. XIII (I, 614b); Lib. VII, hom. IV (I, 745b); Lib. VIII, hom. I (II, 5a–b).

[45] Lib. VII, hom. I (I, 728a); hom. IV (I, 745b).

[46] Lib. V, hom. XIV (I, 462a); hom. XIV (I, 477b & 482b); hom. XIX (I, 523a).

[47] Ibid., hom. XII (I, 464b & 465a–b); hom. XVIII (I, 518a). Cartagena claims that it is altogether possible for a woman to conceive without losing virginity. Such is the case when a girl "attracts" into her body male seeds lying around on seats and in baths! These seeds can fertilize her therefore without her hymen having been broken. The author cites the authority of St. Thomas on this. Lib. VII, hom. XIII (I, 809a–b).

[48] Lib. V, hom. XVI (I, 499a–b); hom. XVII (I, 508a–b); Lib. VII, hom. XIII (I, 709b).

[49] Lib. V, hom. XVII (I, 505b–506b); Lib. VI, hom. XVI (I, 637a).

part in the conception of Christ to consist in providing her blood as
the material for the formation of his body.[50] The Schoolmen also
held that there is an interval of time between the natural generative
act of parents and the actual coming into being of the new person
when the rational soul is infused into the adequately developed
body.[51] Cartagena avers that *mutatis mutandis* there was no such
progression in time in the case of Christ. The moment Mary uttered
her *fiat*, the Word entered into her womb and became man.[52]

4. *Virgo in partu.* And regarding the birth of Christ itself, the
author sees it in conjunction with his conception. Both are holy and
sublime; he was conceived by Mary and was born of her *"virginitate
servata."* Here lies the wonder ot it all, that in conceiving and in giving
birth to Christ, Mary retained her virginal integrity.[53]

It was then a virgin birth.[54] Juan de Cartagena turns to metaphors to express himself. Christ, he says, emanated from the vase
of Mary's virginal womb like oil or perfume, *"instar odoris,"* which
issued forth without doing violence to the flower of her virginity.[55]
In fact, like a sunbeam going through a glass, Christ entered Mary's
womb at his conception and left it at his birth, not only without
damaging the integrity of his virgin mother, but actually sanctifying
and rendering it more radiant and beautiful.[56] And so the birth of

---

[50] Lib. V, hom. VII (I, 425a); hom. XII (I, 466a & b); hom. XIV (I, 480a–b);
hom. XVIII (I, 516b); Lib. VII, hom. III (I, 739a).

[51] Cf. St. Thomas, *Contra Gentiles* II, c. 89; Duns Scotus, *Oxon.* III, d. 16,
q. 2, n. 2: Vives, XIV, 641.

[52] Lib. V, hom. XIV (I, 477b).

[53] Lib. V, hom. XVI (I, 499a–b); Lib. VII, hom. III (I, 743a); Lib. V, hom.
XVIII (I, 517b).

[54] Lib. V, hom. XVI (I, 503a); Lib. VII, hom. I (I, 728a); hom. IV (I,
743b–744a). Cartagena cites Jovianus, Gualterus (Walter of Chateau–Thierry,
† 1249), Molineus (Ch. Dumoulin, † 1566) and the Protestants as asserting that
Mary lost her virginity in giving birth to Christ. Lib. VII, hom. XIII (I, 802b–
803a).

[55] "...faetus, instar odoris, qui absque floris violatione prodit, e thalamo
Virginis egressurus erat." Lib. VII, hom. I (I, 726b). Cf. Lib. V, hom. XVIII
(I, 514a).

[56] "Ad haec sicut radius solaris ingreditur, et egreditur speculum absque
ulla integritatis speculi violatione, ita Christus Dominus per conceptionem uterum Virginis ingrediens, et ab eo per partum instar radii solaris egrediens, virginitate matris suae integritatem non loesit, non labefactavit, non minuit, sed

Christ was not accompanied with the birthpangs due to lesion, but only with a tremendous joy for Mary.[57] Neither was it characterized with the usual bloody outflow.[58] Indeed the mysteries of Christ's virginal conception and birth are beyond reason and surpass our mind.[59]

Cartagena is explicit in affirming that Christ emerged from Mary's womb *"per vulvam"* just like any other normal birth.[60] This is important, otherwise the formal reason of human birth could not be verified, which would then reflect against Christ's true humanity and Mary's real motherhood. On the other hand, the author denies that Christ emerged from her womb by a dilation or distention of her organ. That would have meant that her womb was opened.[61] To the objection that Christ was presented in the temple as the law prescribed, because he opened his mother's womb (Lk 2, 22), the author answers that the law is concerned with first births as such and not with the womb and its aperture in themselves. Christ, being Mary's first child, is therefore said under the letter of the law to have opened her womb, although in reality he was born of her without opening it.[62] A propos opening the womb, Cartagena goes out of his way to try to defend Tertullian, who has been condemned by some theologians for claiming that Mary lost her virginity in giving birth and that Christ truly opened her womb.[63] The author cautions that the man should be interpreted in context. His principal intention was to prove against Marcion that even if Mary conceived virginally, she none-

---

sacravit, ac rutilantem magis, et splendidiorem." Lib. V, hom. XIX (I, 523b). Cf. Lib. VII, hom. III (I, 742b–743a); hom. I (I, 728b).

[57] Lib. VII, hom. IV (I, 744b); hom. II (I, 735a); Lib. VIII, hom. I (II, 7a).

[58] "Illa enim in partu non habuit sordes ex fluxu sanguinis provenientes, cum Virgo manens pareret, et absque ulla Virginei claustri violatione. Et quidem cum opera Spiritus sancti concepisset, ille solus sanguis profluebat a Beata Virgine, qui operis erat ad nutrimentum foetus, quo egresso ab utero totus ille sanguis defluebat ad ubera, ut fieret lac in cibum infantis, et consequenter nullus superfluus sanguis superfuit, ex quo immundities, aut purgationis necessitas oriretur." Lib. VIII, hom. I (II, 6b & 7a–b).

[59] Lib. VII, hom. III (I, 743a).

[60] Lib. VIII, hom. I (II, 7a). Cf. Lib. VII, hom. XIII (I, 804a).

[61] Lib. VII, hom. XIII (I, 807a–b).

[62] Ibid. (I, 805a–b).

[63] Tertullian, *De Carne Christi* 23, 3–4 (CCL 2, 914–915). Tertullian seems to have gone to this conclusion on the belief that without losing physical virginity the mother would not have milk for the infant. Cf. ibid., 20, 6 (CCL 2, 910).

theless really gave birth to Christ, i.e. that Christ was really born of her and was therefore a true man. Tertullian in other words was simply bringing out the *ratio formalis* of Mary's motherhood, under which light she was not a virgin, although in reality she is both a true mother and a true virgin.[64]

How could Christ have come out of Mary's womb without opening it or tearing it? Efforts at explanation have not been lacking. Unacceptable to Cartagena however is the theory that Christ was born of Mary through the natural channel without lacerating her, because he emerged from her not quantitatively but indivisibly as in the Eucharist. Such an explanation does not take into consideration the fact that Christ was in Mary's womb quantitatively and therefore left her womb as he was. Furthermore, such a birth would not be as miraculous as when he, although issuing forth from her womb quantitatively, did not even violate her maidenhood.[65] Likewise to be rejected is the opinion that Christ by his divine power so compressed his body at birth that he emerged from her womb through the natural tiny opening without any dilation necessary. This is no solution, since it renders the birth as such, which is formally in the act of bringing forth the child, no longer supernatural. Also, such an indecent figure of a shrunken Christ is not warranted.[66] Cartagena opts for the traditional explanation based on Christ's power of *"subtilitas."* Through his power of interpenetrability or interjacence Christ left the sealed sepulchre without damaging it. In the same manner he came out of Mary's womb.[67] Does this imply that Mary's role in giving birth to Christ was simple passivity without the normal contractions of a mother's womb, inasmuch as Christ came out of his own power? The author says no. Mary like any other woman giving birth or delivering a baby went through the natural process of muscle–movements to press the child out. But for her it was devoid of any anguish and labor–pains, because by divine power there was no resistance at all between Christ's body emerging on its own and Mary's.[68] The unique and supernatural character of Christ's birth

---

[64] Lib. VII, hom. XIII (I, 805b).

[65] Ibid. (I, 807b).

[66] Ibid. (I, 807b–808a).

[67] "Accepit enim Christus Dominus transeunter, dum vixit, quatuor dotes: ...subtilitatem tandem in egressu, tum ex thalamo virgineo, tum ex sepulchro, cum quibus virtute huius dotis vere se penetravit." Ibid. (I, 808a).

[68] Ibid. (I, 808b–809a).

as Mary remained through it a virgin is perhaps best summarized
by Augustine whom Cartagena quotes: "If there were another like
it, it would not be singular. We confess therefore that God can do
something, which admittedly we cannot fathom." [69]

5. *Virgo post partum*. Mary's virginity was a life–long consecration to God. It was perpetual and was never violated.[70] Christ
was Mary's only child.[71] And that Christ was called the *"primoge-
nitum"* of Mary does not mean there was a *secundogenitum*. The term
simply indicates that Christ was the first child in the sense that he
followed no other child and was preceded by no other child of Mary.[72]
In speaking about the possibility of Christ having a brother, the
author expresses this in a contrary–to–fact condition.[73] The "brothers of the Lord" in the Gospel accounts (Mt 12, 46; 13, 55; and Mk 3,
31; 6, 3; and Jn 2, 12; 7, 5), on the understanding of which the doctrine
of the *virginitas post partum* depends, does not prove, according to
Cartagena, that Mary later on had normal marriage relationship
with Joseph and bore other children, as some heretics like the Anti-
dicomarianites claim. These "brothers" were none other than close
blood relatives of Christ.[74] Cartagena in addition points out that
Mary's fecundity was in no way diminished or worse because of it,
if she had only one child. The fable about the wolf debating with a
lioness illustrates the case. The wolf boasts that she is more prolific
than the lioness, who has only one offspring; she gets always a litter
of cubs. The lioness' reply is: her one young is of much greater value
than the wolf's many cubs. Mary's only child is infinitely more than
all the children of all other mothers together.[75]

---

[69] Augustine, *Epist. 137*, 2, 8 (CSEL 44, 107; PL 33, 519); quoted by Cartagena in Lib. VII, hom. XIII (I, 807b). The author however wrongly claims that
this passage has been cited by the *second* Toletan Synod. It was the eleventh
synod of 675. Cf. DS 533.

[70] Lib. V, hom. XVI (I, 504b); Lib. VII, hom. III (I, 738b).

[71] Lib. VII, hom. XIII (I, 805b); Lib. VIII, hom. VII (II, 48a–b).

[72] Lib. VII, hom. XIII (I, 803b).

[73] "...si Christus Dominus uterinum habuisset fratrem." Lib. V, hom.
XVIII (I, 515b).

[74] Lib. VII, hom. XIII (I, 803a–b). Cf. Josef Blinzler, *Die Brüder und
Schwestern Jesu* (Stuttgart, 1967), esp. p. 145 ff.

[75] Lib. VII, hom. I (I, 728a–b). Cartagena is obviously relying on Pliny's
report (*Hist. Nat.* 8, 16.17) based on Herodotus that a lioness gives birth only
once and to only one cub at that. Cf. A. Forcellini et al., *Lexicon Totius Latini-
tatis*, III (Bononiae, 1966), p. 49.

And in answer to two other veteran heretical arguments against the doctrine that Mary remained a virgin throughout her life, the author charges misinterpretation of Sacred Scripture. Helvidius interpreted the Gospel passage: "And he did not know her until the day she gave birth" (Mt 1, 25) to mean that Joseph did afterwards come to know her, i.e. had carnal relationship with her. Cartagena replies that the preposition "until" is here concerned only with the period up to the birth of Christ and makes no affirmation whatsoever regarding the time after that.[76] Similarly, the second text which reads: "Before they came together she was found to be with child" (Mt 1, 18) does not mean that they later on "were together," i.e. in a sexual union. The passage is affirming clearly only that at the time before Joseph and Mary cohabited in Joseph's house, i.e. before he led her into his own house following the betrothal, he realized she was with child.[77] Mary's perpetual virginity is therefore in no way reflected upon.

B. Reasons for Mary's Virginity

Under this rubric as in the previous chapter, we are interested in the non–scriptural reasons Juan de Cartagena presents in his *Homiliae Catholicae* in support of the doctrine on Mary's perpetual virginity. The author does not claim to have evidence demonstrating her virginity, which is a mystery of faith and which, he says, we can look at only darkly as through a mirror. He intends rather to offer some arguments of congruence, which can compel any sound mind to assent that it is fitting Mary should conceive and give birth to Christ virginally.[78] To be observed is that Cartagena is principally concentrated on the virginal conception and birth and not so much on the *virginitas post partum*. We shall group his arguments into three main groups of reasoning *ex congruentia*, then we shall present his particular arguments directed to pagans.

---

[76] Lib. VII, hom. XIII (I, 806b–807a). Cf. Anton, "Mt 1, 25 und die virginitas B.M. Virginis post partum," *Tübinger theologische Quartalschrift*, 147 (1967) 28–39.

[77] Lib. VII, hom. XIII (I, 804a–b & 806a).

[78] Lib. VII, hom. V (I, 748b–749a). This homily's title is: "Rationes variae proponuntur, quibus non obscure probatur, decuisse Deiparam Mariam non aliter quam inviolata eius virginitate Christum Dominum concepisse et peperisse."

1. *Rationes congruentiae:*

a) In relation to the Father, it is but fitting that the divine Word should be conceived virginally. The Word has been generated in eternity by the Father without any corruption to the divine intellect or the generative power of God. When the same Word took flesh, it is proper that he should be conceived by a mother also without any corruption. Such is the case when his mother's virginal integrity remains unimpaired.[79] *"Conveniens fuit"* was St. Thomas' own conclusion on the matter.[80] Moreover, such a virgin conception manifests God's power. Anselm listed four ways by which God can make man: through the instrumentality of another man and a woman, as is usual; with neither man nor woman, as in the creation of Adam; from a man but without a woman, as in the creation of Eve; and lastly, from a woman without the agency of a man, which until then had not happened yet. And God chose this last way for the conception and birth of Christ to show that this unheard of manner is also subject to God's power.[81]

---

[79] "In eo autem id ostendit, quia sicut Verbum divinum generatur a Patre absque aliqua divini intellectus, seu potentiae generativae corruptione, ita idem Verbum carnem indutum ex matre, inviolato manente virginei claustri sigillo, processit..." Lib. VII, hom. II (I, 749a).

W. Pannenberg, *Grundzüge der Christologie* (Gütersloh, [2]1966), p. 142 f., contends that Christ's pre–existence as found in Paul (Phil 2, 6–7; Col 1, 15–17) and John (1, 1; 17, 5) is irreconcilable with the legends of the virgin birth of Christ. In the NT Christological development this means that the "pre–ministry" Christology centered on pre–existence stands in contradiction to the Matthean and Lucan Christology centered on conception, i.e. that Jesus first became God's Son through Mary's conception. The Church from the very beginning did not find these two Christologies contradictory, and reconciled them in a sequence whereby the Son of God or the divine Word became incarnate in the womb of Mary. This step is itself a genuine development in Christology. What the NT itself has not reconciled are not necessarily irreconcilable in themselves.

But another question arises in this connection. The "high" Christology of the virginal conception seems to indicate in the light of the generally accepted critical theory of a gradual development of explicit NT Christology that the virginal conception is a late Christological theologoumenon. Thus the historicity of this tradition comes in question. Cf. above, footnote 2. A solution could possibly lie in a satisfactory distinction between the *fact* of virginal conception and the *Christology* surrounding it in the accounts of Matthew and Luke. Cf. below, footnote 106. On the critical theory of the development of NT Christology, see Ferdinand Hahn, *Christologische Hoheitstitel* (Göttingen, 1963).

[80] *Summa Theol.*, III, q. 28, art. 1, corp.

[81] Lib. VII, hom. II (I, 750a–b). The reference is to Anselm's *Cur Deus Homo?* II, 8 (PL 158, 405–7).

b) As far as Christ himself is concerned, it is more worthy of him to be conceived and born virginally. Common sense tells any reasoning man that "supposing God's immutable decree, that his son whom he has generated from eternity should be conceived and born in time, it was fitting that his conception and birth be more honorable and pure than all others. He is however more honorable and pure, who does not violate or ruin the woman conceiving and giving birth to him, but leaves her untarnished."[82] It is also characteristic of Christ, who went about doing good and helping others. It stands to reason that in passing through his mother's womb, he did her good rather than wound her.[83] And if a Zacchaeus or a Martha and a Mary were rewarded generously by Christ, because they welcomed him into their homes, and if people have the innate urge to reciprocate others' hospitality, Christ could not have been less munificent towards his own mother. She took him and nurtured him for nine months in her chaste womb. It is inconceivable that he did violence to this sacred home either in entering or in leaving it. Nor is it acceptable to say that perhaps he later repaired whatever impairment he might have caused her. It is easy for him simply to preserve her integrity. Why should he allow it to be damaged at all? [84] Also, it was correct that he who made the law about honoring parents should himself increase, not decrease his mother's honor of virginity. Hence at his birth Christ removed all the pain and rupture ordinarily associated with child–bearing, and instead made it all beautiful and joyful for his mother Mary.[85] In addition, Christ would later be preach-

---

[82] Lib. VII, hom. II (I, 749b).

[83] "...cum Christus numquam legatur damnum aliquod, dum vixit, alicui intulisse, quin potius multis multa bona condonasse... rationi consonum erat, ut dilectissimae matris suae integritati nullum prorsus detrimentum inferret, sed petransiret potius uterum maternum benefaciendo, non laedendo." Ibid. (I, 750a).

[84] "Cum igitur Beata Virgo speciali illo virginei uteri suo hospitio per integros novem menses Christum Dominum suscepisset, summaque sit Christi erga benefactores suos gratitudo, consequens est sacram illam domum non violasse, nec permisisse ad introitum, aut egressum illius iacturam aliquam pati... Nec fas certe est dicere, Christum Dominum post egressum ex matris utero, factam virginei claustri iacturam divina virtute postea reparasse, nam qui eadem facilitate poterat integram illam servare, superfluum sane fuisset illam ortu suo violare, quam confestim redintegrare volebat." Ibid. (I, 751b–752a).

[85] "...decebat valde eum, qui legem de honorandis parentibus condiderat, ne, cum nasceretur, virginitatis honorem in matre minueret, sed potius augeret, quod sane praestitit Christus... in matris tamen partu dolorem non admisit, sed eam potius eximia laetitia perfudit... pulchram illam reddidit..." Ibid. (I, 750b).

ing the merits of virginity. The easier and more effective way of teaching is by example. And the example of Mary's perpetual virginity is certainly more persuasive than any precept.[86]

Cartagena likewise reasons that Christ should be conceived by a virgin mother, so that he could be born without original sin. In terms of the Augustinian theory of the transmission of original sin (which the author earlier rejects!), the normal human conception through the generative act of a man and a woman arousing the sensual appetites occasions the passing on of this sin. Christ, therefore, having been conceived without the operation of a man but by the power of the Holy Spirit only and by Mary, was born without original sin.[87]

c) More related to Mary, it is appropriate that Christ be conceived and born virginally, because like the first Adam made out of the virgin earth that had not been tilled yet, the womb whence the second Adam comes should be intact too.[88] And the virgin mother of

---

[86] Ibid. (I, 750b–751a).

[87] "Decima ratio tandem sit, decuisse Christum Dominum ex matre Virgine oriri, ut etiam ex vi conceptionis peccato originali careret: nam vulgaris modus humanae conceptionis hoc genus peccati perit, conceptio vero ex sola Virgine absque virili opera omnis peccati expers est..." Ibid. (I, 752b).

Ambrose first developed this line of reasoning and Augustine took it up against the Pelagians. Cf. Campenhausen, op. cit., pp. 61–62. See also K. Rahner, "Dogmatische Bemerkungen...," op. cit., p. 140, on this "non sequitur." Against K. Barth's opinion that the virginal conception has something to do with Christ's sinlessness, Pannenberg, op. cit., p. 148, squarely sets himself. Cf. ibid., pp. 371–372.

Cartagena's contemporary, St. Lawrence of Brindisi, saw the matter from another angle and claimed that Mary's Immaculate Conception is more wonderful than Jesus' virginal conception, just as it is more wonderful when sinful parents conceive a child immaculately than when a mother in conceiving a most pure child remains a virgin. Cf. Graef, op. cit., p. 342.

[88] "Octava ratio sit, quia cum primus Adam de terrenus, typum gesserit secundi Adam de coelo caelestis (ut verbis Pauli – 1 Cor 15, 45) oportuit, ut sicut ille ex terra virginea nullius culturae subiecta procreatus fuit, ita etiam Christus ex utero Virgineo, et matre intacta nasceretur." Ibid. (I, 752a).

Elsewhere Cartagena writes: "Sicut enim in formatione Adae non aliae causae concurrerunt, quam Deus, et terra: ille, ut efficiens, haec ut materiam limi subministrans; sic in corporis Christi generatione Deus solum, et Virgo concursum suum adhibuerunt; ille effective viri operam ineffabili modo supplens... sicut etiam terra illa, ex qua procreatus est Adam, virgo erat, utpote quae nullius cultoris semen susceperat; ita virgo erat, et virgo perpetuo mansit, quae semen viri, et peccati corruptionem semper nescivit." Lib. I, hom. III (I, 16a).

Irenaeus in his consistent use of the principle of correspondence and par-

Christ signifies also, as St. Augustine has said, that Christ's members would be born too of a virgin Church by the power of the Holy Spirit. For the Church, whose children are the faithful, is a perpetual virgin who conceives not from a man but from the Spirit, who gives birth not in sorrow but in joy, and who nourishes not with the breast's milk but with her teaching.[89]

2. *Catena Patrum.* Without going into individual details, it should be mentioned here that Cartagena has also pieced together a catena of selected texts from the Fathers and from past and contemporary theologians, to further strengthen his case for Mary's perpetual virginity. Their unanimous consent is in his mind an unbeatable argument against heretics. And to deny their teaching is "the height of temerity, in fact a most clear case of feeblemindedness and insanity." The author's strong language is explained by his belief that the Fathers spoke not just for themselves, but the Holy Spirit spoke in them and thus endowing them with a special authority.[90] In a homily of 30 columns — double the normal length — Cartagena simply quotes from 28 authors in all, beginning with Cyril of Jerusalem and Chrysostom up to Canisius and Baronius. The longest quotation from any one author is taken from five different works of St. Ildephonsus of Toledo.

3. *Adversus Gentiles.* Juan de Cartagena's rather apologetical approach in handling the question of Mary's perpetual virginity, his preoccupation specially with ancient heresies (since the subject is

---

allelism between Adam and Christ, Eve and Mary, was the first one to bring out this detail about the virgin earth and the virgin womb. Cf. *Contra Haer.* V, 21, 1 (PG 7, 1179); Tertullian's imitation in *De Carne Christi* 17 (CCL 2, 903–5).

[89] Lib. VII, hom. II (I, 752b). The reference is to Augustine, *De Sancta Virginitate* 6 (CSEL 41, 239–240). Cf. Vat. II, *Const. on the Church*, n. 63.

[90] "...omnes Sancti Patres, nullo dempto, unanimi consensu, Mariae virginitatem numquam violatam constanter asseverant, quos inficiari velle summa temeritas, perfricatae frontis inditium, execranda inverecundia, immo apertissima fatuitas et amentia est: maxime Christo Domino ad illos dicente: 'Non enim estis vos qui loquimini, sed spiritus patris vestri, qui loquitur in vobis' (Mt 10, 20)." Lib. VII, hom. XII (I, 787b–788a). The title of the homily runs: "De integerrima Deiparae Mariae Virginitate pulchra, et solida ex priscorum Patrum selectioribus monumentis contexitur Catena, quae ob singularem eruditionem, ac uberrimam conceptionum animi copiam, non poterit legenti non utilis esse pariter, et iucunda."

universally accepted, he probably has to resuscitate old "bones" as
fillers and for some excitement), is further underscored by the extra
attention he gives to the pagans. He believes, e.g. that the most
wise author of nature and of grace left unmistakable traces in nature
in support of Mary's virginity. Such testimony from nature both
strengthens Catholic piety and breaks the proud neck of incredulous
pagans.[91] In this, Cartagena is simply taking a page from the Fathers
who in addition to scriptural proofs also gathered materials from nature and pagan mythology to support their contention for Mary's
virginity, as Origen had first done.[92] To make the virgin conception
not to appear too unusual and too marvelous — hence incredible —
efforts were instinctively made by the early apologists to look for
analogies in the examples of animal parthogenesis. The latest developments in today's experimental embryology, e.g. cloning, which
open the possibility of human reproduction without sexual intercourse,
would certainly be a welcome addition to the list. But this quest for
natural parallels is a departure from the emphasis of the evangelists;
for they stress rather the role of the Holy Spirit and regard the whole
mystery as an act of divine power.

a) Parallels from animals. With great credulity, the author
repeats among others the information from Aristotle that an eel
breeds without the help of any male, the report by Augustine that
mares in Cappadocia propagate only with the wind, the expert tip
from Virgil that bees multiply without intercourse, the example by
Basil the Great that vultures conceive in the air without any male
seed, and the observation that woodworms reproduce without the
need of a male.[93]

b) From mythology. Since we are dealing with pagans, says
Cartagena, their own "*fabulosa figmenta*" can provide us with an
argument *ad hominem*. It is widely accepted in pagan mythology
that Vulcan was born of Juno without any father, and that Minerva
came from the brain of Jove without any mother. It is also claimed
that Venus originated from the foam of the sea, Castor and Pollux

---

[91] "Primo tamen adversus Gentiles... stylum acuemus. Equidem cum idem
sit sapientissimus, tam naturae, quam gratiae conditor, voluit in natura ipsa nonnulla relinquere vestigia, quibus et Catholicorum pietas erga virginitatem Mariae
magis iuvaretur, et Paganorum incredulitas, duraque eorum cervix infringeretur."
Lib. VII, hom. III (I, 738b).

[92] Origen, *Contra Celsum* I, 37 (GCS 2, 88–89).

[93] Lib. VII, hom. III (I, 738b–739a).

from an egg, while Deucalion and Pyrrha repeopled the world following the deluge with the stones they threw. "If the pagans think that these monstrous portents, which contradict nature, are worthy of belief, they ought then to judge it more believable that Christ was born of a virgin mother." [94]

c) From the sayings of the Sibyls. To complement the above mentioned cases of unusual births taken from pagan mythology, Cartagena lists too the sayings of the various Sibyls foretelling a coming birth from a virgin. These soothsayers so much revered by the pagans have confirmed too the mystery of Christ's virgin conception and birth. There was the Sibyl of Cumae mentioned by Virgil in his 4th Eclogue, prophesying the golden age and the coming of a virgin. The Sibyls of Erythrea, of Phrygia, of Samia, of Persia, of Delphi, of Libya and of Chimea all said something similar about a virgin feeding a child or god being born of a chaste virgin. The word of their Sibyls should make it more acceptable to the pagans that Christ was born of a virgin. [95]

d) From wonders. The assent of the pagans can be compelled too by the wonders and unusual signs attesting the perpetual virginity of Mary. For instance, the story is told that when the Romans asked the oracle of Apollo how long their massive temple of peace would remain standing, the reply given was: "Until the virgin bears a child." At that the people rejoiced, believing that since the sign indicated is impossible, their temple would then stand in perpetuity. They even wrote at the temple portal: "The eternal temple of peace." On the night Mary gave birth, the temple collapsed. [96] Another prodigy,

---

[94] Ibid. (I, 740a).

Today these instances from mythology, instead of favoring the credibility of the virginal conception, have become possible sources to show that the whole idea might have just been inspired or influenced by some pagan ἱερὸς γάμος. Cf. J. Hasenfuss, "Die Jungfrauengeburt in der Religionsgeschichte," in *Jungfrauengeburt Gestern und Heute*, op. cit., pp. 11–23; A. Vögtle, *Das Evangelium und die Evangelien* (Düsseldorf, 1971), pp. 46–47.

[95] Lib. VII, hom. III (I, 740a–b). The *Oracula Sibyllina* was a 4th century compilation by Christians and Jews of sibylline prophecies with monotheistic and Christian colorings. It was very popular during the Middle Ages and the Renaissance. Cf. *Paulys Real–Encyclopädie* II A, 2, col. 2117–2169.

[96] Lib. VII, hom. III (I, 741a–b). The *Historia Scholastica* by Peter Comestor is cited by the author as reporting this story. This book, one of the most popular in the Middle Ages, was a great summary principally of biblical history. It was used in the schools together with the *Glossa* and the *Sententiae*.

one mentioned also by St. Thomas, was the golden plate unearthed
by Queen Helena and Emperor Constantine with the inscription:
"Christ will be born of a virgin, and I believe in him. O sun, you
will see me again in the time of Helena and Constantine." [97] A more
scholastic sounding incident is contained in the *vita* of St. Aegidius
(† c. 720). According to the narration, a certain master of theology
who had doubts about Mary's virginity once approached the saint,
in order to receive assurance from him. Three times the saint struck
the ground with a staff, each time saying "*Virgo ante partum*,"
"*Virgo in partu*," and "*Virgo post partum*" respectively. And each
time a most white lily sprang out of the ground.[98] Cartagena even
quotes an astrologer, Albumazar († c. 886), to show that heavenly
signs also indicated the virgin conception and birth of Christ.[99]

In the light of these arguments from nature, mythology, the
Sibyls and unusual occurences, the author in his "shadow–boxng"
with the pagans now poses to them a rhetorical question: which is
more credible, the irrational stories of the gods quarreling and mating,
or the story of a virgin conceiving and giving birth? "Believe, o philosopher," he says, "that the Word having assumed flesh in the womb
of the virgin, came forth from the virgin's womb without violating
its seal." [100]

4. *Definita*. Juan de Cartagena holds that the doctrine of Mary's
perpetual virginity has been defined as a dogma of faith in the Lateran Council of 649[101]. The Nicene Creed also affirms that Christ

[97] Lib. VII, hom. III (I, 741b). The reference is to the *Summa Theol.*,
II–II, q. 2, art. 7, ad 3.
[98] Lib. VII, hom. III (I, 742a). Regarding this *vita* of St. Aegidius, see s.v.
in *Catholicisme* V, 19–20.
[99] Lib. VII, hom. III (I, 742a–b).
[100] Ibid. (I, 743a).
[101] "Quare Ecclesia Catholica, tot apertis prophetarum oraculis, ac Evangelicis monumentis innitens veritatem hanc de perpetua virginitate, tanquam
Catholicum fidei dogma diffinivit in V. Synodo cap. 6. et Synodo VI action. II.
in Synodo VII artic. 13 in confessione Tarasii in Concilio Lateranensi sub Martino II
(sic), Canone 3..." Lib. VII, hom. IX (I, 773b–774a).
"Can. 3. Si quis sec. s. Patres non confitetur... Dei genitricem sanctam
semperque virginem et immaculatam Mariam, utpote ipsum Deum Verbum
specialiter et veraciter, qui a Deo Patre ante omnia saecula natus est, in ultimis
saeculorum absque semine concepisse ex Spiritu Sancto, et incorruptibiliter eam
genuisse, indissolubili permanente et post partum eiusdem virginitate, condemna-
tus sit." DS 503. Cf. J. de Aldama, "El canon tercero del Concilio Lateranense

was conceived from the Holy Spirit and was born of the Virgin Mary.[102] The Council of Constantinople in turn refers to her as *"semper virgo."*[103] In his own country, the author recalls, the 11th Council of Toledo (675) defended and acclaimed Mary's inviolate virginity, and, in order to instill firmly this mystery in the mind of the faithful, instituted the Feast of the Expectation of the Birth.[104] In fact, the Church underlines the perfection of Mary's virginity by calling her *"virginitas ipsa."* [105]

It is on the basis of the clear Gospel testimonies and due to the prophetic words in the Old Testament that Mary's perpetual virginity has been defined by the Church. But even prescinding from these scriptural witnesses, Cartagena thinks this doctrine is so undeniably attested by tradition, that every Catholic should believe and profess it.[106]

---

de 649," *Marianum,* 24 (1962) 65–83; idem, "Zur theologischen Würdigung der Lehre von der 'Virginitas in partu' in Laterankonzil von 649," in *Heilige Schrift und Maria* (Essen, 1963), pp. 261–270. Although this Lateran Council is not in the strict canonical sense an ecumenical council, Aldama holds that its affirmation on Mary's perpetual virginity is intended as a dogma of faith. K. Rahner, "Virginitas in partu," op. cit., pp. 178–179, is of the opposite view.

[102] Lib. VII, hom. IX (I, 774b); Lib. V, hom. XII (I, 466a). Regarding the real thrust of these creedal statements to be Jesus' birth and humanity, and not the exact how of his conception, cf. J. N. D. Kelly, *Early Christian Creeds* (London, ²1960), pp. 144–145, 332–338.

[103] Lib. VII, hom. XII (I, 801a).

[104] Ibid., hom. I (I, 726b–727b). Cf. DS 533.

[105] Ibid., hom. IX (I, 774a). The Little Office of the B.V.M. sings: "A Sancta Virginitas, quibus te laudibus efferam nescio, quia quem coeli capere non poterant, tuo gremio contulisti."

[106] "Ex praedictis omnibus in discursu totius huius Libri de integerrima Mariae virginitate colligo, quod cum habeamus firmissimam Ecclesiae Catholicae auctoritatem, et clarissimam nostrorum maiorum, omniumque Sanctorum Patrum ab ipsis etiam Apostolis traditionem, qua, velut inexpugnabili mauro, intemerata Deiparae virginitas adversus quoslibet hostium impetus se tuetur, etiam si sacrae Scripturae testimoniis destitueremur, quae tamen non desiderantur, cum pene innumera, eaque illustrissima adduxerimus, omnes tamen Catholici perpetuam Deiparae pudicitiam, numquamque violatam integritatem constanter profiteri deberemus." Ibid., hom. XIII (I, 811a).

Even if the doctrine of Mary's biological virginity might not have been solemnly defined, it is certainly infallibly taught by the ordinary Magisterium of the Church, having been proposed and believed by the faithful so consistently and universally for some 1600 years. As St. Jerome wrote: "We believe that God was born of a virgin because we read it" (*Adv. Helvidium* 19: PL 23, 213A). In

II. SCRIPTURAL TESTIMONIES

Even as he stresses the long and solid tradition of the Church in believing and professing Mary's perpetual virginity, Cartagena moves with certainty in his exposition of what he considers are apodictic words from Sacred Scripture affirming the doctrine. For the long tradition of the virginal conception stems from its being presented as part of the Christian heritage verified in the Bible. The author finds ten OT passages, some literal, others mystical, in their prophecies about the virgin conception and birth. And the fullfilment of what had been so clearly foretold is duly recorded in the NT. Moreover, Cartagena singles out some images and metaphors from the Bible that are illustrative and confirmatory of the teaching, as he does with the mystery of the Immaculate Conception.

A. PRINCIPAL BIBLICAL PASSAGES

1. *Old Testament prophecies :*
a) Genesis 3, 15. "I will make you enemies of each other: you and the woman, your offspring and her offspring. It will crush your head." This first glimmer of salvation in Sacred Scripture is a special prophecy given by God's providence so early in history to affirm the virginity of the future mother of God, and thus, so to say, to provide for Mary's inviolate purity a shield against all coming attacks by heretics. In spite of the variation of the readings: "He will crush your head" as in the Greek version, or "She will..." as in the Vulgate, which differences logically divide the opinions of the Fathers, it is commonly held that the passage foretells the virginity of the Mother

---

the light of today's discussion, however, where this teaching is questioned by Christians who do not deny the divinity of Christ — unlike the earlier opponents of the doctrine therefore — the question comes up whether the virginal conception might yet turn up as a test case of the limit of the Church's magisterial infallibility. Would this teaching come to the point when one has to distinguish between the valid theological reflection of faith *that* God intervened in the conception of Jesus Christ and a past biological notion *how* God intervened, i.e. through virginal conception? Would this here be an instance of the historical relativity of a doctrinal statement, in the analogy of the theological doctrine that God was specially involved in the creation of man, where the physical imagery of man being formed out of the earth and the woman from the man's body has been "improved" upon by a deeper understanding of evolution? Cf. Brown, art. cit., pp. 12–13.

of God, in that only the seed of the woman is mentioned. Were she
to conceive this son from the seed of a man, the son should have been
declared to be also that of the man and not just of the woman.[107]

b) Leviticus 12, 2. "If a woman being impregnated gives birth
to a body..." would be a useless statement, if it only says what it
outwardly seems to say, i.e. that for a woman to conceive the male
seed is necessary. The special significance of these Scripture words,
other than being merely a clause in the law of purification, rests on
the fact that Mary is exempted from this imperative of nature. She
would be the only woman, who without any male seed would conceive
and give birth to a boy.[108] In addition, it is noteworthy that the following expression: "If she gives birth to a girl..." (12, 5) is quite
different from the first. Why was it not said, "If she being impregnated
gives birth to a girl," as with the giving birth to a boy? It is because
there would be only one woman who would conceive without the
necessity of impregnation and she would have a boy.[109]

c) Proverbs 30, 18–19.

"There are three things beyond my comprehension,
    four, indeed, that I do not understand:

---

[107] "Diligentior, et multo solicitior extitit Dei providentia, virginitatem futurae matris suae a primordiis creationis mundi, singulari oraculo stabiliens, quo
illam velut scuto praemunitam haereticorum iacula laedere nequirent... hoc loco
praedicitur Deiparae Mariae virginitas, cum de solo semine mulieris facta sit
mentio: si enim illa ex viri semine concepta esset, non matris solius, sed viri
praecipue semen diceretur eius filius, per quem ipsa caput serpentis contritura
erat. Huic eleganter Rupert. dixit: 'De quo semine haec dicuntur, nisi de uno
qui est Christus? ipse namque solus ita semen mulieris est, ut non etiam viri
semen sit.' " Lib. VII, hom. VI (I, 753a–b). On the OT and Mary's virginity,
see Johannes Schildenberger, OSB, "Die Jungfräuliche Mutter Maria im Alten
Testament," in *Jungfrauen Geburt Gestern und Heute*, op. cit., pp. 109–136.

[108] "...quibus verbis Divinus legislator excepit B. Virginem, quam sine
suscepto semine, divino spiritu afflante, concepturam praecognoscebat, alioquin
supervacaneum fuisset dicere, 'Mulier, si suscepto semine,' cum naturaliter nulla
possit parere, nisi illud susceperit, voluit igitur in ea lege Mariam excipere, quae
paritura erat sine suscepto semine." Lib. VII, hom. VI (I, 754a).

[109] "Secundum idipsum mihi probat, quod ex ipsa lege palam deprehenditur
ob Marianae virginitatis mysterium, conditionem illam fuisse appositam, sum solum adhibetur in foemina pariente masculum: 'Mulier,' inquit, 'si suscepto semine
pepererit masculum': non vero in muliere pariente foeminam, de qua postea
dicitur: 'Si autem foeminam pepererit.' Cur enim non similiter dixit: 'Si autem
suscepto semina foeminam pepererit?' nisi quia una tantum mulier futura erat,
quae non suscepto semine, masculum erat paritura, ad quam solam excipiendam,
fuit ea particula adhibenda?" Ibid. (I, 754b–755a).

> the way of an eagle through the skies,
> the way of a snake over the rock,
> the way of a ship in mid–ocean,
> the way of a man with a girl."

Cartagena asserts that the last line reads in Hebrew as referring to the way of a man with a virgin, an *almah*, not just a girl. Solomon is here talking about the virgin birth. The man is Christ, who is meant also in the words: "who has mounted to the heavens, then descended?" (30, 4). Christ is the man who even at the moment of birth was not just an infant but a man endowed with reason. An eagle cuts through the skies, a ship ploughs through the sea, a snake scurries over a rock, and they all must part what is before them, in order to pass through. In Christ's passage from Mary's womb, however, there was no seal broken or parted; her virginity remained intact. This is indeed beyond comprehension.[110] Seen from another angle, Solomon could not but confess his ignorance before the wonder of "the way of a man in a virgin," by which without the need of any male seed Christ made his way into the virginal chamber of Mary's womb. She herself would be exclaiming, "How could this be, since I do not know man?" [111]

Following the three above–given prophecies, Cartagena then sets out to interpret the prophet *par excellence* of Christ's virginal conception and birth. As a proponent of Mary's virginity Isaiah has

---

[110] "Voluit ergo Salomon iuxta hanc versionem ibi virginei partus mysterium nobis referare, quod sane difficilius est cognitu, quam aquilae volatus, quam via navis in mari, et colubri semita super petram, haec enim omnia vere scindunt, et dividunt partes corporum, per quae transeunt; in transitu vero Christi Domini, quando per verum partum ex materno utero prodiit, nulla virginei signaculi scissura facta est; et ideo nullum alicuius divisionis vestigium in ea remansit, adeo ut si fingeretur, ipsam matrem negare se peperisse, non esset unde posset mendacii convinci. Iuvatque non parum hanc expositionem, quod in eod. cap. 30. Salomon vere agit de filio Dei, cum dicat: 'Quis ascendit in coelum, atque descendit?' etc. Iuvat etiam, quod Salomon non sine mysterio dixit: 'Viam viri,' non 'adolescentis,' quia scilicet Christus Dominus, de quo agebat, ab instanti conceptionis in utero materno 'vir' fuit, id est, 'homo' praeditus ratione, et discursu, alii vero in eo instanti non 'viri,' sed 'infantes' appellantur." Ibid. (I, 756b–757a).

[111] "Huic autem tertiae viae quartam addit Salomon, quam ingenue se ignorare fatetur, scilicet, 'Viam viri in Virgine,' id est, qua ratione Christus Dominus absque virili semine fecerit sibi viam ad ingrediendum uterum virgineum: nec mirum certe hoc Salomoni difficile sibi visum fuisse, cum eandem difficultatem agnoscens B. Virgo Angelo conceptum Christi ei annuncianti obiecerit: 'Quomodo fiet istud, quoniam virum non cognosco?' " Ibid. (I, 757a).

no peer in the Old Testament. Four passages can be ascribed to him, wherein we are given a glimpse of the mystery to be accomplished in Mary. Foremost among these is of course the text on the *almah*.

d) Isaiah 7, 14. Significantly Matthew pointedly observed, after narrating the angel's message to Joseph that Mary has conceived by the Holy Spirit, that "all this took place to fulfill the words spoken by the Lord through the prophet: 'The virgin will conceive and give birth to a son'" (Mt 1, 22–23). The author claims that the Isaian passage holds the first place among the OT texts supporting the doctrine of Mary's virginal motherhood, since it is a clear prophecy that her virginity would remain inviolate even as she conceives Christ.[112]

It may be objected that in the Hebrew version what the Vulgate translates as *virgo* is, *almah*, which is properly translated as just a young girl. On the contrary, the author maintains, following Jerome's explanation of the word, *almah* is derived from *halam*, which means "to hide," consequently giving *almah* the special connotation of a hidden and intact young girl, a virgin therefore. And when *almah* is written with an aspirate, as it is the case in this Isaian passage, it brings out more unmistakably the meaning virgin, which is the way the LXX translates *almah*, giving witness to an early Jewish interpretation accepted by Matthew. In only two other places in the Bible is *almah* written with an aspirate and in both instances

---

[112] "Inter omnia sacrae Scripturae monumenta ad veritatem hanc catholicam comprobandam, illud quidem principem locum tenere arbitror, quod Isaias Propheta scripsit: 'Ecce Virgo concipiet, et pariet filium, et vocabitur nomen eius Emmanuel'... quibus verbis clare praedixit Isaias inviolatam Mariae virginitatem cum ipsam praegnantem et parientem Virginem compellet." Lib. VII, hom. VII (I, 758b). Cf. ibid., hom. IX (I, 772b).

Among the Fathers, Justin the Martyr was the first to employ this passage to prove against the Jews Christ's virginal conception. *Tryphone* 43, 3–7; 67, 1. Irenaeus, *Contra Haer.* III, 21, 4–5.9, and Tertullian, *De Carne Christi* 4, 20; *Contra Judaeos* 9; and *Contra Marcion* IV, 21, 4, were to reecho and further develop this point.

Cf. Herbert Haag, "Is 7, 14 als alttestamentliche Grundstelle der Lehre der Virginitas Mariae," in *Jungfrauengeburt Gestern und Heute*, op. cit., pp. 137–144, esp. p. 143 f. showing that the Christological meaning given to the passage in the NT is without precedence in Jewish exegesis; Rudolf Kilian, "Die Geburt des Immanuel aus der Jungfrau," in *Zum Thema Jungfrauengeburt*, op. cit., pp. 9–35; A. Vögtle, op. cit., pp. 45–46. On Matthew's custom of adding fulfillment citations from the OT to existing traditions, cf. W. Rothfuchs, *Die Erfüllungszitate des Matthäusevangeliums* (Stuttgart, 1969), esp. pp. 99–100.

it means a virgin. One is the account in Genesis (24, 16) about Rebekah going down to the spring to fill her pitcher with water: "The girl was very beautiful, and a virgin; no man had touched her." The second is in Exodus (2, 8): "And the girl went off to find the baby's own mother," referring to Moses' sister volunteering to look for a nurse for the baby. She was herself just a child of four, and therefore a virgin.[113]

Some understand *"concipiet et pariet"* in relation to the virginity as two different stages which must be taken in *sensu diviso*, i.e. she does not remain a virgin in conceiving and giving birth, granting that she was one before that. However, considering that God wanted to give Ahaz a remarkable sign, a virgin who loses her virginity in having a child would hardly be that extraordinary. God's power was to be manifested in a virgin's conceiving and bearing a child yet remaining a virgin.[114] Still others would say that the prodigy promised by God was not the virgin conception and the virgin birth but the birth itself of the God–man, or, for some, the absence of any male seed was remarkable enough. To the objection, made especially by the *"perfidi Iudei,"* that the passage referred to the mother of King Hezekiah, son of Ahaz, or to the wife of the prophet himself, Origen's answer should suffice: "We ask, who was born during the time of Ahaz, of whose birth it may be said Emmanuel, i.e. God is with us? If none is to be found, evidently that which is said to Ahaz was promised to the house of David, in that it was written, 'From the seed of David would the Savior according to the flesh come.' Indeed it is said that

---

[113] "Halma a verbo Halam derivatur quod 'abscondere,' seu 'celare' significat: igitur Halma idem est apud ipsos, quod 'Virgo abscondita, et intacta,' quod maxime verum habet... quando nomen 'Halma' scribitur cum aspiratione, ut contingit in praedicto loco Isaiae. Ubi observandum est, quod hoc loco excepto nusquam in tota sacra pagina invenitur 'Halma' cum aspiratione, nisi de Rebecca, cum ibat ad hauriendam aquam, et ex contextu patet, tunc Virginem esse, et de Maria sorore Moysis, de qua dicitur: 'Et perrexit Ahalma,' quam etiam constat tunc virginem fuisse, nam... erat parvula quatuor annos habens." Lib. VII, hom. VII (I, 758b–759a).

[114] "Sed contra hoc est, quia ibi Deus promittebat Achaz mirabile aliquod signum... quod autem virgo aliqua pariat, non manens virgo, nullum sane prodigium, aut portentosum signum est, ut ex se constat: verba igitur necessario sunt intelligenda in sensu composito." Ibid. (I, 759b).

"Haec autem divinae potentiae magnitudo in eo certe ostendebatur, quod Virgo manens Virgo conciperet, et pareret." Ibid. (I, 760a).

the sign is from the depths below and the heights above, because he who descends is he who ascends over the entire heaven to rule all." [115] Cartagena further repeats Jerome's calculation that the future king Hezekiah was born nine years before Isaiah's prophecy, which therefore could not have meant him. The author feels so strongly about this text and its interpretation, that he asserts it is sufficient in itself to warrant a definition of the doctrine.[116]

e) Isaiah 53, 8. Varying interpretations have been given to this passage of Isaiah: "Who will explain his descent?" – which translates the Greek and Latin versions, while the Hebrew is uncertain and seems to mean: "Would anyone plead his cause?" But Christian tradition has taken it over to refer to the mysterious origin of Christ. In conceiving and giving birth to Christ, Mary remained a virgin. Indeed, "who will explain his descent?" As Athanasius wrote: "Who will explain his birth? This is he, who was born of a virgin, and as a man appeared on earth, and whose birth according to the flesh is inexplicable. For he is not one who could say that he has a carnal father, because his body was generated not by a man but by a virgin solely." [117]

f) Isaiah 8, 3. "I went to the prophetess, she conceived and gave birth to a son." The author proceeds from the unanimity of the Fathers in expounding these words as speaking of Christ's virginal conception in Mary's womb. It was the Holy Spirit who went to her to overshadow her. And she conceived and gave birth to a son. And Mary is a prophetess, not just because she has prophesied that all generations would call her blessed (Lk 1, 48), but also because she conceived Christ in the manner of prophetical and spiritual infusion

---

[115] Lib. VII, hom. VII (I, 760b–761a).

[116] "Quare crediderim locum hunc Isaiae tanti roboris esse ad Mariae virginitatem astruendam, ut si veritas haec non fuisset iam ab Ecclesia definita, solus ille locus sufficeret ad veritatem hanc, tanquam verissimum fidei dogma in Deiparae Mariae honorem diffiniendam..." Ibid. (I, 763a).

[117] Lib. VII, hom. VIII (I, 764a), where the author also writes: "Gravissimi tamen alii Patres... Isaiae locum ad Christi Domini temporalem ex Maria generationem referunt, quam ex eo capite inenarrabilem, et ineffabilem esse arbitrantur, quod supra totam naturae facultatem facta fuerit, salva et incolumi Deiparae virginitate, adeo ut Isaias hoc tantum mysterium praevidens in admirationem raptus dixerit: 'Generationem eius quis enarrabit?' Et quidem si Christus Dominus communi modo, et ordinaria ratione genitus fuisset a matre, non erat cur Isaias per admirationem in ea verba prorumperet, cum humanae generationis communis propagatio lumine solo rationis facile a philosophis explicetur."

by the power of the Holy Spirit who overshadowed her, just as the gift of prophesying is infused in a prophet by the divine power.[118]

The author rejects the position that the passage is actually talking about the birth of a son to Isaiah. Reduced *ad absurdum*, this opposite view is presented as saying that Isaiah was ordered by God to have two witnesses in his intercourse with his wife, and the child born from this relationship was to receive the name *Maher–shalal–hash–baz*.[119] The obvious confusion lies in having the two witnesses mentioned in verse 2 assigned to verse 3 in which the prophetess was approached and conceived. Actually the witnesses were intended to give legal formality to the act of verse 1 in which as instructed by Yahweh the prophet was to write in some sort of a placard the warning: "The spoil hastens, the plunder comes quickly," the symbolic name to be given to the prophet's son. Another misunderstanding on the part of Cartagena and his authorities stemmed from the mistaken identities and the ensuing miscalculation that neither Uriah nor Zechariah could have been a witness to anything during Isaiah's time, because the first came more than hundred years later, while the second came more than two hundred years later. Actually Uriah was Ahaz's collaborator in his dalliance with Assyrian religion (2 Kings 16, 10–16), while Zechariah was probably the father–in–law of Ahaz (2 Kings 18, 2).

g) Isaiah 9, 6. "And his dominion will be widespread." Even if at first glance these words from the messianic oracle of Isaiah do not seem to be related in anyway to Mary's virginity, a closer scrutiny will show that they say something to illustrate the doctrine. Mary's name in the diction known as *lemarbe* means mistress or ruler, indicating that as the mother of Christ she would be sharing in his

---

[118] "Prophetissam autem, ad quam foecundandam Spiritus Dei accessit, beatissimam Virginem esse, praecitati Patres contestantur, quae mirabile illud edidit vaticinium, dum in suo cantico ex eo, quod concepisset Christum Dominum, praedixit beatam se ab omnibus generationibus praedicandam: 'Ecce enim ex hoc beatam me dicent omnes generationes.' Cum ergo ex accessu Spiritus sancti conceperit, et peperit Maria infantem Iesu, consequens est, salva virginitate illum concepisse, et peperisse. Arbitrorque notanter ad id significandum vocatam fuisse beatam Virginem 'Prophetissam,' ut praenotaret Spiritus sanctus modum corporalis illius conditionis, spiritualis, et Propheticae conceptionis conditionem vaticinium concepit, quam ex divina virtute, sibi divinitus infusa, ita beata Virgo, non aliter concepit Christum Dominum, quam ex Spiritus sancti virtute in ea superveniente." Ibid. (I, 765b).

[119] Ibid. (I, 766a–b).

dominion, so that wherever his kingdom is proclaimed, there her name would be heard too. And to bring out the glory of her name, the author harks once more to the fact that Mary's name in Hebrew has its *mem* close–ended, which is not the usual way, as it would have been, were it found at the end of a word. There must be some secret hidden in this, and none other than that in exception to the normal way of nature Mary would have a child without violation to the seal of her virginity.[120]

h) Jeremiah 31, 22. "Yahweh is creating something new on earth: the woman will surround the man." With this passage from Jeremiah, Cartagena leaves Isaiah and proceeds to three other prophets whose words establish or help establish the truth of the teaching on Mary's virginity. The present text talks about something new, a novelty, which consists in the fact that the woman would conceive and surround the child in her womb and give birth to a son while remaining untouched in her virginity. In the words of Jerome: "The Lord created something new on earth, without any seed, without any intercourse, without any embrace. The woman will surround in the circle of her womb the man, who in spite of the foetal developments by stages and in spite of the fact that he will later seem to progress from infancy to wisdom and age, will really be a perfect man in the woman's womb during the customary months." [121] The generation

---

[120] "...si sensus illorum medullam degustemus, comperiemus multum per omnem modum facere, ad praesens virginitatis Mariae argumentum illustrandum: nam imprimis (ut adnotavit ex veteribus Rabbinis noster Galatinus) in his dictionibus Deiparae Mariae nomen clauditur, quod Hebraicae 'Miriam' dicitur: includi etiam aiunt dictione alia, 'lemarbè' quae 'Domina' interpretatur, ut significaretur dominii, et imperii Christi Domini (de quo ibi agitur) beatam Virginem, tanquam veram eius matrem, valde participem esse futuram... siquidem et Virginis praecipue laus in eo posita est, quod mater sit Messiae, et Messiae splendor in eo etiam eluceat, quod ex matre Virgine fuerit progenitus. Ut vero indicaretur Virginem filium suum, absque reserata virginali eius clausura esse concepturam, et parituram, in medio illius dictionis hebraicae, quae Maria significat, apposuerunt Mem clausam contra eorum usum, et consuetudinem, debebat non esse apertum, quia Hebraei non utuntur Mem clauso in principio, at in medio alicuius dictionis, sed in fine duntaxat, unde cum nusquam alias, nisi in hoc loco, et in Isaiae ca. 7. ubi sermo est de eadem Virgine inveniatur Mem clausum in medio dictionis positum, consequens est aliquod arcanum ibi latere... quod propterea Mem omnino clausum praeter Hebraeorum scribendi rationem appositum fuerit, ut id significaretur praeter totum naturae ordinem Virginem parituram esse, absque virginei sui sigilli violatione." Ibid. (I, 767a–b).

[121] Lib. VII, hom. IX (I, 768a–b). Cf. Lib. V, hom. XVIII (I, 513a–514a).

of Christ in Mary's womb is a semi–creation, since it was not of two
principles of life that he was conceived, namely of a man and of a
woman, but only of a woman. Hence the word "create" was employed. "Will surround" is also indicative of the truth that the woman
is like a closed circle, with no break or opening. For Mary would
conceive and surround her child in her womb in the perfection of
her unbroken virginity.[122] In such a union of motherhood and of
virginity, in a conception without the use of sex, in a birth devoid
of pain, in such novelties and unheard of things, indeed only the Lord
of nature could have been at work.[123]

i) Ezekiel 44, 2–3. "This gate will be kept shut. No one will
open it or go through it, since Yahweh the God of Israel has been
through it. And so it must be kept shut. The prince himself, however,
may sit there..." Although by this door is interpreted by some the
door of knowledge of Sacred Scripture which was closed until Christ
opened it, Cartagena maintains that

> ...many outstanding Fathers, almost all, except for one or
> two, unanimously understand by this door Mary the Mother of
> God, through whom Christ the Lord came to us... they think that
> by the door being closed is to be understood the virginally closed
> womb of Mary. And they add that not without truth did the pro-
> phet say that the door is shut, to mean Mary's integrity not only
> before giving birth and during birth, but also after giving birth...[124]

----

[122] "...consulto dixit: 'creavit,' ut significaret generationem Christi non esse
futura, ex duobus principiis, masculo scilicet, et foemina, instar generationis
aliorum infantium, sed ex uno solo instar creationis, et quia sicut creatio est ex
nihilo, ita generatio Christi, quantum attinet ad virum qui nullus in ea intervenit,
fuit ex nihilo, utpote ex nulla viri materia, atque adeo, quasi semi creatio, ut
ita loquar, licet alioquin ex purissimis Mariae sanguinibus vere fuerit genitus:
tum etiam, quia usurpans verbum illum 'circumdabit' aperte ostendit mulierem
illam undique clausam esse, nam certe circulus, qua parte apertus est, minime
circumdat: igitur cum beata Virgo dicatur a Ieremia circumiens et circumdans
filium suum, consequens est, quod illaesa virginitate illum conceperit. Unde Iere-
mias in praedictis verbis non solum novitatem concipiendi virum, sed et novitatem illam absque iactura virginitatis id praestandi paucis illis perstrinxit."
Ibid. (I, 768b–769a).

[123] "...conceptio est sine venere, partus sine dolore, Virginitas cum mater-
nitate coniuncta, et similes aliae, unde notanter Propheta, non dixit 'novum
creavit Deus,' sed 'Dominus,' ut significaret illum tamquam absolutum Dominum
naturae legibus non astrictum, praedictas omnes novitates naturae facultatem
transcendentes divina sua virtute operari." Ibid. (I, 769a–b).

[124] Ibid. (I, 770a–b).

j) Daniel 2, 34.35b. "While you were gazing, a stone broke away, untouched by any hand, and struck the statue... and grew into a great mountain." The author sees the passage as referring to the coming of Christ, "the corner stone," into the world. Being born of Mary is like being taken from a rock which is not expected to produce anything. For she is a virgin and gave forth Christ "untouched by any hand," i.e. without any man's cooperation in procreating.[125]

2. *New Testament fulfillment:*

Having seen the Old Testament prophecies foretelling Christ's virgin conception and birth, it is time to consider the testimonies of the New Testament. For the fulfillment of the prophecies are related to us as the New Testament speaks of Mary's virginity. The story of the annunciation is pertinent above all.

a) Luke 1, 26–38.[126] The angel's greeting to Mary: *"Ave gratia plena"* means first of all that in Mary is verified too what the Angelic Doctor termed *gratia unionis*, the union of the divine with the human in the person of Christ. In Mary this union lies in the fact that in her womb is the Son of God.[127] What this special union in detail signifies is contained in the words that follow: *"Dominus tecum."* The one and triune God is in Mary. Juan de Cartagena directly addresses her:

---

[125] "...cum ergo ortus Christi Domini valde esset supra totam naturam, utpote ex matre Virgine, ideo Christus dicitur excisus ex petra, quia haec ex sua natura nihil potest producere, itaque Christus, qui lapis angularis est faciens utraque unum, prodiit ex Virgine, quae nomine montis propter sanctitatis eius celsitudinem significator, prodivit autem sine manibus, id est sine viri opera, manus enim amplexum maritalem significare solet..." Ibid. (I, 772a).

[126] Regarding the NT witness on Mary's virginity, see J. Michl, "Die Jungfrauengeburt im Neuen Testament," in *Jungfrauengeburt Gestern und Heute*, op. cit., pp. 145–184; Gisela Lattke, "Lukas 1 und die Jungfrauengeburt," in *Zum Thema Jungfrauengeburt*, op. cit., pp. 61–89; esp. A. Vögtle, "Offene Fragen zur lukanischen Geburts– und Kindheitsgeschichte," in his book *Das Evangelium und die Evangelien*, op. cit., pp. 43–56. In the modern discussion the presence of the virginal conception in the infancy narratives of Luke and Matthew carries no ipso facto guarantee of historicity. For the understanding of the Lucan infancy narrative especially as a Midrash, cf. Rene Laurentin, *Struktur und Theologie der lukanischen Kindheitsgeschichte* (Stuttgart, 1967).

[127] Lib. V, hom. VI (I, 415a).

For 'with you' is the power of the Father, rendering you fecund, so that you may generate a son and be able to say as he does: 'Today I have generated you' (Ps 2, 7); 'with you' is the wisdom of the Son, teaching, disposing and preparing you to be worthy of being his mother; 'with you' is the purity of the Holy Spirit, preserving you an inviolate and most pure virgin as you conceive and bear.[128]

Moreover, the Angel wanted to emphasize that in the mystery of the Son of God being conceived by a virgin, God's *potestas dominativa*, his sovereign power, it at work as expressed by the word *"Dominus."* God is in a way violating the ordained course of nature in having a virgin, while remaining so, conceive and bear a son. But God is the Lord and "nothing is impossible to God" (Lk 1, 37).[129]

This inviolate chastity is what is particularly alluded to by the angel's proclamation that Mary is blessed among women. Her chastity though was not simply that of a married woman remaining faithful to her husband nor that of a widow remaining chaste in her widowhood. She was chastely virgin in a singular manner appropriate to the Mother of God.[130] Unheard of was the second blessing meant by the angel, the fusing of Mary's virginity with a fruitful motherhood.[131] "Hence inasmuch as Mary alone of all women had virginity without being non–fruitful, the freedom of the spirit without lacking a partner — for she was truly married to a man — and inasmuch as she was graced with the fecundity of having a child without violation to her virginity, the angel rightly calls her blessed among all women." [132] And so just as God blessed his works at the beginning of creation, now is Mary blessed, the perfect consummation of God's works. For in her womb is the creature united with the Creator, so

---

[128] Lib. V, hom. VIII (I, 431a).

[129] "Consulto ei dixit: 'Dominus tecum,' in memoriam ei revocans supremam, ac omnipotentem Dei facultatem dominativam, qua prout ei libuerit, facile praestare poterat, ut intacta Virgo genitorem suum conciperet, et pareret." Ibid. (I, 434a).

[130] "Primum fuit benedictio, quae ad castitatem conservandam ordinabatur... alia tandem castitas fuit inaudita quidem rara, et digna solum, ut prima eius observatrix esset, quae futura erat Dei Genitrix; haec fuit castitas Virginea, expresso voto stabilita, et nunquam violata." Ibid. (I, 434b).

[131] "Praeter has tamen benedictiones, alia inaudita fuit Virgini collata, quae foecunditatem matris cum gloria virginitatis ei contulit..." Ibid. (I, 435a).

[132] Ibid. (I, 437a).

that she could say "he who created me rested in my tent" (Ecclesiasticus 24, 8).[133]

And when Mary asked the angel, "But how can this come about, since I do not know man?", it was not because she doubted what had just been revealed to her, but simply in order to know *how* two such opposing states as motherhood and virginity could be made to fuse together in the same person. Zealous of her virginity, and at the same time receiving the message that she would conceive and bear a son, she prudently wanted to find out how that could be.[134] The words of the bride in the Song of Songs (5, 3) approximate the situation: "I have taken off my tunic, am I to put it on again? I have washed my feet, am I to dirty them again?" She has given up the right to have children and the affection of a husband with her religious vow of virginity, is she to violate this vow and assume again the right to procreate? [135]

Her faith was strong enough to lead her to believe what the angel said. As Elisabeth exclaimed to her, "Blessed are you who have believed that the promise made by the Lord would be fulfilled" (Lk 1, 45). Like the father of believers, Abraham, who believed that a very old and sterile woman would have an offspring, Mary believed that a virgin would be a mother; Abraham, that the offspring would

---

[133] Ibid. (I, 436a). The quotation from Ecclesiasticus is "qui creavit me, requievit in tabernaculo meo." The Vulgate translation is different from the actual meaning that God is telling personified wisdom to dwell in Israel: "he who created me fixed a place for my tent," as the Jerusalem Bible puts it.

[134] "...B. Virgo, zelo virginitatis, quam ardentissime amabat, audiens se concepturam, et parituram; 'Ecce concipies et paries': licet alioquin nihil mali suspicaretur, quae certo agnoscebat, sanctum Angelum Dei secum loqui, interrogavit, tamen modum, quo illa extrema adeo distantia, Mater, et Virgo, inter copulanda forent..." Lib. V, hom. XI (I, 455b). Cf. Ibid. (I, 459b–460a). See Josef Gewiess, "Die Marienfrage Lk 1, 34," an appendix in Laurentin, op. cit., pp. 184–217.

[135] "Haec verba apte explicari posse arbitror per illa Canticarum 'expoliavi me tunica mea, quomodo induar illa? Lavi pedes meos, quomodo inquinabo illos?' cum enim ait: 'Expoliavi me tunica mea': significat abdicasse a se omnem filiorum sobolem, et eorum procreationem, qua tunc, velut tunica, sterilitatis ignominia tegebatur; cum vero subdit: 'quomodo induar illa?' perinde est, ac si diceret: quomodo propositum virginitatis, voto obsignatum, violabo; iterumque assumam libertatem nubendi? ac tandem subiungit: 'lavi pedes meos, quomodo inquinabo illos?' aperte significat se, per perpetuae virginitatis votum, ab omni viri affectu, et desiderio prorsus alienam esse, et ideo quaesivit: 'Quomodo fiet istud, quoniam virum non cognosco?' " Lib. V, hom. XI (I, 457b–458a).

be from a woman and a man — Mary, that the child would be of a
woman but not from a man; Abraham, that he would be the father of
only a man — Mary, that she would conceive the God–man.[136] It
is further to be noted that in view of the peculiarity of the Hebrew
language, where the present and the future are embraced by the
same tense, when Mary declared "I do not know man," she meant
more than just the fact that she does not have and never had any
knowledge of man. By her words she indicated too that she would
never have any relationship with any man. Her virginity is perpetual.
She intends to remain a virgin.[137]

In the angel's assurance to Mary, the virgin birth would come
about by the power of the Holy Spirit who would come to overshadow her, just as once God overshadowed and covered Mount Sinai
with clouds. Moses communed alone with God; now under the shadow of the Holy Spirit God and Mary alone shared the mystery
transpiring.[138] Overshadowing or covering with one's shadow connotes the embracing and the enfolding of a wife into the arms of a
husband. And the angel used this figure or metaphor to signify that
inasmuch as Mary indicated her renunciation of a husband's embrace

---

[136] "Ecce fatetur Elisabeth, divino spiritu afflata excellentem adeo fuisse
Virginis credulitatem erga arcana ab Angelo sibi revelata, ut in praemium illius
impleta forent in ea omnia, quae Angelus ei pollicitus fuerat." Ibid. (I, 455a).
Cf. Lib. VI, hom. VIII (I, 560b–561b).

Comparing Abraham and Mary, Cartagena writes: "...ille enim credidit,
sterilem nonagenariam parituram, Maria autem virginem futuram esse matrem:
...Abrahae promisa est proles, sed ex foemina, et viro; Virgini autem ex foemina
sine viro: Abraham credidit, purum hominem ab eo fore generandum, Maria
vero, Deum hominem ab ea esse concipiendum..." Lib. V, hom. XI (I, 456b).

On the foundation of the "early Catholic" devotion to Mary expressed in
Elisabeth's μακαρία ἡ πιστευσασα (Lk 1, 45), cf. Franz Mußner, "Lk 1, 48 f.;
11, 27 f. und die Anfänge der Marienverehrung in der Urkirche," Catholica, 21
(1967) 287–294; and Hermann Volk, "Maria, Mater credentium," Trierer theologische Zeitschrift, 73 (1964) 1–21. Cf. Vat. II, Const. on the Church, nn. 53 & 58.

[137] "Ac tandem si Hebraicam linguam consulamus, in qua eadem vox, et
praesens, et futurum pariter tempus denotat, facile inde deprehendemus, quod
cum beata Virgo dixit verba illa supra relata: 'Quoniam virum non cognosco,'
non solum significavit virum nunquam cognovisse, sed neque unquam illum
cognoscituram esse, cum virginitatem suam perpetuo servandam Deo iam conse-
crasset." Lib. VII, hom. IX (I, 773b).

[138] "Sicut enim Deus olim totum montem Sinai obumbrante nube cooperuit,
ita, ut secreta, quae ibi revelabat, soli ipsi et Moysi innotescerent, ita nunc modum virginei conceptus, divini Spiritus obumbratione adeo contexit, ut soli Deo,
et Virgini maneret perspectus." Lib. V, hom. XII (I, 462b).

when she said "I do not know man," it is not the "shadow" of a man, i.e. not the generative cooperation of a husband, that would help bring about the announced conception, but rather the "shadow" of the Holy Spirit. Thus overshadowed by the Spirit, instead of a man, Mary would bear a son, while preserving the integrity of her virginity. As the Song of Songs (1, 16) has it, "Our bed is all green," or as the Vulgate translates this passage, "Our bed is shady," meaning that Christ would be conceived in the bed of a virgin womb by the power of the Holy Spirit, like a shadow preserving her from the heat of lust and retaining intact her virginity.[139] A shadow does not cause any lesion.[140]

Apropos this mysterious manner of conceiving and bearing a child, the author quotes Maldonatus' commentary on Luke wherein it is deduced that Mary was a virgin even after giving birth to Christ. The Gospel account that "she gave birth to a son, and she wrapped him in swaddling clothes" (Lk 2, 7) shows by the facility with which she took care of her son right after birth that the birth, and it was her very first, gave her no pains and that her body remained unbroken *in partu* and afterwards.[141]

---

[139] "...'obumbrare' propriissime dicitur de viro uxorato; tum quia... vir amplexans uxorem, obumbrat illam... Videns ergo Angelus, Mariam respuere umbram viri, a quo esset maritali affectu cognoscenda; dixerat enim: 'quia virum non cognosco' occurrit ei, affirmans, non a viri, sed a Spiritus sancti umbra cooperiendam fore, cuius cooperatrice virtute Dominum conceptura, et paritura erat; atque adeo salva, et incolumi semper permanente eius integerrima virginitate, qua responsione pacatum reddidit Marianum animum, omnem ab eo expellens turbationem. Atque hunc facit locis ille Canticorum 1. nam ubi nostra vulgata legit: 'lectulus noster floridus:' Septuaginta Interpretes verterunt: 'lectulus noster umbrosus:' quibus verbis, 'floridi,' et 'umbrosi:' non obscure significatur, in lectulo uteri virginalis Christum Dominum concipiendum fore Spiritus sancti virtute, ab omni libidinis calore, velut umbra Mariam praeservante, ac salva eius integritate manente; instar plantae florem germinantis." Ibid. (I, 464b).

[140] "...sicut materialis umbra, nullum scissurae detrimentum subiecto, cui inest, infert, sed potius instar umbrae lauri ei salutifera esse solet, sic sacra humanitas Christi, umbra divini radii in opaco virginei uteri corpore formanda, nihil detrimenti Marianae integritati illatura esset." Ibid. (I, 465b).

[141] "Ad haec eruditissimus Maldonatus virginitatem Mariae post partum colligit ex verbis D. Lucae cap. 2. 'Peperit filium suum, et pannis eum involvit,' nam si Christum parturiens violaretur, consequenter instar aliarum parturientium dolores in partu sustinuisset, unde non potuisset expedita manere ad involvendum continuo pannis filium suum; maxime, quod primus partus solet parientem gravius excruciare, et debilitare propter maiorem, ut in plurimum, eius difficultatem: cum igitur B. Virgo filium suum, cum primum natus est, facile potuerit pannis

b) Matthew 1: 16, 18, 25. According to the account by Matthew, when it was found out that Mary was with child, it is specifically underlined that she was with child "through the Holy Spirit" (Mt 1, 18). Cartagena stretches the Vulgate translation a bit to make out from the words: *"Inventa est in utero habens de Spiritu sancto"* the meaning that Christ was found *in* her, because she conceived through the overshadowing by the Holy Spirit, and not somehow introduced from the outside by a man's seed as is normal in a conception.[142] To allay Joseph's perplexity before this mystery, he was told: "Do not be afraid to take Mary home as your wife, because she has conceived what is in her by the Holy Spirit" (Mt 1, 20). Conceiving by the power of the Holy Spirit, her virginity remains inviolate.[143] And so like in the creation of Adam, points out the author, where God and the earth were the sole efficient and material causes respectively and nothing else, only God and the virgin Mary were at work in the generation of Christ's body. For God in an ineffable way did away with the need for a man.[144]

At this point it is good to consider Joseph's exact role in Mary's life of constant virginity. It is beyond doubt that Joseph was called the father of Jesus. Listening to Simeon in the temple, "the child's father and mother stood there wondering at the things that were

---

involvere, et similia alia obsequia ei praestare, non leve inditium est eius post partum virginitatem indicans." Lib. VII, hom. IX (I, 773b).

[142] " 'Inventa est in utero habens de Spiritu sancto,' certe in materno utero communi modo concipiente non invenitur foetus, sed ab extrinseco venit ex virili semine, quia tamen Virgo ex obumbratione Spiritus sancti conceperat, Christus fuit inventus in illa, ut his verbis explicuit D. Hieronym. epist. ad amicum aegrotantem: 'Semen promissum est mulieris, quod secundum hominem Dominus Deus noster est, qui non infusus est in utero, sed inventus, Evangelista confirmante, cum dicit de Maria: inventa est in utero habens.' " Ibid. (I, 773a).

On the Gospel according to Matthew and the question of Mary's virginity, see O. Knoch, "Die Botschaft des Matthäusevangelium über Emfängnis und Geburt Jesu vor dem Hintergrund...," art. cit., pp. 37–59; and A. Vögtle, "Die Genealogie Mt 1, 2–16 und die matthäische Kindheitsgeschichte," in his *Das Evangelium und die Evangelien*, op. cit., pp. 57–102.

[143] Lib. VII, hom. IX (I, 772b).

[144] "Sicut enim in formatione Adae non aliae causae concurrerunt, quam Deus, et terra: ille, ut efficiens, haec ut materiam limi subministrans; sic in corporis Christi generatione Deus solum, et Virgo concursum suum adhibuerunt; ille effective viri operam ineffabili modo supplens; haec materiam foetus, purissimum scilicet sanguinem suppeditans..." Lib. I, hom. III (I, 16a).

being said about him" (Lk 2, 33). After the feast of the Passover,
"the boy Jesus stayed behind in Jerusalem without his parents
knowing it" (Lk 2, 43). And when they found him three days later,
his mother said to him: "See how worried your father and I have
been, looking for you" (Lk 2, 48). But all these references notwithstanding, Joseph was never said to have fathered Jesus. When it
comes to the question of Jesus' actual generation, it is Mary we find
referred to. It was to her that the angel announced, "You are to conceive and bear a son" (Lk 1, 31). And as Matthew recorded, Joseph
was "the husband of Mary, of her was born Jesus" (Mt 1, 16). The
evangelist did not say that Jesus was born "of them," i.e. of Joseph
and Mary, but only of her.[145]

Joseph's role is aptly indicated by the meaning of his name.
Joseph connotes "growth" or "increase." To be the husband of the
mother of God and the legal father of Christ is surely a great increase in his honor. But Joseph also means growth with another
nuance, that is, growth for Mary, because instead of deflowering her
as would be normal in marriage Joseph in taking her as his wife
strengthened and added to Mary's chastity by his own virginity.[146]
Thus, besides being compared to the two cherubs guarding the Ark
of the Covenant (Ex 37, 7–9), in this case guarding the ark of Christ's
sacred humanity, Mary and Joseph in marriage resemble the chaste
union of David and the young girl chosen to look after the ageing
king (1 Kings 1, 1–4). Just as of David and the young girl it was
written that "the king had no intercourse with her," so also in iden-

---

[145] "Notanter dixit, 'de qua,' non 'de quo,' aut 'de quibus,' ut significaret
Christum fuisse genitum ex sola Maria, non ex Ioseph. Si enim ex utro que Christus
natus fuisset, non est, cur Evangelista fugeret dicere, 'ex quo,' vel 'ex quibus'
natus, nec erat cur Matthaeus mutaret stylum, sed postquam dixit: 'Iacob autem
genuit Ioseph,' consequenter oportebat subiungere: 'Ioseph autem genuit Iesum':
cum ergo id non dixerit, manifeste relinquitur Maria non ex viro concepisse."
Lib. VII, hom. IX (I, 772b–773a). Cf. Lib. V, hom. XVII (I, 506a–b).

[146] "Alia etiam ad idem occurrit ratio, quia, cum alii, nubentes virginitate
minuantur et expolientur, ipsi tamen e contra accidit, nam Mariam in uxorem
accipiens, virginitatis suae augmentum suscepit, dum illam ad imitationem suae
sponsae speciali voto firmavit, et constabilivit; qui ergo praeter communem matrimonii consuetudinem in matrimonio, quo non solum diminui, sed poenitus abo-
leri virginitas solet, illius augmentum suscepit, merito *Ioseph*, id est, *adauctus*,
vel *additus* appellatus est." Lib. IV, hom. III (I, 296b). Regarding Joseph's
perpetual virginity, see Lib. IV, hom. XII (I, 364b–366b).

tical words it was said of Joseph and Mary, that "he had not had intercourse with her" (Mt 1, 25).[147] Comparing Mary and Eve, the author notes that the latter was the occasion of the fall of her man, while the former was an aid in the growth of her husband's sanctity; the latter was the first to lose her virginity, the former was the first to consecrate her virginity to God.[148]

c) Galatians 4, 4. St. Paul concurs with Matthew's foregoing statement that Christ was born "of her" solely, when he wrote that Christ was "born of a woman." Were Christ fathered by a man, it would have been stated. The fact however that Paul went out of his way to say that Christ was born of a woman indicates that he is bringing out the absence of any human father in the conception of Christ, and thus asserting Mary's intact virginity.[149]

---

[147] "Adumbrat etiam eiusdem sacri matrimonii miram castitatem connubium illud inter Sunamitem, et Davidem; nam sicut David non ad libidinem, nec ad prolis generationem accepit in uxorem, Sunamitem; unde sacer textus ait: 'et Rex non cognovit eam': sic Ioseph, non ex concupiscentia, nec sobolis procreandae amore, et desiderio ductus, cum beata Virgine nupsit, unde alter Evangelista eadem verba, quae de Davide dicta sunt, refert de Ioseph dicens: 'Ioseph autem non cognovit eam': et sicut illud matrimonium fuit inter Davidem, et Sunamitem, ut illa Regem prae nimia frigiditate algentem iuvenili suo calore foveret, atque calefaceret, sic Ioseph datus est in sponsum Mariae (ut Hieronymus adnotavit) ut eius bonum nomen, et famam foveret, non ut filios ex ea procrearet." Lib. IV, hom. V (I, 311a).

The author holds that both Mary and Joseph were the first to take the vow of virginity and to practise celibacy in marriage. Cf. Lib. IV, hom. VII (I, 323b).

[148] "...illa [Eva] viro suo fuit occasio perditionis, haec [Maria] viro suo adiutorium ad incrementum sanctitatis; illa prima omnium virginitatem perdidit, haec omnium prima virginitatem Deo consecravit..." Lib. V, hom. IV (I, 404b).

[149] "Accedit ad haec testimonium D. Pauli vocantis Christum Dominum 'factum ex muliere,' si enim Virgo Christum Dominum ex viro concepisset, certe cum vir principalius, quam foemina concurrat ad generationem filiis; non erat cur D. Paulus fugeret vocare illum filium viri: vocans igitur illum factum ex muliere, id absque dubio dixit, ut illum humano caruisse patre, atque adeo ex intacta Virgine conceptum indicaret." Lib. VII, hom. IX (I, 773a). The text of Gal 4, 4 is correctly interpreted today as an expression of the radical historicity of Jesus and his mission, stressing the fact that he came from a woman's womb, but without any allusion as to how he was conceived in that womb.

On the absence of any other testimony in the NT regarding Christ's virginal conception and birth, cf. Vögtle, op. cit., pp. 47–50.

B. Biblical Metaphors and Images

Juan de Cartagena believes that to combat the fierce attacks by heretics and Jews and at the same time to shore up the Catholic doctrine of Mary's virginity, the best and most potent weapon is Sacred Scripture itself, especially the various scriptural metaphors and similitudes with which our human mind is assisted by divine wisdom. He intends however merely to offer here a selection of these images.[150]

1. *Fruit–bearing blossoms.* Mary's mysterious coupling of both motherhood and virginity in her person is in the mind of the author signified by the words of Ecclesiasticus 24, 23: "My blossoms bear the fruit of glory and virtue." Virginity and fecundity are inseparable in her. Her fecundity is virginal and her virginity fecund. That is why she is affirming in this text that her virginity, i.e. her blossoms, bears fruit, unlike the non–productiveness of other virgins. But her fruit is a fruit of glory and virtue, inasmuch as she gave birth with the glory of her virginity intact and her virtue inviolate. "Blossoms" standing for her virginity and "fruits" (plural as in the Vulgate) signifying Christ are in the plural because her virginity would actually be the seed of many virgins and Christ the fruit of her womb would be the beginning of many who would be saved.[151]

---

[150] "...opus est contra has truculentas belluas mille arma sumere, inter quae, quia 'gladius spiritus, quod est verbum Dei' (Ephes 6, 17), quo hucusque usi sumus, omnium optimus, et fortissimus est, eodem armorum genere pugnare insistens, ex divinis eloquiis varios tropos, singularesque similitudines depromam, quibus magis inverecunda Haereticorum, et Iudaeorum petulentia retundatur, virginitatisque illius Catholica veritas magis solidetur... et per similia quibus divina eloquia ad humani ingenii imbecillitatem magis provehendam scatent. Quia tamen haec omnia stylo prosequi longissimum esset, quae ex illis selectiora mihi videbuntur, paucis perstringere curabo." Lib. VII, hom. X (I, 774b–775a).

[151] "Ego sane arbitror, illud ibi latere, quod voluit significare, virginitatem suam esse foecundam, non sterilem instar caeterarum Virginum, et ideo flores suos virginitatem eius designantes, dixit esse fructus, quos constat esse foecunditatis non obscurum argumentum: aderat ergo simul in Maria flos virgineae pudicitiae, et fructus maturae foecunditatis. Existimo autem consulto addidisse Deiparam, 'honoris, et honestatis,' ut significaret fructum benedictum ventris sui, cum ex eo per nativitatem erupit, virginis honorem, et honestatem minime laesisse: ac tandem censeo, notanter beatam Virginem vocasse in plurali virginitatem suam 'flores,' et partum eius 'fructus,' quia virginitas Mariae, ut quae

2. *Wheat surrounded with lilies.* The Book of the Song of Songs is as usual a fertile ground for metaphors and images suiting the purpose of the author. There is, for instance, 7, 2: "Your belly is a heap of wheat surrounded with lilies." Its whiteness and fragrance have easily made the lily a symbol of purity among the ancients. Surrounding the virgin womb of Mary, they proclaim its inviolate integrity. Wheat in general symbolizes fertility. Here it means Christ in particular, whom Zechariah calls *"frumentum electorum, et germinans virgines"* (9, 17).[152] So in the sense of the text Mary's virginity surrounds her fecundity like a fortification (*"vallare"* is the word of the Vulgate), so that no harm may come upon it. Thus is her virginity not prejudicial to her fecundity, nor the latter to the former, as would have ordinarily been the case.[153]

3. *Dove.* "Your eyes are doves" (Song of Songs 1, 15). The eyes of "doves" as a compliment to the bride suggest innocence and fi-

---

prima religioso voti cultu Deo fuerit oblata, origo reliquarum fuerit, quae in tot virginibus effulgent, unde licet in se sit unicus, et singularis flos, plures tamen extitit in virtute: et similiter, quia Christus futurus erat radix fructuum innumerabilium, hoc est, innumerorum fere praedestinatorum, qui fructus sunt sanguinis Christi Jesu, ideo merito Deipara non in singulari, sed in plurali vocavit filium suum 'fructus,' non 'fructum'..." Lib. VII, hom. IV (I, 743b–744a).

[152] "...certe spiritus sanctus ut virginei uteri miram puritatem declararet, candidis liliis illum circumdedit; ut autem significaret Mariam undequaque virginem esse mente et corpore, consulto dixit, ventrem eius vallatum esse liliis, quod enim vallatur, undique cingitur." Lib. VII, hom. I (I, 727b–728a).

"...ad idque denotandum sponsus in praecitatis verbis Canticorum, Deiparae Mariae praegnantem ventrem, acervo tritici congruentissime comparavit: 'Venter tuus sicut acervus tritici': nomine 'tritici' Christum intelligit, qui a Zachar, appellatur 'frumentum electorum, et vinum germinans virgines': ipsaque de se dixit: 'Nisi granum frumenti cadens in terram mortuum fuerit, ipsum solum manet,' per quod foecunditatem Mariae aperte significavit, per 'acervum tritici,' eleganter satis designatam: tum quia frumentum symbolum est foecunditatis..." Lib. VII, hom. I (I, 730b). The quotation from Zechariah 9, 17 is translated by the Jerusalem Bible thus: "What joy and what beauty shall be theirs! Corn will make the young men flourish, and sweet wine the maidens." It pictures the dawn of victory and salvation for Israel; through the power of God's presence the earth produces an abundance.

[153] "...'vallare,' idem est ac fossa circumdata lignis fortissimis ac terreo muro locum militum struere... liliis ergo vallatur frumentum, quia foecunditas Mariae a virginitate fuit custodita velut ab exercitu militum armatorum, nec passa est illam quidquam laedi, sicut aliae foeminae laeduntur, in quibus virginitas obest foecunditati, et virginitati foecunditas." Ibid. (I, 728b).

delity. Cartagena sees them as suggestive of Mary's virginity for the reason that a dove after the first mating is supposed never to mate with any other. Mary too never knew anybody else after she had conceived by the Holy Spirit. Or likely, Christ himself the king of virgins is meant by "dove" as it is said in the same book (2, 12): "The cooing of the turtledove is heard in our land," a picture of Christ whose coming and preaching fostered virginity, so much so that the Holy Spirit in extolling Mary's purity compared it here to Christ, her eyes especially signifying this similarity to Christ, the dove. A further inference from the above is that it is through the propitiation of these two doves of purity, Christ and Mary, that sins are forgiven, just like the pair of turtledoves commanded under the old law for the holocaust and for the sacrifice for sin.[154]

4. *A garden enclosed.* "She is a garden enclosed, my sister, my promised bride; a garden enclosed, a sealed fountain" (Song of Songs 4, 12). The symbolism of the "fountain," found also in Proverbs 5, 15–19, is the high value set on any water supply due to the scarcity of water in the Near East. Hence for the bride it means great affection. Applied to Mary, as a woman blessed with fecundity and motherhood she is a garden. But as a virgin she is so to say closed. That is why in naming her a garden enclosed, the implication is there that she is both a mother and a virgin. And she is a sealed fountain insofar as a virgin she did not receive any male seed in order to conceive. And the fact that in a succeeding verse she is called also a

---

[154] "...cum B. Virgo a nullo sponso nisi a Spiritu sancto filium conceperit, ut aperte significant verba illa: 'Inventa est in utero habens de Spiritu sancto': nec post illum alium cognoverat sponsum, cum a Iosepho, semper fuerit intacta, apte Turturi comparatur, quae post primum coniugium nullum alium coniugem agnoscit. Vel dicamus (quod et mihi verisimile est) nomine 'Turturis' in eodem Cantico Canticorum etiam Christum Dominum Virginum Regem, et virginitatis auctorem intelligi, de illo enim, cum in mundo apparuit, dicitur: 'Vox Turturis auditae est in terra nostra.' Ab eius enim adventu, et praedicatione coepit virginitas vigere, et in magno pretio haberi: ut ergo Spiritus sanctus singulari encomio virginitatem Mariae extolleret, Christi Domini integritati, et puritati illam assimilavit, dicens, virginalem eius verecundiam per 'genas' eius significatam, quia in illis praecipue apparet verecundiae rubor, instar Turturis esse, hoc est, instar Christi per Turturem significati: unde non incongrue putaverim propterea Deum in lege veteri iusisse, ut in sacrificio offerretur par Turturum, ut scilicet per illos hi coelestes Turtures, Christus, et Maria, castimoniae virtute insigniores significarentur, intuitu quorum propitiationem peccatorum faciebat." Lib. VII, hom. XI (I, 784b).

"fountain that makes the garden fertile, well of living water, streams flowing down from Lebanon" (4, 15) is no contradiction, because what is asserted is nothing other than that Mary's virginity is joined to her motherhood. She is indeed a sealed fountain which nonetheless is a well of living water. She is the mother of Christ, the spring of living water welling up to eternal life (Jn 4, 14).[155] Elsewhere in using the same passage to support the teaching that Mary was without original sin, the author says that she is a sealed foutain, sealed that is with the seal of virginity. Or, in other words, Mary is called a garden because she is fecund, and a closed garden because of her virginity in conceiving, and a sealed fountain because of her constant virginity after giving birth.[156] Or enlarging on the metaphor of Mary as a closed well, a *"clausus puteus,"* she herself has said, "I do not know man," i.e. she had never been "open" to any man, although she was open to the Holy Spirit by whose power she became a mother. Like a shell completely closed up in its lower part lest it ejects the moisture of the earth, but open in its upper part in order to develop in itself the precious pearl as it receives heavenly dew, so also Mary is "closed" to all lower and earthly inclinations but open to the impulses of the Holy Spirit.[157]

---

[155] " 'Hortum' vocat coelestem sponsam, Mariam propter foecunditatem, 'conclusum' propter virginitatem: itaque 'hortus' fuit, quia mater, 'conclusus,' quia virgo; 'hortus' vero 'conclusus,' quia mater pariter et virgo... Verum si a sponso vocatur Maria 'fons signatus, et clausus,' quomodo infra appellatur ab eodem: 'fons hortorum, puteus aquarum viventium, quae fluunt impetu de Libano?' si enim est 'fons clausus,' quomodo 'aquae fluunt ab ea?' Et si aquarum suarum avara, illas in se conclusus retinet, quo pacto dicuntur ab illa fluere, et communicari? Voluit certe Spiritus sanctus significare in Maria maternitatem cum virginitate coniunctam esse, unde primo vocat eam fontem clausum, aliunde aquas non recipientem, quia ex virili semine non conceperat, ecce virginitatem: vocat deinde eandem hortum aquarum fluentium, quia peperit Christum Dominum: 'fontem aquae vivae salientis in vitam aeternam': ecce foecunditatem." Ibid. (I, 786b).

[156] "Vocat deinde illam 'Hortum conclusum,' ut significaret, animam eius nulli peccato fores aperuisse; fontem vero signatum dicit eam, ut sigillum virginitatis eius designaret. Vel dicamus aliter cum Ioanne Pico super Cantic. libr. 2. cap. 24. vocari Virginem 'hortum' propter foecunditatem, et 'conclusum' propter clausurae virginitatis ante partum, propter eandem vero post partum vocari fontem signatum." Lib. I, hom. XV (I, 72a–b).

[157] "Vel aliter: 'clausus puteus' erat B. Virgo, quia viro numquam patuit, ipsa dicente: 'Quoniam virum non cognosco': aperta autem, et patens Spiritu sancti virtuti illam foecundanti, iuxta verba Angeli: 'Spiritus sanctus superveniet

5. *Sea.* "You strode across the sea, you marched across the ocean, but your steps could not be seen" (Ps 77, 19). Here the author associates the sea, *mare*, with Mary onomatologically. She is the sea entered by God and navigated by him for nine months. She is the sea crossed by him when Mary finally gave birth to Christ. Notwithstanding all this, no trace of Christ's coming and going can be found, because her virginity remained unimpaired. Indeed Solomon could say that he did not understand "the way of the ship in midocean" (Prov 30, 19). For the ship of Christ's humanity passed through Mary without any trace whatsoever.[158]

To close this section about the scriptural images and metaphors illustrating the mystery of Mary's virginity,[159] it may be appropriate to recall that Juan de Cartagena gives another twist to the relationship between her and Sacred Scripture in claiming that she herself is a great sign unfolding for us revelations of the Bible. In interpreting the words of Revelation 12, 1: "Now a great sign appeared in heaven: a woman, adorned with the sun, standing on the moon, and with the twelve stars on her head for a crown," Cartagena affirms that in a mystical manner this passage pictures Mary. For she

---

in te, et virtus Altissimi obumbrabit tibi': unde sicut conchilium ex parte inferiori omnino clausum est, ne terrestrem humorem fugat, ex parte vero superiori apertum est, ut coelestem influxum recipiens pretiosam margaritam in se concipiat; non secus in Deipara Maria inferiori portio animae eius clausa erat omnino non solum libidini, sed et omni terrestri affectui, portio vero superior eiusdem coelestibus imbribus, ac divinis Spiritus sancti influxibus patebat, quibus ipsa plena, et locupletata copiose Ecclesiam Catholicam irrigat. Recte ergo fontem signatum, et puteum aquarum viventium, quae fluunt de Libano, illam vocat." Lib. VII, hom. XI (I, 786b–787a).

[158] "Nemo ignorat Mariam 'mare' interpretari... semitae, quas Deus perambulavit per hoc mare, conceptio quidem, et nativitas fuere, per illam enim intravit in hoc Marianum mare, per novem menses in eo navigaturus, per hanc vero ad Bethlehemiticum portum appulit: has quidem semitas, quantumcumque oculatissime explores, nulla alicuius viatoris vestigia reperies, quia neque ingrediens, neque egrediens Iesus ex Maria, virginem eius integritatem quidquam laesit.

Atque ad hoc mysterium putant quidem allusisse Salomonem, cum dixit difficilem cognitu sibi esse 'viam navis in medio mari,' intelligens per hanc navem, humanitatis Christi naviculam, mare Mariam uteri fulcantem." Ibid. (I, 784a).

[159] Cartagena also used for instance the images of the store of new and old fruits (Lib. VII, hom. IV – I, 744a), a vineyard looked after (Lib. VII, hom. XI – I, 785a), joined thighs (ibid. – I, 785b), a navel needing no drink (ibid. – I, 78a), two breasts (Lib. VII, hom. XI – I, 787a), the order of Melchizedek (ibid. – I, 787b), and Aaron's branch and almond (Lib. II, hom. IV – I, 153b & 149a).

is truly a sign which leads us to the knowledge of things beyond our senses. Through her we come to a knowledge of her son; through her conceiving by the power of the Holy Spirit, we are led to the secret of her virginity, of the divine fatherhood, of her divine motherhood, and of the incarnation of the divine Word.[160]

---

[160] "...merito archipropheta novae legis Ioannes B. Virginem 'signum' vocavit, cum praeter cognitionem sui, in notitiam Verbi incarnati nos faciat venire. Per matrem enim cognoscimus filium, et cum mater pariter sit, et Virgo integerrima, filium Patrem in caelis habere oportet; et cum id non virtute naturae, sed Spiritu sancto adumbrante factum sit, tandem in sanctissimae Triadis, Verbi divini Incarnationis, ac illius B. Virginitatis, Deiparae, et aliorum arcanorum cognitionem peducimur..." Lib. V, hom. XVI (I, 494a).

CHAPTER SIX

THE ASSUMPTION

Juan de Cartagena calls Mary's Assumption into heaven the "*finis et corona*" of the Marian mysteries.[1] This last chapter of our study's Part II will accordingly be centered on this doctrine of the Assumption. Significantly, Cartagena prefaces his discussion of the matter by making his own the words of Pseudo–Augustine:

> Lord, to me it is an honor and to my heart most sacred to speak about the mother of your son and to employ my tongue with words regarding her most holy body. For she alone merited in obedience to receive the God–man, thus being made the throne of God and the court of the eternal king. Since these truths surpass human reason, may your spirit be present to lead us by his inspiration to the whole truth of what must be said. And since what is to be said concerns her body and soul, which he extraordinarily sanctified and conferred grace upon, do not suffer us to say any nonsense but only what is to your praise and glory.[2]

---

[1] Lib. I, hom. VIII (I, 41b). Cf. H. Barré, CSSp, "Immaculée Conception et Assomption au XIIe siècle," in *Virgo Immaculata*, V, op. cit., pp. 151–180. In the modern theology of the Assumption this *junktim* between the Immaculate Conception and the Assumption is very much underlined. Cf. Thomas Philippe, "Immaculée Conception et Assomtpion," in *Etudes Mariale*, 7 (1949) 149; M. D. Koster, OP, "Die Himmelfahrt Mariens gleichsam die Vollendung ihrer Unbefleckten Empfängnis," in *Virgo Immaculata*, op. cit., X, pp. 92–114; T. Gallus, SJ, "Ratio quae intercedit inter Dogmata Immaculatae Conceptionis et Assumptionis B. M. Virginis," ibid., pp. 80–91. On the Assumption as the crowning of Mary's life–offering, see Schillebeeckx, op. cit., pp. 99–100.

[2] Pseudo–Augustinus, *De assumptione beatae Mariae virginis*, 1 (PL 40, 1143), quoted by Cartagena in Lib. XIV, hom. XIII (II, 652b). As to the true authorshpip of this *sermo*, Cartagena himself was not so sure, although he relied heavily on it. He once cites it thus: "Sanctus Pater Augustinus, vel quicumque alius fuit author libelli de Assumptione Virg..." Ibid. (II, 653a). Perhaps this treatise was written by Ambrose Autpert († c. 780). It played a not insignificant role in the history of the doctrine of Mary's Assumption into heaven, repeatedly quoted by most authors, not only because of its alleged authorship by St. Augustine, but also because of its well–reasoned argumentations and presentation of materials. Cf. Carolus Balić, *Testimonia de Assumptione Beatae Virginis Mariae ex Omnibus Saeculis*, I (Romae, 1948), pp. 180–181, 205–210.

The quotation is symptomatic, not only because it betrays the pervading influence Pseudo–Augustine played both in the historical development of the doctrine and in Cartagena's treatment of it, but also because of the stress it places on Mary's divine motherhood, which the author, as we have seen, considers the *principium* whence all her privileges flow.[3]

Before we present Cartagena's scriptural support for the doctrine, we shall again go first into his systematization of the question and its various prolegomena. The preliminary but intimately related ramifications to the Assumption of Mary are handled by the author together with their justifications. He also uses scriptural arguments in connection with these side–topics, which arguments we shall naturally be referring to, inasmuch as they are necessary for the understanding of his positions, say, on Mary's incorruptibility and resurrection. The later section of this chapter will be limited to his use of scripture in testimony of the Assumption of Mary into heaven.

I. SYSTEMATIC TEACHING

A. Nature of Mary's Assumption into Heaven

1. *A brief historical background.*[4] The mystery of Mary's Assumption into heaven had a rather late start in the consciousness or tradition of the Church. It followed those of her virginity and Immaculate Conception much later. The whole matter about the end of her earthly life and its consequences did not seem to be immediately relevant to the early Church. There is no explicit apostolic tradition on the subject. The question and the belief about her glorification in heaven came to be articulated only later.

---

[3] "...ingressus filii Dei in domum Mariani uteri, ac per novem menses, virginalis aulae in hospitium exceptio, principium fuit, et origo, unde copiosissima in eam gratiarum fluenta emanarunt, et praeclarissimis postmodum gloriae dotibus exornaretur." Lib. XIV, hom. I (II, 559a).

[4] Cf. M. Jugie, *La Mort et l'Assomption de la Sainte Vierge. Etude historico-doctrinale* (Città del Vaticano, 1944); G. Jouassard, "L'Assomption corporelle de la Sainte Vierge et la Patristique," in *Etudes Mariales*, 6 (1948) 97–117; A. Müller, "Marias Stellung und Mitwirkung im Christusereignis," in *Mysterium Salutis*, III–2, op. cit., pp. 488–498.

In his time Epiphanius of Salamis († 403) reflected the nebulous state and lack of any certainty about even her death, when he said that perhaps she died and was buried, but perhaps not; anyway, either is possible to God. The thing is: we really do not know anything about her end.[5] Then towards the close of the 5th century apocryphal writings began to circulate to make up for the void in tradition regarding Mary's *"transitus,"* her passing–over. According to these she died but rose again; a variant story claimed that her body was simply transferred to an earthly paradise. It was the common report that she was buried in the Valley of Josephat near Gethsemani.[6] As a result of all this the liturgical feast in commemoration of Mary came eventually to be known as the Feast of the Mother of God's Homecoming, or *Dormitio.* Her death came to be taken for granted. And sermons and liturgical texts further spoke of her bodily assumption into heaven, as in the case of Pseudo–Modestus of Jerusalem († 680), St. Germanus of Constantinople († 733), St. Andrew of Crete († 740), and St. John Damascene († 749). We shall see more of these testimonies below. Suffice it here to say that in the east the teaching about Mary's Assumption into heaven thus became a pious belief, which it is up to the present day.

In the west, Pope Sergius I (687–701) introduced the Feast of the Dormition, although the Transitus legends were rejected by the so–called Decretum Gelasianum. In the 8th century the Feast of the Dormition metamorphosed into the Feast of the Assumption. A controversy then developed when the letter *Ad Paulum et Eustochium* purportedly written by St. Jerome surfaced, giving warning against bold assertions regarding Mary's resurrection.[7] In response, a Pseudo–

---

[5] Epiphanius, *Panar.* 78, 24 (GCS 3, 469 f.; PG 42, 737A); quoted by Cartagena in Lib. XIII, hom. I (II, 514b–515a).

[6] Cf. E. Cothenet, "Marie dans les Apocryphes," in *Maria*, VI (Paris, 1961), pp. 117–148. Mary's burial place is also reported, e.g. in the *Itinera Hierosolymitana Saec. IV–VIII* (CSEL 39, 142.170.203). Incidentally there is a contrary claim that Mary was actually buried in Ephesus. Cf. C. Kopp, "Das Mariengrab in Ephesus?" *ThGl* 45 (1955) 161–188; J. Euzet, "Remarques sur 'Jérusalem? – Ephèse?' de Clemens Kopp," *Divus Thomas*, 60 (Piacenza, 1957) 47–72; G. Caprile, "L'origine della tradizione sulla morte e sul sepolcro di Maria a Gerusalemme," ibid., 63 (1960) 216–221. See also, A. Wenger, *L'Assomption... dans la tradition byzantine du VIe au Xe siècle* (Paris, 1955).

[7] This work was probably by Paschasius Radbert († 865), PL 30, 122–142. See also H. Barre, "La Croyance à l'Assomption corporelle en Occident de 750 à 1150 environ," in *Etudes Mariales*, 7 (1949) 70–73.

Augustinus writing materialized, *De Assumptione Beatae Mariae Virginis*, defending her assumption into heaven.[8] Throughout the Middle Ages these two works were to exert noteworthy theological influence on the whole discussion, with the Pseudo–Augustine eventually gaining the upper hand. By the 17th and 18th centuries, the teaching itself on the Assumption of Mary was no longer debated. What was then in question was the degree of certitude that should be accorded the doctrine.[9] Juan de Cartagena takes up the subject, therefore, at the time when the teaching was already more or less generally accepted, unlike the turbulent controversy then surrounding the question of Mary's Immaculate Conception.

On November 1, 1950 in the Apostolic Constitution *Munificentissimus Deus* Pope Pius XII defined the doctrine of Mary's Assumption into heaven.[10] The solemn definition was preceded by a worldwide petition asking the Pope precisely for such a solemn affirmation of the doctrine. The universality of the belief led to the dogmatic declaration that Mary, having completed her life on earth, was taken body and soul to heaven.[11]

2. *Mary's death.* Even if the Bible has nothing on it, it is the tradition of the Catholic Church that Mary died. Her passing away is celebrated in the liturgy from the earliest times, says Cartagena, and the Fathers have been unanimous about it. In the appropriate words of Pseudo–Augustine: "Calling to mind her human condition,

---

[8] Cf. Barre, ibid., pp. 80–100, and above, footnote 2.

[9] Cf. C. Dillenschneider, "L'Assomption corporelle de Marie dans la période posttridentine," in *Etudes Mariales*, 8 (1950) 71–146.

[10] *AAS* 42 (1950) 753–771. Cf. *DS* 3903; Vat. II, *Const. on the Church*, n. 59. See also K. Rahner, "Zum Sinn des Assumptio–Dogmas," in *Schriften zur Theologie*, I (Einsiedeln, [8]1967), pp. 239–252.

[11] Cf. G. Hentrich & R. von Moos, *Petitiones de Assumptione Corporea B. Virginis Mariae in Caelum Definienda a S. Sedem Delatae*, 2 vols (Città del Vaticano, 1942); C. Balić, *Pro Veritate Assumptionis B.V. Mariae Dogmatice Definienda* (Romae, 1949).

On the fact that the definition did not explicitate *how* Mary's life on earth ended, see F. de P. Solà, "La Muerte de la Santisima Virgen en la Constitución Apostólica 'Munificentissimus Deus', " *Estudios Marianos*, 12 (1952) 125–156. This open question has kept the controversy alive between the *Mortalistas* and the *Immortalistas*. Cf. *Virgo Immaculata*, X; G. Scelzi, "La morte della Madonna in conformita con Cristo sotto l'aspetto teologico," *Divus Thomas*, 62 (Piacenza, 1959) 69–93; T. Bartolomei, "La mortalità di Maria," *Ephem. Mariol.*, 10 (1960) 385–420; L. Ceccarini, *È morta la Madonna?* (Napoli, 1962).

we do not fear to affirm that the mother of God underwent temporary death." [12]

It is important to keep in mind, warns the author, that Mary's death was due to the state of her human nature and not because of original sin, from which she had been preserved. For this teaching on Mary's death was being used by his contemporary *"Maculistas"* to argue to her having had original sin, since death is a result of sin. Cartagena admits of a *"debitum mortis"* in Mary by reason of the human nature she received from Adam, but denies that her death was due to sin.[13] It is in accordance with the law of nature that man should die. Hebrews 9, 27: *"Statutum est hominibus semel mori"* affirms it, as also Psalm 88, –9. Cartagena calls death the *"debiti naturae solutio."* [14]

---

[12] "Ceterum, B. Virginem, pro conditione humanae naturae, vere mortem obiisse: praeter Catholicae Ecclesiae traditionem, quae per totum Orbem terrarum felicem eius transitum, et mortem celebrat, unanimi consensu Patres illam contestantur." Lib. XIII, hom. I (II, 515a).

"Memores conditionis humanae mortem illam temporalem obiisse matrem Dei, dicere non metuimus." Pseudo–Augustinus, op. cit. (PL 40, 1144); quoted by the author, lib. XIII, hom. I (II, 515a–b). Cartagena refers also to Pseudo–Dionysius Areopagita (5th cent.), *De Divinis Nominibus*, c. 3 (PG 3, 682–3); John Damascene, *Encomium in Dormitionem Celebratissimae Gloriosissimaeque ac Benedictae Dominae Dei Genitricis semperque Virginis Mariae*, hom. 2, n. 2 (PG 96, 726); Andreas Cretensis, *In Dormitionem Sanctissimae Deiparae Dominae Nostrae*, oratio 12 (PG 97, 1051–4); Pseudo–Iuvenalis Hierosolymitanus, as reported by Simeon Metaphrastes (10th cent.), *Oratio de Sancta Maria ad Diem 15 Augusti*, n. 43 (PG 115, 560).

The opposite opinion, however, that Mary did not die simply would not disappear from the scene. Thomas Frances de Urrutigoiti, OFM († 1682), relates how a Spanish *Mariale* during his time came out denying Mary's death and thereby earning the condemnation by the Inquisition. Cf. his *Certamen Scholasticum pro Deipara*, IV (Lugduni, 1675), p. 3. Around 1707 the anonymous work from Salamanca, *De Immortalitate B. Virginis Mariae* (edited by C. Balić, Roma, 1948), upheld the same contrary thesis. The controversy dragged on up to the time prior to the definition. E.g., Dominicus Arnaldi, SJ († 1895), wrote repeatedly against the mortalist position. Cf. his *Super Transitu Beatae Mariae Virginis Deiparae expertis omni labe culpae originalis dubia proposita* (Genuae–Mediolani, 1879). See also C. Balić, "Muerte de Maria, de la edad media al siglo XX," *Estudios Marianos*, 9 (1950) 11–121. On the continuation of the controversy even after the definition, see above, footnote 11.

[13] Lib. XIII, hom. I (II, 515b). St. Augustine, e.g., taught that Mary died "propter peccatum," in his *Enarratio in Psalmum* 34, n. 3 (PL 36, 335). For the reply of Ambrosius Catharinus against his Dominican confratres of the same persuasion, see Balić, *Testimonia de Assumptione*, II (Romae, 1950), pp. 126–7.

[14] Lib. XIII, hom. I (II, 516b; cf. 516a). That Mary died because of her

There are various reasons why it was proper that Mary should undergo death. First of all, it was to refute all sorts of heresies originating from the Christological controversies that Mary was not really human and therefore neither was Christ. Mary died like any other mortal. Secondly, her conformity with her son makes it appropriate for her to die, just as he did. Thirdly, it is fitting that Mary should not lack the rewards and prerogatives earned by the saints through death, by reason of which emoluments death becomes indeed precious. Fourthly, her endurance of death is an encouragement for for us to bear it patiently. And lastly, Mary was not freed from death, so that through it she could deposit riches of satisfaction in the Church's treasury.[15]

Mary did not have a violent death, or one due to some illness; neither was her death accompanied by fear and afflictions. She died *"ex ardenti divini amoris febre,"* and according to the old tradition, at the age of 72 and was buried in Jerusalem in the Valley of Josaphat.[16]

---

human condition was also taught by St. Germanus of Constantinople, *In Sanctae Dei Genitrici Dormitionem*, sermo 2 (PG 98, 358). St. Andrew of Crete, loc. cit., reasoned to Mary's death on the ground of the "lex naturae," alluding too to Ps 88, 49.

[15] Lib. XIII, hom. I (II, 516a–b). All these reasons in the same order and with similar expressions have been given by Bernardinus de Bustis († 1500), *Mariale*, sermo 1: De Assumptione Mariae, pars 4 (Argentinae, 1498). Cartagena probably just enlarged on him.

Germanus of Constantinople reasoned that Mary died to demonstrate the reality of Christ's human nature taken from her; op. cit., sermo 1 (PG 98, 346). Andrew of Crete said the same; loc. cit., oratio 13 (PG 97, 1082). The last reference is from St. Thomas, *Summa Theol.*, III, q. 26, art. 3, ad 1.

[16] "Beatam Virginem nullo morbo laborasse, dolorem in morte nullum sensisse, nec doemonis horribilem vultum intuitam, sed ex ardenti divini amoris febre obiisse: cuius obitus triplex circumstantia, realis praesentiae Christi, loci, et temporis, hoc est domicilii, inquo degebat, anni, mensis, diei, et horae, in qua e vita discessit, ex doctrina antiquorum Patrum aperitur." Lib. XIII, hom. IV (II, 527b ff.). Cartagena is also aware of the claim that Mary was buried at Ephesus. Cf. Lib. XIII, hom. V (II, 537b.538a–539b). Suarez says too that Mary died out of love; op. cit., XXI, 1, 4–11.

The *De Immortalitate B. Virginis Mariae* mentioned above in footnote 12 and which was most probably written by Ignacio de Camargo, SJ († 1722), cites Cartagena on Mary's resurrection on the third day (p. 224; the reference is to Lib. XIII, hom. VII, II–554b, not hom. IV as is given in Balić's edition) and on her age at the end as 72 (p. 231; Lib. XIII, hom. IV, II–536b, not Lib. XII as in Balić).

That Mary's death is not asserted by Sacred Scripture is underlined by the author himself. But the common consent of the Church says that she died. And such a testimony even on the human level deserves faith. Besides, we do not have to have an infallible certitude in everything.[17] In addition, Cartagena repeats the words of Julianus Pomerius († 500) to the effect that the Gospel accounts are intentionally silent in this regard, so as to enflame more the devotion of the faithful to Mary in their desire to know more about her life and death. Inasmuch as she was the mother of God, however, the sanctity of her life and death should be obvious.[18]

3. *Her incorruptibility.* That Mary died is logical enough. But she could not have undergone the natural consequences of death. After such a life of grace and after such an accomplishment as opening for us the fountain of salvation, it is inconceivable that she was subjected to the opprobrium of corruption after dying.[19] As St. Paul pointed out to the Galatians (6, 7–8), "Where a man sows, there he reaps: if he sows in the field of self–indulgence he will get a harvest of corruption out of it; if he sows in the field of the Spirit he will get from it a harvest of eternal life." Mary's harvest of the eternal reward cannot be compared with just that of a just man. Inasmuch as she sowed the most select seeds, she obtained for them not just the hundredfold fruit of life eternal but also the incorruptibility of her body. On this Cartagena relies on the authority of John Damascene, Germanus of Constantinople, Pseudo–Melitus, Nicephorus Callistus, and Guilelmus Peraldus.[20] The last mentioned, for example,

---

[17] "Firmiter igitur statuta veritate, communi Ecclesiae consensu recepta de obitu Beatissimae Virginis... Circa quae permulta me dicturum polliceor, quae tametsi Canonicis scripturis non sint constabilita, gravissimorum tamen Doctorum auctoritate sunt contestata: quibus fidem humanam non adhibere, (nec enim in omnibus infallibilis certitudo quaerenda est) indisciplinatae mentis, et protervi animi non obscurum argumentum esse reor." Lib. XIII, hom. I (II, 516b–517a).

[18] Lib. XIII, hom. I (II, 514a). Cartagena is probably quoting Pomerius' lost *De Natura Animae* second–hand from Isidore of Sevilla. Cf. s.v. "Pomerius," *DThC*, XII, 2537–43.

[19] "Propter haec ergo tam heroica, ac memoranda gesta, inter alia pleraque munera, quibus Christus Dominus genitricem suam cumulavit, illud silentio minime praeterendum censui, quod in sepulchro corpus eius emortuum iacens corruptionis, et foetoris opprobrio non macularetur." Lib. XIII, hom. VII (II, 552a).

[20] Ibid. The first four references are to:

"At quamvis sacratissima et felix anima tua, ut fert naturae sors, a bea-

explained the words of Song of Songs 1, 16: *"tigna domorum nostra-rum cedrina"* to be showing that Mary's body never suffered corruption. "The beams of our houses are of cedar," i.e. of hard, non–decaying wood. It is in the plural, because the houses exempted from the law of corruption are both Jesus' and Mary's bodies. For he was the bone of her bone and the flesh of her flesh, and the fact that he was free from corruption meant that Mary too was preserved from it.[21] This line of reasoning adopted by Cartagena stemmed from

---

tissimo et immaculato corpore tuo disiungatur ac corpus legitimae sepulturae mandetur, non tamen in morte perseverat nec corruptione dissolvitur." Ioannes Damascenus, op. cit., hom. 1, n. 10 (PG 96, 715). In hom. 2, n. 14 (PG 96, 742) he also wrote: "Necesse fuit eius quae in partu virginitatem sine labe servaret, incorruptum etiam post mortem corpus servari." It is to be noted, however, that Cartagena himself does not quote here the words of John Damascene. It is possible that he is referring (also) to the Pseudo–Ioannes Damascenus, an excerpt from the so–called *Euthymiaca Historia* somehow inserted into the second of the three homilies on the Assumption by John Damascene, and which since the 16th century had been a reading in the Roman Breviary for the 18th of August precisely under the name of John Damascene. Cartagena observes that John Dama-scene *quotes* the *Historia Euthymiaca* in his sermon! Cf. Lib. XIII, hom. III (II, 523b). Part of the pertinent passage reads that the apostles upon finding Mary's tomb empty could only think that: "cui placuit ex Maria Virgine in persona propria carnem sumere, et hominem ex ea fieri et nasci... eidem placuit et ipsius, postquam migravit, corpus incorruptione et translatione ante communem et uni-versalem resurrectionem honorare." (PG 96, 750).

"Neque enim fieri poterat ut quae Dei capax vasculum esses, emortuum corpus corrumpente diffueres pulvere." And "Tuumque illud corpus virginale totum sanctum est, totum castum, totum Dei domicilium ut ideo quoque quidem ceu humanum, ad summam incorruptionis vitam sit immutatum." Germanus Constantinopolitanus, op. cit., sermo 1 (PG 98, 347 & 346).

" Et ait Dominus: 'Exsurge, amica mea et proxima mea; quae non sumpsisti corruptionem per coitum, non patiaris resolutionem corporis in sepulcro.' " Pseudo–Melitus, *Transitus Sanctae Mariae*, c. 17 (PG 5, 1231–40). This tract was purportedly written by Melitus, Bishop of Sardis, to answer the heretical teachings of a certain Leucius. Either Syriac or Greek in the original, it is variously dated from the 4th to the 6th century.

Nicephorus Callistus Xantopulus (14th cent.), *Historiae Ecclesiasticae Libri* 18, lib. 15, c. 14 (PG 147, 46), where he concludes that Christ took his mother's immaculate body "in loca quaedam caelestium regionum lucidissima et a cor-ruptione alienissima."

[21] "Cur dicit, non tantum domui tuae, sed domorum nostrarum? Quia non tantum domui Iesu, sed, et domui Mariae hoc privilegium commune fuit, eo quod Iesus os ex ossibus et caro ex carne Mariae fuit. Ideo enim corpus Mariae propter corpus filii, cum corpore filii a generalis lege corruptionis exceptum,

Pseudo–Augustine. Being born of her, Jesus who honored her so much in life honored her also in death. He could and he did preserve her from the natural disintegration due to human nature. He himself did not experience such corruption, and he did not permit Mary to undergo it. *"Caro enim Jesu, caro Mariae est."* [22]

Closely connected with this argumentation is the principle widely used by the Scholastics: *"Decuit, ergo fecit,"* which harks back apparently to Pseudo–Augustine. Christ was all–powerful; to him was given all the power in heaven and on earth. "If therefore he wanted to preserve the integrity of his mother with the purity of virginity, why would he not preserve her from the corruption of decay?" It is unbelievable that the body whence Jesus took the human flesh would be given as food to the worms. [23] This whole line of reasoning will also be used by the author, following Pseudo–Augustine, in his argument from congruence for Mary's assumption into heaven.

And to further strengthen his contention, Cartagena offers images, *"imagines eam adumbrantes,"* featuring this bodily incorruptibility of Mary in the pages of Sacred Scripture. The ark described

---

perpetuae imputribilitatis gratia conservatum fuit." Guillelmus Peraldus, OP ("de Petra alta" † c. 1270), *Sermones per Annum: In Assumptione Beatae Mariae Virginis,* in *Opera Omnia Guilielmi Alverni,* II (Parisiis, 1674), p. 445 f. The sermons of Guillelmus Peraldus have been mistakenly attributed to Guilielmus Alvernus. Quoted by Cartagena, Lib. XIII, hom. VII (II, 552a–b). Cf. Schneyer, op. cit., pp. 155–156.

[22] "Qui in vita prae caeteris Mariam gratia sui conceptus honoravit, pium credere est, singulari salutatione eam in morte et speciali gratia honorasse. Potuit enim eam tam a putridine, quam a pulvere alienam facere, qui ex ea nascens, Virginem eam potuit relinquere. Putredo namque, et vermis opprobrium est humana conditionis, a quo opprobrio cum Iesus sit alienus, et natura Mariae excipitur, quam Iesus de ea assumpsisse probatur. Caro enim Iesu, caro Mariae est." Pseudo–Augustinus, op. cit., c. 5 (PL 40, 1145), quoted by the author, Lib. XIII, hom. VII (II, 552b). This and following quotation from Pseudo–Augustinus have already been employed by Cartagena in connection with the Immaculate Conception. Cf. above, p. 170.

[23] "Data est mihi omnis potestas in coelo, et in terra. Si ergo voluit integram matrem cum Virginitatis servare pudore, cur non velit incorruptam a putredinis servare foetore?" Pseudo–Augustinus, loc. cit.

"Illud sacratissimum corpus, de quo Christus carnem assumpsit, et divinam naturam humana univit, non amittens, quod erat, sed assumens quod non erat, ut Verbum, Caro, hoc est, Deus homo fieret escam vermibus traditum, consentire non valeo, dicere pertimesco, in communi forte putredinis futurum de vermibus pulvere." Ibid., c. 6 (PL 40, 1146), quoted by Cartagena, Lib. XIII, hom. VII (II, 552b–553a).

in Exodus (25, 10) and ordered by Yaweh to be made of acacia wood aptly prefigured the heavenly ark of Christ's body, the womb that bore him. The Septuagint version brings this out clearer with its *"de lignis imputribilibus"* in place of the Vulgate's *"de lignis setim."* The "ark" that bore the body of Christ is also of incorruptible material. Secondly, the fate of Rahab's house (Joshua 6, 22–25) is a figure of Mary's sacred house, her virginal body. Rahab concealed the messengers in her house and for this deed her house was spared from the fire. Mary with her *"Fiat"* welcomed into herself the greatest messenger of all and for this she was freed from all burning and corruption.[24] In Mary is hence fulfilled the blessing uttered by David (Ps 120, 8): "The Lord guards your coming and your going, now and for always." She came into the world, conceived without original sin, even if every other mortal "sinned in Adam," and she left this world exempted from the general rule that dust returns to dust.[25] In another context the author interprets Apocalypse 12, 1 as showing that in having the moon, the symbol of changeability and mutability, under her feet, Mary is being pictured enjoying immutability and incorruptibility in her body just like Christ. Corruption never touched her.[26]

---

[24] Ibid. (II, 553a).

[25] "Fateamur ergo impletam plene benedictionem quam Serenissimus Rex David Beatae Virgini impertivit, cum ei dixit: 'Dominus custodiat introitum tuum et exitum tuum ex hoc, nunc, et usque in saeculum.' Duo pericula, aeque gravissima subire coguntur omnes mortales, ex primo Parente per naturalem generationem propagati. Primum est in principio vitae, cum peccati originalis labe inquinantur iuxta universalem Pauli regulam: 'Omnes in Adam peccaverunt.' Secundum est in fine vitae, cum corpora vitali aura destituta corrumpuntur, et in pulverem rediguntur, iuxta praescriptum illud generale statutum, 'Pulvis es, et in pulverem reverteris.' Regius ergo Propheta cupiens ab his periculis B. Virginem divinitus eripi, dixit: 'Dominus custodiat introitum tuum': id est, conceptionem tuam ab omni labe peccati originalis. Per conceptionem enim intravit in hunc Mundum; subdit deinde: 'Dominus custodiat exitum tuum': hoc est, praecaverat, ut cum ab hac mortali vita exieris, sententiam illam non experiatur; 'Terra es, et in terram ibis: pulvis es, et in pulverem reverteris.' Hodie igitur cernere completam in B. Virgine." Ibid. (II, 554a).

[26] "Ut ergo Spiritus sanctus significaret omnia haec mutabilitatis genera a Virgine supplantari, ideo lunam, quae mutabilitatis symbolum est, sub pedibus eius calcandam apposuit; nec enim unquam obnoxia fuit mutationi gratiae ad peccatum, quae mater gratiae est, et ab instanti suae conceptionis impeccabilis facta fuerat; nec etiam mutationis sui corporis in pulverem particeps unquam fuit, quae incorruptionis singulari privilegio donata extitit, instar corporis Christi..." Lib. II, hom. III (I, 144b).

But the argument *"instar mille,"* as far as the author is concerned, demonstrating why Mary could not have suffered corruption after her death lies in the fact that Christ lived for nine months in her body. Is it conceivable at all that the body which was preserved in virginity, so that it would not be generating men, should now be allowed to generate worms? Or, is the body that was not handed over to any man to be handed over to the worms? [27]

4. *Her resurrection.* Mary's Christ–bearing body was graced not only with incorruptibility but also with the immortality of the resurrected, after the example of Christ who after three days exchanged the garments of mortality to rise up in splendor and glory.[28] The Fathers taught this, especially John Damascene, Simeon Metaphrastes, (Pseudo–) Augustine, and even earlier (Pseudo–) Dionysius Areopagita.[29]

---

[27] "Illa denique una ratio, quae mihi instar mille est in eiusdem argumento comprobationem, quod Christus Dominus totius incorruptionis, et integritatis fons, sacrum illud corpus inhabitasset; si enim corpora balsamo delibuta, incorrupta servantur, quis quaeso dubitavit, Marianum corpus, quod novem mensium intervallo coeleste illud divini Verbi balsamum ex aeterni Patris mente distillatum tulit, omnis corruptionis expers servatum fuisse?... Et quidem si Christus Dominus adeo intactam voluit matrem, ut nec ex proprio viro filios conciperet: qua ratione, quaeso si noluit ex ea generari homines, voluisse credendus est, ut generarentur vermes, nisi velis, quod hominibus negavit, vermibus concessisse?" Lib. XIII, hom. VII (II, 553b).

[28] "Porro non solum Christiferum illud Deiparae Mariae corpus incorruptionis dono, sed immortalitatis, et gloriae fulgoribus coepit coruscare; nam Resurrectionis Christi Domini exemplari aemulata, intra triduum, sicut ille, depositis vetustis mortalitatis indumentis splendoris, et gloriae, amicta vestibus resurrexit." Ibid. (II, 554b).

[29] Ibid. The references are to:

"Necesse enim erat ut quod e terra conflatum erat ad terram reverteretur, atque in caelum transmitteretur post corporis in terra depositionem purissimam vitam accipiens. Necesse enim erat ut quemadmodum aurum, terra deposita et caliginosa mortalitatis mole, carne in morte velut in fusura incorrupta et pura atque incorruptionis fulgore rutilanti e monumento resurgens indueretur." Ioannes Damascenus, op. cit., hom. 3, n. 3 (PG 96, 758). Cf. above, footnote 20.

"Et illud [sepulchrum] quidem fuit apertum; thesaurus autem nequaquam erat in eo; sed solae erant vestes, in quibus fuerat conditus, quomodo etiam in eius Filii resurrectione." Simeon Metaphrastes, op. cit., n. 43 (PG 115, 560). It is not explicitly stated here that Mary rose from the dead. However, Iuvenalis the Archbishop of Jerusalem is mentioned to be saying that: "Siquidem quod ex ea natum erat, totam eam Verbum ad se transtulit, et voluit eam apud se et esse, et perpetuo simul vivere." Ibid.

From the Bible we have Psalm 131, 8 saying: *"Surge Domine in requiem tuam, tu et arca sanctificationis tuae."* This text has been understood by some to mean not just Christ's resurrection but also that of his ark, Mary. It is as if David was saying:

> As you, Lord Jesus, rose from the dead and reign in glorified body in your heavenly resting place, seated at the right hand of the Father, so make that the ark of your holiness, namely the most blessed mother, in whose womb you were concealed as in a mystical ark, may rise up effulgent with gifts of glory.[30]

Moreover, it is because Mary has risen that the Psalm's following verse: *"Sacerdotes tui induantur iustitiam, et sancti tui exultent"* may accordingly be interpreted to mean the Church's rejoicing in her liturgical celebration of Mary's resurrection and its consequence in the growth of her sanctity.[31] In addition, Cartagena finds still another scriptural text insinuating the resurrection of Mary. It is the Gospel account of Christ's visit to Bethany (Lk 10, 38–42). *In sensu allegorico*, the sisters Martha and Mary are the body and soul of the Blessed Virgin, joined together by mutual natural love. Separated by the sword of death, the body of the Blessed Virgin, represented here by Mary who vacated the active role, wants to be reunited to its beloved soul and so calls out: "Lord, do you not care that my sister has left me lying alone in the tomb? Please tell her to help me, to vivify me and return to my partnership, so that together we may serve you reigning glorious in heaven." In her favor the body of the Blessed Virgin could claim the care and love a son owes his mother (Tobit 4, 3). And the formulation of the request shows this nuance of obligation on the part of the son: *"Non est tibi cura...?"* [32] Having

---

Pseudo–Augustinus, op. cit., c. 6 (PL 40, 1146).

"Caeterum tametsi Virgo mater natura legibus fuit obnoxia, tametsi mortem degustavit, tametsi ut homo, in sepulchro est deposita, natura tamen fines, atque terminos superavit, et excessit: neque sepulchrum, et mortalitas eam in potestate sua retinere potuit." Pseudo–Dionysius Areopagita, op. cit. (PG 3, 682).

[30] Lib. XIII, hom. VII (II, 556b).

The author lines up: John Damascene, op. cit., hom. 3, n. 3 (PG 96, 758); "Illuminatus Doctor Mayron," i.e. Franciscus de Mayronis, OFM († c. 1328), a leading disciple of Duns Scotus, and who wrote on the Assumption in his *Sermones de Sanctis* (Basel, 1498).

[31] Lib. XIII, hom. VII (II, 556b).

[32] "Verum, et hoc idem resurrectionis Deiparae Mariae argumentum, secundum sensum allegoricum, video in hodierni Evangelii lectione insinuatum,

fulfilled the *debitum mortis*, Mary's body could therefore lay claim to be reunited with her soul. And she did rise again, just like her son who extended to her his own right to rise again from the dead after the third day, and because she could not be the true mother of God unless her body and soul are united.[33]

5. *Her assumption and glorification in heaven.* Rising from the dead, or, more correctly phrased, raised from the dead, Mary in her glorified body was assumed into heaven, in a reunion of her body and soul. It is this assumption of Mary into heaven in her body that is celebrated by the Feast of the Assumption. To say that it is the assumption of her soul that is the object of the celebration is a futile evasion, says Cartagena.[34]

---

dum nobis proponit sorores duas Mariam, et Martham, quarum altera, scilicet Martha, enixe postulabat a Christo Domino, ut praeciperet Mariae, ut ipsam associaret et adiuvaret: 'Domine non est tibi cura, quod soror mea reliquit me solam ministrare? Dic ergo illi, ut me adiuvet.' In sensu allegorico, sorores istae sunt caro, et anima B. Virginis, quae mutuo naturali amore erant coniunctae. Illis autem ancipiti mortis gladio separatis, caro Virginis per Mariam, quae activae vitae vacabat, apte praefiguratam, ardenter cupiens, ut dilecta eius anima ei reuniretur, eamque associaret, ait quaerula quadam voce: Domine non est tibi curae, quod soror mea reliquit me solam in sepulchro iacentem? Dic ergo, ut me adiuvet, vivificans me, et ad consortium meum rediens, ut simul tibi coelesti in gloria regnanti ministremus. Et quidem ad hoc beneficium obtinendum, duplicem rationem videtur caro B. Virginis in sui favore producere. Prima est, cura, quam filius debet habere honoris, et commodi suae matris. Dicens enim: 'Non est tibi cura,' perinde fuit, ac si diceret: nun filii mi, matris tuae sollicitam curam non geris, Spiritu sancto dicente Tob. 4. 'Honorem exhibebis matri tuae.' Quod si Eccles. cap. 41. ait: 'Deo est cura de omnibus'; portiori iure cura est tibi habenda de matre tua, Apostolo dicente, 1. Timoth. 5. 'Si quis suorum, et maxime domesticorum curam non habet, fidem negavit.' Addens autem: 'Quia reliquit me solam,' hoc est separatam, et divisam per mortem a consortio animae secundam rationem affert, quod iam persolverit debitum mortis, iuxta Pauli promulgatam legem: 'Statutum est hominibus semel mori.' Cum igitur ex una parte huic communi conditionis humanae debito, B. Virginis caro iam satisfecisset, et ex alia, ad pietatem filii pertineret, sollicitam curam donoris materni gerere, ideo B. Virgo utramque rationem tangens, postulat non relinqui solam, sed iterum per resurrectionem, animae associari, et reuniri; non est tibi curae, quod soror mea reliquit me solam in sepulchro?" Ibid. (II, 556b–557b).

[33] Ibid. (II, 557b).

[34] Lib. XIV, hom. XIII (II, 658a–b). Cartagena is here closely repeating the words of Suarez, op. cit., XXVII, a. 2, d. 21, 2, 4.

Gregorio de Jesus Crucificado, "La Asuncion en la Teología española," *Estudios Marianos*, 6 (1947) 361, comments on Cartagena's use of other authors:

She rose by divine power from the night of death, which she submitted to only temporarily. And she was assumed into heaven and placed at the right hand of the Son, with the highest gift of beatitude to the soul and to her body most pure the strength of immortality.[35]

Above all the choirs of angels and over the whole heavenly city, this immaculate woman has been appropriately constituted, body and soul, as *"universalis omnium domina."* [36] Cartagena is here placidly maintaining the Catholic tradition of calling Mary a queen, whose classic expressions are found in the *Salve Regina* and *Regina coeli*, a language strongly objected to by the Reformers. "Hence in heaven," the author goes on, "no one is gazed upon above the mother except the son, no one wondered at more than the queen except the king, no one venerated above the mediatrix except the mediator alone." [37] These words by Cartagena brings out an aspect of Mary's role in heaven which he extensively develops.

In heaven Mary is both a queen and a mother for us. If Eve our first mother conceived us in the deformity of original sin, God's providence has it that we be spiritually regenerated by Mary the mother of God, to conform us to the image of her son. Thus, the devil's words in the Garden of Paradise: *"Eritis sicut Dii"* have contrary to his own expectation become true. We are "gods" by participation, since all the adoptive children of Mary are *"Dei per gratiam et charitatem."* [38] In a comprehensive view which includes the Incarnation

---

"El P. Cartagena se ocupa de la Asunción nada menos que en 27 largas homilías, de las cuales la trece tiene un estricto valor teológico, ya que viene a ser un tratado completo sobre el misterio, aunque tiene el defecto de presentar como proprias opiniones y afirmaciones que, evidentemente están tomadas de otros autores."

[35] Lib. XIV, hom. XIV (II, 675a).

[36] Ibid. (II, 670b). Cf. G. Jouassard, "Royauté de Marie et Assomption," in *Maria et Ecclesia*, V (Romae, 1959), pp. 173–189.

[37] Ibid. (II, 672a).

[38] "Divina tamen Redemptoris nostri providentia factum est, ut Maria Dei Genitrix nos etiam spiritualiter regeneraret, et reficeret, conformesque redderet imagini filii sui, qui cum pariter etiam sit filius Dei naturalis, non falso, ut Eva iuxta suasionem Diaboli: 'Eritis sicut Dii,' sed veraciter nos vero Deo parenti nostro similes reddit... Maria, quae mater esse perhibetur divina, utpote mater eius, qui Deus est per essentiam, consequens est, ut quos parturit foetus, dii sint, per participationem... omnes filii Mariae sint Dei: naturalis quidem, et primogenitus, Deus per naturam, reliqui vero adoptivi, Dei per gratiam, et charitatem." Ibid. hom. XV (II, 677a).

in Christ's salvific action, Cartagena explains that our spiritual regeneration is attributed also to Mary insofar as it is possible only because of Christ's own generation in time, conceived in Mary's womb by the power of the Holy Spirit and with her cooperation. So, just as the first generation could not have taken place without her causality, our spiritual generations are said to be by her also, i.e. immediately through her intercession, so that *"quoad esse supernaturale"* Mary is together with Christ our source: Christ alone as the savior, and Mary as his special instrument.[39] The author goes on:

> ...she takes us in as adoptive children, when from the cradles of infancy we are made clean by the bath of sacred baptism. She offers to God our prayers which are like the crying of children. With the assurance of divine mercy she strengthens and toughens those who are vacillating and swaying away from eternal salvation, in fact even those who are already despairing. She feeds us hungry ones with the food and drink of the body and blood of her only son in the Eucharist. Finally, through her intercession she magnanimously grants us spiritual life, and like a most loving mother she abundantly furnishes us everything needed for its preservation.[40]

Mary in heaven is then *"mater omnium viventium."* [41] She is especially sollicitous of sinners, unceasingly pleading for them and begging

---

[39] "...omnes spirituales illae generationes vim omnem, et efficacitatem sanctificandi animas acceperunt ab unica illa, et suprema Christi temporali generatione, in utero eius virtute Spiritus sancti et Mariae cooperatione facta. Unde sicut conceptio ipsa, et nativitas Christi minime fuerunt absque Virginis causalitate, et idcirco non solum Deo, sed ei etiam debet tribui; ita similiter omnes spiritualiter generationes per Christum factas merito etiam 'suas' vocat B. Virgo, quia ad omnes mediate per filium, immediate vero per seipsam deprecative, sicut Christus imperative concurrit. Unde sicut totum genus humanum quoad esse vitae naturalis, duplicem primum parentem habuit Adamum, et Evam; ita quoad esse supernaturale duplex agnoscit vitae spiritualis primordium, Christum scilicet, et Mariam; quia licet solus Christus Dominus sit Salvator mundi, ipsa tamen multum cooperata est, tanquam praecipuum eius instrumentum ad nostram omnium salutem..." Ibid. (II, 677b–678a). On Mary's role as Christ's *coadiutrix*, see above, pp. 171–175.

[40] Ibid. (II, 678b). Cf. R. Gagnebet, OP, "Le mode d'exercise de la royauté de Marie au ciel à l'égard des hommes viateurs," in *Maria et Ecclesia*, V, op. cit., pp. 201–221; S. Wenceslas, OFM, "La coopération de Marie et de l'Eglise à la rédemption selon les Pères de l'Eglise," ibid., IV (Romae, 1959), pp. 38–45; I. de la Inmaculada, OCD, "El misterio de la corredencion," ibid., pp. 206–214.

[41] Lib. XIV, hom. XV (II, 679a); Lib. I, hom. II (I, 7a). For Mary as "mater

divine mercy in their behalf.[42] She is our most powerful *"Advocata"* in the heavenly court.[43] And her beneficence embraces everyone, even those who are non–believers, those suffering in purgatory, the damned (some of whom, explains Cartagena, could be recalled to mortal life to do penance and therefore could still be saved), and even the angels whose joy could be magnified by the sight of the Incarnate God and his mother.[44] Mary gloriously assumed in heaven is indeed *"universorum Reginam tam coelestium, quam terrestrium, et infernorum."* [45]

B. Reasons for Mary's Assumption

1. *Testimonies by the Fathers and theologians.* In a replay of Salmeron with some additions from Canisius and Baronius, Cartagena proceeds to base the doctrine of Mary's Assumption into heaven on the testimonies of writers from the patristic time to the Middle Ages.[46] Quotations are given from John Damascene,[47] Pseudo–Athanasius,[48] Andrew of Crete,[49] Pseudo–Augustine,[50] Pseudo–Gregory of Nazianzen,[51] Germanus of Constantinople,[52] Cosmas Hie-

---

omnium fidelium," cf. Lib. V, hom. VI (I, 417a–b); Lib. VII, hom. XIII (I, 803b). See also Vat. II, *Const. on the Church*, nn. 53 & 58.

[42] Lib. XIV, hom. XVI (II, 684a–689a); hom. XVII (II, 690a–698b).

[43] Lib. XIV, hom. XVI (II, 699a–704b).

[44] Ibid. (II, 704).

[45] Lib. XIV, hom. XV (II, 679a).

[46] Lib. XIV, hom. XIII (II, 654b–658a). Cf. A. Salmeron, op. cit., XI, tr. 37 & 38, pp. 299b–300a, 306a–309b, 311a; P. Canisius, *De Maria Virgine*, lib. 5, c. 2: IX, pp. 64–69; C. Baronius, *Martyrologium Romanum ad Novam Kalendarii Rationem et Ecclesiasticae Historiae Veritatem Restitutum*, ad 15 augusti (Romae, 1598), p. 399.

[47] John Damascene, loc. cit. Cf. A. Schumpp, "Zur Mariologie des hl. Johannes Damascenus," *Divus Thomas*, 2 (Freiburg, 1934) 22–234.

[48] Pseudo–Athanasius (7th cent.), *Sermo in Annuntiationem Sanctissimae Dominae Nostrae Deiparae* (PG 28, 938).

[49] Andreas Cretensis, op. cit., oratio 13 (PG 97, 1082–3). Cartagena quotes also from Andrew of Crete's "sermo. quodam alio de dormitione Virginis nondum edito, habetur tamen in Vaticana Bibliotheca" Lib. XIV, hom. XIII (II, 655b), which description and the following quotation he took over from Salmeron, op. cit., p. 308a.

[50] Pseudo–Augustinus, op. cit.,

[51] Pseudo–Gregorius, *Tragedia de Christo Patiente* (PG 38, 336).

[52] Germanus Constantinopolitanus, op. cit.

rosolymitanus,[53] Amedaeus Lausannensis,[54] Nicephorus Callistus,[55] Michael Glycas,[56] and Leo the Philosopher.[57] Furthermore, references are made to Pseudo–Dionysius,[58] Gregorius Turonensis,[59] Pseudo–Timotheus Hierosolymitanus,[60] Pseudo–Iuvenalis,[61] Richard of St. Victor,[62] Pseudo–Hugo of St. Victor,[63] Maximus Taurinensis,[64] Simeon Metaphrastes,[65] Absalom of Springiersbach,[66] Pseudo–Petrus Damianus,[67] and Honorius Augustodunensis.[68]

2. *Consent and tradition of the universal Church.* By the argument *"ex consensu et traditione universalis Ecclesiae"* Cartagena understands the practise of the universal Church and the present unanimity of theologians. The Scholastic authorities mentioned as teaching the

---

[53] Cosmas "hymnographus" Hierosolymitanus (8th cent.), whom Cartagena quotes indirectly from Glycas. Cf. below, footnote 56.

[54] Amedaeus Lausannensis († 1159), *De B. Virginis Obitu, Assumptione in Caelum, Exaltatione ad Filii Dexteram,* hom. 7 (PL 196, 1342). The author mistakenly named him *"Andreas* Monachus Cistercensis et Episcopus Lausaniae."

[55] Nicephorus Callistus, op. cit., lib. 2, c. 22 (PG 145, 814).

[56] Michael Glycas (12th cent.), *Annales,* pars 3 (PG 158, 439).

[57] Leo VI, imperator Constantinopolitanus et philosophus († 911), *Oratio 14,* (PG 107, 162–3).

[58] Pseudo–Dionysius Areopagita, op. cit., c. 3 (PG 3, 682–3).

[59] Gregorius Turonensis († 593), *Libri Miraculorum,* lib. 1: De gloria beatorum martyrum, c. 4 (PL 71, 708).

[60] Pseudo–Timotheus Hierosolymitanus (5th cent.), *Oratio in Prophetam Simeonem* (PG 86, 246–7).

[61] Pseudo–Iuvenalis Hierosolymitanus, quoted both by John Damascene and Simeon Metaphrastes. Cartagena is quoting him from Simeon Metaphrastes. Cf. below, footnote 65.

[62] Richard of St. Victor († 1173), *Explicatio in Cantica Canticorum,* c. 42: De assumptione Mariae et eius laudibus (PL 196, 523–4).

[63] Pseudo–Hugo of St. Victor, *De Assumptione et Decem Praeconiis Mariae semper Virginis* (PL 177, 807–8). This is an appendix of uncertain origin included among the works of Hugo of St. Victor.

[64] Maximus Taurinensis († 466), *Sermones de Assumptione* (PL 57, 865–7). The authorship here is doubtful.

[65] Simeon Metaphrastes, op. cit., n. 43 (PG 115, 560).

[66] Absalom of Springiersbach († 1203), *In Assumptione Gloriosae Virginis Mariae,* sermo 44 (PL 211, 255). Cf. A. Thome, *Die "Sermones festivales" des Absalon v. S...* Lic. Diss. (Trier, 1951).

[67] Pseudo–Petrus Damianus = Nicolaus Claraevallensis († c. 1776), *De Assumptione B. Mariae Virginis* (PL 144, 717).

[68] Honorius Augustodunensis († 1136), *Speculum Ecclesiae,* De assumptione S. Mariae (PL 172, 991–4).

doctrine of Mary's Assumption into heaven are: St. Thomas Aquinas,[69] Pseudo–Bonaventure,[70] and John Gerson,[71] plus the unnamed *"universi Scholastici et moderniores Doctores."* But what renders the doctrine so solid, as far as the author is concerned, is the universal Feast of her Assumption. This liturgical celebration, witnessed to by the Fathers already mentioned above, is for the Church a matter of precept and obligation.[72] This fact decides for the author the theological note he will be giving the doctrine below.

Relying on Baronius, Cartagena meets the objection that both Augustine and Jerome in the works *De Assumptione Beatae Mariae Virginis* and *Ad Paulam et Eustochium* actually seem to doubt Mary's assumption with the observation that textual criticism has shown that we are not dealing here with the real Augustine nor with the true Jerome.[73] (And this after the author himself has repeatedly quoted especially Pseudo–Augustine!) But, he goes on, granting for the sake of argument that these two works doubted the assumption of Mary into heaven — which they actually do not, and which they in reality strengthen with arguments, especially Augustine — what during those times was not yet sufficiently investigated and discussed does not necessarily have to remain in doubt and uncertainty forever. Where there was no common consensus then, there is now.[74] And in a significant sentence, affirmative of the development of dogma, Cartagena asserts that "The Catholic Church, like the dawn, grows

---

[69] Thomas Aquinas, *Summa Theol.*, III, q. 27, art. 2 corpus.

[70] Pseudo–Bonaventure, *Speculum B. M. Virginis;* which item Cartagena simply took from Salmeron. Bonaventure did not write this work. Cf. the preface of Bonaventure's *Opera Omnia* I (Ad Claras Aquas, 1882), p. xvi.

[71] John Gerson, *Sermo de Conceptione B. Mariae Virginis*, *Opera Omnia* V (Paris, 1521), p. 111; cf. *Oeuvres complètes*, op. cit., p. 481.

[72] Lib. XIV, hom. XIII (II, 658a–b). This argument from the liturgy was convincing to many theologians of the 17th century and determined in many cases the theological note accorded the teaching of Mary's Assumption. Cf. B. Capelle, "Le témoignage de la liturgie," in *Etudes Mariales*, 7 (1949), pp. 35–62; G. de Jesus Crucificado, art. cit., p. 369.

[73] Lib. XIV, hom. XIII (II, 659b–661a). The references are to Pseudo–Augustinus, op. cit., c. 1 (PL 40, 1143) and to Pseudo–Jerome, op. cit., n. 2 (PL 30, 127).

[74] "Nec enim, quod illa aetate non erat satis discussum, aut exploratum necesse est perpetuo indiscussum, et ambiguum manere; modo enim de Virginis Assumptione adest universalis consensus Ecclesiae, qui tamen tunc non vigebat." Lib. XIV, hom. XIII (II, 661a).

everyday in the knowledge of the truth. She in fact attributes to it [the doctrine of Mary's Assumption] all the certitude that can be given to this truth, short of that which a definition carries with it."[75]

3. *"Ex variis rationibus, et urgentissimis coniecturis."* From a number of texts drawn from Sacred Scripture and from other propositions *ex congruentia*, Cartagena next makes inferences *a fortiori* establishing the appropriateness and reasonability of Mary's Assumption into heaven. The silence of Scripture about her end and her glorification should not be construed, cautions the author, to mean that this whole matter is of no great moment. Scripture is leaving to the reason of man to delve deeper into the question in the spirit of the principle: *Credo ut intelligam.* For the authority of truth is rich, and in a diligent examination it reveals itself.[76]

a) The honor is logically Mary's. Her body and soul had been overshadowed by the Holy Spirit (Lk 1, 35) and she was full of grace. In fact a woman exclaimed in public that her womb was blessed (Lk 11, 27). If plenitude of grace corresponds with plenitude of glory, Mary's fullness of grace in body and soul should mean also her fullness of glory in both body and soul. Moreover, for this fullness of glory to be effected she did not need to wait until the universal resurrection. If she could merit the immediate changing of the water into wine in Cana, she could merit too the speedy glorification of her body. She fulfilled every wish of her son on earth; she merited thereby the fulfillment not only of her desired glorification of the body but also the innate and natural longing of the soul to be united to its body.[77]

---

[75] Ibid.

[76] "Quia quaedam, scriptura sancta veris indagationum studiis quaerenda reliquit, quae non sunt superflua aestimanda, dum vera indagatione fuerint patefacta: foecunda est enim veritatis authoritas, et dum diligenter discutitur, de se gignere, quod ipsa est, cognoscitur." Pseudo–Augustinus, op. cit., quoted by author in Lib. XIV, hom. XIII (II, 653a).

[77] "Manifestum est supervenisse Dei virtutem, non solum in animam, sed in corpus Deiparae, plenitudine gratiae ei proportionata illam cumulantem... Plena erant gratia viscera, et ubera Mariae, ut coram omni populo ingenue falsa est mulier illa, quae exclamans dixit: 'Beatus venter, qui te portavit, et ubera, qua suxisti.' Cum igitur plenitudinem gratiae correspondeat plenitudo gloriae, certe cum Deipara Maria plenitudine gratiae obtinuerit in anima pariter, et in corpore, aequum erat, ut ei in utroque corresponderet plenitudo gloriae... B. Virgo meruit accelerationem conversionis aquae in vinum... satis utique cum ratione coniunctum esse censendum est, accelerationem gloriae sui corporis similiter meruisse.

In addition, to connect this teaching with those of the two earlier chapters, Mary was immaculate in the womb of her mother, and she gave birth to Christ as a virgin and devoid of any pains. It is not credible after such privileges that her most holy body was later handed over to the worms.[78]

Mary deserves this honor more than anybody else could be said to deserve any such honor from God. For instance, the Gospel according to Matthew (27, 52–53) narrates that "The tombs opened and the bodies of many holy men rose from the dead, and these, after his resurrection, came out of the tombs, entered the Holy City and appeared to a number of people." What happened to these holy men afterwards? They ascended into heaven with Christ, said the Fathers.[79] "If God therefore has by him in heaven the bodies of some of his servants endowed with glory and immortality, it would be unbelievable if he were to deny this distinct privilege to the body of his own mother." [80] And if honorable mention and thorough investigations and veneration were given to the following: Martha's house where Christ visited, the manger where he lay as a newborn babe, Nazareth, the cross, and the sepulchre where he was laid, how much more should honor be accorded to the mother, in whose womb Christ was conceived and harbored? [81] And when one thinks of it, isn't it significant that Mary's body had never been located? Notwithstanding the popular devotion to her and the veneration given to her greater than that given to other saints, God has not revealed where her body has been interred. If it really were still here on earth, Christ would not have

---

Etenim B. Virgo adeo sollicitam curam exhibuit in implenda in omnibus et per omnia voluntate filii sui, ut per illam mereretur impleri sibi non solum appetitum elicitum glorificationis sui corporis, sed et naturalem, innatum, et congenitum, quem anima habet ad unionem cum suo corpore." Ibid. (II, 664a–b).

[78] Ibid. (II, 663r). Cf. A. Plessis, "La Virginité de Marie et son Assomption corporelle," in *Etudes Mariales*, 7 (1949), pp. 125–137.

[79] The author refers to Origen, Clement of Alexandria, Epiphanius, Ambrosius and Anselmus, apparently getting this argument from Pseudo–Jerome, op. cit. (PL 30, 127–8), because the quotation Cartagena attributes to Sophronius: "veri testes isti non essent, nisi ad immortalem vitam fuisset eorum resurrectio" is nothing but a paraphrase of Pseudo–Hieronymus, who also cites Acts 2, 23 in this connection as Cartagena does. Cf. Lib. XIV, hom. XIII (II, 661b).

[80] Ibid. (II, 661b–662a). Cf. Rahner, art. cit., pp. 244–245, on the text's eschatological import.

[81] Ibid. (II, 662b).

deprived it of the honor that would have been showered upon his mother, when her body was located.[82]

b) It is to be expected of Christ, that he would so honor his own mother. It is a divine precept to honor one's parents (Ex 20, 12; Deut 5, 16; Mt 15, 4; Eph 6, 1). And Christ came to fulfill the law, not to abolish it (Mt 5, 17). He honored his parents (Lk 2, 51). And if Christ on the brink of death thought of his mother (Jn 19, 26–27), he would certainly think of her also afterwards. And he did; he honored and glorified her body and soul in heaven.[83] Along the same line, all impoliteness is foreign to Christ. And it is lack of urbanity to divest his mother of her precious body, her garment. She in his coming have him his body; he in his home could not have taken away her body. He not only gave it back to her, but returned it decorated with beauty, immortality and all sorts of gifts.[84] Moreover, Christ has said, "If a man serves me, he must follow me, wherever I am, my servant will be there too" (Jn 12, 26). Mary served him. She gave him her own flesh and blood, nourished him, accompanied him in life, and suffered with him at his death. She is there also now where he is.[85]

c) For our sake. This gift of the Assumption of Mary manifests

---

[82] "Cum igitur Beatae Virginis corpus dignius multo sit cultu, et veneratione prae omnibus aliorum Sanctorum corporibus, nemo sibi persuadebit, Christum Dominum hoc honore privasse corpus matris suae, si in terra permansisset." Ibid. (II, 662a).

[83] "...divinum praeceptui est de honorandis parentibus. Exod. 20. Deuter. 5. et Matth. 15... Cum igitur Christus Dominus non venerit solvere legem, sed adimplere, manifestum est, non solum Patrem honorasse... sed et matrem etiam; unde et honoravit eam in vita, in omnibus ei obediendo... Honoravit eam prope mortem commendans illam discipulo Ioanni: honorasse ergo illam post mortem iustum erat. Nec sufficit dicere, honorasse eius animam, quia praeterquam corpori etiam matris honor debetur, et beneficentia ut habetur... Honoravit igitur, et glorificavit corpus, et animam." Ibid. (II, 662b–663a). Absalom of Springiersbach, op. cit., sermo 44 (PL 211, 255–6) had argued in the same manner.

[84] Lib. XIV, hom. XIII, (II, 664b).

[85] " 'Qui mihi ministrat, me sequatur, et ubi ego sum, illic, et minister meus erit,' consequens est, ut Virgo Deipara, quae prae omnibus aliis impensius Christo in carne sua ministravit: sanguinem ei praebens, ut verbum caro fieret: lac ei propinans, ut natam prolem nutriret: pueritiam illius alens, in vita eius illum concomitans, in passione compatiens, in morte assistens modo illa sit cum Christo, ut ubi ille est, ibi sit vigilantissima eius ministratrix." Ibid. (II, 664b–665a). The author picks up this argument from Pseudo–Augustinus, op. cit. (PL 40, 1146–7), whom he quotes at some length in rounding up this argumentation.

God's power, wisdom and fidelity to his promise. It is to the honor of the son, as it is the glory of the mother. It is to the pride of the angels. And for us, it is the strengthening of our faith, the encouragement to our hope, the nourishment for our piety, and the preservation of the assurance that everything, her Assumption too, is actually for our sake.[86]

4. *Certa doctrina.* Juan de Cartagena admits that for Abulensis the teaching that Mary was assumed in her glorified body into heaven was merely a probable opinion.[87] Cajetan and Soto considered it a *pia sententia*,[88] while Cano, Cordoba and Baronius said that to deny it would be a temerity.[89] Catharinus, on the other hand, claimed that the doctrine is *de fide* and its denial heretical.[90]

First of all, Cartagena lists the doctrine of Mary's Assumption into heaven as one of those singular privileges of hers which the Roman Church (*"quae magistra est omnium Ecclesiarum"*) teaches even without any expressed scriptural testimony for it.[91] Secondly, although this bodily assumption of Mary into heaven is not a *de fide* doctrine inasmuch as it has not been defined yet by the Church,

---

[86] Lib. XIV, hom. XIII (II, 663b–664a). Here Cartagena is again simply repeating Salmeron almost verbatim. Cf. Salmeron, op. cit., XI, tr. 38, p. 312b.

This orientation *ad extra* of Mary's grace of the Assumption and its context within the plenitude of her grace (cf. above, footnote 77), are today "modern" facets of the mystery being underscored by theologians. Cf. Koster, art. cit., pp. 94–95; Philippe, art. cit., pp. 149–156; Dillenschneider, art. cit., p. 134; and G. de Jesus Crucificado, art. cit., p. 367.

[87] Alphonsus Tostatus, *Commentaria in Matthaeum*, q. 230: *Operum*, XXIII Venetiis, 1718), p. 138. Cartagena makes this and the following references in Lib. XIV, hom. XIII (II, 658b).

[88] Thomas Caietanus de Vio, OP († 1534), *Tractatus de Conceptione Beatae Mariae Virginis ad Leonem Decimum*, c. 1: *Opuscula*, II (Venetiis, 1594), p. 71.

Dominicus Soto, OP († 1560), *Commentariorum... in Quartum Sententiarum Tomus Secundus*, d. 43, q. 2, a. 1 (Venetiis, 1584), pp. 466b–467a.

[89] Melchior Cano, OP († 1560), *De Locis Theologicis*, op. cit., lib. 12, c. 10 (Bassani, 1746), pp. 392b–393a.

Antonius de Cordoba, OFM († 1578), *Quaestionarium Theologicum*, lib. 1, q. 17, sec. 1 (Venetiis, 1604), p. 150b.

Caesar Baronius († 1607), *Annales Ecclesiastici*, ad an. 48, I (Venetiis, 1705), p. 300a.

[90] Ambrosius Catharinus, OP († 1553), *Annotationes in Commentaria Caietani*, lib. 4 (Lugduni, 1542), pp. 288–289.

[91] Lib. I, hom. XIX (I, 99b–100a).

nonetheless to deny it is clearly erroneous, an *"error in fide,"* because it would be against the *sensus Ecclesiae*. The Feast of Mary's Assumption is celebrated universally by the Church and is obligatory for the faithful, giving the likelihood that the feast originated in apostolic times. Hence the teaching is no less certain a doctrine than her Immaculate Conception.[92] In this, Cartagena numbers himself among the avant–garde of his time in claiming the highest certainty, short of a definition, for the doctrine of Mary's Assumption into heaven.

II. SCRIPTURAL ELUCIDATIONS

Juan de Cartagena explicitly states that the Church teaching on the Assumption of Mary, although certain, is not backed up by any *testimonium scripturae*. But as in the case of the mystery of Mary's Immaculate Conception, the author holds that the doctrine is somehow contained in Sacred Scripture, even if only in the mystical sense. Thus he has entitled Book XIV's 12th homily: *"Adductis variis sacrarum literarum locis, in sensu mystico explicatis, gloriosam Deipa-*

---

[92] "Ut tamen in re hac meam sententiam luculenter aperiam assero, quod licet veritas haec non sit de fide... quia revera nec est ab Ecclesia definita, nec adest testimonium scripturae, aut tibi firma traditio, quae infallibilem faciat fidem: illam tamen negare, plane mihi videretur erroneum, quia pugnat cum omnium Catholicorum sensu, nemine contradicente, seu cum communi Ecclesiae Catholicae iudicio, quae Assumptionem Virginis in corpore solemni ritu colendum omnibus fidelibus proponit, et praecipit. Nihil autem reipsa falsum Ecclesia Catholica, quae spiritu veritatis regitur, colendum potest praecipere fidelibus. Accedit, quod in ritibus Ecclesiasticis, cuius initium non invenitur, ab Apostolis manasse creditur, ut unanimi consensu docent Theologi... Quare existimo, non minus certam esse in Ecclesia Catholica Assumptionem Virginis in corpore glorioso, quam sanctificationem eiusdem in utero materno, cui dissentire erroneum iudico propter rationem tactam." Lib. XIV, hom. XIII (II, 659a). The "error in fide" is in this homily's title. Ibid. (II, 652b).

The opinion of Suárez is here literally reechoed by Cartagena. Cf. Suárez, op. cit., q. XXVII, a. 2, d. 3. And the position of these two former Salamanca professors explicitly reflects in turn that of Catharinus, which set the tone in the up–swing trend of the certitude being then given to the doctrine of Mary's Assumption. Cf. C. Dillenschneider, art. cit., pp. 74–75. See also Bernardo Aperribay, OFM, "La muerte y la Asuncion de la Virgen en los representantes de la mariología franciscano–española," *Verdad y Vida*, 6 (1948) 263–284.

Marcelinus Siuri († 1734), *Theologia Scholastico–positiva de Novissimis, Variis Tractatibus Exposita et Illustrata* (Valentiae, 1707), tr. 30, c. 3, nn. 84–5, p. 560b, cites and agrees with the above position of Cartagena.

rae Virginis Assumptionem illustrare conamur," and 13th homily:
*"Beatam Virginem in Coelum assumptionem in corpore glorioso, ex
sacris Scripturae secundum sensum mysticum... demonstramus..."* [93]
Of what we have already seen of the author's "illustrations and elucidations" of doctrines from the Bible it is clear that we are not
dealing with exegesis in the sense of today's *Bibelwissenschaft* but
with some form of *"eisegesis."* The following Part III will be concerned
with this matter.

Unlike his treatment of the scriptural elucidations for Mary's
Immaculate Conception, Cartagena is rather brief with regards the
illustrations from the Bible for the doctrine of Mary's Assumption
into heaven. He does not devote any homily–long explanation for
any particular text, but instead piles them up one after the other in
a couple of homilies. We shall just give these texts and their interpretations. There will not be any division between principal texts
and images, because here Cartagena does not indicate any.

1. *Song of Songs 3, 6.* As before, the rich spring giving forth
abundant material for mystical interpretation is the Book of the
Song of Songs. The present text reads: "What is this coming up from
the desert like a column of smoke, breathing of myrrh and frankincense and every perfume the merchant knows?" This well–known
passage is claimed by Cartagena to point to the mystery of Mary's
Assumption into heaven. One may well wonder how Mary assumed
into heaven can be compared to a column of smoke. Smoke has traditionally symbolized vanity and instability. Anyway, the author
takes it that, as the LXX has it, the angels were the ones asking the
question.[94] And "coming up from the desert" means coming up from
the world. Mary leaves the world behind her to rise up to higher joys,
hence Richard of St. Victor's further explanation that *"per desertum"*
could well be understood as *"per desertionem,"* because for the sake
of Christ Mary turned her back on everything.[95] Another interpre-

---

[93] Lib. XIV, hom. XII (II, 645b) and hom. XIII (II, 652b): "Ex locis sacrae
Scripturae in sensu mystico expositis iuxta SS. Patrum sententiam." Cartagena
is in this whole section heavily dependent on Salmeron, op. cit., XI, tr. 37,
p. 304a ff.

[94] Lib. XIV, hom. XII (II, 646b–647a).

[95] "Per 'desertum' primo possumus intelligere cum Richardo Victorino
super hunc locum, 'mundum,' quia vel a suis amatoribus saepe deseritur, et con-

tation of the desert was given by Guilelmus Peraldus: it stands for virginity, which was formerly very much neglected and "deserted" in the ancient preoccupation with fertility and posterity. So Mary went up through this desert of virginity, consecrating it to God in order that she may be a fitting dwelling place for him, thus spurning the malediction heaped upon the childless but likewise earning in the process the world's benediction: "Blessed are you among women." [96] And she is like a column of smoke, *virgula fumi*, which is born of a fire and goes spiralling up in search of a higher place. Mary aflame with the divine love is carried up like a fragrant smoke to the supreme heights.[97] And she breathes of myrrh and frankincense and every known perfume, signifying thereby that she possesses all the sweet spiritual odors that God, like a perfume merchant, can provide. Her fragrance is spiced by myrrh and frankincense, bitter sorrow

---

temnitur; vel quia seipsum deserit... Unde cum B. Virgo prae omnibus sanctis, mundum spreverit, ac affectu penitus, etiam cum Mundi incola ascendere dicitur... Secundo, explicatio Richardi mihi non displicet, dum ait, 'Per desertum' idem esse ac si diceretur, 'Per desertionem,' quia Beata Virgo, omnia propter Christum deserendo facta est propter Christum, omnium domina." Ibid. (II, 647b). The reference is to Richard of St. Victor († 1181), *Explicatio in Cantica Canticorum*, c. 42: De assumptione Mariae et eius laudibus (PL 196, 523–4).

[96] "Tertio, per 'Desertum' apte intelligenda venit virginitas, ut ingeniose interpretatus est Guillelmus. Quid enim antiquis diebus tam neglectum, atque desertum, quam Virginitas... Ecce virginitas illis temporibus prae amore sobolis, et metu maledicti, quam ex osa, et abominabilis, et quam deserta res fuerit. Per hoc igitur virginitatis desertum Beata Virgo ascendit, quia perpetuam Deo vovens virginitatem, ut dignum Deo fieret habitaculum, maledictionem illam non exhorruit. Unde factum est, ut salva virginitate semen in Israel faceret, et benedictionem illam amplissimam reciperet. 'Benedictionem omnium gentium dedit illi', per quam, singulari miraculo mater Dei facta est. Unde doctissimus Guillelmus dixit: 'Maria amore incorruptionis parata est a sua gente elogium maledictionis incurere; et ecce salva incorruptionis gloria, totus ei mundus proclamat: Benedicta tu in mulieribus." Lib. XIV, hom. XII (II, 647b–648a). On Guilelmus Peraldus, cf. above, footnote 21.

[97] "Congrua sane comparatio Virgini in coelum assumptae: tum quia sicut fumus ex ignis nascitur, et continuo altiorem locum petit; ita B. Virgo, amoris igne succensa, velut fumus aromaticus in superna per coelestia desideria ferebatur. Tum quia, sicut fumus in sublime evectus se subtrahit aspectui; ita B. Virgo in Coelum assumpta, oculis Apostolorum se subduxit. Tum quia, ut recte observavit Guillelmus in commentario huius loci, 'Beata Virgo, instar virgula fumi ex aromatibus fuit, recta per actionem, fragrans per bonam famam sursum erecta per mentis sinceram intentionem.' " Ibid. (II, 648a).

and sweet–scented love, inasmuch as she shared too in the passion and death of her son.[98]

2. *Song of Songs 2, 10.* "*Surge, propera amica mea, columba mea, et veni.*" These words are an illustration also of Mary's Assumption into heaven. In a long quotation from Guilelmus Peraldus the author re–echoes the interpretation that here Christ is calling his mother Mary to rise up and join him. In her love for him she in effect died with him too, and now she is to resurrect like him and be with him in the glory of immortality. She in her fecundity is like a dove, and lovely in her virginity. And she is being summoned to feast, to rejoice and to reign with her son.[99] Adding his own idea to the above, Cartagena proceeds to say that Christ finding it unbearable to reign in heaven without his mother, invites her to join him.

> Once I came to you to be incarnated by you; now come to me to be glorified by me. Once I reposed in your tabernacle; now come to rest in my tabernacle. Arise therefore from the mound of death to the summit of happiness; arise from corruptibility to incorruptibility; arise from the earth into heaven. Come from battles to your triumph, from tears to joy, from pursuits and labors to everlasting rest.[100]

It is appropriate that Mary should be addressed as a dove. The dove set free from the ark of Noah did not find any place where to rest, until it returned back to the ark. Likewise Mary during her whole sojourn on earth could not find a perfect place where she could

---

[98] "Subiungunt tandem: 'Universi pulveris pigmentarii,' ad significandum nihil defuisse spiritualium aroma tum ei, quae coelestium charismatum fontem genuerat. Sane pigmentarius iste, Deus est de quo Iacobus Apostolus inquit: 'Omne datum optimum, et omne donum perfectum desursum est, descendens a Patre luminum' quasi dicat, omne spirituale pigmentum a summo illo pigmentario est. Quia tamen moris est, huic magno pigmentario pigmenta, quae largitur, in pulveres contundere ad maiorem usum, et suaviorem fragrantiam, variis pressuris iustos exercens, ut bonum Christi odorem latius spargant eos contundit. Id certe praestare non praeter misit in Virgine, in qua omnia virtutum aromata ad maiorem redolentiam, variis tribulationibus fuerunt contusa; maxime cum universis filii cruciatibus materno affectu communicabat; quorum sane aromata duo praecipue nominantur, myrrha amari doloris, et thus flagrantis, et fragrantis amoris, quia quantum amabat, tantundem in filii passione dolebat; atque ita thuris, et myrrhae odorem aequaliter spibat." Ibid. (II, 648b).

[99] Ibid. (II, 649a–b).

[100] Ibid. (II, 649b).

rest. And knowing that she would find rest only in heaven, she cried out to God: "*Emitte manum tuam de alto, et libera me de aquis multis.*" [101] And she was heard and that is why she could truly say: "He sends from on high and takes me, he draws me from deep waters" (Ps 17, 17). "He draws me" is "*assumpsit me*" in Latin. The eternal Father sent the Son to meet the mother and take her into the heavenly kingdom, just like Noah extending his arm to take the dove into the ark, after it failed to find anywhere else to go (Gen 8, 9). And the fact that Jesus took Mary into heaven body and soul is signified by the appellation "dove." In Leviticus 1, 14–17 doves are offered to God without being cut into separated parts, unlike a bull, a lamb or a goat destined for sacrifice. So also it pleased God that after death Mary should be offered to him whole, body and soul, in heaven.[102]

3. *Song of Songs 7, 1.* "How beautiful are your feet in their sandals, O Prince's daughter!" These words are seen also to indicate the doctrine of the Assumption of Mary into heaven. When Moses

---

[101] "Beata ergo Virgo in Coelo agnoscens esse requiem suam, ad eam pervenire cupiens, ad Deum clamabat cum patre suo Davide, dicens: 'Emitte manum tuam de alto, et libera me de aquis multis.' Exaudita fuit pro sua reverentia, deprecatio eius, et impletum est in ea, quod idem David praedixerat, eodem Psalmo: 'Misit de summo et accepit me, et assumpsit me de aquis multis.' " Ibid. (II, 650a). Cartagena refers to the words: "Emitte manum tuam de alto, et libera me de aquis multis" as also from Psalm 17 as the words: "Misit de summo, etc." But the supplicatory form is not found at all in the Vulgate nor in the Hebrew. The parallel version of this psalm found in 2 Samuel 22 does not contain them either.

[102] "Etenim aeternus Pater misit Christum Dominum de excelso folio suo, ut ascendenti Virgini obvius fieret, et occurente sibi universa curia coelesti: illam ad secum conregnandum assumeret, et in aeternam requiem introduceret. Quod mihi praeclare significatum videtur in sequentibus verbis: 'Extenditur Noe manum, et apprehensam intulit in arcam.' Sane manus haec extensa Christus fuit qui a Patre missus, in occursum venit matri suae, ut eam susciperet, et in folio gloriae suae collocaret. Adverte tamen oportet, quod ad significandum assumptam fuisse matrem a filio secundum corpus, et animam, notanter vocavit illam, 'columbam,' alludens ad illud Lev. 1. ubi legimus, quod cum boves pecora, et alia animalia in sacrificium Deo offerebantur, in variis partes dividi praecipiebantur,... Cum vero offerebatur, columba divisionem, seu sectionem in varias partes illius prohibebat Dominus... At licet ita etiam id contingerit Beatae Virgini, transacto tamen triduo mortis illius, placuit. Domino hanc columbam integram sibi offerri, absque divisione partium, ut corpore, et anima gloriosa in Coelum migraret." Ibid. (II, 650a–b).

approached to look at the strange sight of the burning bush (Ex 3, 1–6), he was ordered to take off his shoes. To be in the presence of God, one must take off first the sandals, so to say, of one's bodiliness. That is why with reason can the bridegroom extoll the sandalled feet of Mary as she enters into heaven. For she enters into the presence of God in her glorious body, unlike other saints who must first be stripped of their bodies. And that she is called the prince's daughter gives the ground for her singular privilege. She could enter into the presence of the Lord as she is, body and soul, because she is the daughter of the prince. And in this connection, only the king and the queen usually enter into the palace riding a horse. Christ and his mother, as the king and the queen, entered into heaven borne by the horse, as it were, of their bodies, while other mortals must leave theirs behind.[103]

4. *Psalm 47, 4.* This very first text handled by the author to connote the Assumption is better translated by Pagnini : *"Deus in domibus eius notus, ad elevationem,"* than by the Vulgate: *"Deus in domibus eius cognoscetur, cum suscipiet eam."* That is, God is made manifest through his power in performing Mary's *elevatio,* her assumption into heaven. God's might is known enough in creation, but the

---

[103] "Verba illa sponsi in suo epithalamio: 'Quam pulchri sunt gressus tui in calceamentis, filia Principis,' non obscure mihi indicant Assumptionem Virginis in corpore glorioso. Apte hunc locum explicari posse arbitror per illum alium. Exod. 4. (sic) ubi legimus, quod Moyses cupiens miram illam visionem rubi videre: cum ad eam videndam appropinquaret, prohibitus est a Domino accedere, donec exueret se calceamento suo. 'Tolle calceamenta de pedibus tuis,' quasi diceret: si cupis Moyses, videre me, instar ignis ardere, discalceatus accede... Ignis rubi ardens, et lucens, et illum non consumit, expressa imago fuit huius superni ignis significandum Dominus dixit ad Moysem, quod si vellet ad hunc increatum ignem accedere, oportebat illum calceamento corporis expoliari... Merito ergo sponsus laudat gressus Virginis calceatis pedibus in coelum incedentis, quia cum reliqui sancti ascendant in coelum calceamento corporis expoliari (ut enim adnotavit D. Bernardus in comment. huius loci, calceamentum, utpote ex mortuorum aninalium pelli. confectum mortale hoc corpus designat) ipsa tamen corporis sui calceamento ornata, pulchris gressibus intercedens in caelestem aulam proficiscitur. Cum autem sponsus, 'Filiam Principis' B. Virginem compellat, plane mihi videtur huius tam singularis privilegii rationem nobis exhibuisse. Etenim solus Rex, et Regina tantummodo in palatium suum Regium ingredi equo vecti consueverunt... Christus vero, et Deipara, tanquam Rex et Regina in Coelum intrarunt equo corporis sui vecti, ceteri vero sancti homines animo tantum, corpore velut equo, in morte deposito, et in sepulchro relicto." Ibid. (II, 653b–654b).

entrance of Mary into the eternal beatitude in her glorious body makes the divine power more evident also in his own house.[104]

5. *Psalm 131, 8.* "*Surge Domine in requiem tuam, tu et arca sanctificationis tuae.*" Two Byzantine theologians, Nicephorus Callistus Xantopulus and Michael Glycas, are cited by the author as interpreting this passage to mean Christ's and Mary's heavenly rest in their glorified bodies.[105] Thus Christ as it were is being addressed :

> Rise up by reason of humanity which alone is capable of resurrection, you and also the ark of your holiness, that is Mary your mother, in whom as in a mystical ark of testimony were contained the rod, the tablets of the law, and the manna, that is the Son of God the Father, the power of God, wisdom, and the most sweet manna of mercy.[106]

And as regards the ark, just as once it received a new cart (1 Sam 6, 7), so also it can be said of Mary, the mystical ark, that in her

---

[104] "Verba illa Davidica: 'Deus in domibus eius cognoscetur, cum suscipiet eam' Assumptionem Deiparae Mariae non obscure praesignasse mihi videntur... Caeterum, per haec omnia cognoscebatur Deus extra propriam domum suam: hodierna autem die cum B. Virgo in coelum suscipitur, singulari modo cognoscetur, et innotescit illius magnificentia in propria eius domo. 'Deus in domibus eius cognoscetur, cum suscipiet eam, scilicet in aeterna beatitudine, ut notat glossa interlinearis, ubi notanda est singularis versio Pagnini, qui in hunc modum praedicta verba transfert: 'Deus in domibus eius notus, ad elevationem.' Quid clarius potuisset dici ad significandum Dei potentiam valde innotuisse, cum Beata Virgo ad Coeli cacumina super angelos fuit elevata..." Lib. XIV, hom. XII (II, 645b–646b).

[105] "Quod vero divinum hoc Dei Genitricis corpus resurrecturum fuerat, propheta quoque David praedixit: 'Exsurge, inquiens, Domine, tu et arca sanctificationis tuae.' " Nicephorus Callistus Xantopulus, op. cit., lib. 2, c. 23 (PG 145, 815). The author cites c. 13 (sic). Lib. XIV, hom. XIII (II, 653a).

"Consimili nimirum modo et ipsam Dei Matrem ex mortuis resurrecturam fuisse quo Filius resurrexerat, multo ante beatus ille Davides huiusmodi verbis significaverat: 'Surge, Domine, in requiem tuam, tu et arca sanctificationis tuae.' Nam quia norat Davidis eam quae Christum utero suo gestasset ac illam ipsam ob causam arca sanctitatis esset atque nuncuparetur, eodem pacto resurrecturam e sepulcro quo et natus ex ipsa Christus Dei Filius et Deus resurrexit, idcirco non abs re consimilem utriusque resuscitationem ex mortuis multo ante pictura quadam expressit. Etenim, ni res ita se haberet, non sane posteaquam dixerat: 'Surge, Domine,' subiecisset: 'Et arca sanctificationis tuae.' Quapropter hac quidem in parte amplius haesitare noli." Michael Glycas, *Annales*, op. cit., (PG 158, 439). Ibid.

[106] Lib. XIV, hom. XIII (II, 653a–b).

assumption into heaven she was fitted, so to say, with a new cart, her glorified body.[107]

6. *Psalm 44, 10.* "*Adstitit Regina a dextris tuis in vestitu deaurato, circumdata varietate.*" St. Athanasius is mentioned by Cartagena to be of the opinion that these words speak of Mary's Assumption into heaven in her glorious body.[108] And the author concurs, because no queen is greater than Mary, the Mother of God, who bore the king of the universe, and because nobody else other than Christ's mother endowed with grace above all creatures can be truly said to stand at the right hand of God, and finally because nobody else could be so richly clad as her glorified body.[109]

7. *Psalm 86, 2.* "The Lord prefers the gates of Zion to all the tabernacles of Jacob." In the mystical sense the city here referred to is Mary, raised up on a mountain, i.e. exalted over both the Church militant and the Church triumphant.[110] The two gates are birth and death : normally the coming in original sin and the going back to dust. God watched over these two in Mary. There must be a corres-

---

[107] "Idipsum etiam confirmat, quod olim in figura praecepit Deus, quod arca Domini portaretur posita super plaustrum novum. Quid enim aptius significare potest, quam quod mystica arca Maria in die assumptionis posita fuit in plaustro corporis sui, novis et gloriosis dotibus exornato?" Ibid. (II, 653b).

[108] Actually it is Pseudo–Athanasius, whom Cartagena is referring to and later quotes, ibid. (II, 655a): "Ea nunc ut Regina assistens a dextris filii ubique regnantis, quasi in vestitu deaurato, incorruptionis, et immortalitatis circumamicta et variegata, sacris et solemnibus verbis celebratur: non quidem secundum, aut quasi sine corpore, et carne assistat, sed quod induta sit incorruptibilitate, et immortalitate. Variegata rursus est quantum attinet ad ossa sanctissima, quae eius carnem suffulciunt: nam ex carne eius, et ex ossibus eius, veluti ex veteri Adamo, novus iste Adam, ut viscera eius expleret, costam sibi finxit, nimirum istam incarnationem, eamque semel indutam perpetuo gestat: ac proinde, ista nova Eva, mater vitae, appellatur, variegataque permanet ad primitias vitae immortalis omnium viventium." This direct quotation by the author varies somewhat from the text of Pseudo–Athanasius, op. cit. (PG 28, 938).

[109] "S. Athanasius sermone de Sanctissima Deipara, prope finem, tomo tertio, de eadem Virginis Assumptione in corpore glorioso intelligit, et merito quidem, nam quaenam alia proprie magis Regina, quam Maria, quae Regem universorum peperit? et quaenam alia verius dici potest adstare a dextris Dei, quam Genitrix ipsius, cui maiore gloriae charismata prae omnibus aliis contulit? et quidnam aliud potest esse vestitus ille deauratus, quam corpus Mariae glorificatum?" Lib. XIV, hom. XIII (II, 653b).

[110] Lib. XIV, hom. XI (II, 637b).

pondence and harmony between them, the beginning and the end.[111] Mary came and was born immaculately. She died and went into the heavenly paradise. In dying she did not sustain corruption, but after three days imitated her son and was transferred to his right hand, her soul putting on the garment of her immortal body.[112]

8. *Ecclesiasticus 24, 18.* "*Quasi palma exaltata sum in Cades.*" Cartagena understands this exaltation applied to Mary as referring to her Assumption, inasmuch as Cades, according to him, means "*translatio.*" Hence Mary's Assumption connotes actually her transfer from the Church militant to the heavenly and triumphant Church.[113] She is the mystical palm, which however cannot even with its height surpass the cedar tree, i.e. Christ. For although she is enthroned above all angels and men, she still does not overtake Christ either in glory or in his innate incorruptibility. Also, Christ rose up to immortal life much ahead of her.[114]

9. *Genesis 2, 18.* "It is not good that the man should be alone." God said these words in Paradise and consequently gave Adam his companion Eve. In the mystical sense these words are true too of the Second Adam and the Second Eve, Christ and Mary. The two together in their glorified bodies are the first inhabitants of the heavenly Paradise. Mary is there too where the New Adam is.[115]

10. *Numbers 13, 24–26.* The Scout sent to reconnoiter the land of Canaan came back with the vine branch and its cluster of grapes to demonstrate the produce of the country. To one meditating this holy text the suggestion is that Christ, as the cluster of grapes, and

---

[111] Ibid. (II, 641a).

[112] Ibid. (II, 644a–b).

[113] " 'Quasi palma...,' hoc est, in assumptione mea, quia *Cades* interpretatur *Translatio*. Quis autem non videat Deiparae assumptionem, nihil aliud fuisse, quam translationem quandam eiusdem ex hac militanti ad coelestem, et triumphantem Ecclesiam?" Lib. XIV, hom. VIII (II, 614b).

[114] Ibid. (II, 618a–b).

[115] "...Dominus dixit: 'Non est bonum, hominem esse solum,' et ideo dedit ei consortium simile sibi, unde Adam, et Eva primi fuerunt introducti in Paradisum, ut habitatores, et incolae illius; reste in sensu mistico adumbrari intelligemus secundum Adam, et secundam Evam, Christum, et Mariam primos fuisse habitatores in corpore glorioso coelestis Paradisi." Lib. XIV, hom. XIII (II, 653a).

his mother, as the vine branch from which the cluster hangs, are now glorified body and shoul. They are shown here to make us realize how wonderful our heavenly promised land is.[116]

11. *Exodus 14, 15–31.* The waters parted to let the sons of Israel through, and as Moses again stretched out his hand over the sea, the sea returned to its bed engulfing the Egyptians. Through death Mary's soul too parted from her body, but they later were reunited by Christ to confound the enemy.[117]

12. *1 Samuel 30, 24.* It was once made into a law among the Israelites that those who stay with the baggage receive as much share in the booty as those who go down to the battle. Similarly, although Christ alone fought the battle of Calvary and alone won victory over the enemy, Mary remained behind with the baggage, with the cross, the crown of thorns, the nails, and the linen cloth. And just as Christ was recognized victor through the glorification of his body, so also Mary deserved to be remunerated body and soul with her son.[118]

---

[116] "Rursus palmes qui, ut Numerorum 13 legimus, fuit cum botro pariter adductus ex terra promissa ad cognoscendam terrae bonitatem, quid aliud eleganti sacrarum literarum meditatori insinuat, quam Christum, tanquam botrum, et matrem tanquam palmitem, ex quo pendebat, corpore et animo iam glorificatos nobis esse ostensos, ut coelestis promissae nobis terrae bonitatem, virtutemque agnoscamus, tanquam dulcissimos eius fructus." Ibid. (II, 653b). Except for the first few words, this excerpt from the author is a word for word repetition of Salmeron, op. cit., p. 304.

[117] "Item mare rubrum divisum ad ingressum filiorum Israel, et postea unitum contra Pharaonem et Aegyptios, Maria sorore Moysi in tympano cantante, quid est iuxta spiritum, nisi anima Mariae a corpore eius divisa per mortem; et rursus per Christum, quasi per virgam Moysis unitam, confusis doemonibus, ac invidis Iudaeis?" Ibid. (II, 653b).

[118] "Tandem lib. 1. Reg. c. 30. legimus praecepisse Dominum, ut parta victoria in bello, aequale praemium reportarent pugnantes in illo, et qui remanebant ad sarcinas, et supellectilia exercitus custodienda. Non dissimiliter, quamvis solus Christus Dominus in praelio montis Calvariae cum hoste pugnaverit, et eundem expugnaverit... ipse enim solus sanguine suo nos redimit, et hostem devicit... Ipsa tamen Virgo Deipara remansit quasi ad sarcinas, et supellectilia supremi Ducis Christi servanda: ipsa custodivit crucem, clavos, coronam, linteum quo erat praecinctus ad celanda, quae natura propalare veretur. Unde simili praemio quo Christus invictissimus dux fuit remuneratus per glorificationem sui corporis, meruit B. Virgo in Caelum ascendens, remunerari. Regnat igitur cum filio mater animae, et corporis gloriosis dotibus insignita." Ibid. (II, 654b).

13. *Matthew 10, 41.* "Anyone who welcomes a prophet because he is a prophet will have a prophet's reward." Juan de Cartagena thinks this NT passage can be properly accommodated to argue for Mary's Assumption into heaven. First of all he understands "a prophet's reward" as obviously the reward that a prophet himself would receive from God for his function as a prophet. In the light of this meaning, since Mary welcomed in and offered the hospitality of her womb for nine months to our Redeemer, it would be nothing but correct that she should receive the Redeemer's reward, which is Christ's exaltation and bodily glorification in heaven. Having cooperated in the redemption of mankind, Mary too shares in this glorification in heaven body and soul.[119]

14. *Apocalypse 12, 1.* "Now a great sign appeared in heaven: a woman, adorned with the sun." This vision of the woman expresses for the author clearly enough Mary's Assumption into heaven body and soul. John saw a woman adorned with the sun. Now a woman is only so body and soul, and either the body or the soul by itself would be only a part of a woman and not the whole woman. That is why it is easy to understand that the sacred writer is here picturing Mary glorified body and soul in heaven.[120]

---

[119] "...cum Deipara Maria hospitio uteri sui per novem menses Redemptorem mundi suscepisset, aequum erat, ut sicut qui prophetam recipit in nomine Prophetae, mercedem Prophetae accipit, non secus ipsa qui recepit Redemptorem in nomine Redemptoris, mercedem Redemptoris, quantum decebat eius matrem acciperet. Merces autem Redemptoris sanguinem pro nobis in patibulo Crucis effundentis, exaltatio fuit sui nominis, et gloria corporis, ita ut immortalis gloriae dotibus donatus in anima, et corpore in Coelum scanderit. Simili ergo praemii genere gaudet Virgo, tantoque huiusmodi premio Redemptoris Deiparam decebat remunerari, quanto manifestius est, ipsam ad Redemptionem generis humani cooperatam fuisse, praebendo Christo sanguinem, quo mediante, tanquam unico precio, ipse solus genus humanum redemit." Lib. XIV, hom. XII (II, 651a–b).

[120] "...visio illa Ioannis... non obscure mihi exprimere videtur assumptionem Deiparae Virginis secundum animam, et corpus: quia idem Ioannes aperte testatur, se vidisse ibi Virginem iam suscitatam dum ait: 'Mulier amicta Sole.' Etenim cum nec anima seorsum, nec corpus seorsum 'mulier' dici possit, sed pars duntaxat mulieris, plane mihi significasse videtur, vidisse Mariam corpore, et anima constantem, splendidissimisque gloriae dotibus conspicuam." Ibid. (II, 651b). Cf. H. Gollinger, *Das "großen Zeichen" von Apokalypse 12* (Würzburg, 1971), p. 27 ff., on Mary as the woman according to some interpretation; and p. 35 f., on the pericope's scant connection with the mystery of the Assumption.

PART THREE

JUAN DE CARTAGENA'S BAROQUE SCRIPTURISM

We have tried in Part I to present as completely as possible the life and works of Juan de Cartagena. To appreciate the complexities of his principal work, the *Homiliae Catholicae*, we have looked at its structural dynamics — its composition, orientation and characteristics. Then in Part II we have attempted a doctrinal examination of Cartagena's homilies through a representative sampling of his major theological accomplishment, his Mariology, especially with regards the dogmas of Mary's Immaculate Conception, her perpetual virginity, and her Assumption into heaven. Efforts have been made particularly to set in relief the author's use of Sacred Scripture in his treatment of the Marian Mysteries. It is the purpose of Part III to project Juan de Cartagena in the context of his *Zeitgeist*. We want to understand the man and his scripturism in the light of the historico–cultural and theological factors contributing to the peculiar biblical dimension of his homilies. Here is a case of a 17th century Scholastic theologian turning to Sacred Scripture in homilies to proclaim the glories of the Blessed Virgin Mary. How did he do it ?

"Baroque" is here taken not in its derogatory connotation of something stylistically exaggerated and bizarre, but in the sense of the Western culture of the 17th century. We use the term here in a manner distinctive enough to situate Cartagena on a theologico–cultural map.[1] In response to the crisis brought on by the Protestant Reformation, the Catholic Church of the 16th century experienced a surge of renewal and self–consciousness. This gave impetus to a further development out of the Italian Renaissance. In theology, the Baroque period which followed the Tridentine start at self–

---

[1] Cf. L. Lenhart and F. Stegmüller, "Barock," in LThK, I, 1258–1265. On the history of the term baroque, see Benedetto Croce, *Storia della Età Barocca in Italia* (Bari, 1929), p. 20 ff.

reformation closely coincided at its high–point with Juan de Cartagena's own mature years as a theologian, i.e. from the end of the
16th century to the middle of the 17th century. We shall in this
final part of our study try to see how typical of his time Cartagena was.

We shall first present him within the context of the "rediscovery"
of the mystical interpretation of Sacred Scripture. Then we shall show
his scripturism in the light of Baroque homiletics. And our whole
study of Juan de Cartagena will be concluded with a brief resume.

CHAPTER SEVEN

CARTAGENA'S USE OF SACRED SCRIPTURE

In the introduction to Part II, we said that Cartagena's use of Sacred Scripture more than anything else can give us an understanding of the man as a theologian. By sheer bulk alone Scripture plays a dominant role in the presentations of the *Homiliae Catholicae*. Without much comment, we have already offered his orchestration of Sacred Scripture in connection with Mary's Immaculate Conception, her virginity, and her Assumption into heaven. Without any critique, we have noted his generous employment of the mystical interpretation. Now we would like to examine the mechanics of Cartagena's scripturism, i.e. his methodology in using and explaining the sacred texts. Cartagena was not an exegete *ex professo ;* he never gave a clarification of the hermeneutics he was employing. We can nonetheless, so to say, draw a trawl through his homilies to gather from them pertinent materials.

It is time then for us to focus our attention on Juan de Cartagena's mode of Scripture interpretation. What did he understand exactly by mystical sense? Why did he resort to it? What theological thoughts were behind such an approach to the word of God?

A. SENSUS LITERALIS

Like most theologians of his time Cartagena accepts that in the use of Sacred Scripture priority is to be given to the *sensus literalis*. It should be established first before anything else.[2] The literal sense is the meaning historically affirmed by the sacred words. As St. Thomas Aquinas points out, "In everything that Scripture thus passes on, the truth of history should be taken as the fundament, and the spiritual expositions are to be built upon it." [3] Cartagena follows this generally accepted principle, and gives first the literal sense of the text he is dealing with before going into its spiritual sense.[4]

---

[2] Lib. I, hom. XV (I, 75b).

[3] Thomas Aquinas, *Summa Theol.*, I, q. 102, art. 1; Cartagena, ibid. Cf. M. Reyero, *Thomas von Aquin als Exeget* (Einsiedeln, 1971), pp. 153–168.

[4] In Lib. I, hom. XV, e.g., Cartagena tries to settle first the question as

As for its use, the literal sense of Scripture, since it is clearly intended by the Holy Spirit, has decisive and probative force with regards to matters of faith.[5] Echoing Salmeron, the author admits that this sense alone has convincing argumentative value when it comes to dealing with the *"rebelles Haereticos."* [6] In his own use of the literal sense as *dicta probantia*, for example, Cartagena confesses that Sacred Scripture does not *"loco aliquo expresso"* affirm Mary's Immaculate Conception and her incorruptibility and bodily Assumption into heaven.[7] On the other hand, he claims that Scripture expressedly, i.e. literally, speaks about Mary's perpetual virginity, first of all in the prophecy of Isaiah that a virgin would conceive and bear a son,[8] and then in the explicit words of the Gospel accounts that the Holy Spirit himself would overshadow her and that Mary was later found to be with child "through the Holy Spirit." [9] The doctrine is therefore historically and literally founded on *"tot apertis prophetarum oraculis, ac Evangelicis monumentis."* [10]

To determine what he thinks to be the literal sense, Cartagena makes some attempt to utilize textual criticism, linguistics and history. He weighs different version and readings, giving preference naturally to the Vulgate sanctioned by Trent. Nevertheless he makes judicious comparisons with the Septuagint or with Pagninus' or Vatablus' translations.[11] Obviously not in command of either Greek or Hebrew beyond what he must have acquired as a Jesuit student, the author never makes any original Greek citation, and with Hebrew he has done so only in the case of the word *almah*.[12] All other

---

to whether there was really a "paradisum voluptatis" as related in Genesis, before mystically interpreting the word in relation to Mary's Immaculate Conception. Cf. also Lib. I, hom. XV (I, 80b–81a). Another example is the homily entitled: "Singula haec verba: Magnificat anima mea Dominum: secundum literalem, et mysticum sensum pulchre explicantur." Lib. VI, hom. X (I, 588a).

[5] Cf. Lib. I, hom. XIX (I, 99b). See Salmeron, *Commentarii*, op. cit., Prolog. XIX, p. 340b.

[6] Lib. XIV, hom. XIII (II, 653a). Salmeron, loc. cit.

[7] Lib. I, hom. XIX (I, 100a).

[8] Lib. VII, hom. VII (I, 758b).

[9] Lib. V, hom. XII (I, 462b) and Lib. VII, hom. IX (I, 773a).

[10] Lib. VII, hom. IX (I, 773b).

[11] Lib. VII, hom. VI (I, 753b); Lib. I, hom. II (I, 11a); Lib. I, hom. IV (I, 22a); Lib. I, hom. XI (I, 55a); Lib. I, hom. XIII (I, 65b & 70b).

Regarding the author's preference for the Vulgate, cf. above, chapter III, footnote 31.

[12] Lib. VII, hom. VII (I, 758b–759a).

references to Hebrew versions or peculiarities are indirect, apparently in dependance on some other professional linguists.[13] Going into historical backgrounds, he recalls for instance the Jewish custom regarding the "coming together" or cohabitation of the newly married,[14] and the social scope of the term "brother" among the Jews.[15]

But true to the level of hermeneutics during his time, Cartagena often interprets a word by itself, rather than a whole passage or text and in the context of the whole work. Thus, to cite a couple of instances, he squeezes the word *Dominus* in the angel's salutation to Mary to draw from it legal elaborations that do not seem warranted by the context. Or he bears down on a phrase like "of her" was born Christ, as expressed by St. Paul in his letter to the Galatians, to base his whole interpretation on it.[16] This "word–exegesis," however, is not yet so bad in Cartagena, as it would later be in the century, earning the derisive name of *sensus commaticus*. Moreover, as we shall see in the next chapter, the method is all in conjunction with the so–called *conceptus* preaching.

B. SENSUS MYSTICUS

While acknowledging the primacy of the literal sense in interpreting Scripture, Cartagena knows only too well that it is not sufficient for his pastoral purpose of proclaiming the mysteries of the faith, about which the following chapter on homiletical purpose will be concerned. As we have already observed, he has to admit that not everything being taught about Mary is backed up by expressed words from the sacred pages. It is here that the *sensus mysticus* plays such a pivotal role in the *Homiliae Catholicae* that it becomes a dominant factor in the work.

The author holds the thesis that the same words of Scripture may contain not only literal but also mystical meanings.[17] This mystical sense comes only after the literal and cannot replace it.[18] Although in matters of faith the mystical sense does not make a weighty argument, it is nonetheless of great importance because of

---

[13] Lib. VII, hom. IX (I, 773b).

[14] Lib. VII, hom. XIII (I, 804a–b).

[15] Lib. VII, hom. XIII (I, 803a–b).

[16] Lib. V, hom. VIII (I, 434a); Lib. VII, hom. IX (I, 773a).

[17] Lib. XIV, hom. I (II, 559a).

[18] Cf. above, footnote 4.

the Church's own use of it and because many respected theologians
have recourse to it.[19] The divine wisdom disposing of everything
knew that some hidden mysteries would later offer a lot of difficulties
to believers. Therefore God through various types and images and
metaphors has made it easier to the human mind to grasp such mysteries. The figures in Scripture are much like a finger pointing to the
truth of the mysteries involved.[20] The mystical sense then has a va-
luable religious pedagogical intent. It assists the human mind of a
believer to grasp divine mysteries. In addition, the author is of the
mind that by means of these scriptural comparisons and figures the
shamelessness of the heretics and the querulousness of the Jews can
be checked and the faithful made stronger in the truth.[21] For the
mystical sense nourishes the piety of the people.[22] "It edifies them,
because it is true, and the author of Scripture indicates through his
Church that it is not just catering to superstitions but to the truth." [23]
With its informative value is closely bound the ascetical value of
the mystical sense.

In his homilies Cartagena is rather vague as to what exactly
he understands by mystical sense. He uses the term itself quite
frequently.[24] He comes up too with expressions like *"mystica intelligentia,"* [25] *"mystica interpretatio,"* [26] *"mystice intelligere,"* [27] and *"mys-*

---

[19] Lib. I, hom. XIX (I, 99b).

[20] "Consuevit Divina Sapientia, quae suaviter omnia disponit, obscura quaedam arcana, quae multis difficilia creditu futura praenovit, variis Tropis, ac fi-
guris praedelineare, ut hac ratione humana ruditas miram rei figuratae ad figuram
consonantiam observans, facilius eis assentiret. Praevidens ergo Deus quorumdam
fluctuantes animos, imo et negaturos fore immaculatam Matris suae Conceptionem,
voluit, ad eos in hac veritate firmandos, ac stabiliendos, varios Tropos, ac figuras
praemittere, quae illam velut digito commostrarent." Lib. I, hom. VII (I, 34a).

[21] "...ex divinis eloquis varios tropos, singularesque similitudines depromam, quibus magis inverecunda Haereticorum, et Iudaeorum petulantia retundatur, virginitatisque illius Catholica veritas magis solidetur." Lib. VII, hom. X
(I, 774b). Didacus Stella prescribed the allegorical sense for preaching on the
same ground. See his *De Modo Concionandi Liber* (Coloniae, 1586), p. 6b.

[22] Lib. XIV, hom. I (II, 559a). Salmeron, loc. cit.

[23] Lib. XIV, hom. XIII (II, 653a).

[24] E.g., Lib. I, hom. II (I, 9a); Lib. I, hom. XII (I, 62b); Lib. V, hom.
XVI (I, 494a); Lib. VI, hom. V (I, 555a); Lib. XIV, hom. XI (II, 637b); Lib.
XIV, hom. VI (II, 601a).

[25] Lib. I, hom. VIII (I, 37b).

[26] Ibid. (I, 38a).

[27] Lib. I, hom. VI (I, 31b).

tice accommodari." [28] Or in his expositions he refers to things as mystical, like *"mystica arca"* and *"mysticum templum."* [29] He contrasts the mystical and spiritual with what is historical and literal, and uses it interchangeably with *"allegoricus"* and *"intellectualis."* [30]

1. *Salmeron's influence.* Cartagena never explicitates in so many words what he means by the mystical sense; he simply uses it and practices it. It spills over the pages of his work. Its comprehensive scope and applicability renders its vagueness, due to the absence of any systematic explanation, all the more intriguing, if not frustrating. For the theory of the *sensus mysticus* we turn to another Spaniard, a former Jesuit colleague of the author, Alfonso Salmeron. The influence of this man on Juan de Cartagena is deep and far–reaching. Our foregoing considerations have sufficiently shown the author's many references to him, not to mention the instances where Cartagena without any acknowledgment simply borrows from him.

According to the time's hermeneutics characterized by the revival of spiritual exegesis, Sacred Scripture has two principal senses, the literal and the mystical. Under the mystical are grouped the allegorical, the tropological, and the anagogical.[31] Salmeron defined the mystical sense as *"qui designatur ex rebus ipsis vere gestis per voces expressis, ex intentione Spiritus sancti."* [32] It is what is meant by the

---

[28] Lib. I, hom. IV (I, 24b).

[29] Lib. I, hom. VI (I, 32a & b); Lib. I, hom. VII (I, 35b); Lib. VI, hom. VIII (I, 577a); Lib. I, hom. XII (I, 60b); Lib. I, hom. XVI (I, 88a); Lib. III, hom. II (I, 250b); Lib. XIV, hom. VI (II, 601b); Lib. XIII, hom. VII (II, 556b).

[30] Lib. I, hom. XV (I, 75b); Lib. XIII, hom. VII (II, 556b & 557a).

[31] John Cassian's († c. 435) distinction of the four senses of the Scripture: 1) the historical or literal, 2) the allegorical, 3) the moral or tropological, and 4) the anagogical or eschatological, in his *Collationes*, 14, 8 (PL 49, 964), eventually gave birth to the famous couplet from the Middle Ages:
"Littera gesta docet, quid credas allegoria;
Moralis quid agas, quo tendas anagogia."
Jerusalem is the well–known example of these four senses: historically, it is the Jewish city; allegorically, the Church of Christ; tropologically, the soul of man; and anagogically, the heavenly city. The couplet itself is attributed to the Dominican Augustinus de Dacia († 1282). Cf. H. de Lubac, *Exégèse Médiévale*, I, p. 129 ff.

[32] Salmeron, op. cit., Prolog. XIX, p. 340. He defines the literal sense as "qui spectatur ab Spiritu sancto, et per voces proprias, aut translatas immediate exprimitur, aut per res ipsas vocibus interdum non expressas immediate assumitur." Ibid. Cf. Prolog. VII, p. 73b.

"things and deeds" verbally noted in Sacred Scripture and intended by the Holy Spirit. Prophetical visions and parables are not included, since they properly belong to the literal sense. Not every text of Scripture has a mystical sense, although they all have literal meaning.[33] That in some scriptural text a mystical interpretation can also be drawn out of the literal sense is explained by the companion of St. Ignatius to be founded on God's distinctive art of speech with man. God, so to say, uses three sets of alphabets to communicate with men. The first is the verbal alphabet normally used in human communication and literature. The second is the symbolical alphabet of things, as in a parable, for instance, by which we are led to higher significations. And the third alphabet, exclusive and proper to Sacred Scripture, can be termed the salvation history alphabet, by which mysteries of Christ and his Church are foreshadowed and delineated in the persons, things and events of both the Old and New Testaments.[34] In this last mentioned alphabet *"ex intentione divina,"* which is the basis of the mystical sense, we can see that for the Spanish exegete the mystical sense is in principle not really different from what we call the *sensus typicus*.[35] But only in principle, because in practise the mystical sense is more inclusive. Interestingly, Salmeron pictured Sacred Scripture as *"liber ille involutus, qui erat scriptus intus, et foris"* – borrowing the expressions of Ez 2, 10 and Apoc 5, 1. Exteriorly the Bible speaks through words, interiorly through things themselves; exteriorly and openly in the New Testament, interiorly

---

[33] Ibid., Prolog. XIX, p. 342a–b.

[34] "Quomodo igitur asserimus, homines et vocibus, et rebus per illas significatis alias res indicare? Dicendum est triplex esse veluti alphabetum, quo Deus ad nos loqui voluit. Primum est vocum sive verborum: secundum est alphabetum inferiorum rerum pro arbitrio confictarum ad alias res grandiores, et excellentiores a posite significandas... Deus vero in sacris literis, non tantum verbis, sed et proverbiis, et perpertuis rerum allegoriis, et parabolis in utroque Testamento, ad nos erudiendos, et a vitiis avocandos saepe uti consuevit. Tertium Alphabetum, et sacris literis tantummodo proprium, est rerum vere gestarum ab hominibus, quibus maxima Messiae, et sponsae suae Ecclesiae mysteria in factis, et historiis Veteris Testamenti, vel Novi adumbrare, et delineare voluit. Hoc autem sola Divina arte, et sapientia alphabetum inventum est." Ibid., Prolog. VII, pp. 72b–73a.

[35] "Deinde statuendum ut solidum sensum, qui elicitur in primo, et secundo alphabeto, literalem sive historicum; sensum vero in tertio, solum esse mysticum et spiritualem." Ibid., p. 73a. Regarding the mystical sense as also typical, cf. ibid., p. 73b.

and latently in the Old Testament.[36] The accomodated use of the two above Scripture passages to elucidate the meaning of the mystical sense is already a widened understanding of it. It shows firstly an understanding of allegory, which due to the frequency of its use becomes equivalent to the mystical sense, that can interpret anything in the OT to be symbolizing a divine truth or mystery. In effect, the mystical sense, i.e. the allegorical sense, becomes a wide–ranging metaphor, which evidently goes beyond a mere typology.[37] Salmeron also asserted that allegories are also found in the NT, which taken in conjunction with the above definition of allegory means that technically anything and everything in Sacred Scripture can be allegorized or mystically interpreted.[38] This inclusive and broad latitude of the mystical sense is further enhanced by a built–in extensiveness and pluriformity of things mystically under consideration. Salmeron differentiated the literal from the mystical sense in that the former is very limited as far as meaning is concerned. The latter on the other hand does not only have the allegorical, tropological and anagogical significations of one and same thing, but also contains in each of these three divisions as many possibilities and variations as a thing can have different qualities, relations and applications.[39] We shall be treating this aspect in our consideration below of the profundity of God's word.

The danger of an arbitrary and merely subjective mystical interpretation of the sacred pages is obvious enough. Hence Salmeron himself had to give a warning against any forced and unfounded extraction of mystical sense.[40] Incidentally, Erasmus spoke up too against the same danger of wholly imagining the mystical sense. He

---

[36] Ibid., p. 69a. Similarly Augustine taught: "In vetere novum latet, et in novo vetus pateat." *Quaest. in Heptateuchum*, 2, 73 (PL 34, 625). Cf. de Lubac, op. cit., 177–187.

[37] Salmeron defines scriptural allegory so: "Illa est, quando res, quae corpore gestae, aut gerendae sunt, ut symbola, et figurae aliarum rerum assumuntur, ut Christi, et regni eius; sive quod hic habet in Ecclesia militante, sive eius quod habet in triumphante." Ibid., p. 75b.

[38] Ibid., Prolog. XIX, p. 345a.

[39] "Hinc sit ut sensu literales paucissimi existant, mystici vero non solum diversarum specierum, ut Allegoriae, Tropologiae, et Anagogiae, sed etiam unius, et eiusdem speciei quam plurimi: nam plures possunt esse allegorici, et anagogici, et plures tropologici: quod contingit ob varias rerum virtutes, et variam rationem ad diversas res applicandi." Ibid., p. 342b.

[40] Ibid., Prolog. VII, pp. 71b–72a.

would accept the mystical sense as far as typology is concerned even for dogmatic argumentation, but not the open–door allegory to which it has been in practise reduced, which he thought is good only for oratorical purposes.[41] Salmeron, without paying attention to this distinction by Erasmus, sharply replied against the Rotterdamer's comment that some Fathers have a "playful" inclination for allegories, by saying that the new exegetes themselves (including Erasmus, of course) are indulging in a destructive game.[42] It seems that Eramus had been classed as a vocal opponent of the mystical sense precisely because of his narrower understanding of it in opposition to Salmeron's, for instance.

2. *All–inclusive allegorizing.* In the light of the above understanding of the mystical sense according to Salmeron, on whom the author relies, we can now better comprehend Cartagena's own employment of it in his *Homiliae Catholicae*. Salmeron provided the theory for Cartagena's practise. Under the term *sensus mysticus* the author includes practically everything not belonging to the historical or literal sense. The scope of the spiritual interpretation spans then for him an extended sort of typology, accommodation and take–all allegory. In effect, anything in the Bible can be mystically expounded. Let us cite some examples. In the spirit of the typology between Adam–Eve and Christ–Mary, the author applies Genesis 2, 18: "It is not good for man to be alone" in the mystical sense as foreshadowing Christ's loneliness in heaven and Mary's subsequent assumption and reunion

---

[41] Erasmus, *De Ratione Concionandi* (Basileae, 1544), pp. 643 & 670; against fantasizing, pp. 663 & 648; for allegory in preaching, pp. 641, 673 & 675.

[42] Salmeron, op. cit., p. 69b. Cf. M. Neumayr, *Die Schriftpredigt im Barock* (Paderborn, 1938), pp. 49–50.

Re. Patristic exegesis' mystico–allegorical tendencies and its endurance through the Middle Ages, cf. H. de Lubac, *Exégèse Médiévale*, I–V (Paris, 1959–1964); Beryl Smalley, *The Bible in the Middle Ages* (Notre Dame, 1964); S. Spicq, *Exquisse d'une Histoire de l'Exegese Latine au Moyen Age* (Paris, 1944); R. Brown, "Hermeneutics," in *The Jerome Biblical Commentary* (London, 1968), II, 605–623, and his *The 'Sensus Plenior' of Sacred Scripture* (Baltimore, 1955), pp. 29–67; Henri Crouzel, "Spiritual Exegesis," in *Sacramentum Mundi*, I (London, 1968), 201–207.

The Reformers vigorously objected to spiritual exegesis, but were themselves not above employing it. Cf. Victor Baroni, *La Contra–Reforme devant la Bible* (Lausanne, 1943); J. Lecler, "Littéralisme biblique et typologie au XVIe siecle," *Recherches de science religieuse*, 51 (1953) 76–95; R. M. Grant, *The Bible and the Church* (New York, 1948), pp. 111–114; de Lubac, op. cit., II, 427–453.

with him.[43] Proverbs 8, 22–24, which the author takes to be speaking of the uncreated Wisdom or the Word Incarnate being with God from all eternity, to his mind can in the mystical sense be easily "adapted" to Mary to show her own eternal predestination to sinlessness, just as the Church in her liturgy has often "accommodated" this text to her.[44] This is then a case of a mystical accommodation of a text sanctioned by Church practise. Apocalypse 12, 1, the great sign of a woman with the sun, Cartagena points out, although held by many commentators to be referring to the Church, is also taught by others to be picturing Mary in the mystical sense.[45] This is an instance of a Marian mystical interpretation of a NT text, as based on the authority of some Fathers and theologians. Of this sort are the many passages from the Song of Songs and the Psalms explained by Cartagena in the mystical sense as applying to Mary, on the authoritative words of the Fathers and *Doctores* especially of the Middle Ages.[46] And inasmuch as Cartagena was not a professional exegete but in this regard more of a compiler, in most cases his mystical interpretations or adaptations are presented on the authority of others.

Particularly abundant in his homilies are his mystical understanding and allegories of biblical personages, things and happenings, packaged as *"metaphorae et similitudines."* [47] An illustration is the *"terra alleviata"* of Zabulon (Is 9, 1). Meaning a tax–exempted piece of land in the literal sense, it is mystically understood as Mary who is also "alleviated," i.e. never burdened by original sin.[48] In this manner, Cartagena can entitle a homily presenting a string of such biblical images ranging from the neck to sandalled feet, from a lily to Hebrew horsemen, thus: *"Varia sacrae Scripturae loca, ad eandem illibatam Virginis Conceptionem illustrandam, secundum mysticam intelligentiam pulchre explicantur."* [49] Or, in his treatment of Mary's

---

[43] Lib. XIV, hom. XIII (II, 653a).

[44] Lib. I, hom. II (I, 9a). Cf. above, pp. 180–185. Cf. T. Barosse, "The Senses of Scripture and the Liturgical Pericopes," *Cath. Biblical Quart.*, 21 (1959) 1 f.

[45] Lib. V, hom. XVI (I, 494a). Cf. above, p. 298.

[46] Cf. e.g., above, pp. 185 ff., 261 ff., 290 ff. See F. Ohly, *Hohelied–Studien. Grundzüge einer Geschichte der Hohenliedauslegung des Abendlandes bis um 1200* (Wiesbaden, 1958).

[47] Cf. below, footnote 91. See Hans–Jörg Spitz, *Die Metaphorik des geistigen Schriftsinns* (München, 1971).

[48] Lib. I, hom. VI (I, 31a–b).

[49] Lib. I, hom. VIII (I, 37b). Cf. above, p. 193 ff.

virginity he has a homily with the title: "*Variae metaphorae, egregiae-que similitudines, et divinis eloquis depromptae eandem Deiparae Mariae virginitatem mirifice confirmant.*" [50] In this prolific use of extended metaphors and comparisons, to which in many cases the mystical sense has been reduced, Cartagena does not always have to call on some authorities. Giving free reign to his own acumen and imagination, he has composed quite a generous list.

In his Marian homilies Cartagena looks for the mystical sense of a text not just when in the literal interpretation it talks of somebody or something else other than Mary and her mysteries. Even when in the literal sense the subject is Mary, the author still develops the mystical explanation. He does so, for example, with the Magnificat.[51] The mystical sense is for him not a second choice when nothing else is there, but a way of approaching the sacred words by its own right. Also, the mystical interpretation he gives is not always necessarily in relation to Christ or Mary. The pharaoh's soldiers stuck in the Red Sea (Ex 15, 4–5), for instance, are mystically seen by Cartagena as men born in original sin.[52]

Cartagena justifies this practically unbounded enthusiasm for the mystical sense in its widest extension of metaphor by summoning the Pauline word that "the letter kills, the spirit however gives life" (2 Cor 3, 6).[53] St. Augustine gave the same justification for his more–than–literal exegesis, as did many other theologians of the 17th century.[54]

C. Mira Profunditas

Juan de Cartagena's preoccupation with the *sensus mysticus* rests on a particular vision or understanding of Sacred Scripture as God's word. Particularly strong during the Miggle Ages, this attitude towards the Bible was carried over to the 17th century by the survival of spiritual exegesis. [55] It is an attitude of wonder before the immense

---

[50] Lib. VII, hom. X (I, 774b). Cf. above, p. 260 ff.

[51] Lib. VI, hom. X (I, 588a). Cf. also Lib. VI, hom. XIII (I, 614a) and Lib. VI, hom. V (I, 555a).

[52] Lib. I, hom. II (I, 14a).

[53] Lib. XIV, hom. I (II, 560b).

[54] Augustine, *De Doctrina Christiana*, I, III, c. 5, n. 9 (CCL 32, 82).

[55] As the first shock of the Reformation was over, the more–than–literal sense, which never really disappeared as shown by the works of Johannes Driedo

profundity and unfathomable riches of Sacred Scripture. It could not be like other literature with one set meaning. God never makes anything so ordinary; he rather has given men a book containing more mysteries than meet the eye. True, the Bible has a literal sense just like any other book. But it has too a deeper sense, the spiritual, which is singular to itself. The literal or historical meaning of the sacred words are, as Rabanus Maurus put it, just the foundation of a structure or like the milk necessary for beginners or infants; the foundation must be built upon, and the grown–up must receive more than just milk.[56]

This deeper meaning of the word of God, by which it surpasses worldly wisdom, is based on the fact that in the Bible *"non solum voces, sed et res significativae sunt."* [57] God speaks to men not just with words, as do men to men, but also through things and creatures.[58]

(† 1535), Alfonso Salmeron († 1586), Francisco de Toledo († 1596) and Francisco de Ribera († 1591), made a telling come–back. Cornelius a Lapide († 1637), e.g., filled his commentaries with spiritual interpretation inspired by the Fathers who were once more being emphasized. Jansenism, typified by Pascal, also accepted the traditional division of Scripture meanings into literal and mystical. Then the Pietistic movement within Protestantism itself went tapping Scriptures for ascetic wealth through broad typology and accommodation, as exemplified by J. Cocceius († 1669). Cf. R. Guelluy, "L'évolution des méthodes théologiques à Louvain d'Erasme à Jansenius," *Revue d'Histoire Ecclesiastique*, 37 (1941) 71–80; J. Steinman, "Entretien de Pascal et du Père Richard Simon sur les sens de l'Ecriture," *Vie intellectuelle* (March, 1949) 239–253; Baroni, op. cit., pp. 418–419.

[56] "Mater quippe sapientia per hos adoptionis filios pascit, conferens insipientibus (incipientibus) atque teneris potum in lacte historiae... Dum enim haec, de qua loquimur, sacra Scriptura verba historiae simpliciter narrat, quasi inchoando fundamentum aedificii jactat..." R. Maurus, *Allegoriae in Universam Sacram Scripturam* (PL 112, 849A & D).

[57] Richard of St. Victor, *Excerptiones* II, 3: De scripturae divinae triplici modo tractandi (PL 177, 205B). Cf. his *Speculum Ecclesiae* (PL 177, 375B); Hugh of St. Victor, *De Scripturis et Scriptoribus Sacris*, 3 (PL 175, 12A): "Habet enim sacrum eloquium proprietatem quamdam ab aliis scripturis differentem, quod in eo primum per verba quae recitantur de rebus quibusdam agitur, quae rursum res vice verborum ad significationem aliarum proponuntur."

Cf. de Lubac, op. cit., I, pp. 119–128; F. Ohly, "Vom geistigen Sinn des Wortes im Mittelalter," *Zeitschrift für Deutsches Altertum und Deutsche Literatur*, 89 (1958) 1–23.

[58] "Voces ex humana, res ex divina institutione significant. Sicut enim homo per voces alteri, sic Deus per creaturas voluntatem suam indicat." Richard of St. Victor, *Speculum Ecclesiae* (PL 177, 375C). Creation is "opus Dei, quod numquam desinit esse, in quo opere visibili invisibilis sapientia creatoris visibiliter scripta est." Hugh of St. Victor, *De Arca Noe Morali*, II, 12 (PL 176, 643D).

Alphabetum rerum was Salmeron's name for it. Nature is theophanous and sacramental; it has symbolic density that can reveal God to men. Alanus ab Insulis expressed this belief in the mystical depth of things, when he wrote about the rose:

> *Omnis mundi creatura*
> *Quasi liber et pictura*
> *Nobis est et speculum;*
> *Nostrae vitae, nostrae mortis,*
> *Nostri status, nostrae sortis*
> *Fidele signaculum.*
> *Nostrum statum pingit rosa,*
> *Nostri status decens glosa,*
> *Nostrae vitae lectio.*[59]

In Sacred Scripture the signification of a *res* must be distinguished then from the literal meaning of its *vox*. For a thing has also a symbolic function by which we are led to something beyond it – a *symbolum* that is in the definition of Hugh of St. Victor as *"collatio idest coaptatio visibilium formarum ad demonstrationem rei invisibilis propositarum."* [60]

The signification of a thing can in itself be multiple and varied, insofar as it can have different properties and characteristics. Thus, a thing can have a signification according to its nature and another according to its form.[61] Moreover, a thing can have bad qualities side by side with its good qualities, and therefore it can have another set of spiritual meanings *"in malam partem,"* just as, as it is often said, there are words which can be written with golden or with black ink.[62]

This view of the world harks back to the words of St. Paul in Rom 1, 20. Cf. also Johan Huizing, *Herbst des Mittelalters* (Stuttgart, 1953), pp. 216–217.

[59] Alanus ab Insulis, *Anticlaudianus* (PL 210, 579A). Cf. M. D. Chenu, *Théologie au douzième siècle* (Paris, 1957), pp. 162–163.

[60] Hugh of St. Victor, *Expos. in Hier. Cael.* III (PL 175, 960). On the significance of this "demonstratio," cf. Chenu, op. cit., pp. 162 & 185–187.

[61] "Voces non plus quam duas aut tres habent significationes. Res autem tot possunt habere significationes, quot habent proprietates... Res duobus modis significant, natura et forma. Natura, ut nix, quia frigida est, exstinctionem designat libidinis. Forma, quia candida est, munditiam designat boni operis." Richard of St. Victor, *Excerptiones*, II, 5: De significatione vocum et rerum (PL 177, 205D). Cf. Cartagena, Lib. XIV, hom. I (II, 560b).

[62] "Dentes et tetris et aureis litteris scribuntur in hac pagina." J. B. Pitra, *Spicilegium Solesmense* II (Paris, 1855), p. 212. Cf. ibid., pp. 251, 499 & 504.

"Una eademque res non solum diversam, sed et adversam aliquando in

Now, the determination of these properties and qualities of a *res* given in Sacred Scripture, in order to arrive at their deeper meanings, is a process of uncovering what is seemingly hidden. Cartagena pictures the effort as *"a literae cortice sensum elongare,"* peeling off the literal or verbal shell to come upon the spiritual meaning.[63] His expressions are many, like *"de variis sacramentis latentibus sermonem instituere," "abdita mysteria referare," "aperire singularia arcana quae latent in verbo illo,"* etc., but they all connote the same idea that to get at the deeper spiritual meaning of the sacred words, one is trying to bring to light something masked and hidden.[64] One is sure it is there, but still one must search for it. In this connection, it is remarkable how the word *arcana* becomes a leitmotif of Cartagena's *Homiliae Catholicae*. His homilies purport to expound the secrets of the faith about Mary. And these sacred *sacramenta, mysteria* and *arcana* hidden in the words of Scripture are what he intends to bring to light by means of mystical interpretation.

D. Apparatus for the Mystical Sense

To uncover significations of a *res* apart from its *vox*, the Middle Ages had come up with a number of apparatus which were in wide use even during the time of Cartagena.

1. *Emblematic example books.* In his resort to biblical *"metaphorae et similitudines"* to illustrate Mary's Immaculate Conception,

---

scriptura sacra significationem habere potest." Pseudo–Hrabanus, *Allegoriae* (PL 112, 850B). Salmeron gave many examples of this. Op. cit., Prolog. XIX, pp. 348b–352b. Cartagena himself quotes examples from Anselm. Lib. XIV, hom. I (II, 560b).

The anonymous writer from Clairvaux (Pitra, op. cit., II, 156) provides an illustration of such a catalogue in verse of a thing's qualities "in bonam partem" and "in malam partem" alike:

"Est mare diffusum, fervens, salsum atque profundum,

Absorbens, fluidum, lucidum, foetens et amarum

Atque procellosum, rugit, gignitque periclum."

[63] Lib. XIV, hom. I (II, 560b). Cf. Alanus ab Insulis' similar expression in his *De Planctu Naturae* (PL 210, 451CD): "In superficiali litterae cortice falsum resonat lyra poetica, sed interius auditoribus secretum intelligentiae altioris eloquitur, ut exteriore falsitatis abjecto putamine, dulciorem nucleum veritatis secrete intus lector inveniat."

[64] Lib. I, hom. XVI (I, 85b); Lib. II, hom. VI (I, 169b); Lib. V, hom. XVI (I, 494a); Lib. VI, hom. XIII (I, 614b).

for instance, Cartagena himself says that he is relying on the *"rerum naturalium historiographi."* [65] The works of these historiographers, the emblematic example books so popular during the Middle Ages, were intended to assist in ferreting out the deeper significations of the sacred words. Among the titles we have already given above in Chapter Three with the list of Cartagena's sources for his homilies are Bartholomaeus Anglicus' *Liber de Proprietatibus Rerum* and Petrus Berchorius' *Inductorium vel Reductorium Morale de Proprietatibus Rerum.* A pioneer in the field was Rabanus Maurus' *De Universo,* which the author himself described as *"de sermonum proprietate et mystica rerum significatione."* [66]

To illustrate how these encyclopedic books went about their task of enumerating a thing's qualities, let us cite Thomas Cantipratanus' († c. 1270) *De Naturis Rerum* in its description of the moon, which he also applied point by point to Mary:

> *Sunt ergo isti versus et lunae proprietates: Humorum mater, solisque refrigerat aestum; Eclipsim patitur, Phoebo faciente recessum; Huic sol dat lumen; tenebras de nocte relidit; Illustrat mundum, sol pristina quando revisit; Inter planetas magis haec terris propiavit; Crescit, decrescit, candet, tempus mediavit.* [67]

---

[65] Lib. I, hom. XVI (I, 84a); Lib. I, hom. X (I, 53b); Lib. I, hom. III (I, 19a); Lib. I, hom. VIII (I, 38b–39a & 42a–b); Lib. I, hom. XIV (I, 73b). Cf. above, pp. 139–140.

During the Middle Ages, the liberal arts, the Trivium and the Quadrivium, all served in finding out the spiritual sense. As Richard of St. Victor put it: "Omnes itaque artes subserviunt divinae sapientiae et inferior scientia recte ordinata ad superiorem conducit. Sub eo igitur sensus, qui inter voces et res versatur, continetur historia, et ei subserviunt tres scientiae, dialectica, rhetorica, grammatica. Et sub eo sensu, qui inter res et facta mystica versatur, continetur allegoria. Et sub illo, qui est inter res et facienda mystica, continetur tropologia. Et his duabus subserviunt arithmetica, musica, geometria et physica." *Excerptiones* II, 4 (PL 177, 205C).

"Septem liberales artes huic scientiae subserviunt. Trivium ad significationem vocum, quadrivium ad rerum significationem respicit." Hugh of St. Victor, *De Scripturis* 13 (PL 175, 20C). Cf. de Lubac, op. cit., I, pp. 74–94.

[66] Hrabanus Maurus, *De Universo,* praefatio (PL 111, 9B).

[67] Thomas Cantipratanus, *De Naturis Rerum,* XVII, 3 (Pitra, II, 63 ff.). Cf. Cartagena's employment of such descriptions: Lib. III, hom. IV (I, 261a–b); Lib. XIV, hom. V (II, 594a–596b); Lib. II, hom. III (I, 143a); Lib. I, hom. XI (I, 56a–b).

In addition, since not only things, but also persons and places and events carry spiritual significations, appropriate compilations were also available, like Antonius Rampegolus' *Figurae Bibliorum* on biblical personages, the anonymous *Speculum Exemplorum Magnum*, and Robert Holcot's *Moralitates*.

2. *Onomastics.* Also, for the purpose of spelling out the *sensus mysticus* encapsuled in names and words, a special etymology had been developed, which is more theological than philological. A classic example of this onomastics is Mary's own name. Cartagena writes in this regard that "we shall lay open the mysteries contained in every letter making up Mary's name, and we shall diligently unravel what lies hidden in the various significations." [68] He terms this an argument from "*ethymologia et allusione vocabuli.*" [69] In his words, it is an "*ethymologia (quae) ad sapientiam et docendi munus refertur.*" [70]

To give some examples, Maria, i.e. *mare*, a large body of water or a "*congregatio aquarum,*" means in its mystical interpretation an "*aggregatio virtutum et charismatum.*"[71] Another word mystically connoting something for Mary is "*stella*" which came from *stare* and hence is aptly attributed to her in the title, *Stella Maris*, since it signifies her "stability" and permanence in God's grace.[72] Similarly containing spiritual significations are the names: Joseph, Esther, Anna, Joachim, etc.[73]

But this special etymology as Cartagena's statement of intention above indicates is concerned not only with a whole word or name as such, but also with every single letter composing a name, when it

---

[68] Lib. II, hom. VI (I, 169a).

[69] Ibid. (I, 169b). Cartagena reasons to its importance in that God himself modified Abraham's and Sarah's names (Gen 17, 5 & 15), and Christ gave Peter's (Mt 16, 18), because particular connotations are in play. He cites too St. Jerome's *Liber Interpret. Nominum Hebraicorum* (PL 23) and St. Isidore of Seville's *Ethymologia* as testifying to the importance and usefulness of onomastics. Cf. Jan Heller, "Namengebung und Namendeutung," *Evangelische Theologie,* 27 (1967) 255–266.

[70] Lib. X, hom. X (II, 276a).

[71] Lib. II, hom. VII (I, 172a–b). Cf. Lib. I, hom. X (I, 50a); Lib. I, hom. XIII (I, 67b).

[72] Lib. II, hom. VII (I, 175a). Cf. W. Delius, *Geschichte der Marienverehrung* (München, 1963), pp. 9–10.

[73] Lib. IV, hom. III (I, 296b); Lib. I, hom. IX (I, 44b–45a); Lib. I, hom. X (I, 48b).

is possible. Thus, for instance, the letter M of the name Mary is Mem in Hebrew, which is written in Mary's name alone without any opening or break at the bottom, to signify her virginity.[74] The second letter is A or Alef, meaning doctrine, thus bringing out the fact that Mary is not only the teacher of truth but also the mistress of sanctity. And so on.

3. *Symbolic arithmetic*. Another aspect of this interest in the mystical significations of names or words manifests itself in the effort to decipher them through a symbolic arithmetic. Cartagena also turns to this method, for instance, in the case of Mary's name. He relates that among the Jews a creature of God above all other creatures is believed to contain in itself the perfection of all others, and it is called Mitatron. This Mitatron is Maria, having in herself the perfection of all other creatures. And how come Maria is identified with Mitatron? Well, both names give the same number 999.[75] This fascination with numbers was taken seriously. For Salmeron, for example, numbers in Sacred Scripture are carriers of mysteries, not of human invention, but *"Spiritus Sancti arte, et sapientia nob's insinuata."* [76]

4. *Distinctiones*. Another help in finding the spiritual meaning of things in Sacred Scripture were the dictionaries already mentioned when dealing with the sources Cartagena utilized for his homilies. The *Dictionarii* and *Distinctiones* were systematically arranged commentaries along the allegorical and moral lines about things, persons and what–have–you, interspersed with biblical, patristic and other quotations. The earlier types arranged their words according to the order of occurrence, say, in the Psalter, much like a text commentary. Much later they came to be ordered according to groups or according to some hierarchical system. Thus, words dealing with God are set together, then comes the group of entries concerning man, animals, and so on. The type which prevailed was the alpha-

---

[74] Lib. VII, hom. VII (I, 760b); Lib. VII, hom. VIII (I, 767b).

[75] Lib. XIV, hom. XVI (II, 686b–687a). The author quotes from Franciscus Georgius (Zorzi) Venetus', OFM, *De Harmonia Mundi Totius Cantica Tria*, I, t. 5, c. 7 (Venice, 1578), which was placed on the Index for its Neo–Pythagorean cabalistic mysticism. Cf. Lib. I, hom. II (I, 7b). See also Chenu, op. cit., pp. 163–164.

[76] Salmeron, op. cit., Prolog. XX, p. 357b. Cf. de Lubac, op. cit., IV, pp. 7–40.

betically arranged, like Thomas of Pavia's *Distinctiones Bovis* and Nicholas of Byard's *Dictionarius Pauperum*.[77] Another example of such a publication which came later and was extensively used during Cartagena's time was Santes Pagnini's *Isagoge ad Mysticos Sacrae Scripturae Sensus* (Lyon, 1536) or Hieronymus Lauretus' *Silva seu potius Hortus Floribus Allegoriarum Totius Sacrae Scripturae* (Barcelona, 1570).[78]

E. Obscuritas Sacrae Scripturae

The above mentioned encyclopedic books so widely propagated and used so long were intended primarily as aids in explaining the Bible. Based on the belief that the sacred book must have something more to say than just its literal meaning, no stones were left unturned in the search for Scripture's deeper message. Compilations and dictionaries offered their users spiritual interpretations of things, persons, words and events recorded by the sacred pages. Being God's book, the Bible must have a mystical dimension to it, distinguishing it from secular literature.

Even theology got into the act, or better said, theology manifestly adopted the distinction between the *vox* and the *res significata*, which in the Middle Ages opened the door to a flurry of allegorization in exegesis.[79] In Cartagena's own time the Jesuit Maximilianus Sandaeus, for instance, came out with a book *De Theologia Symbolica* (Moguntiae, 1623), concerned with questions like: "Are all things created, in order to be symbols of the divine secrets & of God's perfections?" Under this perspective, which was but a carry–over from the Middle Ages' *"Omnis mundi creatura / Quasi liber et pictura,"* as Alanus ab Insulis had versified the idea, the things of this world are like shells nursing within them deeper realities. They are signs of things beyond themselves. Creation is a book of nature, written in the *alphabetum rerum*, communicating to men transcendental truths,

---

[77] Cf. above, p. 138.

[78] Cf. F. Ohly's introduction to Lauretus' *Silva seu potius Hortus Floribus Allegoriarum Totius Sacrae Scripturae*, Nachdruck der 10. Ausgabe (München, 1971).

[79] Thomas Aquinas, *Summa Theol.*, I, q. 1, art. 9. Cf. de Lubac, op. cit., pp. 266–267; M. D. Chenu, "Histoire et allégorie au douzième siècle," in *Glaube und Geschichte*, Festgabe J. Lortz, II (Baden–Baden, 1958), pp. 59–71.

sacramentalizing divine secrets. In Cartagena's own description, the world is a theatre or studio filled with God's "creations," every single one of which reveals something of the divine artist, as does Mary, the instance, the most perfect of all his works.[80] There is nothing in this world, which through comparison and allegory cannot be related to something else and thus "manifest" something else. These things must only be studied, so that they can yield their spiritual and deeper significations.

With such a pervasive sense of being surrounded literally by *sacramenta* and *arcana* waiting to be uncovered, even non–biblical literature metamorphosed into springs of mystical meanings. Homer, Virgil and Ovid, among others, were subjected to a search of the Christian and spiritual dimension they surely contain according to divine providence. Cartagena himself resorts to such moralizing and allegorical interpretation of Ovid, tracing in his verses Christian themes.[81] Baptizing pagan literature is what Cartagena has called reclaiming gems of truth from "unlawful possessors." [82] Example books like John of Wales' *Expositio seu Moralitates Fabulorum Ovidii*, also known as *Ovidius Moralisatus*, and the *Gesta Romanorum Moralisata* typified this development.

The *"profunditas"* of Sacred Scripture which triggered off this hectic investigation of its mysteries and wonders through mystical exposition actually means in part the *"obscuritas sacrae Scriptuae."* Notwithstanding the humanistic advances in linguistics and history, and in spite of the new–found interest in biblical languages, the Bible remained in itself a mystery. Textual and form criticism, biblical history and archaeology, and a more thorough grasp of the biblical languages were then still things to come. With his expectations heightened by the honest belief that Sacred Scripture is a treasure of divine truths, and yet confronted by the seeming obscurity of Scripture due to the limitations of his biblical science, a theologian of the 17th century like his brother in the Middle Ages could only try to scale the wall separating him from his goal by the available and venerable means. Salmeron thus counselled that one should search for the mystical sense, when the text gives the first impression

---

[80] Cf. above, p. 187.

[81] Lib. I, hom. XVIII (I, 94a); Lib. I, hom. XIX (I, 107a). Cf. Chenu, *Théologie au douzième siècle*, op. cit., pp. 164–165.

[82] Cf. above, pp. 130–131.

of being barren and empty! [83] *"Quaecumque scripta sunt ad nostram doctrinam scripta sunt"* (Rom 14, 4) justified both for the Middle Ages and for the Baroque period the belief that every word of Scripture must somehow teach us, if not literally, then mystically. And this recourse to spiritual exegesis, partly due to exigency, indicates too the necessity of word–exegesis and the use of rhetoric in interpreting the Bible, as we shall discuss in the next chapter.

A question remains to be answered in connection with the generous use of allegory in the mystical interpretation of Scripture. Is this mystical sense characteristic of the Bible any different from what we mean by allegory in secular literature? Were the commentators and exegetes of the Middle Ages and of the 17th century not involved with the visualization through personification or *Verdinglichung* of some abstract idea or mystery of the faith as they piled up the mystical meanings they claimed to have discovered in Scripture? An essential difference between scriptural allegory and literary allegory lies in the fact that the first is concerned with a *revelatio* or a *spiritualis notificatio*, as Hugh of St. Victor clearly explained it.[84] Literary allegory on the other hand, in the examples of the Middle Ages' *The Romance of the Rose* and *The Faerie Queene*, or the Baroque *Pilgrim's Progress* by J. Bunyan, or the modern *The Allegory of Love* by C. S. Lewis, G. Orwell's *Animal Farm* and the recent bestseller *Jonathan Livingston Seagull* by R. Bach, is an effort to present an idea in a stylistic garb masquerading what is being communicated.[85] Scriptural allegory is essentially revelation of what is hidden, a fathoming of Sacred Scripture's *mira profunditas*, a breaching of its *obscuritas*, an uncovering of its *arcana*.

F. Mariology and Spiritual Exegesis

The foregoing exposé of Cartagena's scripturism with the stress on the mystical or allegorical shows its direct descent from the spiritual exegesis of the Middle Ages, which in turn was a bequest of the

---

[83] Salmeron, op. cit., Prolog. XX, can. 25.

[84] Hugh of St. Victor, *De Scripturis* (PL 175, 20D). Cf. de Lubac, op. cit., IV, pp. 126–149.

[85] On allegory as a literary or poetic technique, see J. C. Joosen and J. H. Waszink, "Allegorese," in *Reallexikon für Antike und Christentum*, I (Stuttgart, 1950), 283–293.

Fathers. Notwithstanding Renaissance humanism and the Reformation and the subsequent effect of these on biblical studies, spiritual
exegesis Phoenix–like could not be annihilated and kept reappearing
on the theological scene. Cartagena's *Homiliae Catholicae* is a prime
example of this approach to Sacred Scripture, based on the conviction
that it contains *mysteria* attainable only through the mystical sense.

This chapter on Cartagena's use of Sacred Scripture as exemplified in his Marian homilies cannot end without taking up the question
of the relationship between Mariology and spiritual exegesis. Did
Juan de Cartagena resort to a mystical interpretation of sacred texts
in connection with Marian mysteries simply because of the Bible's
obscuritas and the absence of enough explicit words about her, or
simply because, as we shall see in the next chapter, it was then fashionable with Baroque homiletics? Did he have any theological grounds
for such Mariological scripturism? We must admit that Cartagena
does not seem to have any over–all Mariological concept or theory
giving form and orientation to his use of spiritual exegesis. In the
matter of Mary's virginity, for instance, as we have already seen,
although he says that the teaching explicitly rests on the words of
the Bible, he still turns to mystical accommodations of what are in
themselves totally unrelated texts. It is not for reason of pure necessity that he turns to the mystical sense, therefore. He knows of
the Fathers' typology of Mary–Eve and Mary–Church, but he gives
this line of thought no extra attention. Consciously, in order to illustrate Marian teachings and to confirm them in the mind of the faithful,
he seems to have sought merely to compile as many texts of Sacred
Scripture as possible which have been Mariologically interpreted or
accommodated one way or another by earlier and contemporary
authors. Cartagena was not sophisticated beyond his time. The
present main Mariological themes of Mary as the daughter of Sion
or as the symbol of the People of God or of Israel are later refinements.[86]

Did Cartagena however hold any special affinity between Mariology and spiritual exegesis? This very question is at least impli-
citly considered in the *Homiliae Catholicae*. Noting that Sacred Scripture leaves many things unsaid about Mary, Cartagena believes this

---

[86] Cf. R. Laurentin, op. cit., p. 168 ff.; L. Deiss, *Maria, Tochter Sion* (Mainz,
1961); H. Cazelles, "Fille de Sion et théologie mariale dans la Bible," *Etudes
Mariales,* 21 (1964) 51–71.

to be not without reason.[87] The silence of Scripture should actually serve as an incentive for theologians to investigate deeper and study further her mysteries.[88] For the Church does not watch passively over a collection of truths, but is rather in the process of continuously growing *"instar aurorae"* in what she knows, for instance, about our Blessed Virgin Mother.[89] That the Church teaches certain doctrines about her, e.g. her Immaculate Conception and Assumption into heaven, which are not explicitly and literally supported by Sacred Scripture, offers no insurmountable difficulty for Cartagena, since he believes that biblical *metaphorae et similitudines* are like indicators of the truth.[90] He means by it that after having reasoned out the congruence and appropriateness of a certain teaching, one can easily find illustrations in Sacred Scripture confirmatory of it.

As we have seen, this theologically inductive method is based on the belief that the Bible communicates to us more truths from God than we can guess at. And it must not be forgotten that Cartagena's presupposition limits this procedure to believers. It is only out of faith that one can "read into" Scripture. And it is only to and for believers that it appeals and bears fruit. It strengthens their faith; it confirms, and enlarges on, what they already believe. Ultimately it is an application of the maxim: *Credo ut intelligam.*

This above procedure of utilizing Sacred Scripture in order to proclaim Mary's mysteries and to confirm the faithful in their beliefs about her has to go of its very nature beyond the literal sense. To "actualize" the Bible in connection with Mary for his readers, Cartagena turns to the mystical sense of scriptural texts. His Mariological *mystica intelligentia* is broader than just typology.[91] It includes typological application to Mary of OT personages and events, but in such a comprehensive way that it really is allegorical. At times, Cartagena's allegorical reading into the sacred texts to illustrate Marian mysteries is highly arbitrary, based apparently on an imaginative use of *Distinctiones* and emblematic example books. But fundamentally, behind Cartagena's free and imprecise employment of the mystical sense, a weakness partly inherited from the Middle Ages,

---

[87] Cf. above, pp. 178–179.
[88] Cf. above, pp. 274–275.
[89] Cf. above, p. 284.
[90] Cf. above, footnote 20.
[91] Cf. Bernhard Langemeyer, "Konziliare Mariologie und bibliche Typologie," *Catholica*, 21 (1967) 295–316.

lies a thinking represented by the *Theologia symbolica* of the 17th century and, earlier, of the 12th.[92] It differentiates itself from the causal thought structure of Scholastic theology and philosophy, in that it places the emphasis on the symbolic inter–relationship of things. It is neo–Platonic, as opposed to the Aristotelian. It holds that on the level of symbol and not only of causality a certain correspondence exists between things, as between analogues. This theology proceeds from the primal truth that God is the creator of everything. On this ground alone is there a certain unity of being in the world; things compare with one another and they reflect one another, with God as the ultimate point of reference. The more two beings harmonize with one another, the more do they re–present each other. The objective of this symbol theology is the deepening of knowledge about something through its "re–presentation" and symbolization in another. By means of such a reflection elsewhere, one improves on what one already knows.

Cartagena's use of metaphors, figures and images culled from Sacred Scripture to illustrate and confirm what is already taught or speculated on regarding Mary is in principle *Theologia symbolica*. Taking off from the historical and causal datum of Scripture that Mary is the mother of Jesus Christ, Cartagena knows that he has to go beyond this *principium* of any Marian grace to say "more" about her. He rounds off the other Marian data of tradition and of Scholastic theology by availing himself of the comparative and symbolical

---

[92] Cf. above, pp. 207 ff. Salmeron understands by it the use of the spiritual sense in a theology, which is not polemical or argumentative, but edificatory for the faithful. Op. cit., Prolog. XIX, p. 340b. Cf. J. Danielou, "Symbolisme et théologie," in *Interpretation der Welt*, ed. H. Kuhn (Würzburg, 1965), pp. 663–674.

In Cartagena's early years as a theologian, in opposition to the more common opinion that the use of the mystical sense should be limited to homiletical and ascetical purposes, the thesis was also represented that it actually should be the main stay of theology, as claimed, for instance, by Coimbra's Antao Galvão († 1609). A *Theologia symbolica* seems to be his objective. Cf. Klaus Reinhardt, "Theologie als Interpretation der Heiligen Schrift bei Antao Galvão OESA (ca. 1559–1609) und Pedro Luíz Beuther SJ (1538–1602)," in *Portugiesische Forschungen der Görresgesellschaft*, 11 (1973) 7–8, 10–12. Other Portugese theologians of the same mind as to the importance of the mystical sense were: Hector Pinto, Luis de Sotomayor, Sebastiao Barradas and Brás Viegas. Cf. F. Stegmüller, *Filosofia e Teologia nas Universidades de Coimbra e Evora no Século XVI* (Coimbra, 1959), pp. 21–29, 77–82; Reinhardt, art. cit., p. 13, adds to this group João de Payva and Manoel de s. Jerónimo.

images and figures of Scripture, illustrating these other contents of tradition.

This *theologia symbolica* of the 17th century, however, in its intimacy with spiritual exegesis and its excesses, can hardly be identified with the *Symboldenken* proposed by A. Müller for Mariology.[93] Although they may coincide in their basic suppositions, the latter is strictly typological in its biblical scope, while the former is really a freewheeling allegory. For the old spiritual exegesis of the Fathers and of the Middle Ages, even in its revival in the Baroque period, seems often unconcerned about being so outlandish and totally foreign to the intention of the sacred writer even when viewed from the over–all standpoint of salvation history.

Second thoughts are being had nowadays over this question of the Fathers' allegorical exegesis.[94] Biblical form and historical criticism may well succeed in determining the writer's intention, but it has yet to take into full account the heuristic factor of the community's faith, to which the sacred writer's own testimony of faith is originally addressed. Also, the Fathers have only "actualized" for their own believing communities the living message of the sacred pages, and this, on the ecclesiological belief that the Holy Spirit continuously guides both the Scripture interpreter and the receiving community. The same Spirit it was who "inspired" the NT communities. Does this reality mean anything in today's literal exegesis? Are we over–doing the stress on the historical in Sacred Scripture at the expense of other, no less real, dimensions, such as the emotional and the symbolical? Especially with regards Mariology is this inter-

---

[93] A. Müller, "Marias Stellung und Mitwirkung im Christusereignis," in *Mysterium Salutis*, op. cit., pp. 394–397. W. Pannenberg, op. cit., p. 144, views this effort by Müller rather favorably and believes in a symbolic frame of thought for Mariology.

[94] Cf. Adolf Smitmans, "Anfragen der Väterexegese and die historisch-kritische Methode," in *Versuche mehrdimensionaler Schriftauslegung*, ed. Helmut Harsch & Gerhard Voss (Stuttgart–München, 1972), pp. 62–69. French–speaking exegetes have particularly been involved in this regard, especially in connection with structural exegesis and existential hermeneutics. Cf. Michael van Esbroeck, *Hermeneutik, Strukturalismus und Exegese* (München, 1968); *Exegese im Methoden Konflikt*, ed. X. Leon–Dufour, (München, 1973), esp. p. 210 ff., on Paul Ricoeur's "Sprache und Theologie des Wortes." For a "defence" of spiritual exegesis, see Henri Crouzel, "Grounds for Spiritual Exegesis," in *Sacramentum Mundi*, op. cit., I, 202–204.

est in a more–than–literal exegesis alive.[95] Only in some form of spiritual exegesis, whether in strict typology couched in *Symboldenken* or in some sort of *sensus plenior,* can the major ramifications of the mystery of God's grace in Mary be traced in Sacred Scripture.

---

[95] Cf. Enrique de Sdo. Corazón, "Sobre el sentido 'plenior' y su aplicación en mariologia," in *Maria in Sacra Scriptura,* II (Romae, 1967), pp. 81–104; Gabriel Roschini, "De usu regulae quartae Tychonii in mariologia biblica," ibid., III, pp. 141–171. On the sensus plenior in general, cf. R. Brown, *The Sensus Plenior of Sacred Scripture,* op. cit.; his article, "The Sensus Plenior in the last ten years," *Catholic Biblical Quarterly,* 25 (1963) 262–285; Joseph Coppens, "Levels of Meaning in the Bible," *Concilium,* 3/10 (1967) 62–69; Louis–Marie Simon, "Le sens scripturaire plénier," *Maria in Sacra Scriptura,* I (1967), pp. 105–116.

CHAPTER EIGHT

CARTAGENA AS A BAROQUE PREACHER

We have seen above in Chapter III that Juan de Cartagena intends his *Homiliae Catholicae* to be an aid–book for preachers, presenting abundant materials compiled and arranged thematically according to the chronology of the Marian mysteries. His desire is to make a pastoral contribution *"pro cibandis fidelibus"* by explaining certain topics about the Catholic faith and by setting aright the morals of men.[1] This twofold goal of theological information and of moral formation is achieved by and through the word of God proclaimed in preaching. We have discussed above in the previous chapter Cartagena's predominant utilization of the mystical interpretation of Sacred Scripture. We have tried to see this characteristics of Cartagena's use of the Bible in the context of spiritual exegesis in the 17th century and in terms of the particular understanding of the Bible underlying such a more–than–literal exposition of Scripture. In this present chapter we want to investigate his scripturism in the light of the ministry of preaching. We shall see how his inclination for the mystical sense is to a great part dictated by Baroque homiletics. We shall first examine Cartagena's idea of homiletics and its special articulation in the so–called *conceptus* homily. Then we shall consider the whole tendency or trend as a manifestation of the Baroque *Zeitgeist*.

I. CARTAGENA'S HOMILETICS

A. THE INDISPENSABILITY OF GOD'S WORD

In a very personal affirmation of what preaching means to him, Cartagena claims that it is a reflection of the procession of the Holy Spirit from the Father and the Son, and should therefore beget the same Spirit in the hearts of men.

> I remember having said more than once, as I preach to the people, that the preacher's use of the Word of the Gospel should be in

---

[1] HCUCRA, Dedication. Cf. above, pp. 108–109.

the people similar to the uncreated Word of the eternal Father, which could not but produce the Holy Spirit. So also the preacher's presentation of the Word of the Gospel should not only instruct the intellect of the hearers, but should beget in their will the Holy Spirit.[2]

It is consequently necessary that the preacher should remain a proclaimer of the Gospel. He is not simply an orator, nor may he adulterate God's Word. Cartagena observes,

> Alas, to the deprivation of the faithful nowadays, we know of not a few preachers of the divine Word who are "adulterers of the Word of God," if I may so speak with St. Paul. For just as an adulterer is not committed to the generation of an offspring but seeks only his own pleasure, in like manner a preacher, who does not really try to enthrone God in the souls of his hearers... but strives only to foster his own self–esteem... In these calamitous times is the Church suffering from a very great loss, because preachers seek more to be orators than to be heralds of the Gospel, turning to profane and theatrical expressions, rather than to Gospel words.[3]

These lines from Cartagena explain why his *Homiliae Catholicae* is so overwhelmingly scriptural. Ultimately intending to reach the faithful even if only vicariously through the preacher–users of his work, he keeps himself indeed as close as possible to God's own Word. As we have seen in Chapter III, Cartagena composed his homilies under the auspices of positive theology, with all its emphasis on Scripture and the Fathers and its strong pastoral and kerygmatic connotations.[4] God's Word is the preacher's sword, says Cartagena, quoting St. Paul on the efficacy of Scripture.[5] But it is unlike other swords which kill and wound. The sword of God imparts life and raises up. As the dialogue between Lazarus and Abraham (Lk 16, 29ff) demonstrates, the Word of God preached by Moses and the prophets is more powerful and effective than the words of a dead man returning to life.[6] Further availing himself of Scripture's self–testimony, the

---

[2] Ibid., lib. XV, hom. XV, col. 106.

[3] Ibid.

[4] Cf. above, p. 113 ff.

[5] Lib. XV, hom. XXI (III, 189b), quoting Eph 6, 17.

[6] "Ecce, quomodo cum alii gladii trucident, et occidant, gladius verbi Dei vivificat, et resuscitat, in quo certe mira eius effulget et utilitas, et efficacia... Ecce, quam magna sit Verbi Dei efficacia; cuius virtutem tantam esse agnovit

author points out that God's Word is for the soul food and nourishment. Amos 8, 11 pictures hunger and thirst for the Word of God, while Christ himself says that "man lives not by bread alone, but by every word that comes from the mouth of God" (Mt 4, 4).[7] Moreover, in view of his purpose of presenting to the faithful the mysteries of faith, Sacred Scripture becomes indispensable in that it is the touchstone which either establishes a teaching's truthfullness or uncovers its falsehood.[8] Sacred Scripture is the primary and essential *locus theologicus.*[9]

B. A Return to the Bible

Cartagena's insistence on the Word of God for the preacher is but a reflection of the return to the Bible following the Council of Trent. In 1563, the year Juan de Cartagena was born, the Council passed what the Council Fathers themselves considered to be their greatest single reform, the seminary decree of the 23rd Session, the 18th chapter on reform.[10] Ordering the establishment of seminaries for the training of the clergy, the study of Sacred Scripture, theological books and the homilies of the saints, among others, was made regulatory. The newly founded Society of Jesus particularly embodied these provisions of Trent. We have seen that both as a Jesuit student and as a professor of theology Cartagena had to show himself adept on the Bible.[11] But if the *lectio* or study of the Sacred Books became part and parcel of theological training, it was in con-

---

Abraham, ut non dubitarit dicere, quod etiam si quis ex mortuus ad illos veniret, et enarraret horribilia gehennae tormenta, quae ipse patitur, non maiorem haec narratio habitura esset efficaciam, quam Verbum Dei praedicatum a Moyse, et Prophetis. Certe viva vox habet nescio quid latentis energiae." Ibid. (III, 191b).

[7] Ibid. (III, 195b).

[8] HCUCRA, lib. VI, hom. I, col. 6: "Est enim sacra Scriptura veluti lapis Lydius, sive index, qui doctrina, aut revelationis veritatem, aut falsitatem detegit."

[9] M. Cano, op. cit., Lib. XII, c. 3. Cf. Albert Lang, *Die Loci Theologici des Melchior Cano und die Methode des dogmatischen Beweises* (München, 1925), p. 91 ff.

[10] Cf. *Handbuch der Kirchengeschichte, IV: Reformation, Katholische Reform und Gegenreformation*, hrsg. I. Iserloh, J. Glazik, H. Jedin (Freiburg, 1967), pp. 516 & 524.

[11] Cf. above, pp. 20 & 23.

junction with the *praedicatio* of the same, as Trent's earlier decree on preaching brings out.[12]

The Archbishop of Vienna's long memorandum on the forthcoming Council to Pope Paul III in June of 1543 gives an enlightening summary of the situation then urgently calling for reform. Too many preachers, the archbishop wrote, were unqualified to teach orthodox doctrine. They often neglected Sacred Scripture and instead satisfied themselves with stories and fables. Recondite theological questions were on the other hand preferred by some preachers to wholesome moral instruction. Thus the sermons went over the head of the people, instead of providing them with the simple and salutary truths of the faith which are the staple of a good Christian life.[13] The Council's Session V, chapter 2 and Session XXIV, chapter 4 accordingly legislated on the needed reform of preaching, emphasizing training and a turn to the Bible.

The reform principles of Trent received teeth and were worked out in detail especially by St. Charles Borromaeus' Third Provincial Synod of Milan in 1575, whose *Instructiones Praedicandi Verbi Dei* had great vogue throughout Europe for the next two hundred years at least.[14] Preachers, who were put under close supervision, were especially warned against outlandish interpretations of Sacred Scripture and the excessive use of allegories. If allegories there must be, let them be drawn from approved sources only. In the spirit of the Protestant Reformation, the homiletics of the 16th century was unequivocal in giving primacy to the Word of God. Diego de Estella or Didacus Stella, OFM († 1578), for instance, in his *De Modo Concionandi Liber* advised the preacher even to a daily reading of Scrip-

---

[12] *Concilium Tridentinum*, ed. Societas Goerresana (Freiburg, 1911), V, p. 241 ff. Cf. Johann Rainer, SJ, "Entstehungsheschichte des Trienter Predigtreformdekretes," *Zeitschrift für katholische Theologie*, 39 (1915) 256–317, 465–523; Schneyer, op. cit., pp. 234–235.

[13] *Concilium Tridentinum*, XII, p. 407. As early as 1516, the 5th Lateran Council already ordered the preaching of Sacred Scripture according to the approved interpretations by the Fathers. On the time's situation on preaching, see Antonio Cañizares Llovera, *Santo Tomás de Villanueva. Testigo de la predicación española del siglo XVI* (Madrid, 1973), p. 86 ff.

[14] For the synod's *Instructiones Praedicationis Verbi Dei*, cf. Achille Ratti, *Acta Ecclesiae Mediolanensis*, II (Milan, 1890) col. 1207–1248. See also Joseph Connors, SVD, "Saint Charles Borromeo in Homiletic Tradition," *The American Ecclesiastical Review*, 138 (1958) 9–23; H. Caplan and H. King, "Latin Tractates on Preaching: a Booklist," *Harvard Theological Review*, 42 (1949) 185–206.

ture plus collecting a private scrap–book of alphabetically ordered citations and insights.[15] Another Franciscan preacher and professor of sacred eloquence at Ara Coeli in Rome, Francesco Panigarola († 1594), drew from Trent's decrees and the writings of Borromeo and combined them with a running paraphrase of Demetrius Phalereus' treatise on style for his posthumously published *Il Predicatore* (Venice, 1609). Another architect of 16th century homiletics was Luis de Granada, OP († 1588), who was of the same tone in urging the indispensability of Scripture for the ministry of preaching in his book *Ecclesiasticae Rhetoricae sive de Ratione Concionandi* (Lisbon, 1576 ; in 1594 it came out in Cologne bound together with Didacus Stella's work).[16] This basic dimension of preaching as far as the use of Sacred Scripture is concerned is perhaps best expressed by the Jesuit Carolus Regius († 1612) :

> Since the preacher therefore is a preacher of the divine Word and an instrument of God for the good of souls... through the ministry of God's Word, it is obvious that Sacred Scripture, inasmuch as the divine Word is contained in it, must be where he finds his proper and acknowledged material.[17]

C. CONCEPTUS HOMILY

The above–mentioned works on homiletics represent the immediate stage preceding the further development of the early Baroque period. They called for a strong use of the Bible in preaching, more or less to the tune of Trent's decrees. And they were the outstanding texts on homiletics which Cartagena doubtless read and used. But judging from Cartagena's use of Sacred Scripture in his *Homiliae Catholicae*, his homiletics betrays elements of the typical middle–17th–century homilies, although still in its inchoate form. For if in theology Cartagena lived during the Baroque highpoint, in homiletics he exemplifies only the beginning. A point of illustration is the matter of *conceptus* homily, which in its advanced stage represents High Baroque, but which as found in Cartagena was still in its early development.

---

[15] Didacus Stella, *Modus Concionandi* (Coloniae, 1594), c. 13.

[16] Cf. J. Connors, "Homiletic Theory in the Late 16th Century," *American Ecclesiastical Review*, 138 (1958) 316–332.

[17] Carolus Regius, *Orator Christianus* (Romae, 1612), p. 131.

The 1617 Ingolstadt German translation of Juan de Cartagena's homilies on the Magnificat, originally a book of the *Homiliae Catholicae*, carried the title *Zwanzig schöner ausführlicher Concept, über der glorwürdigesten Himmel Königin Mariae, hochheiliges Lobgesang: das Magnificat genandt*.[18] The word *Concept* or *Konzept*, from the Latin *conceptus* and better known in homiletics in the Italian translation *concetto*, had been defined by Emmanuele Tesoro († 1677) in his classic book on High Baroque homiletics as "a deeply reflective thought, only suggested by the divine Spirit, brought to light by the human intellect in a shrewd manner and supported through the words of some holy writers."[19] Tesoro stressed the fact that it is a product of intellectual shrewdness, somehow having to do with the divine Spirit and sacred writers. A more precise definition was given like a historical hindsight by Ignaz Weitenauer, SJ († 1783), who wanted to defend the already bygone Baroque homiletics. As he succinctly put it, "*Conceptus significari solet animadversio ingeniosa in aliquem Divini Codicis locum.*"[20] The reference to Sacred Scripture is vital. A Scripture text is the heart of a concetto; it is what it is all about. It is human interpretation of a sacred word or text in connection with or in relation to something else.

To return for a moment to the German translation with the title description of *Concept*, it is significant that that early an entire book of homilies should be so understood and presented. Or was it precisely because of having been written along the line of the concetti homilies that Thobias Hendschel thought of capitalizing on the new mode in preaching by offering to a wider audience some of his fellow Franciscan's homilies? At that time the literary category of *conceptus* productions was still very young. St. Theresa of Avila's († 1558) *Conceptos del Amor de Dios* was one of the earliest, as was Alonso de Ledesma's († 1623) *Conceptos espirituales*.[21] At the turn of the 17th

---

[18] Cf. above, pp. 88–89.

[19] E. Tesoro, *Il Cannocchiale Aristotelico o sia Idea dell'Argutia et ingeniosa Elocutione* (Roma, 1664), p. 79; quoted by Pirmin Hasenöhrl, OFM, "Die Concetti-predigt," *Kirche und Kanzel*, 3 (1920) 57.

[20] I. Weitenauer, SJ, *Subsidia Eloquentiae Sacrae*, V (Augsburg, 1764–9), p. 114. Hasenöhrl, loc. cit., gives this definition as from Wallafrid Hillinger, OMRecol, *Ars bene dicendi de suggestu ecclesiastico seu Rhetorica sacra* (Augsburg, 1770), p. 97, who actually took it from Weitenauer.

[21] Cf. João Mendes, "Conceito," in *Enciclopédia Luso–Brasileira de Cultura*, V (Lisboa, 1967) 1198–9. "Conceptismo" as founded by Alonso de Ledesma and

century the style of the *conceptus* was relatively a newcomer and far from being the highest concretization of the Baroque homiletics.

Anyway, if Cartagena is here in the avant–garde of a new form, a definite non–uniformity among his homilies is also noticeable. Of the 28 homilies in Liber VI from which the *Zwanzig schöner Concept* was drawn, Hendschel chose 20, dropping the rest.[22] In a work as exhaustive and wide–ranging as Cartagena's *Homiliae Catholicae* it is inevitable that some of the homilies would be principally essays on Patristic teachings, Scholastic discussions, historical reconstruction, or apologetical argumentations.[23] But these homilies are of a supplementary type, designed to complete and round out the author's presentation and explanation of scriptural texts. A historical background, the support of the Fathers, the refinements by the Scholastics, and, where necessary, the refutation of heretical positions are simply called for in a thorough disquisition of Catholic doctrines. But by and large the *Homiliae Catholicae* is a presentation of Cartagena's reflections on Sacred Scripture seen in the light of and ordered according to Marian mysteries.

In Cartagena's own mind there is no doubt at all that his homilies are basically *conceptus*. The titles are revealing: *"...varia eruditione, ac uberrima conceptuum copia prosequimur," "variis animi conceptio-*

---

as exemplified by Francisco de Quevedo is sharply dismissed by James Fitzmaurice-Kelley, *A History of Spanish Literature* (London, 1898), p. 299, as a school of "metaphysical conceits, philosophical paradoxes, and sententious moralisings, as of a Seneca gone mad," and in p. 302, as a style of "the flashy epigram, the pompous paradox, the strained antithesis, the hair–splitting and refining in and out of season." Cf. also below, footnote 63.

[22] E.g., Lib. VI, hom. I (I, 529) is partly entitled: "...prius tamen difficultates, quae circa eius historiam occurrunt, enodamus, in illa verba: Exurgens Maria abiit in montana, cum reliquis Mariae Visitationem enarrantibus." Ibid., hom. IV (I, 543): "Ostenditur iterum Christus Dominus in utero matris festinasse, ut Ioannem sanctificaret; cuius occasione SS. Patrum testimoniis palam sit, quam sit Deus ad miserendum proclivis et velox. De misericordia autem in hac visitatione divinitus collata gaudent Ioannes, Elisabeth, Zacharias, Deipara Maria, Christi humanitas, imo et beatissima Trinitas." Hendschel omitted these homilies.

[23] For Patristic homilies, cf. Lib. I, hom. III (I, 14a); Lib. III, hom. I (I, 244); Lib. IV, hom. VI & X (I, 317a & 343b). Scholastic: Lib. I, hom. IV (I, 19b); Lib. VII, hom. XV (I, 811a); hom. XVI (I, 840); Lib. XIV, hom. XX (II, 708a). Historical: Lib. IV, hom. I to V (I, 284 ff.); Apologetical–controversial: Lib. VII, hom. III & XIII (I, 738b & 802b); Lib. XVI, hom. IX (III, 279); or a potpourri of everything: Lib. I, hom. XIX (I, 99a); Lib. VIII, hom. XII (II, 84); Lib. XI, hom. I (II, 316); Lib. XIV, hom. XIII (II, 652b).

nibus tam humana, quam sacra eruditione explicantur," "variis animi conceptionibus elucidantur verba illa," "variis animi conceptionibus perpulchre explicatur." [24] At times the terms *conceptus* and *conceptio animi* themselves are not used, but only implied in expressions like: *"singulari eruditione deducitur," "erudite exponi," "pulchre explicantur," "varia eruditione disseritur."* [25] At other times the *conceptio animi* is explicitly linked up with metaphors, e.g. *"Metaphoram palmae multiplici eruditione, variisque animi conceptionibus elucidare conamur in illa verba..."* [26] Thus the connection between the mystical interpretation of Scripture texts, as Cartagena makes it inclusive of metaphors and comparisons, and his employment of concetto or *conceptiones animi* is spotlighted. Every *conceptus* is for him about some words from the Bible. It is not just some sort of clever thought whatsoever used as an argument, as Cartagena's Jesuit contemporary homiletic writer Regius understood it.[27] As Weitenauer's definition has it, a *conceptus* is an ingenious reflection about a sacred text. A homily therefore composed of *conceptiones animi* is basically an architectonic organization of a number of ingenious ruminations on scriptural words grouped around and hinging on a main topic or idea.[28]

D. The Art of the Ingenium

We are not interested here in the pure construction of a *conceptus* homily but rather in its formal object, the presentation of a subject through scriptural reflections. Again, let it be remembered

---

[24] Lib. I, hom. IX (I, 43a); Lib. II, hom. III (I, 141a); Lib. IV, hom. VII (I, 321b); hom. XI (I, 355b); hom. XII (I, 362b); Lib. VI, hom. VII (I, 566a); Lib. XIV, hom. V (II, 589b); Lib. XV, hom. IX (III, 85a).

[25] Lib. I, hom. VI (I, 29a); hom. VIII (I, 37b); hom. XV (I, 75a); Lib. II, hom. IV (I, 145b); Lib. X, hom. VII (II, 249b); Lib. XII, hom. X (II, 500a).

[26] Lib. XIV, hom. VIII (II, 614b). Cf. Lib. II, hom. VII (I, 172a); hom. IX (I, 188a); Lib. VII, hom. XII (I, 787b).

[27] Regius, op. cit., p. 401, talks of amplifying on a scriptural text with "varia argumenta, et ut vulgo solemus dicere, conceptus varios."

[28] Cf. Hasenöhrl, art. cit., pp. 64–66; Mendes, "Conceito predicavel," in *Enciclopedia Luso-Brasileira de Cultura*, op. cit., 1199; L. Signer, OMCap, *Die Predigtanlage bei P. Michael Angelus von Schorno, O.M.Cap. Ein Beitrag zur Geschichte des Barockschrifttums* (Assisi, 1933), pp. 80–84; Neumayr, op. cit., p. 132 ff. Schneyer, op. cit., p. 299, warns against exaggerating the singularity of the concetti homilies in the Baroque literature.

that Cartagena's homilies are not actually preached as they are, nor are they intended to be delivered as they are. Thus, although like any unit of writing his homilies have a beginning, a middle and an end, he does not always adhere to the traditional division of parts into *exordium* or *introductio*, *propositio* and *divisio*, sometimes *dispositio*, *narratio*, *confirmatio* or *probatio*, and at the end, the *epilogus* into *adhortatio*, *commotio affectuum* and *repetitio*.[29] Often Cartagena begins his homilies immediately with the consideration of the metaphor or text announced by the title. Many times a homily simply picks up the thought where it was left by the previous homily, and so on. In other words, a homily in the *Homiliae Catholicae* can oft be what is normally considered the body of a sermon, i.e. the development of a theme. He always ends however with a varied formula of glory to God, or to Mary and/or Joseph.

The intellectual element we want to see in his *conceptus* homilies lies not in their harmonization of parts or in the orchestration of a multiplicity of concepts around a main theme, but in the art of arriving at a *conceptus* itself. To come upon a beautiful reflection about a sacred text or word is an exercise of the faculty of *ingenium*. It is what makes a reflection *ingeniosa*, cunning, shrewd, clever, as Weitenauer's definition has it. Cartagena himself connects the *conceptus* with the *ingenium*. He entitles a homily so: *"Prosequimur idem argumentum... multiplici eruditione tam ex sacra scriptura, quam ex sanctis Patribus, ac ingenti conceptuum copia palam demonstramus."* [30] The *ingenium* was the magic word of the Baroque period, an incarnation of its spirit. It is the intellectual capacity of intuition, acumen and sagacity, the ability to penetrate the deep meanings and connotations of the object under consideration, and the agility much like a juggler in combining and separating and exchanging with the subject even what seems most unrelated to it.[31] From the titles cited above, Cartagena clearly associates this ability of the intellect with what he calls *eruditio*.

It is this intellectual power of his *ingenium* which Cartagena pictures sailing out into the deep ocean of Marian mysteries, as he begins

---

[29] For the normal Scholastic sermon structure, cf. Arendt, op. cit., pp. 33–60; Th.–M. Charland, OP, *Artes Praedicandi* (Paris–Ottawa, 1936), pp. 111–226; A. Lecoy de la Marche, *La Chaire française au moyen âge* (Paris, 1886), pp. 289–307.

[30] Lib. XV, hom. XX (III, 173b). Cf. also Lib. V, hom. VIII (I, 429b).

[31] Neumayr, op. cit., p. 136.

his undertaking to present and explain to the faithful the *arcana Mariae* through his *Homiliae Catholicae*.

> Taken up by a daring piety to Mary, I shall strive to announce to the whole world her sacred mysteries under the inspiration of the Divine Spirit (as I hope to be inspired by God's supreme liberality). For although Mary may be a most deep ocean, and the skiff of my *ingenium* can and ought rightly to fear rocks, sandbanks, overhanging cliffs and whirlpools in its navigation, Mary is however known to be the star of the ocean. Hence, although as a deep ocean she is frightening, however, as the star of the ocean she draws to herself, guides, illuminates and enlightens, and promises a most favorable sailing without storms.[32]

And later in discussing Mary's virginity, Cartagena sees his own *ingenium* as merely paving the way for the more felicitous intellectual power and piety of others, who are coming after him. The pursuit itself of explaining doctrines through his *ingenium* he describes as delightful and pious.

> Now in entering a more difficult area, we shall use for the same argument some extraordinary and untried scriptural texts, with which by chance we may open the way, so that others endowed then with a more felicitous *ingenium* and greater piety may seek out other texts (for this art of searching is delightful and pious), with which the truth of this Catholic teaching may more firmly cleave to the mind of the faithful...[33]

By means of one's ingenuity therefore motivated by piety one can discover texts of Sacred Scripture for the purpose of explaining and supporting mysteries of our faith. One can by means of it disclose divine secrets, as the author affirms of David's wisdom, for instance. In an exercise of his own ingenuity, Cartagena interprets the comparison of King David to a *"tenerrimus ligni vermiculus"* (2 Sam 23, 8), indicating "a sharpness of intellect, by which the secrets of the divine law are arrived at, and even if they are difficult, they are laid open nonetheless by searching and by the application of a most unassuming *ingenium*." [34]

---

[32] Lib. I, hom. I (I, 4b–5a).

[33] Lib. VII, hom. XI (I, 783b).

[34] Lib. X, hom. X (II, 277b). The Scripture text is found only in the Vulgate.

E. In the Service of Hermeneutics and Homiletics

It is through the instrumentality of his *ingenium* that Juan de Cartagena forms his *conceptiones animi* or reflections on some sacred texts. In addition to the teaching words of the Church, of the Fathers and of theologians, he has set out to explain the mysteries of Mary's life by further enriching on the literal meaning of the sacred pages through his own mystical reflections on the same and other words from Scripture. The technique by which one can ingenuously come upon or turn up such a *conceptus* or rumination has been thoroughly catalogued by later homileticians. Let us see the list put together by Weitenauer for the *fontes conceptuum*.[35] Although the sources listed below belong more to the time of the High Baroque, their use dates back very early.

The 12 classic *fontes* with examples from Cartagena are as follows.

1. *Conceptus a particula.* The angel's *"Dominus tecum"* (Lk 2, 28) to Mary sollicited from the author a series of reflections on just who is "with" Mary and how.[36] Or Mt 1, 18: *"inventa est in utero habens de Spiritu sancto"* evokes the reflection that since she conceived by the power of the Holy Spirit and not from the outside by a male seed, Christ was simply found "in" her.[37]

2. *Ex numero grammatico nominis.* The *"ex qua"* (not *"ex quibus"*) of Mt 1, 16 shows that Christ was conceived by Mary without any action on the part of Joseph.[38] Or Eccl 24, 23: *"Flores mei fructus honoris et honestatis"* in its plural *"flores"* stands for the many virgins who would be imitating Mary who is here speaking, while the plural *"fructus"* includes not just Christ her son but all who would be redeemed by him.[39]

3. *A tempore verbi grammatico.* Mary's "I do not know man" (Lk 2, 34) denotes according to the peculiarity of the Hebrew language not only the present, but also the future. Hence she has not

---

[35] Hasenöhrl, art. cit., pp. 131–133, referring to Hillinger, another belated defender of Baroque homiletics. The real source is Weitenauer, op. cit., pp. 115–152. Gelasius Hochenleutner, OMRef, *Modus et Praxis Utiliter Concionandi* (Augsburg, 1724), p. 605 f., also discussed the same but less completely. So also I. Wurz, SJ, *Anleitung zur geistlichen Beredsamkeit*, I (Wien, 775), pp. 191–2.

[36] Lib. V, hom. VIII (I, 431a–b).

[37] Lib. VII, hom. IX (I, 773a).

[38] Lib. VII, hom. IX (I, 772a).

[39] Lib. VII, hom. IV (I, 744a).

only never known any man carnally; she would never have any sexual relation with any.[40]

4. *A verborum ordine vel eorum trajectione.* Eccl. 24, 27: *"In me gratia omnis viae et veritatis."* Mary's grace, which includes her preservation from original sin, is a *"gratia viae,"* i.e. she received it while on her way and not at the end of her life, and *"gratia veritatis,"* i.e. this grace is all truth, meaning that her Immaculate Conception is most true.[41] Or, Psalm 24, 10: *"Universa via Domini misericordia et veritas,"* indicates mercy first, thus demonstrating that out of mercy God preserved Mary from sin, otherwise considered in justice alone or in the first place, she should have been born in sin like the others.[42]

5. *Ab epitheto.* Song of Songs 6, 9's *"acies bene ordinata"* signifies a well protected front and rear, otherwise an army with exposed ends would not be well ordered. For Mary it means that her *antiguardia*, i.e. her conception, was protected against the devil of original sin, and her *retroguardia*, i.e. her death, was protected too from the ignominy of corruption.[43]

6. *Ab affine vocabulo.* Gal 4, 4 says of Christ *"factum ex muliere."* Why did he not say that Christ was a *"filium viri"*? Doubtless it was to indicate that Christ lacked a human father and was conceived by Mary virginally.[44] Or, Prov 8, 22: *"Dominus* (not *Deus*) possedit me"* signifies that the Lord possessing Mary has absolute dominion to dispense her from the universal law of original sin.[45]

7. *A voce ambigua.* Song of Songs 3, 6's *"virgula fumi"* coming up from the desert is made applicable to Mary by saying that she is Aaron's *"virga"* blossoming by God's grace in the Tent of Testimony.[46]

8. *A metaphora seu similitudines.* This is a great favorite of Cartagena, and of the Baroque period in general. As is profusely illustrated in Part II, Mary is not only the throne of Solomon, or the ark of Noah, she is also like a lily, a cedar, etc.

9. *A comparatione vocabulorum inter se.* Psalm 84, 2 uses *"avertisti"* in describing God's action to prevent Jacob's captivity, and in

---

40 Lib. VII, hom. IX (I, 773b).
41 Lib. I, hom. XII (I, 61b).
42 Lib. I, hom. II (I, 11b–12a).
43 Lib. I, hom. XI (I, 59a).
44 Lib. VII, hom. IX (I, 773a).
45 Lib. I, hom. II (I, 9a–b).
46 Lib. I, hom. XIV (I, 73b).

verse 3 *"remisisti"* regarding the people's iniquity. So also, Mary's slavery under original sin was hindered or prevented by God, while ours was only taken away; she was preserved, we were cleansed of it.[47]

10. *A praetermissione.* That Sacred Scripture says nothing about Mary's parents just indicates that she was not conceived in sin like the rest of men. It is then to her greater glory.[48]

11. *A lectione variante.* The Protoevangelium's *"ipsum"* (in the Hebrew version) or *"ipsa"* (in the Vulgate) demonstrates by their very variance that Christ with Mary conquered the devil and saved us : Christ principally, Mary only in a subsidiary role.[49]

12. *A comparatione huius loci cum alio.* The Davidic city[50] or the citadel of Jonathan[51] were strongly guarded and impregnable against the enemy. The mystical city of David or citadel of Jonathan, i.e. Mary, is also impregnable against the devil. That is to take this 12th *fons* topographically. But literarily it means more the "harmonization" of two different Scripture texts. Thus, Gen 8, 9's dove from the ark of Noah which could not find any place where to alight is completed by Psalm 17, 17, which speaks of God sending from on high and taking someone, drawing this someone from deep waters, i.e. Mary, the dove.[52]

From the foregoing examples of the *fontes conceptuum* it should be beyond doubt what a tremendous influence the *conceptus* way of interpreting sacred texts must have had on Cartagena's exegesis, or more correctly, on his "eisegesis," his reading *into* Scripture words. It was supposed to assist him put together the development of a theme for preaching purposes, but it underlay too what we have considered in the previous chapter as his mystical understanding of the Bible. He could find a given text's deeper, spiritual meaning with relative ease by putting to work his *ingenium* or perspicacity. During the Baroque period when the mystical sense was highly valued, the *conceptus* homily was also proportionately estimated. Interestingly, for instance, in the Jesuit *Ratio Studiorum* the professor of Sacred Scripture was reminded that allegories and moralizations are not to be omitted, if they contain something *"ingeniosum*

---

[47] Lib. I, hom. III (I, 16a–b).
[48] Lib. II, hom. II (I, 133b–134a).
[49] Lib. I, hom. III (I, 16b–17a).
[50] Lib. I, hom. VI (I, 29a).
[51] Lib. I, hom. VII (I, 36a–b).
[52] Lib. XIV, hom. XII (II, 649a–b & 650a).

et perspicax" in them, in view precisely of the students' later preaching ministry.[53] It is no accident that in Part II's presentation of Cartagena's use of Sacred Scripture in connection with the doctrines of Mary's Immaculate Conception, perpetual virginity, and Assumption into heaven, biblical images, comparisons and similes are preponderant. If metaphor is the mother of poetry, so is it too of the *conceptus*. And as Cartagena himself points out, through such resemblances and metaphors, with which Sacred Scripture abounds, God carries and helps forward our weak human *ingenium*.[54]

The formal method of rhetoric, with its many rules on how to handle a given text, as exemplified by the above–mentioned *fontes conceptuum*, has therefore become an ever–ready assistant not just to homiletics but also to hermeneutics, to the hermeneutics inclined to the more–than–literal sense of Scripture. In this hermeneutics surviving from the Middle Ages, when the *sacramenta* and *arcana* of the sacred words are hidden behind the *obscuritas Sacrae scripturae*, one can always search for the text's spiritual and deeper meaning by using one's *ingenium* to turn up *conceptus*. St. Augustine's saying in this regard became an appeal for such an action: "*Nihil igitur vacat, omnia inuunt, sed intellectorem requirunt.*" [55] And so, where before not enough biblical citations could be given to support a particular subject, now through the *ingenium*'s *conceptus* there can always be practically as many as one may care to have.[56] The very obscurity of a text has in fact become a rich possibility for a preacher. And although the resulting *conceptiones animi* or mystical interpretations do not carry much dogmatic weight in argumentation especially with heretics, for which they are not intended anyway, nonetheless they edify the faithful and assist in clarifying and confirming teachings about the faith. Cartagena explicitly states that it is out of Christian piety that such mystical meanings are discovered in the sacred texts,[57] and also that in this the Christian piety of believers is nourished.[58]

---

[53] *Ratio atque Inst. S.J.*: Reg. Prof. S. Scripturae, n. 15; Pachtler, II, op. cit., p. 70 f.

[54] Lib. VII, hom. X (I, 774b).

[55] Augustine as quoted by Weitenauer, V, op. cit., p. 114.

[56] Neumayr, op. cit., p. 148.

[57] Lib. I, hom. XIX (I, 100b). Re a similar approach by the Seraphic Doctor, cf. J. Guy Bougerol, OFM, *Introduction à l'étude de S. Bonaventure* (Paris, 1961), pp. 126–7.

[58] Lib. XIV, hom. I (II, 559a).

As a contemporary author put it, the goal of the preacher to raise up and put in order the morals of men is served well by the mystical interpretation of sacred passages.[59] For it edifies and strengthens.

It is clear that the emblematic and example books, the *distinctiones* and the *dictionarii*, we have discussed above, had great popularity originally and principally with preachers. They helped in searching out the secrets of the Bible, not just for the sake of studying it, but in order to herald the faith through the explanation of Scripture. The interpretation of Scriptures has always been closely linked with preaching. The encyclopedic reference books of the Middle Ages served well in providing the preacher–"exegete" with points for rumination with which he could build up some *conceptiones animi*. Here we see clearly enough the fact that the level and the direction of the exegesis of the time tends to be in direct proportion to the homiletics. If preaching is preaching the Word of God, the preacher ultimately has to fall back on the achievement and apparatus of the exegete. To the extent therefore that professional exegesis during the time of the Baroque period had not yet really overcome the deeply–rooted spiritual orientation of antiquity and of the Middle Ages, the preacher's own interpretation of Scripture could only be of the same class. The revival of the more–than–literal sense of Sacred Scripture during the 17th century had to manifest itself also in homiletics. The question as to which had the greater impact: exegesis determining homiletics, or homiletics dictating exegesis, loses its moment when taken in the context of the whole cultural environs, which called and craved for the mystical and the ingenious. But before we go into that, let us first consider the abuses that in the end gave the Baroque its bad reputation.

F. ABUSES

As in the case of the mystical interpretation of Sacred Scripture, warnings too had not been lacking with regards the possible abuses of the *conceptiones animi* in preaching. In 1613 the Jesuit General Aquaviva, for example, officially came out against the straining after *concetti* in preaching.[60] The situation started to get worse when the *argutezza* or *argutia* became the fashion of the day. Claimed to be

---

[59] Regius, op. cit., p. 394.

[60] Aquaviva, *De Formandis Concionibus* (Romae, 1613), c. 2, n. 7.

the nerve–system of a Baroque sermon, *argutia* has been defined as *"dictum quoddam acutum seu formula quaedam dicendi a communi ratione valde remota."* [61] What it affects basically is the language as an instrument of the *ingenium*, or of man's cleverness. The trick is to be stunning and smart in speech, unexpected and pointed. The cultivation of unusual constructions and odd expressions developed into a self–serving *stylus acuminosus*, the bizarre that became identified with the Baroque. Thus, from the earlier preoccupation of man's *ingenium* to uncover *conceptus*, some satisfied themselves later with the more superficial and extreme *argutia*. Thus a single metaphor ingeniously reflected upon and mystically interpreted was metamorphosed into a convoluted analogy with unbelievable trimmings and verbal arabesques. The preacher's main concern seemed to have become the applause and the acclaim of his hearers. The practise was so endemic, that the Jesuit Francisco de Isla († 1781), whose *Fray Gerundio* lampooned the style so effectively that it precipitated the demise of Baroque preaching, spoke of the *"mal gusto de los ingenios"* as an *"enfermedad contagiosa."* [62] The seemingly insatiable craving for the new and the unusual, carried to absurd lengths and artificiality, unavoidably turned crude, grotesque and gibberish, a degeneration to *culteranismo*. [63] Moreover, associated with this abuse

---

[61] Aloysius Juglaris, SJ, *Ariadne Rhetorum* (Monachii, 1658), p. 141. E. Tesoro's lyrical song of love for the *argutezza* with its almost divine creativity is most revealing especially in its sonorous Italian original: "...l'argutezza, gran madre d'ogni ingegnoso concetto / chiarissimo lume dell'oratoria, e poetica elocutione / spirito vitale delle morte pagine / piacevolissimo condimento della civil conversatione / ultimo sforzo dell'intelleto / vestigio della divinità nell'animo humano. Non è fiume si dolce di facondia, che senza questa dolcezza, insulso, e dispiacevole non ci rassembri... gli angeli istessi, la natura, il grande Iddio nel ragionar con gli huomini, hanno spresso con argutezze, ò verbali, ò simboliche, gli hor più astrusi ed importanti secreti. Ma non solamente per virtù di questa divina pito, il parla degli huomini ingegnosi tanto si differentia da quel de' plebei, quanto il parlar degli angeli da quel degli huomini; ma per miraculo di lei, le cose mutole parlando / le insensate vivono / le morte risorgono / le trombe, i marmi, le statue da questa incantatrice degli animi ricevendo voce spirito e movimiento, con gli huomini ingegnosi, ingegnosamente discorrono. In somma, tanto solamente è morto; quanto dale' argutezza non è avvivato." Quoted by Neumayr, op. cit., p. 137. Cf. J. Mendes, "Conceptismo," in *Enciclopédia Luso–Brasileira de Cultura*, op. cit., 1194–6.

[62] Cf. Neumayr, op. cit., p. 152.

[63] Cf. Pfandl, op. cit., p. 249 ff.; Fitzmaurice–Kelley, op. cit., p. 283 ff. The latter, p. 300, compares *conceptismo* with *culteranismo* thus: "the latter played

of the *ingenium* was a voracious mangling of sacred texts.[64] To look for the *acuminosum*, single words were completely taken out of context and dissected in a veritable *"anatomia sacrae paginae."* [65] As the archcritic of the *conceptus* homily, François Fénelon († 1715), put it : "How bad it is for a preacher to want an inventive and brilliant head, by which he has to speak with all the dignity and power of the Holy Spirit, whose words serve him."[66]

II. THE SPIRIT OF THE BAROQUE

To fully comprehend why the more–than–literal interpretation of Sacred Scripture made a comeback in spite of Renaissance humanism and contrary to Reformation demands, and to understand more deeply why the *sensus mysticus* and the *conceptiones animi* are so dominant in a work like Juan de Cartagena's *Homiliae Catholicae*, one has to try to gauge the depths of the Baroque soul and let the spirit of the time speak for itself. In this last section of our last chapter we shall round off our consideration of Cartagena's scripturism in his Marian homilies. We have seen his use of Sacred Scripture from the hermeneutical and homiletical viewpoints, and have discussed the theological background to such a preoccupation with the mystical sense. We have also said something of the psychological and stylistic reasons behind the orientation both to the mystical and the ingenious. Now we want to suggest that all this was in a way but a manifestation, a phenomenon of the Baroque *Zeitgeist*. We intend therefore to take a brief look at the cultural milieu in which Juan de Cartagena thrived.

A. THE BAROQUE THIRST FOR ARGUTIA

The mystical sense became for the preacher almost indistinguishable from the *conceptiones animi* during the 17th century. Both

---

with words, the former with ideas. A bizarre vocábulary was enough for a man to pass as *culto;* the *conceptista* must be equipped with various learning, and must have a smattering of philosophy."

[64] Cf. Pachtler, op. cit., p. 114 f.

[65] Weitenauer, op. cit., V, p. 152.

[66] F. Fénelon, *Gespräche über die Beredsamkeit im allgemeinen und über die Kanzelberedsamkeit im besonderen* (München, 1819), p. 164.

were products of the human intellect moved by Christian piety and
emanating from faith. Both were in search of Sacred Scripture's
deeper meaning. In the leeast analysis both were an exercise of man's
mental power. Both were in effect a refusal to give up in the confrontation with the obscurity of the Bible. Both were to fall victim to the
march towards the hollow formalisms and exaggerations of the *argutia*. If a common characteristic can be assigned to Baroque music,
painting, architecture and literature, it is in artistic ornamentation
to the point of floridness.[67] This phenomenon in literature was intimately related with the thirst for *argutia*.

The "mental food" provided by the mystical sense and the
conceptiones animi did not satisfy for long. Like anything habit–
forming, the craving for "bigger trips" soon showed itself. Gradually
the content, the message of the sacred word uncovered through spiritual exegesis hand in hand with the *ingenium*, gave way in importance to the form and the expression, the *argutia*. The manner of
communicating the message turned out to be more stimulating and
hence was eagerly sought after. This development occurred first in
secular literature, with its unrestrained worldliness. As the Jesuit
Aloysius Juglaris writing in 1658 in his *Ariadne Rhetorum* commented about the *argutia*, "our age loves it so much." [68] A few years
earlier the stanch defender of Ciceronian eloquence, Albertus de Albertis, SJ, pictured for us a feet–stomping and cat–calling audience
interrupting a speaker whose piece is not *"argutiolis"* enough.[69]
And a manual for this *conceptista* rhetoric was the *Agudeza y Arte de
Ingenio* (1642), which was written by the Aragonese Jesuit Baltasar
Gracián († 1658). A certain addiction to magniloquence, spiced with
pointed and bizarrely dressed thoughts, had set in.

This contemporary inclination for metaphors and convoluted
analogies, and for vivid and picturesque speech naturally could not
be ignored by homiletics. As Rodulphius a Tossignano, in his edition
of the *Dictionarium Pauperum* for preachers, expressed it: *"translatis
et alienis magis delectemur verbis, quam propriis."* [70] That is why, in

---

[67] Cf. Maurice Ashley, *Das Zeitalter des Barock* (München, 1968), pp. 104–5.

[68] Juglaris, op. cit., p. 141.

[69] Albertus de Albertis, SJ, *In Eloquentiae quum Profanae, tum Sacrae
Corruptores Actio* (Mediolani, 1651), p. 13.

[70] Rodulphius a Tossignano (Nicholas de Byart), *Dictionarium Concionatorum Pauperum Auctoris Incogniti* (Friburgi, 1602), c. 16. Cf. Regius, op. cit.,
p. 239.

addition to the metaphors drawn from Scripture, Virgil's Bucolics, for instance, became popular as a source for more outlandish metaphors. Thus, if the Renaissance resurrected the pagan literature of antiquity, the Baroque appropriated them. The relation between the hearers and the speaker/preacher turned into an ever rising tension between expectation and satisfaction. The more unlikely and unexpected the comparison or the connection ferreted out by the speaker's ingenuity, the greater the wonderment and the applause on the part of the audience. The use of the *ingenium* and the display of the *argutia* degenerated into a demonstration of the speaker's ability and into satisfying the listeners' craving. And one somehow gets the impression that Cartagena himself is playing it along this rule, when he entitles his homilies with such self–advertising phrases as: *"singulari eruditione deducitur,"* or *"perpulchre explicantur."*

But what is essential in all this, the degeneration notwithstanding, is that it was taken as an intellectual exercise. It was not simply an epidemic of over–stimulated phantasies. It was all seen as *ars*, an art enthroned. It was in fact considered a technique approaching divine creativity, by which what was before hidden is laid bare, what was non–existent even is called to life, what was in darkness drawn to light.[71]

B. To Fathom All Depths

The basic intellectual element of the baroque thirst for *argutia* as an exercise of man's *ingenium* reflects very closely the time's pervading desire to fathom all depths. The Renaissance and the Reformation had liberated man from the strait–jacket of the Middle Ages. Individualism was born.[72] And man's newly won self–consciousness received a tremendous boost in the achievements of the 16th century: the discoveries and conquest of overseas lands, the development of mercantilism and trade, the progress in mathematics, physics, medicine and astronomy. Man by the 17th century had a taste of his power to study and analyse the world around him, its laws and manifestations. Daring and encouraged, scientists and

---

[71] Cf. above Tesoro's rhapsodized description, footnote 61; Karl Vossler, *Lope de Vega und sein Zeitalter* (München, ²1947), pp. 48–49.

[72] Edith Simon, *Ketzer Bauern Jesuiten – Reformation und Gegenreformation* (Hamburg, 1973), pp. 181–2.

thinkers set out to widen still more the horizon of man and to challenge him to fathom all depths. His confidence on man's intellectual power urged him. The road to all knowledge is the human intellect.[73] It is to be trusted; it is capable of grasping and clarifying anything. The Baroque man lived with a terrific metaphysical thirst to unravel all secrets and mysteries.

Religion and theology were not exempted from this striving to master, in which is found the seed of later Baroque absolutism. Sacred Scripture consequently could be explained too. Its deeper, mystical significations could be uncovered by the application of human ingenuity and mental resources. And very important to this thought was the realization that the Fathers and their later commentators had already somehow indicated the way. To be observed too is that in this beginning of rationalism the mystical was accorded a place of its own.

Moreover, man's individuality meant that he developed his capacities to the full. This should be done in one way by the use of *ingenium* in what he encounters, observes, studies and says. Carried into the church, it meant that the preacher was expected to demonstrate his own mental sagacity, and the hearers in turn waited to have their own acumen whetted and satisfied.

But much like an adolescent, with his contradictions and cuteness, his self–conscious bravado and inhibiting inexperience, his daring and awkwardness, the Baroque thinker was both a captive and a free man. He had broken away from the Middle Ages but was not yet fully liberated from its thought–structures and limitations. A definite dualism characterized him. Side by side with his sensuality and abandon to the things of this life was his spiritualism and idealism in search of the simplest and straightest way to God. With his strict formalism in style was coupled his stark realism in the arts. His frightening naturalism and anxiety to please see–sawed with his illusionism.[74] This pot–pourri of antitheses is best illustrated by the country of Juan de Cartagena's origin, Spain, which gave the world the strongest expression of the Baroque as its own literary genius.

---

[73] Wilhelm Schubart, "Vom Geist des siebzehnten Jahrhunderts," in his *Glaube und Bildung im Wandel der Zeiten* (München, 1947), pp. 174–5.

[74] Carl Friedrich, *Das Zeitalter des Barock* (Stuttgart, 1954), pp. 56–57.

C. A SPANISH ORIGIN

The *conceptus* homily or the concetti, despite its name, originated from Spain. It reached Italy through Spanish Naples, and from
Italy it spread out to the rest of Europe. Also, the revival of the
mystical interpretation of Sacred Scripture was represented for the
greater part by Spanish exegetes and theologians. Spain was the
driving force to Baroque developments.

The Spanish society of the 16th century had produced a brilliant civilization, as rich in cultural accomplishments as it was poor
in economic achievement. And Spain was particularly strong in the
field of literature. The great literary figures of this age were almost
all contemporaries of Juan de Cartagena: Miguel Cervantes (1547–
1615), whose *El ingenioso hidalgo Don Quixote de la Mancha* (1605)
portrays so humorously the antithesis to the Baroque; Luis de Góngora (1561–1627), chaplain to the king and founder of the *"estilo
culto"* or *culteranismo*, synonymous with exuberance and unrestraint
in arts, typified by cultivating artificial antitheses, violent transpo-
sitions, verbal inventions, exaggerated and licentious metaphors — to
charm *"los cultos,"* the cultivated; Lope de Vega (1562–1635), the
prolific poet and dramatist of more than 1,500 plays, whose realism
was eminently Spanish in its strength but whose anxiety to please
at any cost was also eminently Spanish in its weakness; Tirso de Molina (1571–1648), the poet–priest; Francisco de Quevedo (1580–1645),
the satirist; and later Pedro Cálderon (1600–1645), the great dramatist. All these writers gave fullness and form to the qualities of the
Baroque.[75] They mirrored in their works the tension between idealism
and spirituality on the one side and passionate sensuality and eroti-
cism on the other, between formalism and profuse ornamentation
on one hand and strong naturalism of the other. Their extreme illusionism that this life is but a dream, echoed for all times by Calderon's *La vida es sueño* and in William Shakespeare's (1564–1616)
Macbeth, was inescapable. In Calderon's idealized interpretation of
existence, his characters are really allegorical types of men and women; he reveals a brilliant pageant of abstract and mystic emotions,
not the ignoble real life. In his *autos sacramentales*, exposing the Eu-
charistic mystery through allegorical characters, abstractions are
wedded to the noblest poetry and doctrinal subtleties are embellished

---

[75] Ibid., pp. 63–70.

with miraculous ingenuity. Calderon expressed the full genius of his age.[76]

Originally religious in inspiration and based on the realization of God's transcendence as the only reality, the stark Spanish Baroque illusionism was greatly influenced and deepened by the situation in the land. Toward the end of the 16th century, the fulcrum of Europe had started to shift from the Mediterranean, from Spain and Italy, northward.[77] The mighty Castilian kingdom was sagging under its own weight. The invicible Armada proved ineffecient and the fight against international Protestantism also. The economy was in crisis; and the failure of leadership was beyond repair.[78] The imperial triumph was giving way to imperial defeat. The days of heroism were being replaced by the days of *desengaño*. There was only a precarious balance between optimism and pessimism, enthusiasm and irony. And the moral and emotional involvement of the intellectuals seemed to have stimulated them in a creativity that reflected the national tragedy.

In their flight from the real and the commonplace, their illusionism manifested itself in the voracious craving for symbolism and the other-wordlly. A side development was the frenzied abandon in the artificiality of Góngora's cultism. Another sign was the "retreat" to the intellect. With the emphasis on individualism, each should develop his intellect and higher powers to the greatest extent. This ideal was contained in the word *ingenio*.[79] Also, the world was seen as a theatre, in which we are bitplayers. Each man should play his role to the hilt and with flare. We play for the bravos and applause, to please our audience. Another typically Spanish manifestation of this illusionism was the still higher retreat to mysticism.[80] It was no matter of chance that all the great mystics of Spain lived during the latter part of the 16th century: St. Theresa († 1582), Juan de la Cruz († 1591) and Luis de Granada († 1588).[81] A graphic illustration of

---

[76] Cf. Max Kommerell, *Beiträge zu einem deutschen Calderon*, I (Frankfurt am Main, 1946); Fitzmaurice–Kelley, op. cit., pp. 317–332.

[77] Cf. Pierre Chaunu, *Europäische Kultur im Zeitalter des Barock* (München, 1968), p. 31 ff.

[78] Cf. J. Elliott, op. cit., p. 285 ff.; Pfandl, op. cit., pp. 211–214; Chaunu, op. cit., p. 102 f.

[79] Cf. Pfandl, op. cit., pp. 236–239.

[80] Cf. Josef Gregor, *Das spanische Welttheater* (München, 1943), p. 168 ff.

[81] Cf. Bataillon, op. cit., p. 750 ff.

this illusionist ambivalence is perhaps best suggested in a strange juxtaposition by El Greco's *"Burial of the Count of Orgaz,"* painted during Juan de Cartagena's early religious life in 1586. The withdrawn faces of the witnesses to the miracle seem only partially of this world.

The foregoing very brief summary of the cultural and literary development in Spain intended to give a glimpse of the historical circumstances that contributed to the shaping of the Baroque *Weltanshauung* giving soul to the thoughts and orientation of Juan de Cartagena, *"Hispanus"*. That much of what is accepted as characterizing the 17th century developed first and more fully in Spain, makes it clear why Cartagena possessed such a strong inclination to the mystical and the ingenious in his *Homiliae Catholicae*. He was a child of his time and of his land.

CONCLUSION

Our study allows us to make the following conclusions:

Juan de Cartagena (1563–1618) of the city of Madrid entered the Society of Jesus in 1581 and was ordained a priest in 1590. From a teaching post in León, he became a professor of theology at Salamanca in 1596–7. His brief professorial tenure there ended unhappily in connection with an effort to counter the influence of Francisco Suarez, with whom Cartagena had been identified. Assigned to teach in Valladolid, Cartagena eventually joined the Franciscan Observants in 1602. From 1606 to 1616 he was a theology professor of high repute in San Pietro in Montorio in Rome. In mid–1618, apparently due to an epidemic, the *emeritus* theologian died in Naples while on a mission for the Pope.

Cartagena made a name for himself as a devoted and prolific writer in the service of the Holy See, especially during the troubles with the Republic of Venice and in the course of the controversy *"de auxiliis."* A personal friend of Pope Paul V, Rome's initiative to reward him with a Spanish bishopric did not bear fruits.

His writings show a wide range of interest, from a purely Scholastic treatise like his *Selectarum Disputationum in Quartum Sententiarum* (1607), to papal apologetics like *Pro Ecclesiastica Libertate, et Potestate Tuenda* (1607) and *Propugnaculum Catholicum de Iure Belli Romani Pontificis adversus Ecclesiae Iura Violantes* (1609), to moral issues like *Disputatio Insignis Utilis Valde ac Pernecessaria ad Extirpandum Quoddam Latentis Simoniae Vitium* (1607), to spirituality as his *Praxis Orationis Mentalis* (1618). But his main work is the four volumes of his *Homiliae Catholicae* (1609–1616). The wide distribution throughout Europe of his *Homiliae Catholicae* with its many translations and many reprintings testify that Cartagena achieved his purpose of giving a sourcebook to preachers, on the mysteries of Christ and of Mary and Joseph.

Regarding his Mariology, he taught that Mary's Immaculate Conception meant a presevation from a *debitum contrahendi peccatum originale,* in an echo of Duns Scotus and of Suarez. Together with the avant–garde of his time, he considered the doctrine to be *definibilis.* He connected this Marian privilege with her eternal predestination to be the Mother of God and Christ's *coadiutrix* in the work of salvation.

Mary's virginity was *ante partum, in partu, post partum.* It was a physical integrity throughout, prepared for by her vow of virginity. This doctrine is for Cartagena a defined dogma.

The dignity that was Mary's as the mother of Christ, the principle whence all her graces flow, preserved her from corruption after her death. She was taken up to heaven body and soul, and now intercedes before God for us all as the *mater omnium viventium.* The doctrine of the Assumption is *certa,* as is her Immaculate Conception.

With regards his use of Sacred Scripture, Cartagena acknowledged the primacy of the literal sense, which alone has dogmatic value. But his real interest lies in the mystical sense. With the exception of the mysteries of Mary's divine motherhood and her virginity, Sacred Scripture is silent about her graces: the Immaculate Conception and the Assumption. The Bible can speak of these other Marian mysteries only in the mystical sense, which for Cartagena meant actually a wide–ranging, practically all–inclusive allegorical interpretation of Scripture texts applied often arbitrarily to Mary. He considered this Mariological use of biblical *"metaphorae et similitudines"* illustrative and confirmatory of what we believe about her.

Hermeneutically, Cartagena was dependent on Alfonso Salmeron's mystical exegesis and reflects the revival of Patristic and medieval biblical interpretation in the post–Tridentine period. The approach was based on the belief of Sacred Scripture's *mira profunditas* having more to communicate to us than what the letters say. It was also dictated by Scripture's *obscuritas.*

Even if the *Homiliae Catholicae* does not offer ready–made homilies but rather thematically developed materials, it manifests characteristics of Baroque homiletics with its emphasis on the *conceptus* and the use of the *ingenium.* These *conceptiones animi* are in effect the *mystica intelligentia* of Sacred Scripture Cartagena presented in illustrating his explanations of Mary's graces. His method in coming upon these *conceptus* or ingenious reflections on the sacred words is the same as the process of looking for the deeper, spiritual meaning of Scripture texts.

Cartagena's *Homiliae Catholicae* reflects the interdependence between homiletics and hermeneutics in the Baroque period. It exemplifies the new found confidence in the ability of the human intellect to fathom all depths. Thus Cartagena's inclination for the ingenious and the mystical just proves him to be the *"Hispanus,"* for these Baroque developments originated and flowered in Spain.

To proclaim the mysteries of the faith, Cartagena spoke the language of his time and culture. His thoughts and especially his way of using Sacred Scripture should be seen as the product of a particular society and was meaningful to such a society. To understand him and do him justice, we have to see in this context the justification, say, for his particular way of interpreting Scripture. For basically Sacred Scripture has always to be "re–interpreted" to communicate its message to any given time. A language of faith is historically conditioned.[1]

We have said in the introduction to this study that our purpose was to reduce the question mark enveloping Juan de Cartagena. We wanted to understand him as a theologian and as a preacher of the faith to the Christians of his own time. We hope we have at least reduced the size of that question mark.

---

[1] Cf. E. Schillebeeckx, "The Crisis in the Language of Faith as a Hermeneutical Problem," *Concilium*, 9/5 (1973) 31–45.

SELECT BIBLIOGRAPHY

I. PRIMARY SOURCES

A. Cartagena's Works Used in This Study

Cartagena, J. de, *Homiliae Catholicae Universa Christianae Religionis Arcana* (Romae, 1609; Coloniae, 1614).

Homiliae Catholicae de Sacris Arcanis Deiparae Mariae et Ioseph, I–III (Coloniae, 1613–1616; Coloniae, 1625).

Propugnaculum Catholicum de Iure Belli Romani Pontificis adversus Ecclesiae Iura Violantes (Romae, 1609).

Zwanzig schöner ausführlicher Concept, über der glorwürdigsten Himmerl Königin Mariae, hochheiliges Lobgesang, das Magnificat genandt, transl. by Thobias Hendschel (Ingolstadt, 1617).

Praxis Orationis Mentalis ad Faciliorem Eius Usum Reddendum (Coloniae, 1618).

Conciones Quadragesimales in Sacrosancta Evangelia (Parisiis, 1632).

De Sufficientia et Efficacia Divinae Gratiae (*Verdad y Vida,* 86, pp. 200–219).

Regulae Quaedam Proponuntur Apprime Necessariae Valdeque Utiles ad Definiendam Veritatem Praesentis Controversiae de Efficacia Divinae Gratiae (Ibid., 220–227).

Referuntur Varia Testimonia Scholasticorum Doctorum in Favorem Sententiae Asserentis Omnes Actus Liberos Humanae Voluntatis Praedefiniri et Praedeterminari a Efficaci et Absoluta Voluntate (Ibid., 227–231).

B. Literature Directly or Indirectly Referring to Juan de Cartagena

Archivum Romanum Societatis Jesu, manuscripts: *Catalogus Triennialis Castellanus* 14, f. 23, f. 29, f. 165, f. 248, f. 324, f. 380.

Epistolae Virorum Illustrium SJ, V. 96, f. 215.

Castell. Epist. Gener. 1588–1603, Cast. 6, f. 288, f. 292, ff. 293–4, ff. 295–6, f. 300.

Hispania, 2.

Historia Societatis, 54.

Alençon, E. d', "Marchant, Pierre (1585–1661)," *DThC*, IX, 2004–6.

Amann, E., "Jean de Carthagena," *DThC*, VIII, 754–5.

Antonio, N., *Bibliotheca Hispana Nova sive Hispanorum Scriptorum qui ab anno 1500 ad 1684 Floruere Notitia*, ed. by T. Antonio Sanchez, J. Antonio Pellicer & R. Casalbon, I (Matriti, 1783).

Bayle, P., *Dictionnaire Historique et Critique*, II (Amsterdam, [5]1740).

Bibliotheca Catholica Neerlandica Impressa 1500–1727 (The Hague, 1954).

Bihl, M., "Friars Minor," *The Catholic Encyclopedia*, IV (New York, 1913), 281–298.

Biografía Eclesiastica Completa, "Cartagena," III (Madrid–Barcelona, 1850), 464–5.

The British Museum Catalogue of Printed Books, IX (Ann Arbor, 1946).

Castro, M. de, "Juan de Carthagène," *Catholicisme*, VI (Paris, 1967), 595–6.

Catalogue Général de Livres Imprimés de la Bibliothèque Nationale, 79 (Paris, 1931) & 194 (Paris, 1966).

Catalogus Bibliothecae Bunauianae, III–1 (Lipsiae, 1755).

Cerreto, S. M. de, *Annales Minorum*, 25 (Quaracchi, [2]1934).

Dausquius, C., *Sancti Iosephi Sanctificatio extra uterum seu Binoctium adversus F. Marchanti Minoritae Exprovincialis Inanias. Item Aplysiarum F. Minorum audom. Spongia* (Lugduni, 1631).

Diccionario Enciclopedico Hispano–Americano, "Cartagena, Juan de," IV (Barcelona, 1888), 322.

Ferrier, S. de, *Le Catholique d'Estat ou discours des alliances du Roy Tres–Chrestien* (Paris, 1625).

Jöcher, C., *Allgemeines Gelehrten Lexicon*, I (Leipzig, 1750).

Grabmann, M., *Die Geschichte der katholischen Theologie seit dem Ausgang der Väterzeit* (Freiburg im Br., 1933).

Gubernatis, D. de, *Orbis Seraphicus, Historia de Tribus Ordinibus a Seraphico Patriarcha S. Francisco Institutis*, III (Romae, 1684).

Laurus, I. B., *Theatri Romani Orchestra... Dialogus de Viris Sui Aevi Doctrina Illustribus* (Romae, 1625).

Lipenius, M., *Bibliotheca Realis Theologica*, I–II (Francofurti ad Moenum, 1685).

Marchant, P., *Sanctificatio S. Josephi Sponsi Virginis Nutriti Iesus in Utero, asserta pro R.P.F. Joanne Cartagena Ordinis S. Francisci olim in Academia Salmanticensi professore, et in urbe de mandato Sanctissimi Generali lectore contra R.D. Claudii Dausquii Tornacensis Canonici calumnias* (Brugge, 1630).

Martinez, P. de Alcantara, "La Inmaculada Concepción según las Doctrinas de Juan de Cartagena y Juan Serrano, O.F.M. (s. XVII)," *Virgo Immaculata*, VII–2 (Romae, 1957) 209–241.

Peers, E. Allison, *Studies of the Spanish Mystics*, I–III (London, 1951[2], 1930, 1960).

Renedo, A., *Escritores Palentinos*, I (Madrid, 1919).

San Antonio, J., *Bibliotheca Universa Franciscana*, II (Madrid, 1732).

Sbaralea, H., *Supplementum et Castigatio ad Scriptores Trium Ordinum s. Francisci a Waddingo, Aliisve Descriptos*, II (Romae, 1921).

Sdo Corazón, E., "La paternidad josefino en los escritores españoles de los siglos XVI y XVII," *Estudios Josefinos*, 6 (1952) 152–178.
"Razon de prioridad y preeminencia entre el matrimonio y la paternidad de S. José, segùn Juan de Cartagena y Fray Melchor Prieto, O.M.," *Estudios Josefinos*, 13 (1959) 62–90.

Stegmüller, F., "Carthagena, Johannes de," in *Lexikon der Marienkunde*, I, ed. Konrad Algermissen et al. (Regensburg, 1960), 1067–72.

Tejera, J. P. & R. de Moncada, *Biblioteca del Murciano o Ensayo de un Diccionario biográfico y bibliográfico de la Literatura en Murcia*, I (Madrid, 1924).

Toda y Güell, E., *Bibliografia Espanyola D'Italia*, II (Escornalbou, 1928).

Trottier, A., *Essai de Bibliographie sur saint Joseph* (Montréal, 1968).

Vasquez, I., "Fr. Juan de Cartagena (1563–1618). Vida y Obras," *Antonianum*, 39 (1954) 243–301.
"Ineditos de Juan de Cartagena," *Verdad y Vida*, 86 (1964) 189–231.
" Nueva Documentos de Fr. Juan de Cartagena, OFM, sobre las controversias de auxiliis," *Antonianum*, 40 (1965) 319–325.

Wadding, L., *Annales Minorum*, 25 (Quaracchi, 1934).
Scriptores Ordinis Minorum (Romae, 1650: Unveränderter Nachdruck, Frankfurt/Main, 1967).

Willaert, L., *Bibliotheca Janseniana Belgica*, I (Brussels–Paris, 1949).

II. SECONDARY SOURCES

A. MARIOLOGY

Aldama, J. de, *De Quaestione Mariali in Hodierna Vita Ecclesiae* (Romae, 1964). Bibliotheca Mariana moderni aevi. Pontificia Academia Mariana Internationalis.
"El canon tercero del Concilio Lateranense de 649," *Marianum*, 24 (1962) 65–83.
"Zur theologischen Würdigung der Lehre von der 'Virginitas in partu' im Laterankonzil von 649," in *Heilige Schrift und Maria* (Essen, 1963), pp. 261–270. Mariologische Studien II.
"Nuevos documentos sobre las tesis de Alcalá," *Archivo Teológico Granadino*, 14 (1951) 134–157.
"El mérito condigno de la maternidad divina de Nuestra Señora en la teología de los s. XVI–XVII," *Archivo Teológico Granadino*, 25 (1962) 179–224.

Aperribay, B., "La muerte y la Asuncion de la Virgen en los representantes de la mariologia franciscano–española," *Verdad y Vida*, 6 (1948) 263–284.

Bachelet, X. Le, "Immaculée conception dans l'Eglise latine après le concile d'Ephèse," in *DThC*, VII, 979–1218.

Balić, C., *Testimonia de Assumptione Beatae Virginis Mariae ex Omnibus Saeculis*. Pars prior: ex aetate ante Concilium Tridentinum (Romae, 1948). Pars altera: ex aetate post C. Tridentinum (Romae, 1950). Bibliotheca Assumptionis B. Virginis Mariae, I–II.
Theologiae Marianae Elementa Ioannis Duns Scoti, Doctoris Mariani (Sibenici, 1933).
Pro Veritate Assumptionis B.V. Mariae Dogmatice Definienda (Romae, 1949).
"Die Corredemptrixfrage innerhalb der franziskanischen Theologie," *Franziskanische Studien*, 39 (1957) 238–244.
"De significatione interventus Scoti in historia dogmatis I.C.," *Virgo Immaculata*, VII–1 (1957) 74–95. Acta Congressus Mariologici–Mariani Romae 1954 celebrati. 8 vols. (Romae, 1955–58).
"Muerte de Maria, de la edad media al siglo XX," *Estudios Marianos*, 9 (1950) 11–121.

Barre, H., "La Croyance à l'Assomption corporelle en Occident de 750 à 1150 environ," *Études Mariales*, 7 (1949) 63–123.

Beumer, J., "Die marianische Deutung des Hohen–Liedes in der Früh-scholastik," *Zeitschrift für katholische Theologie*, 76 (1954) 411–439.

Bonnefoy, J.-F., "Marie indemne de toute tache du péché originel," *Virgo Immaculata*, XI (1957) 1–62.
"La negacion del 'debitum peccati' en Maria," *Verdad y Vida*, 12 (1954) 103–171.

Brandenburg, A., "De mariologia ac cultu Mariae apud protestantes," in *De Mariologia et Oecumenismo* (Romae, 1962), pp. 479–516. Ed. by Pontificia Academia Mariana Internationalis.

Brlek, M., "Legislatio O.F.M. circa Doctorem Immaculatae Conceptionis," *Virgo Immaculata*, VII–3 (1957) 188–226.

Brosch, H. J. & J. Hasenfuss, ed., *Jungfrauengeburt Gestern und Heute* (Essen, 1969). Im Auftrag der deutschen Arbeitsgemeinschaft für Mariologie.

Brown, R., "The Virginal Conception of Jesus," *Theological Studies*, 33 (1972) 3–34.

Campenhausen, H. v., *Die Jungfrauengeburt in der Theologie der alten Kirche* (Heidelberg, 1962).

Canisius, P., *Mariae Sacrosanctae et Deiparae Virginis Vita*, brevius comprehensa a P. Vogt, SJ (Taurini, 1933).

Capelle, B., "Le Témoignage de la liturgie," *Études Mariales*, 7 (1949) 35–62.

Carvajal, L., *Declamatio Expostulatoria pro Immaculata Conceptione* in P. Alva y Astorga, *Monumenta Antiqua Seraphica pro Imm. Conceptione* (Lovanii, 1665), pp. 464–518.

Cazelles, H., "Fille de Sion et theologie mariale dans la Bible," *Études Mariales*, 21 (1964) 51–71.

Cole, W., "Scripture and the Current Understanding of Mary among American Protestants," *Maria in Sacra Scriptura*, VI (1967) 95–161. Acta Congressus Mariologici–Mariani in Republica Dominicana anno 1965 celebrati. 6 vols. (Romae, 1967).

Cothenet, E., "Marie dans les Apocryphes," *Maria*, VI (1961) 117–148. Ed. by H. du Manoir.

Deiss, L., *Maria, Tochter Sion* (Mainz, 1961).

Delius, W., *Geschichte der Marienverehrung* (München, 1963).

Dietz, I. M., "Ist die Hl. Jungfrau nach Augustinus 'Immaculata ab initio'?" *Virgo Immaculata*, IV (1955) 61–112.

Dillenschneider, C., "L'Assomption corporelle de Marie dans la période posttridentine," *Études Mariales*, 8 (1950) 71–146.

Duncker, P., "Auctoritas S. Scripturae et praevia sanctificatio B.V. Mariae iuxta S. Thomam," *Virgo Imm.*, VI (1955) 92–102.

Frank, K., et al., ed., *Zum Thema Jungfrauengeburt* (Stuttgart, 1970).

Gagnebet, R., "Le Mode d'exercise de la royauté de Marie au ciel à l'égard des hommes viateurs," *Maria et Ecclesia*, V (1959) 201–221. Acta Congressus Mariologici–Mariani in civitate Lourdes anno 1958 celebrati. 6 vols. (Romae, 1959).

Gallus, T., *Interpretatio Mariologica Protoevangelii Posttridentina usque ad Definitionem Dogmaticam Immaculatae Conceptionis*, pars prior (Romae, 1953).
"Ratio quae intercedit inter Dogmata Immaculatae Conceptionis et Assumptionis B.M. Virginis," *Virgo Imm.*, X (1957) 80–91.

Geenen, G., "Eadner, le premier théologien de l'Immaculée Conception," *Virgo Imm.*, V (1955) 90–115.

Gewiess, J., "Die Marienfrage Lk 1, 34," in R. Laurentin, *Struktur und Theologie der lukanischen Kindheitsgeschichte* (Stuttgart, 1967).

Gössmann, E., *Die Verkündigung an Maria im dogmatischen Verständnis des Mittelalters* (München, 1957).

Gräber, R., *Die marianischen Weltrundschreiben der Päpste in den letzten hundert Jahren* (Würzburg, ²1954).

Graef, H., *Maria eine Geschichte der Lehre und Verehrung* (Freiburg, 1964).

Inmacula, I. de la, "El misterio de la corredencion," *Maria et Ecclesia*, IV (1959) 206–214.

Jesus Crucificado, G. de, "La Asunción en la teologia española," *Estudios Marianos*, 6 (1947) 354–378.

Jouassard, G., "Marie à travers la Patristique," *Maria*, I (1949) 71–157.
"L'Assomption corporelle de la Saint Vierge et la Patristique," *Études Mariales*, 6 (1948) 97–117.
"Royauté de Marie et Assomption," *Maria et Ecclesia*, V (1959) 173–189.

Jugie, M., *La Mort et l'Assomption de la Sainte Vierge. Étude historico-doctrinale* (Città del Vaticano, 1944).

Koster, M. D., "Die Himmelfahrt Mariens gleichsam die Vollendung ihrer Unbefleckten Empfängnis," *Virgo Imm.*, X (1957) 92–114.

Künneth, F. W., "Maria im Glabenszeugnis der Kirche Evangelisch–Lutherischer Reformation," *Maria in Sacra Scriptura*, VI (1967) 5–13.

Langemeyer B., "Konziliare Mariologie und biblische Typologie," *Catholica*, 21 (1967) 295–316.

Laurentin, R., *Struktur und Theologie der lukanischen Kindheitsgeschichte* (Stuttgart, 1967).

Macali, L., "La Dottrina dell'Immacolata nei Grandi Scotisti OFM Conv. dei Secoli XVI–XIX," *Virgo Imm.*, VII–2 (1957) 44–98.

Martinez, P. de Alcantara, "La Redención Preservativa y el Débito Remoto," *Salmaticensis*, 1 (1954) 301–337.
"La redención de Maria y los méritos de Cristo," *Estudios Franciscanos*, 55 (1954) 195–254.
"La corredencion y el débito según los teólogos salmantinos," *Virgo Imm.*, XI (1957) 196–253.

Mückshoff, M., "Die mariologische Prädestination im Denken der franziskanischen Theologie," *Franziskanische Studien*, 39 (1957) 288–502.

Müller, A., *Ecclesia–Maria* (Freiburg, ²1955).
"Maria Stellung und Mitwirkung im Christusereignis," in *Mysterium Salutis*, ed. Johannes Feiner & Magnus Löhrer (Einsiedeln, 1969), III–2, pp. 393–510.
"Maria," in *LThK*, VII, 25–32.

Murphy, J., "The Development of Mariology," *The American Ecclesiastical Review*, 138 (1958) 89–103, 158–172.

Mußner, F., "Lk 1, 48 f; 11, 27 f und die Anfänge der Marienverehrung in der Urkirche," *Catholica*, 21 (1967) 287–294.

Napiorkowski, Stanislaw, "The Present Position in Mariology," *Concilium*, 3/9 (1967) 52–62.

Nicolas, M. J., "De transcendentia Matris Dei," *Maria et Ecclesia*, II (1959) 73–87.

Plessis, A., "La Virginité de Marie et son Assomption corporelle," *Études Mariales*, 7 (1949) 125–137.

Rahner, K., "Die Unbefleckte Empfängnis," in *Schriften zur Theologie*, I (Einsiedeln, 1962) 223–237.

"Zum Sinn des Assumptio–Dogmas," ibid., 239–252.

"Virginitas in Partu," *Schriften zur Theologie*, IV (Einsiedeln, 1964), 173–205.

Recio A., "La Inmaculada en la predicación franciscano–española," *Archivo Ibero–Americano*, 15 (1955) 105–200.

Riedlinger, H., "Maria–Kirche in den marianischen Hohenliedkommentaren des Mittelalters," *Maria et Ecclesia*, III (1959) 241–289.

Roschini, G., "Il problema del 'debitum peccati' in Maria Santissima," *Virgo Imm.*, XI (1957) 343–355.
"De usu regulae quartae Tychoni in mariologia biblica," *Maria in Sacra Scriptura*, III, 141–171.

Sdo. Corazón, E., "Sobre el sentido 'plenior' y su aplicación en mariologia," *Maria in Sacra Scriptura*, II, 81–104.

Sagués, P., "Doctrina de Immaculata B.V. Mariae Conceptionis apud P. Ludovicum de Carvajal, O.F.M. († 1552)," *Antonianum*, 28 (1943) 141–162, 245–270.

Schelke, K. & O. Semmelroth, "Maria," in *Handbuch theologischer Grundbegriffe*, III (München, 1970), 115–126.

Schillebeeckx, E., *Mary, Mother of the Redemption* (London, 1964).

Schmaus, M., "Mariology," in *Sacramentum Mundi*, III (London, 1969) 376–390.

Sericoli, C., "Ordo Franciscalis et Romanorum Pontificum acta de immaculata BMV conceptione," *Virgo Imm.*, II (1956) 99–152.

Solà, F. de P., "La Muerte de la Santisima Virgen en la Constitución Apostólica 'Munificentissimus Deus'," *Estudios Marianos*, 12 (1952) 125–156.

Unger, D., "S. Irenaei doctrina de Maria, socia Iesu in recapitulatione," *Maria et Ecclesia*, IV (1959) 67–140.

Varela, D., "La Mariologia en los Autores españoles de 1600 a 1650," *Estudios*, 7 (1951) 249–295.
"Exencion del débito según los mariologos españoles de 1600 a 1650," *Ephemerides Mariologicae*, 1 (1951) 501–526.

Villalmonte, A. de, "La immaculada y el débito del pecado," *Verdad y Vida*, 12 (1954) 49–101.

Vogt, B., "Duns Scotus, Defender of the Immaculate Conception," *Virgo Imm.*, VII-1 (1957) 220–240.

Vögtle, A., "Mt 1, 25 und die virginitas B.M. Virginis post partum," *Tübinger theologische Quartalschrift*, 149 (1967) 28–39.

Volk, H., "Maria, Mater credentium," *Trierer theologischer Zeitschrift*, 73 (1964) 1–21.

Uribe, A., "La Inmaculada en la literatura franciscano–española," *Archivo Ibero–Americano*, 15 (1955) 201–495.

Wenceslaus, S., *De B. Virgine Maria Universali Gratiarum Mediatrice*. Doctrina Franciscanorum ab an. 1600 ad an. 1730 (Romae, 1953). "La Coopération de Marie et de l'Eglise à la rédemption selon les Pères de l'Eglise," *Maria et Ecclesia*, IV (1959) 38–45.

Wenger, A., *L'Assomption de la T.S. Vierge dans la tradition byzantine du VIe au Xe siècle. Études et documents*. (Paris, 1955).

B. Hermeneutics

Arias Reyero, M., *Thomas von Aquin als Exeget* (Einsiedeln, 1971).

Baroni, V., *La Contre–Reforme devant la Bible* (Lausanne, 1943).

Barosse, T., "The Senses of Scripture and the Liturgical Pericopes," *Catholic Biblical Quarterly*, 21 (1959) 1–23.

Blinzler, J., *Die Brüder und Schwestern Jesu* (Stuttgart, 1967).

Brown, R., *The Sensus Plenior of Sacred Scripture* (Baltimore, 1955). "The Sensus Plenior in the last ten years," *Catholic Biblical Quarterly*, 25 (1963) 262–285. "Hermeneutics," in *The Jerome Biblical Commentary* (London, 1968) II, 605–623.

Caplan, H., "The Four Senses of Scriptural Interpretation and the Mediaeval Theory of Preaching," *Speculum*, 4 (1929) 282–290.

Coppens, J., "Levels of Meaning in the Bible," *Concilium*, 3/10 (1967) 62–69.

Criado, R., "El Concilio de Trento y los estudios biblicos," *Razon y Fe*, 131 (1945) 151–187.

Crouzel, H., "Spiritual Exegesis," in *Sacramentum Mundi*, I (London, 1968), pp. 201–207.

Garcia, Juan, L., *Los Estudios Biblicos en el Siglo de Oro de la Universidad Salmantina* (Salamanca, 1921).

Gollinger, H., *Das "große Zeichen" von Apokalypse 12* (Würzburg, 1971).

Grant, R., *The Bible in the Church* (New York, 1948).

Hahn, F., *Christologische Hoheitstitel* (Göttingen, 1963).

Heller, J., "Namengebung und Namendeutung," *Evangelische Theologie*, 27 (1967) 255–266.

Lauretius, Hieronymus, *Silva seu potius Hortus floribus allegoriarum totius S. Scripturae* (Barcelona, 1570: Nachdruck–München, 1971).

Lecler, J., "Littéralisme biblique et typologie au XVIe siècle," *Recherches de science religieuse*, 51 (1953) 76–95.

Leon–Dufour, X., ed., *Exegese im Methoden Konflikt* (München, 1973).

Lubac, H. de, *Exégèse Médiévale*, I–IV (Paris, 1959–1964).
Histoire et Esprit. L'intelligence de l'Ecriture d'après Origène. (Paris, 1950).

Muñoz Iglesias, S., "El decreto tridentino sobre la Vulgata y su interpretacion por los teólogos del siglo XVI," *Estudios Biblicos*, 5 (1946) 137–169.

Ohly, F., "Vom geistigen Sinn des Wortes im Mittelalter," *Zeitschrift für deutsches Altertum u. deutsche Literatur*, 89 (1958) 1–23.

Reinhardt, K., "Theologie als Interpretation der Heiligen Schrift bei Antão Galvão OESA (ca. 1559–1609) und Pedro Luis Beuther SJ (1538–1602)," *Portugiesische Forschungen der Görresgesellschaft*, 11 (1973) 1–25.

Rothfuchs, W., *Die Erfüllungszitate des Matthäus–Evangeliums* (Stuttgart, 1969).

Salmeron, A., *Commentarii in Evangelicam Historiam et in Acta Apostolorum*, I–XII (Coloniae, 1602 ff.).

Schillebeeckx, E., "The Crisis in the Language of Faith as a Hermeneutical Problem," *Concilium*, 9/5 (1973) 31–45.
"Exegese, Dogmatik und Dogmenentwicklung," in *Exegese und Dogmatik*, ed. H. Vorgrimler (Mainz, 1962), pp. 91–114.

Simon, L.-M., "Le Sens scripturaire plénier," *Maria in Sacra Scriptura*, I (1967) 105–116.

Smalley, B., *The Study of the Bible in the Middle Ages* (Notre Dame, 1964).

Smitmans, A., "Anfragen der Väterexegese an die historisch–kritische Methode," in *Versuche mehrdimensionaler Schriftauslegung*, ed. H. Harsch & G. Voss (Stuttgart, 1972), pp. 62–69.

Spicq, C., *Esquisse d'une histoire de l'exégèse latine au moyen âge* (Paris, 1944).

Spitz, H.-J., *Die Metaphorik des geistigen Schriftsinns* (München, 1971).

Stegmüller, F., *Repertorium Biblicum Medii Aevi*, I–V (Matriti, 1940 ff.).

Steinmann, J., "Entretien de Pascal et du Père Richard Simon sur les sens de l'Ecriture," *Vie intellectuelle* (March 1949), 239–253.

Vögtle, A., *Das Evangelium und die Evangelien* (Düsseldorf, 1971).

C. Homiletics

Arendt, P., *Die Predigten des Konstanzer Konzils* (Freiburg, 1933).

Belluco, B., *De Sacra Praedicatione in Ordine Fratrum Minorum* (Roma, 1956).

Charland, T.-M., *Artes Praedicandi* (Paris–Ottawa, 1936).

Connors, J., "Homiletic Theory in the Late 16th Century," *The American Ecclesiastical Review*, 138 (1958) 316–332.
"Saint Charles Borromeo in Homiletic Tradition," ibid., 9–23.

Fenelon, F., *Gespräche über die Beredsamkeit im allgemeinen und über die Kanzelberedsamkeit im besonderen* (München, 1819).

Hasenöhrl, P., "Die Concettipredigt," *Kirche und Kanzel*, 3 (1920) 56–67, 130–3, 193–202.

Juglaris, A., *Ariadne Rhetorum* (Monachii, 1658).

Lecoy, de la Marche, A., *La Chaire Française au moyen âge* (Paris, [12]1886).

Neuemayr, M., *Die Schriftpredigt im Barock* (Paderborn, 1938).

Rainer, J., "Entstehungsgeschichte des Trienter Predigtreformdekretes," *Zeitschrift für katholische Theologie*, 39 (1915) 256–317, 465–523.

Ratti, A., *Acta Ecclesiae Mediolanensis*, II (Milan, 1890).

Regius C., *Orator Christianus* (Romae, 1612).

Schneyer, J. B., *Geschichte der katholischen Predigt* (Freiburg, 1969).

Stellae, D., *De Modo Concionandi Liber* (Coloniae, 1586).

Weitenauer, I., *Subsidia Eloquentiae Sacrae*, V (Augsburg–Freiburg, 1764).

Wurz, I., *Anleitung zur geistlichen Beredsamkeit*, I (Wien, 1770).

Zawart, A., *The History of Franciscan Preaching and of Franciscan Preachers (1209–1927)* (New York, 1928).

D. Baroque Period & Culture

Ashley, M., *Das Zeitalter des Barock* (München, 1968).

Chaunu, P., *Europäische Kultur im Zeitalter des Barock* (München, 1968).

Croce, B., *Der Begriff des Barock* (Zürich, 1925).
Storia della Età Barocca in Italia (Bari, 1929).

Elliott, J. H., *Imperial Spain 1469–1716* (Middlesex, Pelican edn, 1970).

Fitzmaurice–Kelley, J., *A History of Spanish Literature* (London, 1898).

Friedrich, C., *Das Zeitalter des Barock* (Stuttgart, 1954).

Gregor, J., *Das spanische Welttheater. Weltanschauung, Politik und Kunst der grossen Epoche Spaniens* (München, [2]1943).

Hausenstein, W., *Vom Genie des Barock* (München, 1956).

Hocke, G. R., *Manierismus in der Literatur* (Rowohlts deutsche enzyklopädie, Reinbeck bei Hamburg, 1959).
Die Welt als Labyrinth (Rowohlts deutsche enzyklopädie, Hamburg, 1957).

Huizinga, J., *Herbst des Mittelalters* (Stuttgart, [7]1953).

Krailsheimer, A. J. (ed.), *The Continental Renaissance 1500–1600* (Pelican Books, 1971).

Lang, H., "Barock als Lebenswelt," in *Bayerische Barockprediger* (München, 1961), ed. by Georg Lohmeier.

Lenhardt, L. & F. Stegmüller, "Barock," in *LThK*, I, 1258–65.

Mendes, J., "Conceitismo. Ceonceito. Conceito predicável," in *Enciclopédia Luso–Brasileira de Cultura*, V (Lisbao, 1967) 1194–9.

Schubart, W., *Glaube und Bildung im Wandel der Zeiten* (München, 1947).

Signier, L., *Die Predigtanlage bei P. Michael Angelus von Schorno, OMCap., ein Beitrag zur Geschichte des Barocks Schrifttums* (Assisi, 1933).

Simon, E., *Ketzer, Bauern, Jesuiten – Reformation und Gegenreformation* (Hamburg, 1973).

Vossler, K., *Lope de Vega und sein Zeitalter* (München, [2]1947).

E. Others

Alba, Duque de, et al., ed., *Documentos inéditos para la Historia de España*, I (Madrid, 1936).

Andres Martin, M., *Historia de la Teologia en España (1470–1570)*, I (Roma, 1962).

Astrain, A., *Historia de la Compañia de Jesus*, III–IV (Madrid, 1909 & 1913).

Barth, K., *Einführung in die evangelische Theologie* (Zürich, 1962).

Bataillon, M., *Erasmo y España* (Mexico, 2nd Spanish edn, 1966; & the French edn, Paris, 1937).

Bougerol, J., *Introduction à l'étude de Saint Bonaventure* (Paris, 1961).

Browe P., "Die religiöse Duldung der Juden im Mittelalter," *Archiv für katholische Kirchenrecht*, 118 (1938) 3–76.

Cañizares Llovera, A., *Santo Tomás de Villanueva. Testigo de la predicación española del Siglo XVI* (Madrid, 1973).

Cano, M., *De Locis Theologicis* (Venetiis, 1567).

Castro, M. de, "Manuscritos franciscanos de la Biblioteca Nacional de Madrid," *Archivo Ibero–Americano*, 19 (1959) 269–329.

Catechism, A New: Catholic Faith for Adults (New York, 1967).

Chenu, M.-D., *La Théologie au douzième siècle* (Paris, 1957).

Congar, Y., *Das Mysterium des Tempels* (Salzburg, 1960).
" Théologie," *DThC*, 15, 341–502.

Constitutiones Societatis Iesu Anno 1558 (Romae, 1558).

Daniélou, J., "Symbolisme et théologie," in *Interpretation der Welt*, ed. H. Kuhn (Würzburg, 1965), pp. 663–674.

Decreta Congregationum Generalium Societatis Iesu (Antwerpiae, 1635).

Duhr, B., *Die Studienordnung der Gesellschaft Jesu* (Freiburg i. Br., 1896).

Gerson, J., *Oeuvres complètes*, V (Paris, 1963), ed. P. Glorieux.

Getino, A., *El Maestro F. Francisco de Vitoria y el Renacimiento filosófico–teológico del siglo XVI* (Madrid, 1914).

Grabmann, M., *Mittelalterliches Geistesleben* (München, 1926).

Guelluy, R., "L'Evolution des méthodes théologiques à Louvain d'Erasme à Jansenius," *Revue d'Histoire Ecclesiastique*, 37 (1941) 31–144.

Hanapis, N., *Virtutum Vitiorumque Exempla* (Coloniae, 1544).

Heredia, B. de, "La enseñanza de s. Tomas en la Compañia de Jesus durante el primer siglo de su existencia," *Ciencia tomista*, 11 (1915) 388–408, 12 (1916) 34–48.

Hervieu–Léger, D., "The Crisis in Doctrinal and Kerygmatic Language," *Concilium*, 9 (1973) 19–30.

Hurter, H., *Nomenclator Literarius Theologiae Catholicae*, I–III (Oenipotente, ³1903–6).

Inauen, A., "Stellung der Gesellschaft Jesu zur Lehre des Aristoteles und des hl. Thomas vor 1583," *Zeitschrift für katholische Theologie*, 40 (1916) 201–237.

Iparraguirre, I., "Nuevas formas de vivar el ideal religioso (siglos XV y XVI)," in *Historia de la Espiritualidad*, II (Barcelona, 1969), 143–247.

Jedin, H., *Geschichte des Konzils von Trient*, II (Freiburg, 1957). "Reformation: Katholische Reform und Gegenreformation," in *Handbuch der Kirchengeschichte*, IV, ed. E. Iserloh, J. Glazik, H. Jedin (Freiburg, 1967).

Joosen, J. & J. Waszink, "Allegorese," *Reallexikon für Antike und Christentum*, I (Stuttgart, 1950), 283–293.

Kelly, J., *Early Christian Creeds* (London, ²1960). "Die Konstitution vom anglikanischen Standpunkt aus gesehen," in *De Ecclesia*, ed. G. Barauna, II (Freiburg, 1966) 526–535.

Kleinhans, A., "De Vita et Operibus Petri Galatini," *Antonianum*, 1 (1926) 145–179, 327–356.

Kolbe T., *Die symbolischen Bücher der evangelisch–lutherischen Kirche* (Gütersloh, 1912).

Lang., A., *Die Loci theologici des Melchior Cano und die Methode des dogmatischen Beweises* (München, 1925).

Lejarza, F. & A. Uribe, *Introducción a los origines de la observancia en España. Las reformas en los siglos XIV y XV* (Madrid, 1958).

Leturia, P., "Sentido verdadero en la Iglesia militante," *Gregorianum*, 23 (1942) 137–168.

Loyola, I. de, *Geistliche Übungen* (Freiburg, 1951).

Menendez y Pelayo, M., *Historia de los heterodoxos españoles* (Madrid, 1928).

Monumenta Historia Societatis Jesu. Monumenta Paedagogica, I (Matriti, 1901), ed. Caecilius Gomez Rodeles, et al.

Pachtler, G. M., *Ratio Studiorum et Institutiones Scholasticae Societatis Jesu*, I (Berlin, 1887).

Pannenberg, W., *Grundzüge der Christologie* (Güterloh, ²1966).

Pitra J. B., *Spicilegium Solesmense*, II & III (Paris, 1855).
Analecta Sacra, II (Paris, 1884).

Pou y Marti, J., "Felipe III y los santuarios franciscanos de Italia,"
Archivo Ibero–Americano, 3 (1915) 212–233, 4 (1916) 74–89, 214–241.

Pozo, C., *Fuentes para la Historia del Método teológico en la Escuela de
Salamanca*, I (Granada, 1962).

Ratzinger, J., *Einführung in das Christentum* (München, 1971).

Sainz Rodriguez, P., "Introduccion," in Alain Guy, *El Pensamiento Fi-
losofico de Fray Luis de Leon* (Madrid, 1960).

Scorraille, R. de, *François Suarez*, I–II (Paris, 1912).

Serna, V., "Un comentario inedito de Miguel Marcos a la cuestion 23 de
la Suma de Santo Tomas de Praedestinatione," *Archivo Teologico
Granadino*, 19 (1956) 235–435.

Serry, J. H., *Historia Congregationum de Auxiliis Divinae Gratiae* (Antwerpiae, 1709).

Sicroff, A., *Les Controverses des statuts de "Pureté de Sang" en espagne du
XVe au XVII Siècle* (Paris, 1960).

Sommervogel, C., *Bibliothèque des écrivains de la compagnie de Jésus*
(Bruxel–Paris, 1890 ff.).

Stegmüller, F., "Gnadenstreit," *LThK*, IV, 1002–7.

Suarez, F., *De Mysteriis Vitae Christi*, in *Opera Omnia*, XIX (Paris, 1890).

Tridentinum Concilium, edn Goerresiana, V (Freiburg, 1911), IX (1930).

Vansteenberghe, E., "Molinisme," *DThC*, X, 2166 ff.

Vasquez, I., "El arzobispo Juan de Rada y el molinismo. Sus votos en
las controversias 'de auxiliis'," *Verdad y Vida*, 20 (1962) 351–396.

Vatican II, The Documents of, ed. W. Abbott (New York, 1966).

Villoslada, R. G., "Un teólogo olvidado, Juan Mair," *Estudios Eclesiasticos*, 45 (1936) 96–109.

Welter, J., *L'Exemplum dans la littérature religieuse et didactique du moyen
âge* (Paris–Toulouse, 1927).